Management – Culture – Interpretation

Edited by
Andreas P. Müller
Stephan Sonnenburg

The book series of the Karlshochschule International University explores new ideas and approaches to management, organizations and economy from a cultural and interpretive point of view. The series intends to integrate different perspectives towards economy, culture and society. Therefore, management and organizational activities are not seen as being isolated from their context, but rather as context-bound and dependent on their surrounding cultures, societies and economies. Within these contexts, activities make sense through the allocation, the interpretation and the negotiation of meanings. Sense-making can be found in performative processes as well as the way social meaning is constructed through interactions. The series seeks innovative approaches, both in formulating new research questions and in developing adequate methodological research designs. We welcome contributions from different interdisciplinary and collective ways of thinking and seeking knowledge which focus on the integration of "Management – Culture – Interpretation".

Edited by
Prof. Dr. Andreas P. Müller
Prof. Dr. Stephan Sonnenburg

Karlsruhe, Germany

Stephan Sonnenburg · Desmond Wee
(Eds.)

Touring Consumption

Springer VS

Editors
Stephan Sonnenburg
Karlshochschule International University in Karlsruhe
Germany

Desmond Wee
Karlshochschule International University in Karlsruhe
Germany

Management – Culture – Interpretation
ISBN 978-3-658-10018-6 ISBN 978-3-658-10019-3 (eBook)
DOI 10.1007/978-3-658-10019-3

Library of Congress Control Number: 2015939897

Springer VS

Printed on acid-free paper

Springer VS is a brand of Springer Fachmedien Wiesbaden
Springer Fachmedien Wiesbaden is part of Springer Science+Business Media
(www.springer.com)

Acknowledgements

First, we wish to thank all the participants of the 'Touring Consumption' conference at Karlshochschule International University for their inspiring presentations and insightful discussions. In particularly, we would like to thank our keynote speakers Jørgen Ole Bærenholdt, Steve Miles and John Urry; it was truly a great honor. Second, we want to express our wholehearted gratitude to David Sixt for his inexhaustible support towards making this book happen. Finally, we would like to say a big thank you to all the authors who helped in making 'Touring Consumption' possible. We hope that the book will be of value to students, academics and practitioners alike. We would also like to take this opportunity to show our appreciation to the Journal of Consumer Culture for its decision to keep the itinerary of touring consumption moving. A Special Issue stemming from 'Touring Consumption' will be published in 2016.

Stephan Sonnenburg and Desmond Wee
Editors

Contents

Touring Consumption: Itineraries on the Move 9
Stephan Sonnenburg / Desmond Wee

Revitalizing Forgotten Place Brands through Touring Consumption: The Case of The Old London Underground Company 21
Melodena Stephens Balakrishnan

Pilgrimage Tourism in Consumer Society: Foot Pilgrimages to the Jasna Góra Sanctuary in Częstochowa 57
Felicjan Bylok / Leszek Cichobłaziński

Facets of Mobility 77
Ulrich Gehmann

Spectral Touring: Subject, Consumption, and the 'Wound' of the Photograph 97
Sourav Kargupta

Fashion and the Mobile Body: The Value of Clothing and Fashion for Merleau-Ponty's Concept of Chiasm 117
Ian W. King

De-+-Touring through Embodied 'Inter-Place' 133
Wendelin Küpers

Developing Branding Strategies based on Automatic Behavioural System for Mega Event Tourism, The Olympics 161
Erica Liu

Protecting the European Medical Tourist: A New Challenge for the E.U. Law? 185
Fernando Peña López

**How Tall Can the Acacia Grow?
Cityscapes between Conviviality and Mass Invasion** 201
Florin Mureşanu / Monica Mureşanu

**The ACACIA Paradox: Built Heritage Conservation
versus Increasing Tourism** 229
Florin Mureşanu / Monica Mureşanu

The Legally Pluralistic Tourist 261
Roy Andrew Partain

**The Hidden Dimensions of Cultural Consumption
within the Framework of Tourism Mobility** 285
Tamara Rátz / Viktória Kundi / Gábor Michalkó

**Towards a New Role Model of the
Contemporary Architectural Tourist** 303
Jan Specht

Notes on Contributors 319

Touring Consumption: Itineraries on the Move

Stephan Sonnenburg / Desmond Wee

Moving towards touring consumption

Tourism has become a significant area of scholarship especially given the industry's product development opportunities on a global scale. However, the emphasis placed on such research has largely been from a supply-side perspective, reviewing economic value within market segments. What needs to be explored is the shift towards the agencies of the tourist/traveler as consumer, and consumption as being embodied as a moment of practice in continuous states of touring. The ways in which we consume in our contemporary world is becoming increasingly complex and fascinating, especially as we consider enhanced economies, technologies and competencies. Inasmuch as consumption is commonly construed in terms of demand and supply, it is also pertinent to explore consumption as an inherent part and productive activity of the everyday (de Certeau 1984).

In this sense, consumption and its relation to markets and culture can be considered in terms of social practices and as a phenomenon to understand processes involved in the creation and reproduction of practices. Warde (2005) relates consumption not as a practice in itself, but a moment in every practice in which appropriation occurs within practices and determines how practice is organized. It becomes apparent that practice accommodates both the holistic role of habituation alongside notions of agency, embodiment and performance.

Touring in terms of travel, tourism or varying aspects of mobilities contributes substantially to particular conventions and rituals of consumer practices. However, the dynamic agencies of the individual, where the consumer produces and reproduces in the act of consuming, seem to be neglected. We need to understand that production is ultimately an inherent part of consumption, not in terms of both ideas working together, but both being embodied in a unified fashion. We would like to position the consumer as one who consumes in a conscious and reflective way in which we have a kind of consumption that condones "practices of meaning creation and dissemination" (Humphreys and Grayson 2008).

Hence, touring consumption delineates a kind of performance that is not only reproduced, but is productive and emergent in its own right. The more traditional conceptions of tourist, pilgrim, vagabond, refugee, expatriate, international student or business traveler in the tourism sciences and related disciplines are becoming more and more diffused and need to be re-examined against the background of a differentiated, complex and individualized everyday perspective. It is also useful to see this in the light of prosumption (see Campbell 2005) and co-creation (see Prahalad and Ramaswamy 2004).

As an outlook, we would like to consider a 'touristification' of society and everyday life (Picard 1996; Larsen 2008; van der Duim 2007) in which touring as a metaphor and concept (Bal 2002) can be used to encapsulate new forms of mobilities as societal, economic, consumptive or scientific phenomena. Furthermore, we could conceptually refer to a 'touring' turn (see 'cultural turns' in Bachmann-Medick 2014) and ask guiding questions as to what the theoretical and practical impact of a touring turn is on contemporary society and the consumer at large, and how the everyday is shaped by touring. Although the 'everyday' baggage in tourism is seminal, less has been discussed about how the everyday itself is already infused with tourism. It is imperative to go beyond by analyzing tourist practices incorporated in the everyday, whereby "everyday sites of activity are redesigned in 'tourist' mode" (Sheller and Urry 2004: 5) and consider that touring and mobility are already incorporated as topics across the social sciences and humanities as well as in our social lives and consumer practices.

Moving itineraries

This book arose out of a conference, 'Touring Consumption', organized by the Karlshochschule International University in Karlsruhe, Germany in October 2013. It attempts to confront spatial, performative and cultural interrelations between tourism and social/economic behavior by providing a critical platform for articulation and discussion of possibilities, problems and effects of the complexities of 'touring consumption' in our contemporary world. As we conceptualized 'Touring Consumption', rather than defining what we meant by it, we provided only a sketchy framework so that academics from various fields were able to incorporate their background, disciplines, methodologies and idiosyncracies within their presentations and, together, allow a meaning (or meanings) to emerge collectively. This worked apparently, as demonstrated through the sheer quality of the presentations and papers. But what was even more convincing were the spaces and times allocated for dialogue, both formal and informal, in which participants felt as if they were not discussing the conference thematic, but engaging it by living it.

We wanted to follow on from this to provide a similar impulse in the writing of the sketch and the editing of this book. Once again, instead of discussing what we mean by touring consumption with 'precision', we wanted to allow nuances and subtleties, and thought we would project the onus onto you, the reader, to assist us in this project. However as editors, we hope to guide you in two ways.

First, we would like to suggest some initial questions to create your own itineraries through the book and its chapters: How can we look at touring consumption as part of practices? To what extent are touring practices performed, enacted and embodied? Who and what is the tourist/traveler in this context as opposed to predisposed ideas of what a tourist already is? How do we position a touristification of society in terms of the everyday? How are agent mobilities organized in our contemporary world?

Second, what we did do is to provide an overall conceptual frame and suggest four possible itineraries in the forms of 'embodiment and experience', 'brand and space', 'performance and form', and 'culture and discourse' in which one could tour the book with. Again these only represent some ways of moving through the text, as we attempt to derive meanings out of all the contributions and reposition them within certain concepts, paradigms and perspectives, as fluid and mobile as possible.

Embodiment and experience

Tourism is all about experience, yet we usually refrain from discussing this in embodied ways. We often rely on the tourist gaze (Urry and Larsen 2011) as an othered experience, one which involves a trained eye and skilled appreciation. Perhaps we need to reconsider how this gaze is manifested in the form of a de-exoticised experience, that is, translated from what is often construed of as extraordinary into an ordinary form of existence that is part and parcel of the everyday. McCabe contextualises this when he writes that the tourist experience is a metaphor of the social world and more, "since it mirrors and replicates that everyday world, along with the social concerns of ordinary members of society" (2002: 62). We need to consider how everyday life is practiced and that leisure and tourism is constitutive of this.

Pearce had already in 1988 written about the habitual nature of our holiday experiences as a kind of 'mindlessness'. But how are the mundane activities of our everyday lives incorporated within our holiday, especially our decision making process as a consumer? At what stage are the ordinary things that we do memorable? Tourism is thus about being in the world and making sense of it. By incorporating the everyday, we also at the same time rely on a kind of reflexiveness that passively coerces us to acknowledge that embodied practices and experiences cannot be underestimated in the ways in which we understand how tourism is practiced (Obrador Pons 2003; Ateljevic et al. 2007; Larsen 2008, Wee 2012). Instead of dealing directly with the fuzzy distinction between tourism and the everyday, what we need to consider is the peripheral, that which makes the event meaningful.

Smith et al. iterate that the "processes of embodiment and experience are *moments*...in which we redefine our lives – when a meaning or belief is put at risk or we find ourselves reliving a memorable event" (2012: 5). Another way in which to consider embodiment is to refer to the tourist.

> "The places and spaces of tourism each present us with complex sets of expectations and norms that must be adhered to by the tourist. We might question how we – as embodied tourists – act in such ways as to reproduce the larger structures of society..." (Hannam and Knox 2010: 58)

Both *Küpers* and *King* engage embodied insights in their work with particular reference to a phenomenology of embodiment incorporating space, place and body. *Küpers* provides a theoretical framework for a critical understanding of embodied place and space in relation to touring and mobility, which is conceived as body-mediated movement that moves through inter-places. He proposes the notion of de-touring as an alternative metaphor and concept for an inter-placed mobility and finally, an ethos of 'engaged letting-go' ('Gelassenheit') as a relational inter-p(l)acing practice. *King* appropriates Merleau-Ponty's notion of chiasm and projects this onto the world of fashion and the clothed body. However it is the facilitation of their mobility, explored through aesthetics and the body and the tactility of fabric that makes the crucial step towards a realization of being. Interestingly, clothing (amongst many other things) is also 'regulated' during the foot pilgrimages to the Jasna Góra Sanctuary in Częstochowa, where women are not supposed to be scantily clad. For *Bylok and Cichobłaziński*, this performance is also at the same time a means of resisting fashion and the consumption of pleasure. They further develop the notion of practices, in contextualising pilgrimage tourism, how consumer society is ascribed to and embodied through walking and the development of 'communitas' and walking across liminal space.

In contrast to the pilgrimage, *Mureşanu and Mureşanu* take us onto an urban sphere to demarcate a kind of tourism in which the local communities provide counter discourse to an experience of place as an articulation of the multifaceted tourist resources that produce and adapt themselves together with local inhabitants. This is exemplified by metaphor to the mutual dependencies between the Acacia and the giraffe in the African savannah, or at least a 'chemistry' involving local communities and the greater global tourist flow. The historical contextualization and the rendering of local voice, most striking in 'Das Venedig Prinzip' and 'Carcelona', question the gaps between conviviality and mass invasion. Another paper by the *Mureşanus* elaborates the paradox inherent in built heritage conservation versus increasing tourism, revealing the problems arising for the heritage sites presented as touristic opportunities in Romania. By looking at UNESCO sites (and wannabes) as case studies, they ask the extent to which heritage sites need to enforce protection against the tourists in order to ensure their (potentially both heritage sites and tourists) preservation and how this might impact the tourists' experience. In this sense, this experiential nature is inasmuch a consumption of heritage, as in the intangible cultural transfer based on embodied encounters in space. By going back to Hannam and Knox's (2010) quote above, perhaps it is necessary to envision, to fear and to embrace vampire giraffes guarding temples against embodied tourists.

Brand and space

Brands could be described as touring phenomena which move in a 'polylogue' (Sonnenburg 2009) or a "process of interagency" (Kozinets et al. 2004: 658) between various brand stakeholders. The consumer increasingly has an active role during the brand itinerary, accordingly they can be regarded as 'prosumers' (Toffler 1980), 'produsers' (Bruns 2008) or 'bricoleurs' (Holt 2002). In brand polylogues, they create and swap content in conformist and even nonconformist ways (Sherry et al. 2006: 18). The brand itinerary moves if the consumers are motivated to engage themselves in it and if the brand content carries meaning and gives meaning to their lives and (inter)actions:

> "Meaning defines brands, and people make meaning. People make meaning through social means: they make meaning through their interaction, through the institutions they have created and maintained, through accommodation and negotiation with marketers, through rumors, through politics, and often in reaction to a disruption in the social sphere. Brands are meaning." (O'Guinn and Muniz 2010: 133)

Brand meaning is more and more created by space. Buildings, streets, squares, cities or regions could be regarded as spaces for (touring) consumption (Miles 2010). These spaces increasingly become, de facto if not de jure, brands (Sherry 1998), in other words, 'branded spaces' (Sonnenburg and Baker 2013). One may think of icons like the Taj Mahal, the Champs-Élysées, Times Square, Mecca or the Black Forest. Even for companies and their branding, space is increasingly the driver for meaning and reputation, comprising of for example flagship stores, corporate museums and brandparks (Bielzer 2013). Following Arvidsson, we are on an itinerary to "end up living in a well-nigh all-encompassing brand-space" (2005: 236).

Liu emphasizes the importance of brand strategies (for mega events) based on the behavioral pattern of audiences and the contexts surrounding the event. In focusing on the Olympics and its legacies as the desired future of the host city, she details the planning process through a rebranding of the city and managing how tourism is consumed, both in terms of the planned and unplanned experience of consumption. This in turn provides the linkages between creating experiences coherent with the expectations of people. For *Balakrishnan*, touring consumption represents a mobile consumption of place brands reconstructed through tourist associations across space and time and mediated by multi-sensual encounters and experiences. She focuses on the revitalization of forgotten place brands through identifying, bridging and managing gaps that destination marketers need to address, but from a tourist point of view. A seminal way for her is to manage the perceived value of the place brand by providing structured brand choices that allows multiple perspectives to co-exist. Yet in a more critical and ironic way, *Mureşanu and Mureşanu* provide ample examples to question city branding for its economic valuation and contribution to mass tourism. Both their articles play against each other, one in which the modern edifice is being venerated, the other in which old buildings are branded under the name of built heritage conservation, in the light of increasing tourism.

Form and performance

Performance and its 'counterpart' performativity have different roots and streams across disciplines. Speech act theory is starting point for performativity (Austin 1962), ritual and theatre studies for performance (Turner 1982). For the purpose of this introduction and based on an inference by Harwood and El-Manstrly (2012), we use performance to explore why humans carry out specific habits of consumption and to explain social practices as acts of something being performed in everyday life, whereby performance is not primarily meant in the orthodox or formal sense of theatrical performance (Schechner 2002: 110) or within the linguistic context. Performance correlates with embodiment (see the aforementioned itinerary) as both metaphorical concepts are processes of experiencing and meaning-making.

Edensor regards tourism as a shape of performance and he elaborates that:

> "...performance can be conceived in more ambivalent and contradictory terms, can be understood as intentional and unintentional, concerned with both being and becoming, strategically and unreflexively embodied...tourism as performance can both renew existing conventions and provide opportunities to challenge them." (Edensor 2001: 78)

We would add that touring is "a creative interplay of different actors and contexts in the making and performance of tourism experiences" (Richards 2011: 1246). Therefore, travelers and tourists co-creatively produce and reproduce 'something' in the act of touring. The magic takes place at present. Touring consumption can be approached between the poles of performance and *something* which can be described as the form. Scarles argues consumer performances enacted within tourist spaces "are highly regulated and ordered" (2012: 930). This forming is either the cause for the performance, the emergent during the performance or the outcome of the performance. However, we use performance and form not as antipodes, but as interrelations and interdependent incorporations which is illustrated in the term 'per(form)ance': no form without performance and vice versa. Depending on the research focus, the notion of per(form)ance can be differently used in tourism like enactment, being, transformation, negotiation or efficiency (Harwood and El-Manstrly 2012). This is reflected in some contributions of this book.

Balakrishnan, *Specht* and *Rátz, Kundi and Michalkó* had clear formal modes of research engagement; they had specific places in mind, yet these places were contingent in the ways they were appropriated. *Balakrishnan* focused on the disused London underground and she used the case of the Old London Underground Company (TOLUC) to understand the re-development of abandoned stations, along with a re-imagination on how to bridge the gaps between use(d) and reuse. *Specht,* on the other hand, was above ground and incorporated the architecture of various cities to develop an urban and contemporary framework in which various forms of tourists could be distinguished. His example of Qianmen Street in Beijing highlighted the role of 'renewed buildings' constructed to resemble the style of late Qing dynasty and questions a reflective notion of authenticity aimed back at the various typologies of the cultural tourist as consumer. *Rátz, Kundi and Michalkó* also start off in the same vein, but highlight the kinds of data lost especially in regards to the liminality of conventional tourism per(form)ances in Hungary. While *Specht's* cultural tourist is highly visible and distinguishable, *Rátz, Kundi and Michalkó's* tourist has become concealed or invisible. Be it the invisible tourist, the omnipresent tourist or the potential tourist, it becomes clear then that the places in which they inhabit will be reproduced through various encounters and enactments in fluid per(form)ances.

Culture and discourse

Discourse can be seen in terms of travel and mobilities as products of social relations and dealing with the making and unmaking of cultural meanings (see Jaworski and Pritchard 2005). Ultimately, it is tourist discourse that shapes leisure and travel experiences, especially if we consider how culture is marketed in the tourism industry. This can be portrayed as tourism image and examined through the systems of discourse that shape the creation and production of the image (Morgan and Pritchard 1998). It is also within these discourses that power is regulated through shifting global structure and signification processes in the ordering of information. It becomes clear that culture is commodified for tourism, yet as Löfgren emphasizes, that "standardized marketing does not have to standardize tourists" (1999: 8) and that the uniqueness of personal travel experience should not be understated.

Franklin states that "…tourist things tend to be significant only in what they represent; as a meaningful set of signs and metaphors..." (2003: 97). It is necessary to understand how discourse is reproduced and interspersed with culture through construction of self and others. One way to consider this is through a kind of materiality (Haldrup and Larsen 2006), that tourist practice is inherently linked to material culture and physical sensations, as enhanced by objects, technologies and machines. To project this at a meta-level, Ingold writes:

> "Understood as a realm of discourse, meaning and value inhabiting the collective consciousness, culture is conceived to hover over the material world but not to permeate it. In this view, in short, culture and materials do not mix; rather, culture wraps itself around the universe of material things, shaping and transforming their outward surfaces without ever penetrating their interiority." (Ingold 2000: 53)

Rátz, Kundi and Michalkó examine the role of culture as a consumption component within a framework of tourism mobilities in space. They do this by exploring how festivals and other cultural events in Hungary remain hidden as a consequence of inadequate data collection, despite the economic and social contribution of culturally motivated trips to the individuals' quality of life and the destinations' and attractions' demand and revenue characteristics. It is apparent that material (and immaterial) resources of culture become important especially since they lend themselves to notions of memorability, despite the cultural tourists' invisibility to destination decision makers. For *Specht*, new forms of the cultural tourist needs to be reformulated so that important measures regarding the development and marketing of attractions and destinations are not left to chance. He positions the tourist within tourism theory relating to patterns of consumption and delineates the contemporary architectural tourist, a role that goes beyond the art and cultural tourist. With this typology in place, he appeals to developers, marketers and managers to be aware of developing roles, and their interdependencies, in order to have a deeper understanding of specific consumers and target groups.

Another kind of material discourse can be framed along the lines of legislation, as seen by both *Partain* and *Peña López*. *Partain* presents the raw notion of law as a consumptive act of tourism and situates law as acts of authenticity and belonging alongside other traditional acts of culture and identification. Yet when law is consumed as a tourist good, then it needs to be redefined as an act of belonging to the other, in which authenticity is sought outside one's normal legal culture. He explores if law can be seen as a ritual performance (see the aforementioned itinerary) that tourists could participate in, as much as they might in other aspects of culture. *Peña López* focuses on European Union law and the mobilities involved in medical tourism and their ability to produce transcendental changes in the regulation of medical treatment in both host and receiver nation. This project is inherently multidimensional, not in the least because it works on very clearly material practices such as abortions, assisted suicides and embryo cryopreservation, but the scope of what these entail, not only borders on the availability of medical treatment, the costs, the quality or even the wait, but on the moral and ethical constrains that hold a nation state together.

Kargupta postulates theoretical conjectures on Marx and Derrida, and the intentionality of internal transactions between the 'postmodern subject' and the 'touring subject' in the context of the act and desire of touring. He philosophizes on the fragmentary self and how such a divided self can recover to produce a locus of perception organized around dispersed perceptions of the outside as experience of touring. What interests *Kargupta* is how the touring site, its objects, representations and images interrupt, resist or write the touring subject, and how the subjectivity of the tourist shapes the 'site' in question in return. *Gehmann's* underlying thesis is that tourism is more than just 'site-seeing' because 'sites' serve special functions and in themselves, become functionalized to a high degree through transformation into products of consumption. Rather than a traditional understanding of *sites*, he contextualizes products, artifacts as sites constructed to fulfill certain functionalities, in which the world becomes a marketable product. These sites also inform the way moving consumers indulge in mobilities and the dependencies towards this in terms of space and time compression.

References

Arvidsson, A. (2005): Brands: A critical perspective. In: Journal of Consumer Culture, 5(2), 235-258.

Ateljevic, I., Pritchard, A. and Morgan, N. (2007): The critical turn in tourism studies: Innovative research methodologies. Oxford: Elsevier.

Austin, J.L. (1962): How to do things with words. Oxford: Clarendon Press.

Bachmann-Medick, D. (2014): Cultural Turns: Neuorientierungen in den Kulturwissenschaften. Reinbek: Rowohlt.

Bal, M. (2002): Travelling concepts in the humanities: A rough guide. Toronto: University of Toronto Press.

Bielzer, L. (2013): Corporate branded spaces: A glance at today's diversity and some historic origins. In: Sonnenburg, S. and Baker, L. (eds.): Branded spaces: Experience enactments and entanglements. Wiesbaden: Springer VS, 89-108.

Böhme, G. (1993): Atmosphere as the fundamental concept of a new aesthetics. In: Thesis Eleven, 36, 113-126.

Bruns, A. (2008): Blogs, wikipedia, second life, and beyond: From production to produsage. New York: Peter Lang.

Campbell, C. (2005): The craft consumer: Culture, craft and consumption in a postmodern society. In: Journal of Consumer Culture, 5(1), 23-42.

de Certeau, M. (1984): The practice of everyday life. Berkeley: University of California Press.

Edensor, T. (2001): Performing tourism, staging tourism. In: Tourist Studies, 1(1), 59-81.

Franklin, A. (2003): Tourism: An introduction. London: Sage.

Haldrup, M. and Larsen, J. (2006): Material cultures of tourism. In: Leisure Studies, 25(3), 275-289.

Hannam, K. and Knox, D. (2010): Understanding tourism: A critical introduction. London: Sage.

Harwood, S. and El-Manstrly, D. (2012): The performative turn in tourism. In: University of Edinburgh Business School Working Papers Series, 5. http://www.research.ed.ac.uk/portal/files/4832557/12_05.pdf, 08.12.2014.

Holt, D.B. (2002): Why do brands cause trouble? A dialectical theory of consumer culture and branding. In: Journal of Consumer Research, 29(1), 70-90.

Humphreys, A. and Grayson, K. (2008): The intersecting roles of consumer and producer: A critical perspective on co-production, co-creation and prosumption. In: Sociology Compass, 2, 1-18.

Ingold, T. (2000): The perception of the environment: Essays on livelihood, dwelling and skill. London: Routledge.

Jaworski, A. and Pritchard, A. (2005): Discourse, communication and tourism. Clevedon: Channel View Publications.

Kozinets, R.V., Sherry, J.F., Storm, D., Duhachek, A., Nuttavuthisit, K. and Deberry-Spence, B. (2004): Ludic agency and retail spectacle. In: Journal of Consumer Research, 31(3), 658-672.

Larsen, J. (2008): De-exoticizing tourist travel: Everyday life and sociality on the move. In: Leisure Studies, 27(1), 21-34.
Löfgren, O. (1999): On holiday: A history of vacationing. Berkeley: University of California Press.
McCabe, S. (2002): The tourist experience and everyday life. In: Dann, G. (ed.): The tourist as a metaphor for the social world. Wallingford: CABI Publishing, 61-75.
Miles, S. (2010): Spaces for consumption: Pleasure and placelessness in the post-industrial city. London: Sage.
Morgan, N. and Pritchard, A. (1998): Tourism promotion and power: Creating images, creating identities. Chichester: John Wiley and Sons.
Obrador Pons, P. (2003): Being-on-holiday: Tourist dwelling, bodies and place. In: Tourist Studies, 3(1), 47-66.
O'Guinn, T.C. and Muniz, A.M. Jr. (2010): Toward a sociological model of brands. In: Loken, B., Ahluwalia, R. and Houston, M.J. (eds.): Brands and brand management: Contemporary research perspectives. New York, NY: Routledge, 133-155.
Pearce, P.L. (1988): The ulysses factor: Evaluating visitors in tourist settings. New York: Springer.
Picard, M. (1996): Bali: Cultural tourism and touristic culture. Singapore: Archipelago Press.
Prahalad, C.K. and Ramaswamy, V. (2004): The future of competition: Co-creating unique value with customers. Boston: Harvard Business School Press.
Richards, G. (2011): Creativity and tourism: The state of the art. In: Annals of Tourism Research, 38(4), 1225-1253.
Scarles, C. (2012): The photographed other: Interplays of agency in tourist photography in Cusco, Peru. In: Annals of Tourism Research, 39(2), 928-950.
Schechner, R. (2002): Performance studies: An introduction. London: Routledge.
Sheller, M. and Urry, J. (2004) (eds.): Tourism mobilities: Places to play, places in play. London: Routledge.
Sherry, J.F. (1998): The soul of the company store: Nike Town Chicago and the emplaced brandscape. In: Sherry, J.F. (ed.): Servicescapes: The concept of place in contemporary markets. Lincolnwood, Ill.: NTC Business Books, 109-146.
Sherry, J.F., Kozinets, R.V. and Borghini, S. (2006): Agents in paradise: Experiential co-creation through emplacement, ritualization, and community. In: Carù, A. and Cova, B. (eds.): Consuming experience. London: Routledge: 17-33.
Smith L., Waterton E. and Watson S. (2012) (eds.): The cultural moment in tourism. Oxon: Routledge.
Sonnenburg, S. (2009) (ed.): Swarm branding: Markenführung im Zeitalter von Web 2.0. Wiesbaden: VS Research.
Sonnenburg, S. and Baker, L. (2013) (eds.): Branded spaces: Experience enactments and entanglements. Wiesbaden: Springer VS.
Toffler, A. (1980): The third wave. New York: Bantam Books.
Turner, V. (1982): From ritual to theatre: The human seriousness of play. New York: PAJ Publications.
Urry, J. and Larsen, J. (2011): The tourist gaze 3.0. London: Sage.

van der Duim, R. (2007): Tourismscapes: An actor-network perspective. In: Annals of Tourism Research, 34(4), 961-976.

Warde, A. (2005): Consumption and theories of practice. In: Journal of Consumer Culture, 5(2), 131-153.

Wee, D. (2012): Touring heritage, performing home: Cultural encounters in Singapore. In: Smith, L., Waterton, E. and Watson, S. (eds.): The cultural moment in tourism: New perspectives on performance and engagement. London and New York: Routledge, 79-96.

Revitalizing Forgotten Place Brands through Touring Consumption: The Case of The Old London Underground Company

Melodena Stephens Balakrishnan

Touring consumption as applicable to place branding

The consumption of a place brand is an interdisciplinary science lying between tourism, marketing, economics, sociology, urban planning, sustainability and psychology which creates challenges for researchers who prefer to dwell in narrowly defined empirical studies (Papdopoulous and Heslop 2002; Fan 2006; Gilmore 2002; Prichard et al. 2011). There is a need for a polydimensional viewpoint in design of research studies. A place brand as defined by Zenker and Braun (2010: 4) is a sum of the networks of association in the consumer's mind developed from the visual, verbal and behavioural expression of a place which itself is based on the aims, communication, values, general culture of the place's stakeholders and the overall place design. To add to this complexity is the issue of mobility in tourism consumption. Today's place consumers want variety as they embrace "a desperate search for experience in a world of ontological excess" (Thamassen and Balle 2012). While constructing a place brand, "*choice*" and choice criteria become important (Erdem and Swait 2004). A tourist can dwell in the range of mobilities (Urry 2000: 157; Sheller 2004) suggesting that place brands need to be endowed with liminality (Edensor 2007:199) as tourism mobilities are "fluid, ambivalent and labile" (Gardiner 2000: 6). Hones and Leyda (2005: 1025) for example suggest that for reinterpreting geography of a place, we need to move away from discrete places and separate scales (local, regional, and national) to a geography of networks (circulatory sites).

To quote Sheller and Urry (2004: 1), "Different mobilities inform tourism, shape the place where tourism is performed and drive the making or unmaking of a tourist destination. Mobilities of people and objects; airplanes and suitcases, plants and animals, images and brands, data system and satellites, all go hand in hand into 'doing' tourism. It also concerns the relational mobilization of memories and performances, gendered and racialized bodies, emotions and atmospheres. Places have multiple contested meanings that offer disruptions and disjunctures. Tourism mobilities involve complex combinations of movement and stillness, realities and fantasies; play and work."

Further while designing a place brand, it is important to restructure consumer demand away from short-run benefit decisions into deferred gratifications (Bogart 1973: 998). For this, a practitioner must be able to find the contact zone and engineer multiple encounters to manage multiple representations (Firat and Schultz 1997). This can be done by managing the touristscape (Edensor 2006) or the "*sensuous concatenation of material forces*' (Wylie 2002: 251). Based on the above theoretical perspective, it is possible to define touring consumption as the mobile consumption of a place brand related through multi-sense encounters (not necessarily at the physical site) which are reconstructed through the associations tourists form across time, people, atmospheres and media by the cognitive and affective rationalization of these encounter experiences.

Briefly this research paper is divided into two parts. The first part explores the theory relevant to how forgotten places can be revitalized through re-imagination using touring consumption. The process of re-imagination is presented as a conceptual model, which looks at four gaps or spaces that need to be bridged. The second part of the article illustrates the case of The Old London Underground Company (TOLUC) which is a project focusing on re-development of abandoned London underground stations. The methodology is grounded research using qualitative data (case study), and is presented as a narrative (e.g. Glaser and Strauss 2009; Charmaz 2014). This study is significant as it is a longitudinal study chronicling a start-up from idea to launch and the 4½ year journey of managing TOLUC from 2011 to 2014. Data was collected through three interviews with the CEO of TOLUC; secondary articles in various media; social media observation and a field visit with the CEO to the Mayor of London's Office. Cross-referencing with existing theory helped provide a robust method for revitalization of abandoned places. The study is presented using storytelling, which is a more creative form of qualitative research that presents an emic (insiders) point of view (Hansen and Kahnweiler 1993; Frank 2008).

This paper contributes to theoretical knowledge of place brands and identifies the gaps destination marketers need to work on to create viable projects for the communities, project stakeholders and final consumers of the project. This paper also adds to our knowledge of the creation of start-ups and theoretically contributes to our knowledge of entrepreneurship. Practically the paper presents a checklist of tools available to start-up projects that manage multiple stakeholders.

Forgotten places need reimagination before revitalization

A review of literature on places whether forgotten, abandoned or requiring revitalization shows a variety of settings (see Figure 1) and they all have one thing in common, that of using the original essence of that place by rethinking our notions of space/space-time (Massey 1999). The preferred methodologies in these studies are the use of single cases. Surprisingly, forgotten places can lie dormant in urban communities, decaying in plain sight as urban planners are unable to assess indicators of distress (Jennings 2012). Though there are many successful revitalization projects of forgotten places, for example, like Canary Wharf in London in 1980, Pittsburgh, USA in 1950, or Central Park, New York in 1909, they all begin by reimagination of the place (for example Cochrane and Jonas 1999; Hall 2004). At the time of this study, there were no scholarly documented studies of abandoned underground stations though abandoned underground air-raid shelters have been the focus of a venture start-up in the past in China (Xiu Li Hawken converted some into shopping malls) and currently there is a consortium looking at Hong Kong's abandoned Kai Tak Airport. Re-imagination can lead to civic engagement (Gordon and Koo 2008) and help re-form relationships with the past and present (Banting 2012).

Reimagining needs to be followed by revitalization. As places are forgotten, employment opportunities are lost, safety decreases and there is a slow degeneration of community areas (Frumkin 2003). Not all revitalization can have positive consequences (Van Hoving et al. 2010). The Bilbao effect (Plaza 2007), the destroying of indigenous populations (Pattullo 1996), loss of sustainability (Pickering and Hill 2007; Gössling 2002), species extinction (Walpole et al. 2000), destruction of foci of site itself (Shakley 1999), or managing the risk of investment (Evans 2014) are some of the documented challenges. This means there are trade-offs and the debate on the whether place-based infrastructure and development programs may be effective at stimulating investment continues (Spencer and Ong 2004). From a subject perspective, it is hard to delineate between the topics of tourism and development (Hoffman 2000) as development often is perceived as civil or infrastructure requirements whereas tourism falls often into the purview of place marketing.

Study setting	Authors
Creation of new spaces	
Non place/empty place to place making	Lavrinec 2011
Abandoned Agriculture lands – rewilding	Navarro and Pereira 2012
Hinterland tourism – create gateways	Zurick 1992
New Fashion City in Brazil in Belo Horizonte, Dubai Global Village	Example: http://foresightinhindsight.com/article/show/262
The Palm, Dubai "urban fascination"	Balakrishnan 2008
Revitalizing infrastructure	
Abandoned mine roadway tunnels – future heating centers	Luo and Chen 2011
Adaptive use of abandoned churches	Ahn 2013
Use of abandoned/forgotten cemeteries	Uslu 2010
Slum Tourism	Durr 2012; Foster 2009; Freire-Medeiros 2009
Industrial heritage – redevelopment/tourism	Edwards 1996; Choi and Lim 2013
Dams – make a recreational and alternative transportation corridor paralleling the river	Laiho and Fizgerald 1998
Old building for archives	Haymond 1982
Disused Bridges – market	Bressi 2001
Revitalization after disaster/riots/extinction	
Tourism after forest fires	Hystad and Keller 2008
Destruction tourism	Gould and Lewis 2007; Strochlic 2012
Toxic tourism – e.g. after Chernobyl	Goatcher and Brunsden 2011; Stone 2013
Revitalization after riots/ghettos – empowerment zones, historical/culture peg	McGuire 1997; Rama 2013; Hoffman 2000
Extinct tourism	Pennisi et al. 2004; Leahy 2008

Revival Through Psychic Stimulus using tools like Cultural/History/mythology	
Dark tourism	Lennon and Foley 2000
Rural tourism	Briedenhann and Wickens (2004).
Tourism with legends /mythology	Hennig 2002, Cohen 2010
Tourism of historical relics	Candelaria 2005
War memorials	Mayo 1988
Commercial decline – revitalization	Sutton 2010; Forbes 2006
Declining central-city districts - ethnically themed revitalization	Ford et al. 2008
Virtual Tourism	Behr et al. 2001
Crime/movie tourism	Sydney-Smith 2006; Yamamura 2009
Shopping/cultural festivals	Getz 1993; Hsieh and Chang 2006; Anwar and Sohail 2004
Trust tourism (Las Vegas – What happens in Las Vegas Stays in Las Vegas)	Wood 2005
Sports/game for tourism and revitalization	Gu 2007; Chapin 2004; Austrian and Rosentraub 2002
Self-discovery through reframing: Religious tourism, romance tourism, self-discovery, retreat, retail therapy	Arnould and Thompson 2005; Creighton 1995; Norman and Cusak (2014)

Figure 1: Studies on abandoned places or places requiring revitalization. (Author)

Bridging gaps to revitalize forgotten place brands

To revitalize a place brand, you must be able to manage gaps from a tourist point of view. There are two key methods of bridging that can be identified from literature. The first is reframing (Schembri 2009; Rama 2013) which is to create a new emotional and cognitive frame of reference. This helps overcome resistance and change the status quo. As emotions tends to dominate decision making, the conditioning a consumer is exposed to prior to the decision can impact the choice or post-experience recall (McClure et al. 2004; Armel et al. 2008; Rajagopal and Montgomery 2011; Esch et al. 2012). Neuromarketing and behavioral economics are showing that decisions are rarely rational and hence reframing can help overcome prior bias or lethargy by infusing energy into a situation (Finuacane et al. 2000; Zaltman 2003; Baars et al. 2003; Ariely 2011;

Pessiglione et al. 2008). With forgotten places, there is an opportunity to rebuild them again or "reconstruct memories" (XuDong and Bell 2005).

The other method is to create a cultural movement (Goodson 2012). Movements are initiated by translating "personal experiences into publicly resonant ones" (Knight 2009:115) and "establish(ing) temporal communities of passers-by, who share the interest of spending some time together, sharing emotions and taking part in something different than everyday routine" (Lavrinec 2011: 64). Movements are emotion based. Research shows that while cognition is important to create change, affect-based attitudes (yours and others), can affect decisions (Epstude and Roese 2011; Gray et al. 2002). While many place brands focus on functionalization for decision making as choice criteria, it is clear during decision making that emotions can take over rationalization affecting the brand associations (Finucane et al. 2000; Burke and Edell 1989). Positive emotions also have a contagion effect on groups (Barsade 2002), which are important for creating cultural movements. However, positive emotions can dissipate suggesting that the challenge in managing place brands is protecting the system from leakages through disenchantment (Moisescu 2006). Most place brands will need constant revitalization or reimagination as the setting of place brands is the dynamic global arena where the resources involved like time and money are finite but customer choice is plenty (Haddad et al. 2011).

Based on the case study, it is clear that to reimagine a space and begin the process of revitalization to create touring consumption mobility, there are four gaps that forgotten places must bridge. These four gaps are:

1. Mental – bringing cognitive and emotional gaps
2. Temporal – bridging past, present and future
3. Physical – making the intangible, tangible
4. Economic – helping with the "valuation of money"

There are various concepts found in literature used for revitalization or re-imagination. The purpose of these concepts can be to create a toolbox that can be used to stimulate thinking and emotions that can engage touring consumption. Reimagination of space needs tools for stakeholder engagement. This requires education (Jickling and Wals 2012), writing (Reynolds 2004; Banting 2012) and storytelling. Storytelling can be used to precondition and give meaning to a brand (Szondi 2007; Scolari 2009; Lichrou et al. 2010). Hope has been found to be a powerful emotion and overlaps with brand charisma according to Smothers (1993). And for generating hope, self-narratives of the "underdog" have been found to be linked with greater motivation towards the cause (Prestin 2013). Another important tool is making the stakeholder a co-creator and hence gets stakeholder buy-in and ownership (Payne et al. 2008). The stakeholder buy-in also increases from a psychological point of view using self-discovery and social alignment as motivators (for example Tung and Ritchie 2011).

The second set of tools is for visualization or "eye-balling". This means increasing tangibility of the project either though the creation of iconic structures (Dempsey 2012), servicescape (Lin 2004), using symbolic reminders like mementos or souvenirs (Balakrishnan 2010) or imagineering technology (Rhinesmith 2013). Branding is a shortcut for visualizing (Pawson 1997). Brand architecture helps in managing mental representations and creates synergy in product portfolios (Douglass et al. 2001; Aaker 2003; Stebringer 2004).

The third set of tools overlaps the first two as it creates an experiential backdrop to reimagination by immersing the customer through technology, writing and servicescape and engaging the customer through interactive displays that use technology or people. Music and lyrics (Botta 2006), media and popular culture like books, movies (Iwashita 2006; Hudson and Ritchie 2006) and mobile gaming (Hoffman 2011) are additional tools being used.

The fourth set of tools is for creating energy. This requires active engagement with media, stakeholders and generation of positive emotions using writing, press conferences, tours and meetings. It overlaps with all the three set of tools and focuses on creating a cultural movement. Perceived choice in the product portfolio creates energy by catering to the variety-seeking behavior (Kemperman et al. 2000) and hedonistic appeal (Bigne et al. 2009; Bigne and Andreu 2004). These engagement tools which can be abbreviated by as E^4 (see Figure 2) help create touring consumption.

The purpose of creating touring consumption is to create brand equity and brand loyalty to the place which result in reputation, relational and venture capital (Goldberg et al. 2003; de Castro et al. 2004; Quelch et al. 2004; Aaker 2009; Balakrishnan 2011). Brand equity is defined from the consumer (stakeholder) point of view and can be considered as the perception or desire that a brand will meet a promise of benefits (see Raggio and Leone 2007). Brand loyalty is the set of meaningful relationships a consumer/stakeholder has with the brand and can bridge involvement at the emotional, behavioral and cognitive levels (Fournier and Yao 1997). At the operational level, brand equity and brand loyalty lead to emotional attachment, positive word of mouth (WOM), positive reputation, brand credibility, satisfaction, positive decisions making behavior (choice, commitment to buy) (see Balakrishnan 2011).

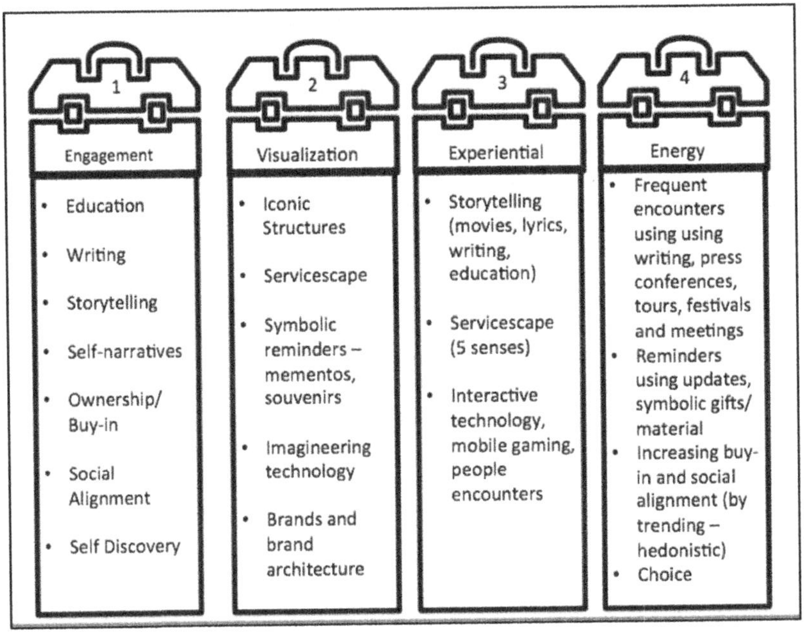

Figure 2: E[4] Re-imagination toolbox: Creating connectivity by initiating movements and precondition. (Author)

Gap 1: Bridging temporal spaces

Decision-making is affected by time or temporal space (Balakrishnan et al. 2011) and can be bridged through emotions by converting intensions to actual behavior (Mohiyeddini et al. 2009). Relevant communications strategies can give form and substance to temporal vistas through specific stories (Castano et al. 2008; Ooi 2001: 190). This may create the phenomena of "timelessness" which according to Mainemelis (2001) is the creation of a psychological, and sometimes physical, space in which one can become totally involved in the task-away from worries, problems, or distractions. While reimagination from past to present can be achieved using education and technology (or "*imagineering*") to create timelessness (Hoffman 2011; Rhinesmith, 2013), revitalization from present to future needs the benefits of the project to be tangible (Rowley and Slack 1999). This is done through engagement strategies using the toolbox described in Figure 1. It has been found that the *strength of the engagement* contributes to the experienced value (Higgins 2006) which leads to various positive consumer behaviors like commitment to buy; positive word of mouth, trust and repeat behavior (Vivek 2009). For example a study found that business engagement on Twitter related directly to consumers' engagement with online word-of-mouth communication, even though the life cycle of a tweet was generally only 1.5 to 4 hours at most (Zhang et al. 2011). Openness in dialogue and active engagement is important to create credibility to bridge temporal spaces (Yang et al. 2010).

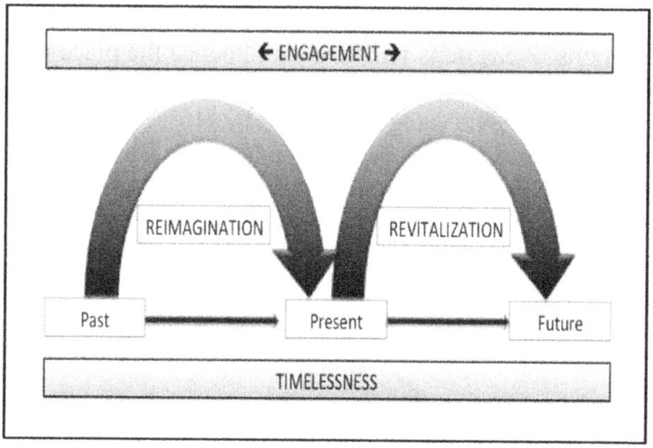

Figure 3: Creating consumption mobility through temporal space. (Author)

Gap 2: Bridging the functional or physical spaces

To bridge the functional space from past to present, the challenge with place revitalization is making the intangible, tangible (Rushton and Carson 1985). The physical environment or servicescape (what you can see, touch and smell) has been found to generate excitement in leisure settings, which affects repatronage intentions and willingness to recommend (Wakefield and Blodgett 1999). Physical attributes lead to place attachment and satisfaction (Stedman 2003). Product attributes contribute to brand equity and brand choice (Myers 2003) and the importance of various attributes peak at different stages of the tourism choice process (Balakrishnan et al. 2011). This makes mobilities between product offerings important. Another objective of bridging the functional or physical spaces is to reduce spatial search. This can be done by giving access to a "*behind the scenes*" tour or self-organized tours using maps or virtual interactive devices (Murphy and Rosenblood 1974).

Visualization of a project, especially one with huge infrastructure costs or requiring community participation needs to be tangible for "*reimagination*" to achieve revitalization. In the place context, consumption mobility takes place across areas of functional, experiential and symbolic elements through the spheres of physical goods, service, experiences and even concepts (Ariely and Norton 2009; Picard 1996). Since perceived choice is important to bridge functional spaces a variety of products should be offered and can be chosen from the portfolio depicted in Figure 4. Since hedonistic characteristics of a space help bridge functional space – tourism products offered must be able to create these pleasurable emotions. Pleasure is temporary and hence the place needs to be able to capture these memories either through pictures, souvenirs and social media narratives (see Bruner 1989; Xiang and Gretzel 2010). Narratives can create (in some cases distort) memories (Garry and Wade 2005) showing how powerful a tool it can be. These strategies help increase perceived value by increasing benefits associated with the place and reducing perceived costs. A model to bridge the functional or physical space is presented in Figure 5.

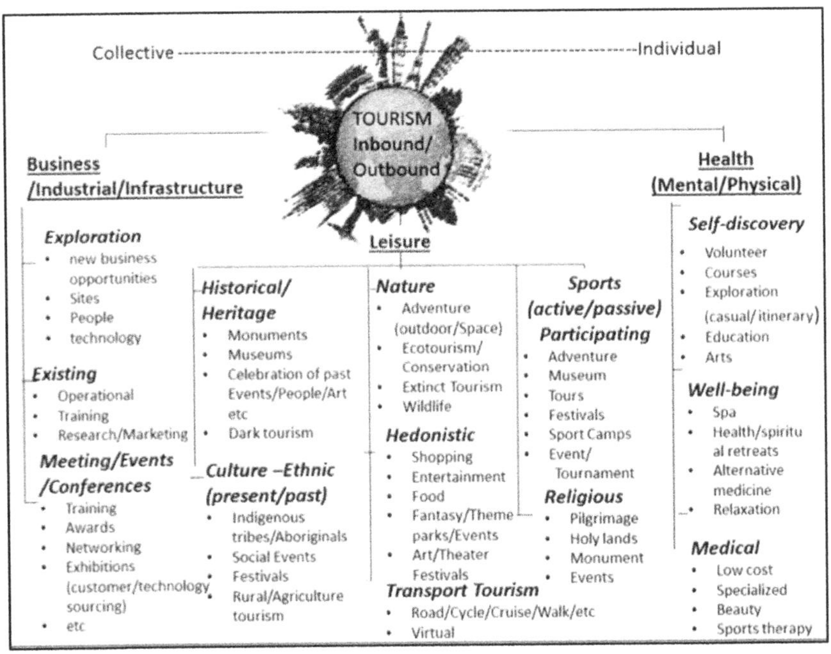

Figure 4: Tourism product portfolio. (Author)

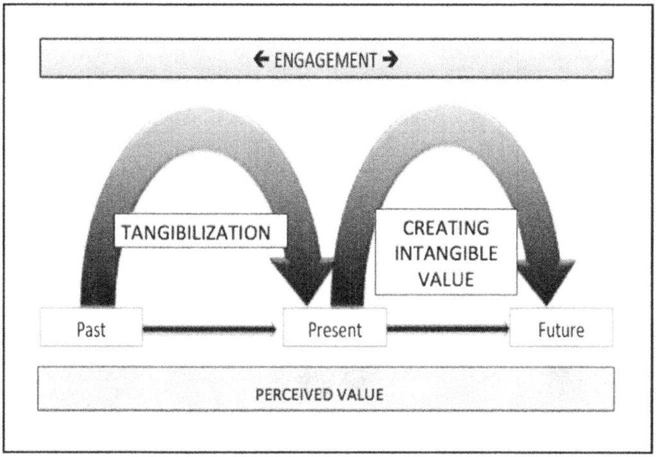

Figure 5: Creating consumption mobility through functional spaces. (Author)

Gap 3: Bridging economic space

To bridge the economic space from past to present, customers conduct a cost benefit analysis, and the value of money becomes a trade-off to experiences and hedonism, often to demonstrate status or the alignment to social group (Phillip and Back 2013). This means a customer may be willing to barter economic value in exchange for additional benefits like self-discovery or even to get social approval. At this stage the relationship is still transactional since the psychic cost may be high. Hence the mental setting may determine the fair exchange for the "*valuation of money*" and the "*imagination of a place*" (Desforges 2001). For new products, the promise of the core service quality and perceived value are more important drivers of customer satisfaction than the actual delivery (relational service quality) (McDougall and Levesque 2000) indicating that the mental setting (or preconditioning) was key to bridging the economic space.

When present to future value is bridged through satisfaction and credibility of the brand experience, consumers show loyalty, repurchase and even shareholders invest more (Phillip and Back 2013; Bigne et al. 2009; Bigne and Andreu 2004; Anderson et al. 2004; Sweeney and Swait 2008). At this stage the demand may outstrip the supply and the competitive arena may get more defined with customers bidding for more benefits. A key to bridge economic space for all concerned stakeholders is to manage the perceived value of the place brand that reviews benefits and costs (Balakrishnan 2011). A model to bridge economic space is presented in Figure 6.

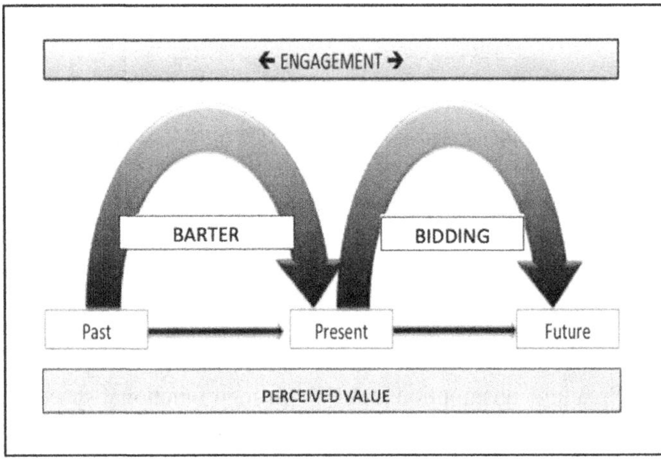

Figure 6: Creating consumption mobility through economic spaces. (Author)

Gap 4: Bridging mental space

When bridging past to the present, you need to engage the customer at the cognitive level. Cognitions refer to mental representations such as knowledge or beliefs. These can create barriers to place consumption decisions because of perceived risk or associated costs in the place brand choice decisions. Information sharing helps reduce these mental barriers (Bettman et al. 1986; Christelis et al. 2010; Johnson et al. 2008; Hottola 2004). The information strategies can be combinations of the classic push (inner motivations) and pull (external place attribute) derived from the factor motivation theory (Crompton 1979).

Place decision-making is not rational (Balakrishnan et al. 2011) and when bridging mental spaces, the heart (affective reactions) takes over mind (cognitive reactions) especially given limited processing time to determine choice (Shiv and Fedorikhin 1999; Bechara 2004). Consumers are attracted to products that enable the enactment of self-discovery and this needs to be consistent in their perception of self or the various social entities which make up the sense of self (Pearce 1985; Joy and Deschenes 2010; Wearing 2004; Keleine III et al. 1993).

Because a destination image is a multi-dimensional concept formed by cognitive and affective evaluations of a place (San Martin and Del Bosque 2008) it needs multiple positions to reimagine spaces (Jickling and Wals 2012; Warde 2005: 131). The challenge is to minimize misrepresentation with reality or the culture shock (Johnson et al. 2008; Hottola 2004; Bandyopadhyay and Morais 2005) and allow multiple representations to co-exist without too much friction. This means providing structured brand choice that allows multiple perspectives to co-exist. Hence we see some overlap with functional space. Bridging the present to future requires maintaining or increasing the affective elements associated with the place (commitment and loyalty) as these are difficult to rationalize (Pritchard et al. 1999: 334; Balakrishnan 2011). A model to bridge mental spaces is presented in Figure 7.

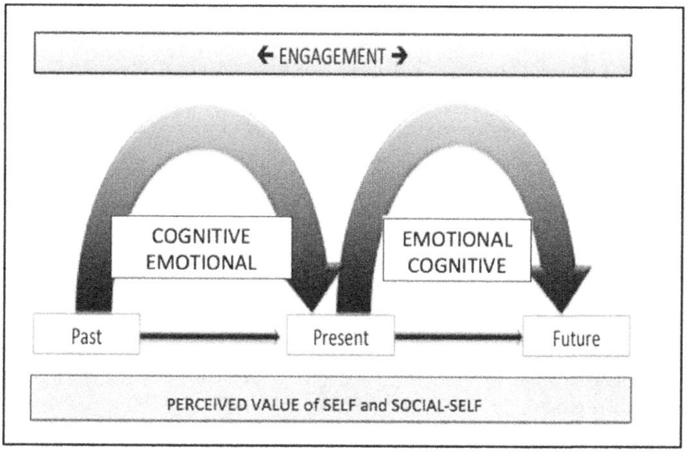

Figure 7: Creating consumption mobility through mental spaces. (Author)

The Old London Underground Company: A case study

The Old London Underground Company (TOLUC) is a British start-up founded by Ajit Chambers, a former executive at JPMorgan Chase. On February 14, 2009 Ajit was cycling past an old shop in a tiny alley. Inside, he found an old map with the original London Underground stations on it. Ajit wanted to contribute in a way to alleviate the credit crunch affecting Londoners. Within a month, he resigned from his job planning to figure out a way to use the disused stations for the economic benefit of the city. These sites were worth about £1 billion in real estate terms. Ajit says he wanted to "…unlock the value of historic underground real estate that had largely been forgotten". Preliminary feasibility studies showed that revitalization of each underground station would require £2.5 million. Revitalization would take 3-5 years at the minimum to make the place safe and secure. His viability tests showed that there was a potential to generate £200 million from the first five active sites. He stated "The project is – was, to reimagine London's cultural landscape... to change the way we see old and disused sections of the UK's capital city....(it) may encourage other global cities to begin to reinvent rundown historical landmarks into economically viable cultural heritage" (Hirani 2013a). Though the project was conceived in 2009, he only got his first offer for investment funding of £200 million in September 2013. The journey (which was documented on his living room wall – see Figure 8) was made arduous by managing the multiple stakeholders with vested viewpoints. He needed to initiate tourism consumption by encouraging mobility across spaces or pre-conceived gaps that blocked progress. The biggest barrier was the fact that an idea does not mean reality was possible.

Figure 8: TOLUC key stages in the development of the company and finalization of plans. (Ajit Chambers)

Managing stakeholders is a big challenge for place branding and touring consumption as it complicates the products that need to be offered. The project was difficult to execute as it involved public private partnerships (PPPs). Private partnerships were forged for investment, community involvement and execution of the project. A key challenge was establishing ownership and managing the integrity of first rights. With government and public sector involvement, authority delineation was more complicated. On one hand was the Mayor of London – Boris Johnson and his very protective bureaucratic government office; members representing political parties; Government offices like the Transport for London (TfL) which owned most underground stations and The Ministry of Defense (MOD). MOD had bought sites like Brompton Road from TfL during the war years and was considering making a massive ROI selling the site to foreign investors (Cecil and Prynn 2014). TOLUC was lobbying against this privatization and had support from some members of the Parliament, media and many champions but the process was diffused as the authority lines and decision makers were not clear in a British bureaucratic set-up.

By 2013, Ajit had managed to get public support from 70 MPs. For example in May 2012, Mike Weatherley, the Conservative Member of Parliament for Hove and Portslade was the primary sponsor moving a motion (No 2853) that congratulated TOLUC on "*...its efforts in opening up London's ghost stations and deep level shelters to the public as a viable enterprise following HM Treasury's Wider Markets Initiative....and supports Ajit Chambers with the next stage of this exciting opportunity for outside investment in the leisure and tourism sector.". The motion also "...recognizes that TOLUC requests assistance from Transport for London to include international press in the site visit for Honorary Members and Lords to visit a ghost station site.*" (Weatherly 2012). David McNeill (TFL Group Corporate Affairs Director) was helping progress the project through all the red tape[1], as the majority of the disused stations were accessible to the operational railway which presented safety issues.

TOLUC's objective was the "*Reimagination and Revitalization of London's portfolio of disused underground space.*" TOLUC needed to create connectivity across various consumptions, to generate positive emotions to reimagine places and change perceptions to overcome barriers to the project. The four consumption experiences TOLUC and Ajit were focusing on bridging were (1) temporal (2) physical (3) economic and (4) mental gaps.

1 http://commutingexpert.com/resurrecting-ghosts-the-return-of-london-undergrounds-abandoned-stations/

TOLUC: Bridging temporal spaces

TOLUC was focusing on bridging the past with the present and the present with the future. The name of the company was a tangible reminder of the past and related to the present London Underground tube representation (see Figure 9). The London Underground is considered the world's oldest subterranean rail network with a rich history accompanying many sites, which has been forgotten. One of the first stations planned to be opened, the Brompton Road Station, part of the Piccadilly Line, was opened in 1906 and then closed temporarily during World War II to be used as a war room and ceased to be used after 1934. It was sold to the MOD shortly after the outbreak of the Second World War, for £24,000 (Subterranea Britannica 2008). Brompton Road was used as the secret underground Command Centre for the anti-aircraft division of the RAF where Winston Churchill frequented. This site was the interrogation site of Hitler's deputy Rudolf Hess who had crash-landed in Scotland in 1941. Another abandoned station, Aldwych, near the theater district was used as a bomb shelter and closed in 1994 (BBC, 2014). These are just some examples.

Ajit planned to open some tunnels as museums – dedicated to great British movements. Few people know that London has the 4th largest fire brigade in the world even though a museum exists. TOLUC plans for one of the tunnels to be a literal walk through time where visitors experience the history of the fire brigade. The exhibits would be interactive allowing customer to pump water and see realistic figures of horse drawn fire brigade carriages. Tales like how the ladder became an important part of the fire brigade or even the great London fire of 1666 which gutted most of the medieval City of London will be retold with tangible reminders. Ajit plans to use Imagineering technology ranging from the passive slides, displays or the more Interactive, experiential or educational ones like rides back into time using 3D movies, holograms, mix of actors and technology that will create an explorative experience. More nostalgic customers could book personal tours. The experience was to be offered 24/7, introducing the concept of "timelessness" which is a phenomena associated with travellers. But the present and future were also being bridged. So for example the tunnel dedicated to British banking would have an interactive wall where comments, suggestions and questions could be written and answers from concerned authorities would be forwarded to the customer's email. It was hoped that crowd sourcing would solve current problems but more importantly would help the public connect with the right people to bypass bureaucracy. In this way TOLUC was fusing past, present and future seamlessly.

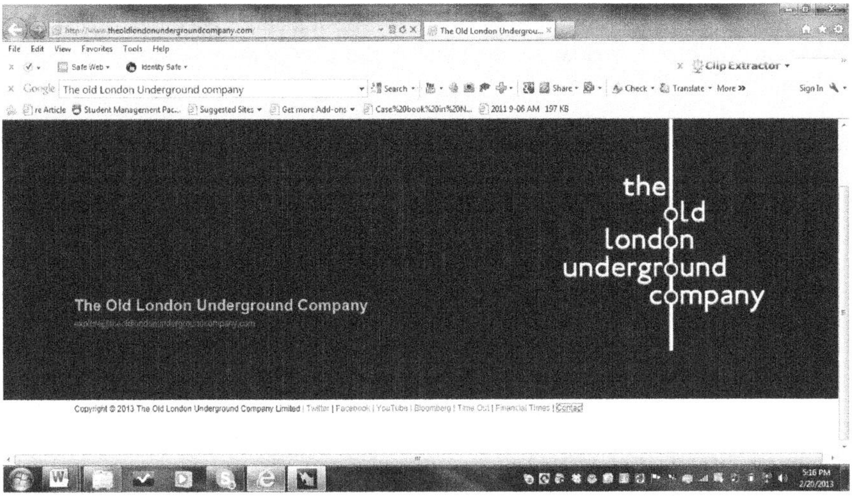

Figure 9: TOLUC – representation. (Ajit Chambers)

Bridging the functional or physical spaces

Ajit had to bridge the Physical gap with respect to investment stakeholders and regulatory stakeholders. In 2009, he spent his last salary to design 12 back boxes with a single golden ticket[2] giving the holder permission to tour the underground (see Figure 10). The first person he wanted to give the box to was the Mayor of London. Ajit cycled to the Mayors Office with an invitation to '*a tourist adventure into the veins of London*'. Ajit said: "*The staff said it looked great – I said it does not exist. I gave these to Time Out Magazine, FT ...(I) put the business card on the wall as a tangible reminder of the progression of work and set a goal – by the time this wall is full, I must have completed this project.*" He created an external presence of project progress through the active use of social media (twitter, Facebook, YouTube) and by giving over 200 interviews using both social media (Wiki, LinkedIn, Skype) and mainstream journalists – like local media TV (BBC) and international press (Bloomberg). The media proliferation was necessary creating a tangible evidence of progress but also maintaining engagement across time – creating a relationship.

2 Similar to Charlie and the Chocolate Factory

In 2009, Ajit stood up in front of the Mayor at a conference in Croydon and promised to create a private and public partnership that would bring in £200 million for the UK economy. From then on, it took 18 months to make the right contacts and build a consortium[3] and by 12th November 2012 – he presented the formal plan to the Mayors office (see Figure 11) and to the Mayor himself on 20th December. In July 2013, he showed his cashiers check to the Mayors Office to show proof of investment. Bloomberg ran a press article on the 200 million investment Ajit was able to bring to the table as early as 2011 and a Canadian TV channel – Global National conducted an interview with his local MP (Spillane 2011 and Global National 2013).

Figure 10: Black box with a gold ticket. (Ajit Chambers)

3 http://www.citmagazine.com/article/1184242/masterplan-transforming-londons-underground-stations-events-space

Figure 11: Formal business plan. (Ajit Chambers)

Each site had a range of product offerings for the final customer. For the final consumer, there were leisure and self-discovery offerings like museums, events, dancing and historical tours; Adventure excursions (like the climbing shafts) and hedonistic products like shopping, food and retail. For the business customers there were events, and meeting/conference venues being offered. Each site had a model where triple redundancy was built into it. The tools TOLUC used were visualization, dialogues and creation of hedonistic experiences giving choice for vicarious consumption. Ajit was getting WOM, generating place attachment and developing credibility through multiple associations and the perception of choice for the immediate stakeholders (history – nostalgia, pride in heritage, future of small business and tourism, economic viability and returns, social impact etc.). TOLUC had loyalists who were championing the cause even at the highest echelons of power.

Bridging economic space

TOLUCs funding methodology was to create ROI through private and public partnerships (PPP) but without the legal expense of creating an overly complex structure. For funding, TOLUC needed to get stakeholder buy-in by agreeing on the "value" of the exchange. The Mayor of London, Boris Johnson, pledged on BBC Parliament TV on December 12, 2011 that '*We will do the project as long as it doesn't cost a penny of public money*'[4]. TOLUC by bringing private funding to the table was able to demonstrate the feasibility of the project.

Ajit worked with Jones Lang LaSalle, so that communities around the proposed sites knew that the value of their property would increase in future as each site was opened. Ajit was able to get the Heritage Lottery Fund to promise £50,000 for each borough, for each site, for each community, to add to the already existing ties with the community, to revitalize the neighborhood by painting signs and hosting and running workshops for that particular underground section. Ajit says "*So it's all about community involvement. Community work has been used many years without having any depth. But after the credit crunch, it is there again... we need to capture it.*" Community involvement was crucial for the success of the plan. He had celebrity support in the form of actors Rupert Everett and Russell Brand. In September 2013, there were rumors that the Brompton site was being sold to a wealthy private international family. Ajit had always said that heritage sites should be accessible to the public and was against their privatization, "*As the battle for Brompton Road begins, the public become a large influence as essentially they own this site as taxpayers.*[5]" He lobbied tugging at emotional sentiment and had support from the Parliament and from inside Downing Street. It was not about the money, it was about the access to the sites by Londoners! TOLUC planned to lease the sites from the government to keep it accessible to the public.

TOLUC runs with the help of professional volunteers. Ajit says "*I'm quite egoistical about details...so I make deals.*" He uses barter – some examples were work in exchange for the sharing of knowledge, contacts, access to his networks – or the tantalizing scoop. Ajit reminisces what he does was similar to the early fire brigade years when beer tokens were given to volunteers to rally in support of the community to put out fires. These tokens were then redeemable at pubs. Some supporters contribute in anticipation of the future returns. International corporations have already realized the potential and are bidding for the right to stage the first event in the site offering sums in the areas of £100,000 and media

4 See video: http://www.youtube.com/watch?v=wq3fNmnYyuA

5 http://www.telegraph.co.uk/history/britain-at-war/10314264/Billionaires-in-bidding-war-for-Brompton-Road-station

companies like MSN have promised to cover the launch event for worldwide consumption.

Some people volunteer because of the need to contribute to the "*Spirit of London*". Ajit has assembled a strategic task team of volunteers like the founder of the visitor-experience led Vinopolis, Duncan Vaughan-Arbuckle; Wing Commander Ian Shaw (ex- MOD/RAF) and John Ross, former CEO of Schneider Electric. Most of the volunteers manage their own costs. Ajit says of his volunteers "*All of those guys, have been through hard times... Generally what happens when someone tells anyone else about this project, people will laugh at me, but the successful people realize that if someone is laughing at you, they are probably laughing at you for a reason, which means there may be a very good chance you may be right. This is a project and product for London Spirit, not specifically for this team to succeed at it but the project itself to keep leaning forwards.*" The value exchange in this case is not monetary.

The consumer target was multinational, Ajit said – "*Not particularly only Londoners created these products in London. This is about how the whole world built it – London and in effect how the whole world built every city with all the collective expertise.*" The funding consortium is international. TOLUCs mental reframing of the cause for multiple stakeholders allowed greater self-discovery, social alignments and created hedonism but not in the same proportions for all stakeholders. The ability to barter was key to keeping the project alive. We see that the valuation (from stakeholder perspective) has increased in time and so has the status of the project. There is a serious commitment to invest resources (not just money but time, energy, networks, talent) and this is also inherent in the reduction of psychic cost of key stakeholders and public.

Bridging mental space

Ajit was the underdog and his narratives seemed to build hope in the hearts of many – whether entrepreneurs or small business owners or even lovers of the old London Underground. Ajit says "*I spent my last paycheck on setting up the business to prove that I was strong enough to do this, even when I thought I was becoming weak. Was it difficult? It was incredibly difficult, constantly difficult, setting up constantly for the last three years, you get incredibly lonely. Not only that, you get incredibly lonely when people who are supposed to be looking after you are the ones that are laughing at you. But as with most things in life, we are not looking for the easy but the difficult things ...so yah, yah, I'm an old man with gray hair and all, because of this.*" Two universities were using TOLUC as educational resources in 2013 – one in Dubai and the other in Cambridge.

Ajit's press policy was to constantly be in contact with influencers and the community. The sites would provide education for history or movie aficionados. "*In London I had a press policy, which was that we would reach out 24 hours a day, even at 4 in the morning, constantly, to the most wealthy self made people in the world.... (for) cross-contamination of the brand... You will hear about it in two places, ...so yah, we went big time on press, internationally first, then locally with radio, then we did a talk show, a little bit of TV background, which wasn't really seen, but if you Google us – you will see us on the Vanessa show. Myself and Russell Brandt's dad, ...now we are going back to national TV. We got Russian TV with a 100 million viewers, Network ten. ABC Australia, the Stage show for NBC...so it is about letting everybody know. A classic example was about how I had someone in Eastern Europe, reading about us in the Lonely Planet and they managed to find the phone number, and call us and say this is brilliant.*"

For urban planners, communities, investors, Ajit talks about unlocking the hidden potential of the sites "*The Project is showing London that urban regeneration does not have to be 'more of the same' and that thinking out of the box will show us the answers that are hidden but blindingly obvious once explored. We are making £1 billion pounds of space available to a city that is desperate for it by simply adding health and safety in an efficient and economic way.*" Hence he is able to present a rational dialogue but it is interspersed with the emotional undertones of his story, heritage of the sites and the people and companies involved. This dual communication leads to a cultural movement that seems to gather momentum with time. From self-discovery it moves to social alignments through the multiple reference frames for various stakeholders through storytelling, education, the immersive and interactive experiences, and thus TOLUC generates positive emotions.

Model – Revitalizing: Forgotten places through tourist consumption

There are areas TOLUC can work on, like emotional bonding through sensory signatures like audio, taste, smell and touch. Most of the focus at this stage before the project is running is on the visual. We do know how strong smell and taste are on linking old memories (Lindstorm 2005). Multiple stakeholders add complexity to place branding as with revitalization projects, funding is always the first major hurdle after permissions. There still exists a gap to bridge spaces between self and social self but this is something for the final consumer, not current stakeholders. Some levels of secrecy are inherent in deal making. The connectivity trade-off in experiences range from limited to extensive, passive or active, immersed or interactive, or delivered or co-created. It depends of the stakeholder and also context, London is far more open than some parts of the world and celebrates small business owners. There are opportunities for spillover – festivals, movies, books, and this opens more new doors.

Figure 12 presents a conceptual model – the GAME Model of Consumption (Gap Action & Mobilization through Engagement), which is an engagement model for creating touring consumption across temporal, physical or functional, economic or mental spaces for tourism consumption. We find to bridge from past to present, the tools used are (1) to help stakeholders prioritize the product mentally, (2) to create visualization and (3) to create experiences. The tools used to bridge present and future revolve around (1) value-exchange reframing, (2) creation of energy and (3) creating visibility. The brand outcomes range from brand equity and brand commitment.

This brings up additional research questions in the area of tourism, consumption, branding and entrepreneurship and can be tested in other cases.

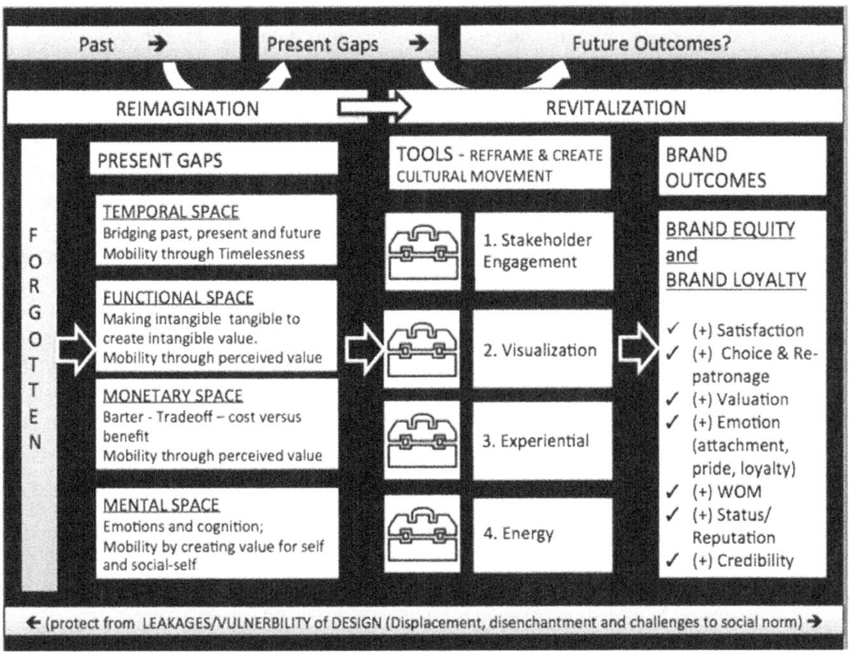

Figure 12: GAME model (gap action & mobilization through engagement) of consumption. (Author)

References

Aaker, D.A. (2003): The power of the branded differentiator. In: MIT Sloan Management Review, 45(1), 83-87.

Aaker, D.A. (2009): Managing brand equity. New York: Simon and Schuster.

Ahn, Y.K. (2013): Adaptive reuse of abandoned historic churches: Building type and public perception. http://repositories.tdl.org/tdl-ir/handle/1969.1/ETD-TAMU-1677, 12.12.2013.

Anderson, E.W., Fornell, C. and Mazvancheryl, S.K. (2004): Customer satisfaction and shareholder value. In: Journal of Marketing, 68(4), 172-185.

Anwar, S.A. and Sohail, M.S. (2004): Festival tourism in the United Arab Emirates: First time versus repeat visitor perceptions. In: Journal of Vacation Marketing, 10(2), 161-170.

Ariely, D. (2011): The honest truth about dishonesty. New York: Harper Collins Publisher.

Ariely, D. and Norton, M.I. (2009): Conceptual consumption. In: Annual Review Psychological, 60, 475-499.

Armel, K.C., Beaumel, A. and Rangel, A. (2008): Biasing simple choices by manipulating relative visual attention. In: Judgment and Decision Making, 3(5), 396-403.

Arnould, E.J. and Thompson, C.J. (2005): Consumer culture theory (CCT): Twenty years of research. In: Journal of Consumer Research, 31(4), 868-882.

Ashworth, G.J. and Kavaratzis, M. (2010) (eds.): Towards effective place brand management: Branding European cities and regions. Cheltenham: Edward Elgar Publishing.

Austrian, Z. and Rosentraub, M.S. (2002): Cities, sports, and economic change: A retrospective assessment. In: Journal of Urban Affairs, 24(5), 549-563.

Baars, B.J., Ramsøy, T.Z. and Laureys, S. (2003): Brain, conscious experience and the observing self. In: Trends in Neurosciences, 26(12), 671-675.

Balakrishnan, M.S. (2008): Dubai–a star in the east: A case study in strategic destination branding. In: Journal of Place Management and Development, 1(1), 62-91.

Balakrishnan, M. S. (2011): Gain the most from your marketing spend on loyalty. In: Business Strategy Series, 12(5), 219-225.

Balakrishnan, M.S., Nekhili, R. and Lewis C. (2011): Destination brand components. In: International Journal of Culture, Tourism and Hospitality Research, 5(1), 4-25.

Bandyopadhyay, R. and Morais, D. (2005): Representative dissonance: India's self and western image. In: Annals of Tourism Research, 32(4), 1006-1021.

Banting, P. (2012): The bioregional imagination: Literature, ecology, and place. In: Interdisciplinary Studies in Literature and Environment, 19(4), 788-789.

Barsade, S.G. (2002): The ripple effect: Emotional contagion and its influence on group behavior. In: Administrative Science Quarterly, 47(4), 644-675.

BBC (2014): The allure of abandoned Tube stations, dated 3 January. http://www.bbc.com/news/magazine-25576814, 15.06.2014.

Bechara, A. (2004): The role of emotion in decision-making: Evidence from neurological patients with orbitofrontal damage. In: Brain and Cognition, 55(1), 30-40.

Behr, J., Froehlich, T., Knoepfle, C., Kresse, W., Lutz, B., Reiners, D. and Ehr J. (2001): The digital cathedral of Siena – Innovative concepts for interactive and immersive presentation of cultural heritage sites. http://www.archimuse.com/publishing/ichim01_vol1/behr.pdf, 02.02.2014.

Bettman, J.R., Payne, J.W. and Staelin R. (1986): Cognitive considerations in designing effective labels for presenting risk information. In: Journal of Public Policy and Marketing, 5(1), 1-28.

Bigné, J.E. and Andreu L. (2004): Emotions in segmentation: An empirical study. In: Annals of Tourism Research, 31(3), 682-696.

Bigné, J.E., Sánchez, I. and Andreu, L. (2009): The role of variety seeking in short and long run revisit intentions in holiday destinations. In: International Journal of Culture, Tourism and Hospitality Research, 3(2), 103-115.

Billig, M. (2005): Sense of place in the neighborhood, in locations of urban revitalization. In: GeoJournal, 64(2), 117-130.

Blackman, A. (2011): London entrepreneur sees a gold mine in developing unused subway-stations. http://www.bloomberg.com/news/2011-09-08/london-entrepreneur-sees-a-gold-mine-in-developing-unused-subway-stations.html, 02.10.2013.

Bogart, L. (1973): Psychology on a large scale: The study of consumption. In: American Psychologist, 28(11), 994-999.

Bottà, G. (2006): Pop music, cultural sensibilities and places: Manchester 1976-1997. In: The ESF-LiU Conference, 121-125, http://www.ep.liu.se/ecp/020/011/ecp072011.pdf, 12.02.2013.

Briedenhann, J. and Wickens E. (2004): Tourism routes as a tool for the economic development of rural areas – vibrant hope or impossible dream? In: Tourism Management, 25(1), 71-79.

Bressi, T.W. (2001): Bridgemarket, James A. Farley building. In: Places, 14(2), 21-22.

Brodie, R.J, Hollebeek, L.D., Jurić, B. and Ilić, A. (2011): Customer engagement conceptual domain, fundamental propositions, and implications for research. In: Journal of Service Research, 14(3), 252-271.

Brown, G., Brown, B.B. and Perkins, D.D. (2004): New housing as neighborhood revitalization place: Attachment and confidence among residents. In: Environment and Behavior, 36(6), 749-775.

Bruner, E.M. (1989): Of cannibals, tourists, and ethnographers. In: Cultural Anthropology, 4(4), 438-445.

Burke, M.C. and Edell, J.A. (1989): The impact of feelings on ad-based affect and cognition. In: Journal of Marketing Research, 26(1), 69-83.

Candelaria, M.A.F. (2005): Angkor sites of Cambodia: The conflicting values of sustainable tourism and state sovereignty. In: The Brooklyn Journal of International Law, 31, 253-269.

Castaño, R., Kacker, S.M. and Sujan, H. (2008): Managing uncertainty in the adoption of new products: Temporal distance and mental simulation. In: Journal of Marketing Research, 45(3), 320-336.

Cecil, N. and Prynn, J. (2014): Disused Brompton Road tube station sold to wealthy Ukranian for £53m, London Evening Standard, dated March 1, http://www.

standard.co.uk/news/london/disused-brompton-road-tube-station-sold-to-wealthy-ukranian-for-53m-9162296.html, 12.05.2014.

Chapin, T.S. (2004): Sports facilities as urban redevelopment catalysts: Baltimore's Camden Yards and Cleveland's Gateway. In: Journal of the American Planning Association, 70(2), 193-209.

Charmaz, K. (2014) Constructing grounded theory. Sage Publications Limited, London.

Choi, J.R. and Lim, D.G. (2013): A case study of cultural space to revitalize local community. In: International Journal of History and Culture, 1(1), 1-14.

Christelis, D., Jappelli, T. and Padula, M. (2010): Cognitive abilities and portfolio choice. In: European Economic Review, 54(1), 18-38.

Cochrane, A. and Jonas, A. (1999): Reimagining Berlin world city, national capital or ordinary place? In: European Urban And Regional Studies, 6(2), 145-164.

Cohen, E. (2010): Dinosaurs in Thai culture and tourism. In: Tourism Culture and Communication, 10(2), 117-135.

Corral-Verdugo, V. (2002): A structural model of pro-environmental competency. In: Environment and Behavior, 34 (4), 531-49.

Creighton, M.R. (1995): Japanese craft tourism: Liberating the crane wife. In: Annals of Tourism Research, 22(2), 463-478.

Crompton, J.L. (1979): Motivations for pleasure vacation. In: Annals of Tourism Research, 6(4), 408-424.

Dangerfield, A. (2012): Brompton Road tube ghost station resurrection plans announced. In: BBC News London, dated 14 April, http://www.bbc.co.uk/news/uk-england-london-17699680, 06.05.2013.

De Castro, G.M., Sáez, P.L. and López, J.E.N. (2004): The role of corporate reputation in developing relational capital. In: Journal of Intellectual Capital, 5(4), 575-585.

Dempsey, K. (2012): Galicia's hurricane: Actor networks and iconic constructions. In: Geographical Review, 102(1), 93-110.

Desforges, L. (2001): Tourism consumption and the imagination of money. In: Transaction of the Institute of British Geographers, 26(3), 353-364.

Douglas, S.P., Craig, C.S. and Nijssen, E.J. (2001): Integrating branding strategy across markets: Building international brand architecture. In: Journal of International Marketing, 9(2), 97-114.

Durr, E. (2012): Slum tourism in Mexico. In: International Journal of Urban and Regional Research, 36(4), 707-24.

Edensor, T. (2007): Mundane mobilities, performances and spaces of tourism. In: Social & Cultural Geography, 8(2), 199-215.

Edwards, J.A. (1996): Mines and quarries: industrial heritage tourism. In: Annals of Tourism Research, 23(2), 341-363.

Edwards, K. (1990): The interplay of affect and cognition in attitude formation and change. In: Journal of Personality and Social Psychology, 59(2), 202.

Epstude, K. and Roese, N.J. (2011): When goal pursuit fails: The functions of counterfactual thought in intention formation. In: Social Psychology, 42(1), 19.

Erdem, T. and Swait, J. (2004): Brand credibility, brand consideration, and choice. In: Journal of Consumer Research, 31(1), 191-198.

Esch, F.R., Möll, T., Schmitt, B., Elger, C.E., Neuhaus, C. and Weber B. (2012): Brands on the brain: Do consumers use declarative information or experienced emotions to evaluate brands? In: Journal of Consumer Psychology, 22(1), 75-85.

Evans, A.M. (2014): No visibility, no artifacts, no problem? Challenges associated with presenting buried sites and inaccessible shipwrecks to the public. In: Scott-Ireton, D.A. (ed.): Between the Devil and the Deep. New York: Springer, 131-139.

Fan, Y. (2006): Branding the nation: What is being branded? In: Journal of Vacation Marketing, 12(1), 5-14.

Firat, A.F. and Shultz II, C.J. (1997): From segmentation to fragmentation: Markets and marketing strategy in the postmodern era. In: European Journal of Marketing, 31(3/4), 183-207.

Frank, A.W. (2008): Why study people's stories? The dialogical ethics of narrative analysis. In: International Journal of Qualitative Methods, 1(1), 109-117.

Finucane, M.L., Alhakami, A., Slovic, P. and Johnson, S.M. (2000): The affect heuristic in judgments of risks and benefits. In: Journal of Behavioral Decision Making, 13(1), 1-17.

Fitzmaurice, J. and Comegys, C. (2006): Materialism and social consumption. In: The Journal of Marketing Theory and Practice, 14(4), 287-299.

Forbes, J. (2006): Using economic development programs as tools for urban revitalization: A comparison of empowerment zones and new markets tax credits. In: University of Illinois Law Review, 2006(1), 177-204.

Ford, L., Klevisser, F. and Carli, F. (2008): Ethnic neighborhoods and urban revitalization: can Europe use the American model? In: Geographical Review, 98(1), 82-102.

Freire-Medeiros, B. (2009): The favela and its touristic transits. In: Geoforum, 40(4), 580-88.

Frith, C.D. and Singer, T. (2008): The role of social cognition in decision making. In: Philosophical Transactions of the Royal Society B: Biological Sciences, 363(1511), 3875-3886.

Ford, L., Klevisser, F. and Carli, F. (2008): Ethnic neighborhoods and urban revitalization: Can Europe use the American model? In: Geographic Review, 98(1), 82-102.

Foster, J. (2009): Slumdog Millionnaire puts slum tourism in the spotlight. In: Asia Development: A Publication of the Asian Development Bank 3, http://development.asia/issue03/feature-01.asp, 14.06.2013.

Fournier, S. and Yao, J.L. (1997): Reviving brand loyalty: A reconceptualization within the framework of consumer-brand relationships. In: International Journal of Research in Marketing, 14(5), 451-472.

Frumkin, H. (2003): Healthy places: Exploring the evidence. In: American Journal of Public Health, 93(9), 1451-1456.

Gardiner, M. (2000): In: Critiques of everyday life. London: Routledge.

Garry, M. and Wade, K.A. (2005): Actually, a picture is worth less than 45 words: Narratives produce more false memories than photographs do. In: Psychonomic Bulletin & Review 12(2), 359-366.

Getz, D. (1993): Planning for tourism business districts. In: Annals of Tourism Research, 20(3), 583-600.

Gilmore, F. (2002): A country-can it be repositioned? Spain-the success story of country branding. In: The Journal of Brand Management, 9(4-5), 4-5.

Glaser, B.G. and Strauss, A.L. (2009): The discovery of grounded theory: Strategies for qualitative research. New Brunswick: Transaction Publishers.

Global National (2013): The Old London Underground company. http://www.youtube.com/watch?v=hAUhgpYVPvk, 06.07.2014.

Gray, J.R., Braver, T.S. and Raichle, M.E. (2002): Integration of emotion and cognition in the lateral prefrontal cortex. In: Proceedings of the National Academy of Sciences, 99(6), 4115-4120.

Grimsey, D. and Lewis, M.K. (2005): Are public private partnerships value for money? Evaluating alternative approaches and comparing academic and practitioner views. In: Accounting Forum, 29(4), 345-378.

Goatcher, J. and Brunsden, V. (2011): Chernobyl and the sublime tourist. In: Tourist Studies, 11(2), 115-137.

Goldberg, A.I., Cohen, G. and Fiegenbaum, A. (2003): Reputation building: Small business strategies for successful venture development. In: Journal of Small Business Management, 41(2), 168-186.

Goodson, S. (2012): Uprising how to build a brand and change the world by sparking cultural movements. USA: McGraw-Hill.

Goossens, C. (2000): Tourism information and pleasure motivation. In: Annals of Tourism Research, 27(2), 301-321.

Gordon, E. and Koo, G. (2008): Placeworlds: Using virtual worlds to foster civic engagement. In: Space and Culture, 11(3), 204-221.

Gössling, S. (2002): Global environmental consequences of tourism. In: Global Environmental Change, 12(4), 283-302.

Gould, K.A. and Lewis, T.L. (2007): Viewing the wreckage: Eco-disaster tourism in the wake of Katrina. In: Societies Without Borders, 2(2), 175-197.

Gu, Z. (2007): Which way to go? Analysis of gaming revenue enhancement approaches for Macau. In: Journal of Revenue and Pricing Management, 6(1), 33-39.

Haddad, L., Hossain, N., McGregor, J.A. and Mehta, L. (2011): Introduction: Time to reimagine development? In: IDS Bulletin, 42(5), 1-12.

Hall, T. (2004): Re(placing) the city: Cultural relocation and the city as centre. In: Westwood, S and Williams, J. (eds.): Imagining cities: Scripts, signs and memories. London: Routledge, 202-218.

Hankinson, G. (2004): The brand images of tourism destinations: A study of the saliency of organic images, In: Journal of Product and Brand Management, 13(1), 6-14.

Hankuk, T.C. and Aggarwal, P. (2003): When gains exceed losses: Attribute trade-offs and prospect theory. In: Advances in Consumer Research, 30(1), 118-124.

Hansen, C.D. and Kahnweiler, W.M. (1993): Storytelling: An instrument for understanding the dynamics of corporate relationships. In: Human Relations, 46(12), 1391-1409.

Haymond, J. (1982): Adaptive reuse of old buildings for archives. In: The American Archivist, 45(1), 11-18.

Hennig, C. (2002): Tourism: Enacting modern myths. In: Dann, G.M.S. (ed.): The tourist as a metaphor of the social world. UK: CABI Publishing, 169-187.
Heung, V.C. and Qu, H. (1998): Tourism shopping and its contributions to Hong Kong. In: Tourism Management, 19(4), 383-386.
Higgins, E.T. (2006): Value from hedonic experience and engagement. In: Psychological Review, 113(3), 439-460.
Hirani, P. (2013a): Pinpointpolitics. http://pinpointpolitics.co.uk/contributors-2/political-researcher/prithvi-hirani/, 14.02.2014.
Hirani, P. (2013b): In: Pinpointpolitics. http://pinpointpolitics.co.uk/?p=3508, 14.02.1014
Hirschman, E.C. and Holbrook, M.B. (1982): Hedonic consumption: Emerging concepts, methods and propositions. In: Journal of Marketing, 46(3), 92-101.
Hsieh, A.T. and Chang, J. (2006): Shopping and tourist night markets in Taiwan. In: Tourism Management, 27(1), 138-145.
Hoeffler, S. and Keller, K.L. (2003): The marketing advantages of strong brands. In: The Journal of Brand Management, 10(6), 421-445.
Hoffman, L.M. (2000): Tourism and the revitalization of Harlem. In: Hutchinson, R. (ed.): Construction of Urban Space, Stamford, CN: JAI Press, 207–23.
Hoffman, B. (2011): Mobile gaming: Exploring spaces and places. In: Cruz-Cunha, M., Varvalho, V. and Tavares, P. (eds): Business, Technological, and Social Dimensions of Computer Games: Multidisciplinary Developments, Hershley: IGI Global,185-199.
Hones, S. and Leyda, J. (2005): Geographies of American studies. In: American Quarterly, 57(4), 1019-1032.
Hottola, P. (2004): Culture confusion: Intercultural adaptation in tourism. In: Annals of Tourism Research, 31(2), 447-466.
Hudson, S. and Ritchie, J.B. (2006): Promoting destinations via film tourism: An empirical identification of supporting marketing initiatives. In: Journal of Travel Research, 44(4), 387-396.
Huffington Post (2012): Aldwych Tube Station: Abandoned station opened for tours, dated March 12, http://www.huffingtonpost.com/2012/12/03/aldwych-tube-station-aban_n_2230732.html, 13.06.2013.
Hystad, P.W. and Keller, P.C. (2008): Towards a destination tourism disaster management framework: Long-term lessons from a forest fire disaster. In: Tourism Management, 29(1), 151-162.
Iwashita, C. (2006): Media representation of the UK as a destination for Japanese tourists: Popular culture and tourism. In: Tourist Studies, 6(1), 59-77.
Jennings, J. (2012): Measuring neighborhood distress: a tool for place-based urban revitalization strategies. In: Community Development, 43(4), 464-475.
Jickling, B. and Wals, A.E. (2012): Probing normative dimensions of environmental education research. In: Stevenson, R. B., Brody, M., Dillon, J. and Wals, A.E.J. (eds): International Handbook of Research on Environmental Education, USA: Routledge Publihers, 74-86.
Johnson, M.S., Sivadas, E. and Garbarino, E. (2008): Customer satisfaction, perceived risk and affective commitment: An investigation of directions of influence. In: Journal of Services Marketing, 22(5), 353-362.

Joy, A., Sherry, Jr G.T. and Deschenes, J. (2010): Re-thinking the relationship between self and other: Levinas and narratives of beautifying the body. In: Journal of Consumer Culture, 10(3), 333-361.

Kahn, B.E. and Isen, A.M. (1993): The influence of positive affect on variety seeking among safe, enjoyable products. In: Journal of Consumer Research, 20(2), 257-270.

Kleine III, R.E., Kleine, S.S. and Kernan, J.B. (1993): Mundane consumption and the self: A social-identity perspective. In: Journal of Consumer Psychology, 2(3), 209-235.

Kemperman, A.D., Borgers, A.W., Oppewal, H. and Timmermans, H.J. (2000): Consumer choice of theme parks: A conjoint choice model of seasonality effects and variety seeking behavior. In: Leisure Sciences, 22(1), 1-18.

Knight, C. (2009): Public art: Theory, practice and populism. Malden: Blackwell Publishing.

Laiho, D.R. and Fitzgerald, P.A. (1998): Rock dam revitalization. In: Civil Engineering – ASCE, 68(7), 60-61.

Lavrinc, J. (2011): Revitalization of public space: From "non-places" to creative playgrounds. In: Santalka: Filosofija, Komunikacija, 19(2), 70-75.

Leahy, S. (2008): Climate change: Tourism at the end of the world, Inter Press Service, dated January 18, http://www.ipsnews.net/2008/01/climate-change-tourism-at-the-end-of-the-world/, 13.03.2013.

Lennon, J.J. and Foley, M. (2000): Dark tourism: The attraction of death and disaster. London: Cassell.

Lichrou, M., O'Malley, L. and Patterson, M. (2010): Narratives of a tourism destination: Local particularities and their implications for place marketing and branding. In: Place Branding and Public Diplomacy, 6(2), 134-144.

Lin, I.Y. (2004): Evaluating a servicescape: The effect of cognition and emotion. In: International Journal of Hospitality Management 23(2), 163-178.

Lindstrom, M. (2005): Broad sensory branding. In: Journal of Product and Brand Management, 14(2), 84-87.

Luo, P. and Chen, N. (2011): Abandoned coal mine tunnels: Future heating/power supply centers, In: Mining Science and Technology (China), 21(5): 637-640.

Mainemelis, C. (2001): When the muse takes it all: A model for the experience of timelessness in organizations. In: Academy of Management Review, 26(4), 548-565.

Massey, D. (1999): Space-time, 'science' and the relationship between physical geography and human geography. In: Transactions of the Institute of British Geographers, 24(3), 261-276.

Mayo, J.M. (1988): War memorials as political memory. In: Geographical Review, 78(1), 62-75.

McClure S.M., Li J., Tomlin D., Cypert K.S., Montague L.M. and Montague P.R. (2004) Neural correlates of behavioral preference for culturally familiar drinks. In: Neuron, 44(2), 379-387.

McDougall, G.H. and Levesque, T. (2000): Customer satisfaction with services: Putting perceived value into the equation. In: Journal of Services Marketing, 14(5), 392-410.

McGuire, D. (1997): Strategic revitalization plan for the West Side Community of Newark, NJ. Center for Urban Policy Research.

McKercher, B., Cros, H. and McKercher, R.B. (2002): Cultural tourism: The partnership between tourism and cultural heritage management. New York: Haworth Hospitality Press.

Mistilis, N. and Dwyer, L. (1999): Tourism gateways and regional economies: The distributional impacts of MICE. In: International Journal of Tourism Research, 1(6), 441-457.

Moisescu, O.I. (2006): A conceptual analysis of brand loyalty as core dimension of brand equity. In: Proceedings of the International Conference, Competitiveness and Stability in the Knowledge-Based Economy, Craiova.

Mohiyeddini, C., Pauli, R. and Bauer, S. (2009): The role of emotion in bridging the intention-behavior gap: The case of sports participation. In: Psychology of Sport and Exercise, 10(2), 226-234.

Murphy, P.E. and Rosenblood, L. (1974): Tourism: An exercise in spatial search. In: The Canadian Geographer/Le Géographe canadien, 18(3), 201-210.

Myers, C.A. (2003): Managing brand equity: A look at the impact of attributes. In: Journal of Product and Brand Management, 12(1), 39-51.

Navarro, L.M. and Pereira, H.M. (2012): Rewilding abandoned landscapes in Europe. In: Ecosystems, 15, 900-912.

Norman, A. and Cusack, C. M. (2014), Religion, Pilgrimage, and Tourism: Critical Concepts in Religious Studies, UK: Routledge, Taylor & Francis.

Okada, E.M. and Hoch, S.J. (2004): Spending time versus spending money. In: Journal of Consumer Research, 31(2), 313-323.

Ooi, C.S. (2011): Dialogic Heritage: Time space and visions of the Nation al Museum of Singapore. In: Teo, P., Chang, T.C. and Ho, K.C. (eds): Interconnected Worlds: Tourism in Southeast Asia, Pergamon, Amsterdam: Elsevier Science Limited, 176-192.

Papadopoulos, N. and Heslop, L. (2002): Country equity and country branding: Problems and prospects. In: The Journal of Brand Management, 9, 4-5.

Pattullo, P. (1996): Last resorts: The cost of tourism in the Caribbean. Kingston: Ian Randle Publishers.

Pawson, E. (1997): Branding strategies and languages of consumption. In: New Zealand Geographer 53(2), 16-21.

Payne, A.F., Storbacka, K. and Frow, P. (2008): Managing the co-creation of value In: Journal of the Academy of Marketing Science, 36(1), 83-96.

Pearce, P.L. and Lee, U.I. (2005): Developing the travel career approach to tourist motivation. In: Journal of Travel Research, 43(3), 226-237.

Pegrum, M. (2012): In the know: Question - Is there a tour of London's disused tube stations?, The Telegraph, dated 20 June, http://www.telegraph.co.uk/sponsored/in-the-know/london-cultural-attractions/9345037/london-underground-tours.html, 21.06.2013.

Pennisi, L.A., Holland, S.M. and Stein, T.V. (2004): Achieving bat conservation through tourism. In: Journal of Ecotourism 3(3), 195-207.

Pessiglione, M., Petrovic, P., Daunizeau, J., Palminteri, S., Dolan, R.J. and Frith, C.D. (2008): Subliminal instrumental conditioning demonstrated in the human brain. In: Neuron, 59(4), 561-567.

Petromilli, M., Morrison, D. and Million, M. (2002): Brand architecture: Building brand portfolio value. In: Strategy & Leadership, 30(5), 22-28.

Phillips, W.J. and Back, K.J. (2011): Conspicuous consumption applied to tourism destination. In: Journal of Travel & Tourism Marketing, 28(6), 583-597.

Picard, M. (1996): Bali: Cultural tourism and touristic culture. Singapore: Archipelago Press.

Pickering, C.M. and Hill, W. (2007): Impacts of recreation and tourism on plant biodiversity and vegetation in protected areas in Australia. In: Journal of Environmental Management 85(4), 791-800.

Prestin, A. (2013): The pursuit of hopefulness: Operationalizing hope in entertainment media narratives. In: Media Psychology, 16(3), 318-346.

Pritchard, A., Morgan, N. and Ateljevic, I. (2011): Hopeful tourism: A new transformative perspective. In: Annals of Tourism Research, 38(3), 941-963.

Plaza, B. (2007): The Bilbao effect (Guggenheim Museum Bilbao). Published in: Museum News. American Association of Museums, 86(5), http://mpra.ub.uni-muenchen.de/12681/1/MPRA_paper_12681.pdf.

Pritchard, M.P., Havitz, M.E. and Howard, D.R. (1999): Analyzing the commitment-loyalty link in service contexts. In: Journal of the Academy of Marketing Science, 27(3), 333-348.

Quelch, J.A., Austin, J.E. and Laidler-Kylander, N. (2004): Mining gold in not-for-profit brands. Harvard Business School Publishing, http://hbr.harvardbusiness.org/2004/04/mining-gold-in-not-for-profit-brands/ar/1, 20.12.2013.

Raggio, R.D. and Leone, R.P. (2007): The theoretical separation of brand equity and brand value: Managerial implications for strategic planning. In: Journal of Brand Management, 14(5), 380-395.

Rajagopal, P. and Montgomery, N.V. (2011): I imagine, I experience, I like: The false experience effect. In: Journal of Consumer Research, 38(3), 578-594.

Rama, E. (2013): Take Back Your City with paint, TED, http://www.ted.com/talks/edi_rama_take_back_your_city_with_paint.html, 12.05.2013.

Reimann, M., Castaño, R., Zaichkowsky, J. and Bechara, A. (2012): Novel versus familiar brands: An analysis of neurophysiology, response latency, and choice. In: Marketing Letters, 23(3), 745-759.

Reynolds, N. (2004): Geographies of writing: Inhabiting places and encountering difference. Carbondale: Southern Illinois University Press.

Rhinesmith, C. (2013), Collaborative design in a virtual world: Using Second Life to re-imagine Boston City Hall Plaza. http://citeseerx.ist.psu.edu/viewdoc/download?doi=10.1.1.93.2362andrep=rep1andtype=pdf, 05.08.2013.

Roehm Jr, H.A. and Roehm, M.L. (2005): Revisiting the effect of positive mood on variety seeking. In: Journal of Consumer Research, 32(2), 330-336.

Rowley, J. and Slack, F. (1999): The retail experience in airport departure lounges: reaching for timelessness and placelessness. In: International Marketing Review, 16(4/5), 363-376.

Rushton, A.M. and Carson, D.J. (1985): The marketing of services: Managing the intangibles. In: European Journal of Marketing, 19(3), 19-40.

San Martin, H. and Rodríguez del Bosque, I.A. (2008): Exploring the cognitive-affective nature of destination image and the role of psychological factors in its formation. In: Tourism Management, 29(2), 263-277.

Schembri, S. (2009): Reframing brand experience: The experiential meaning of Harley-Davidson. In: Journal of Business research, 62(12), 1299-1310.

Scolari, C.A. (2009): Transmedia storytelling: Implicit consumers, narrative worlds, and branding in contemporary media production. In: International Journal of Communication, 3(4), 586-606.

Shackley, M. (1999): Tourism development and environmental protection in southern Sinai. In: Tourism Management, 20(4), 543-548.

Sheller, M. (2004): Mobile publics: Beyond the network perspective: Environment and planning In: Society and Space 22(1), 39-52.

Sheller, M. and Urry, J. (2004): Places to play, places in play. In: Sheller, M. and Urry, J. (eds), Tourism Mobilities. London: Routledge, p. 1-10.

Shiv, B. and Fedorikhin, A. (1999): Heart and mind in conflict: The interplay of affect and cognition in consumer decision making. In: Journal of Consumer Research, 26(3), 278-292.

Silberberg, T. (1995): Cultural tourism and business opportunities for museums and heritage sites. In: Tourism Management 16(5), 361-365.

Spencer, J.H. and Ong, P. (2004): An analysis of the Los Angeles Revitalization Zone: Are place-based investment strategies effective under moderate economic conditions? In: Economic Development Quarterly 18(4), 368-383.

Smothers, N. (1993): Can products and brands have charisma. In: Aaker, D.A. and Biel, A.L. (eds.): Brand equity and advertising. Hillsdale, NJ: Lawrence Erlbaum Associates, 97-111.

Somervuori, O. and Ravaja, N. (2013): Purchase behavior and psychophysiological responses to different price levels. In: Psychology & Marketing, 30(6), 479-489.

Spillane, C. (2011): London entrepreneur sees gold mine in unused subway stations, Bloomberg, dated September 8, http://www.bloomberg.com/news/2011-09-08/london-entrepreneur-sees-a-gold-mine-in-developing-unused-subway-stations.html, 25.07.2014.

Stedman, R.C. (2003): Is it really just a social construction? The contribution of the physical environment to sense of place. In: Society and Natural Resources, 16(8), 671-685.

Strebinger, A. (2004): Strategic brand concept and brand architecture strategy: A proposed model. In: Advances in Consumer Research, 31, 656-661.

Stone, P.R. (2013): The case of Chernobyl In: White L. and Frew E. (eds): Dark Tourism and Place Identity: Managing and Interpreting Dark Places. New York: Routledge, pp. 37, 79.

Strochlic, N. (2012): Tourists in New York flock to see damage wrought by Sandy, The Daily Beast, dated November 2, http://www.thedailybeast.com/articles/2012/11/02/tourists-in-new-york-flock-to-see-damage-wrought-by-sandy.html, 23.03.2013.

Subterranea Britannica (2008): Site name: Brompton Road Station & London's Anti-Aircraft Defenses, http://www.subbrit.org.uk/sb-sites/sites/b/brompton_road/index50.shtml, 12.07.2014.

Sutton, S.A. (2010): Rethinking commercial revitalization: A neighbourhood small business perspective. In: Economic Development Quarterly, 24(4), 352-371.

Sweeney, J. and Swait, J. (2008): The effects of brand credibility on customer loyalty. In: Journal of Retailing and Consumer Services 15(3), 179-193.

Sydney-Smith, S. (2006): Changing places: Touring the British crime film. In: Tourist studies, 6(1), 79-94.

Szondi, G. (2007): The role and challenges of country branding in transition countries: The Central and Eastern European experience. In: Place Branding and Public Diplomacy, 3(1), 8-20.

Thomassen, B. and Balle, M. (2012): From liminoid to limivoid: Understanding contemporary bungee jumping from a cross-cultural perspective, In: Journal of Tourism Consumption and Practice 4(1), 59-93.

Torres, J.F. (2013): Interview - Digital October Knowledge Stream project, dated: 15 February, http://www.youtube.com/watch?v=-ev57cqHoEA, 12.02.2014.

Tung, V.W.S. and Ritchie, J.R. (2011): Exploring the essence of memorable tourism experiences. In: Annals of Tourism Research, 38(4), 1367-1386.

Urry, J. (2000): Sociology beyond societies: Mobilities for the twenty-first century. London: Routledge.

Uslu, A. (2010): An ecological approach for the evaluation of an abandoned cemetery as a green area: The case of Ankara/Karakusunlar cemetery. In: African Journal of Agricultural Research, 5(10), 1043-1054.

Vivek, S.D. (2009): A scale of consumer engagement, Doctoral dissertation, The University of Alabama TUSCALOOSA, http://acumen.lib.ua.edu/content/u0015/0000001/0000096/u0015_0000001_0000096.pdf, 31.07.2013.

Yamamura, T. (2009): Anime pilgrimage and local tourism promotion: An experience of Washimiya town, the sacred place for Anime "Lucky Star" Fans. In: 北海道大学文化資源マネジメント論集= Web-Journal of Tourism and Cultural Studies, 14, 1-9. http://eprints.lib.hokudai.ac.jp/dspace/bitstream/2115/38541/1/paper014.pdf, 31.06.2014.

Yang, S.U., Kang, M. and Johnson, P. (2010): Effects of narratives, openness to dialogic communication, and credibility on engagement in crisis communication through organizational blogs. In: Communication Research, 37(4), 473-497.

Yankovska, G. and Hannam, K. (2013): Dark and toxic tourism in the Chernobyl exclusion zone. In: Current Issues in Tourism ahead-of-print. http://www.tandfonline.com/doi/abs/10.1080/13683500.2013.820260#preview, 31.06.2014.

Yu, H. and Littrell, M.A. (2003): Product and process orientations to tourism shopping. In: Journal of Travel Research, 42(2), 140-150.

Van Hoving, D.J., Wallis, L.A., Docrat, F. and De Vries, S. (2010): Haiti disaster tourism: A medical shame. In: Prehospital Disaster Medicine, 25(3), 201-202.

Walpole, M.J. and Goodwin, H.J. (2000): Local economic impacts of dragon tourism in Indonesia. In: Annals of tourism research 27(3), 559-576.

Wakefield, K.L. and Blodgett, J.G. (1999): Customer response to intangible and tangible service factors. In: Psychology and Marketing, 16(1), 51-68.

Weatherly, M. (2012): Move to open underground ghost stations hailed by Mike, dated 27 April, http://www.mikeweatherleymp.com/2012/04/27/move-to-open-underground-ghost-stations-hailed-by-mike/, 26.05.2013.

Wearing, S. (2004): Examining best practice in volunteer tourism. In: Stebbins, R.A. and Graham, M. (eds): Volunteering as leisure/leisure as volunteering: An international assessment, Wallingford, UK: CABI Publishing, 209-224.

Wood, A.F. (2005): What happens [in Vegas]: Performing the post-tourist flâneur in "New York" and "Paris". In: Text and Performance Quarterly, 25(4), 315-333.

Wylie, J. (2002): Becoming-icy: Scott and Amundsen's South Polar voyages, 1910-1913. In: Cultural Geographies 9(3), 249-265.

Warde, A. (2005): Consumption and theories of practice. In: Journal of Consumer Culture, 5(2), 131-153.

Xiang, Z. and Gretzel, U. (2010): Role of social media in online travel information search. Tourism Management, 31(2), 179-188.

Xudong, Z. and Bell, D. (2005): Destroying the remembered and recovering the forgotten in Chai between traditionalism and modernity in Beijing. In: China Information, 19(3), 489-503.

Zaltman, G. (2003): How customers think: Essential insights into the mind of the market, Boston: Harvard Business Press.

Zenker, S. and Braun, E. (2010): Branding a city: A conceptual approach for place branding and place brand management. Paper presented at the 39th European Marketing Academy Conference, Copenhagen, Denmark. www.placebrand.eu/publications, 23.05.2013.

Zeppel, H. and Hall, C.M. (1991): Selling art and history: Cultural heritage and tourism. In: Journal of Tourism Studies, 2(1), 29-45.

Zhang, M., Jansen, B.J. and Chowdhury, A. (2011): Business engagement on Twitter: A path analysis. In: Electronic Markets, 21(3), 161-175.

Zurick, D.N. (1992): Adventure travel and sustainable tourism in the peripheral economy of Nepal. In: Annals of the Association of American Geographers 82(4), 608-628.

Pilgrimage Tourism in Consumer Society: Foot Pilgrimages to the Jasna Góra Sanctuary in Częstochowa

Felicjan Bylok / Leszek Cichobłaziński

Introduction

In contemporary society, a change in the function of religion is taking place. It is possible to state that the religiousness of consumer society is that of syncretic religiousness as for instance in "a house with a multitude of deities". One such deity is that of the religious market, together with its economic mechanism. This market is characterized by regulations and patterns of procedure with regard to the faithful that are drawn from the consumer market. In truth, this is the result of a change in Western cultures in which the culture of consumption is of an ever-increasing level of importance. The values associated with this are becoming absorbed into religion, which is leading to a change in the relation between the faithful and the church itself. Hence, strategies of attracting the congregation, as well as patterns of religious leadership, or even religious doctrine need to be reconsidered in order to respond to the new conditions.

Consumers and the congregation search for utilitarianism in religion. Indeed, they want to realize their own individualized aims associated with religion. Religion is to help in solving the problems of life and in finding solace. Individualism in religion is a symptomatic indicator of change in the approach to life, in which it is worth striving towards pleasure and happiness. This phenomenon may be termed as a selective approach to religion, which involves the fact that the congregation merely chooses the religious rules that match their lifestyles and aid the achievement of goals and values associated with these lifestyles.

The aim of this paper is to provide a description of the changes in the approach to religion and pilgrimages in contemporary Polish society. Poland is a good example for that kind of observation because foot pilgrimages are still very popular, in particularly, the Jasna Góra sanctuary. The qualitative results of research carried out on the people making pilgrimages to the largest Marian sanctuary in Poland shall be described.

Pilgrimage tourism as a cultural phenomenon

The pilgrimage, according to Urry (2002) is the archetype of tourism. Contemporary tourism follows on from this in which the pilgrim becomes the archetypal tourist.

> "All tourists for MacCannell embody a quest for authenticity, and this quest is a modern version of the universal human concern with the sacred. The tourist is a kind of contemporary pilgrim, seeking authenticity in other 'times' and other 'places' away from that person's everyday life." (Urry 2002: 9)

In this context, a pilgrimage may be perceived as a metaphor of human life, whose essence may be boiled down to the constant "being on the road".

> "'We are pilgrims through time' was under the pen of St Augustine not an exhortation, but a statement of fact. We are pilgrims whatever we do, and there is little we can do about it even we wished." (Bauman 1996: 20)

Nowadays, pilgrimages are made with the aid of all available means of transport, however the custom of foot pilgrimages has been maintained. Foot pilgrimages have their own specifities, which distinguish them from other forms of pilgrimages. The development of pilgrimage tourism is proceeding so rapidly that in some dioceses, there is a Ministry of the Diocese of Tourism and Recreation, e.g. in the Diocese of Gliwice, which mainly deals with the organization of pilgrimages to holy places.[1]

Pilgrimage tourism is that which connects religion and tourism to travelling. The essence of both of these activities is movement. The concept of time in both cases is similar in that it is not ordinary. It is rather time taken out of everyday life and devoid of routine, by means of which the traveller is in a transitional state, metaphorically speaking, which was termed by Victor and Edith Turner (1978) as becoming the liminal phase. In defining a pilgrimage, it is necessary to state the following: "At its most basic, a pilgrimage can be viewed as any travel that involves a religious experience". (Griffin 2007: 18). Hence, a pilgrim differs from a tourist first and foremost, in terms of the aim of the trip being made. The aim of a pilgrimage is of a religious nature and is most frequently to a holy place or sanctuary. What connects a pilgrim with a tourist is that of the experiences which bring new value to their lives. In the case of a pilgrim, this however relates to an experience that is typically transcendent and transcending beyond the boundaries of the temporal world.

1 http://www.pielgrzymki-gliwice.pl/, 20.06.2014.

> "Dilthey viewed experience as an eruption from routine and saw in it an urging toward expression. Turner stresses the disruptions that are cut out of the everyday and sees experience as an isolable sequence marked by beginnings, middles, and endings, as a way in which people tell what is most meaningful about their lives." (Bruner 1986: 13)

Pilgrimage as a liminal space

The aim of a pilgrimage is spiritual change, becoming closer to transcendence and the sacred. It is a process which is transgressive in terms of its essence. The said change occurs in three stages: (1) the phase of freezing the current knowledge and identity, (2) the phase of defreezing the identity up to now, or in other words, the liminal phase (transitional), during which the knowledge up to now loses its value of truism, as well as (3) the phase of freezing new knowledge and new identity. The liminal space thus resembles a purgatory that fulfils the function of cleansing, thereby leading to spiritual transformation. Liminality is hence, a feature of each change and is strictly associated with what Victor Turner terms *rites de passage* (1975: 231).[2] It is essential to underline the fact that the connection of the Marian cult with the liminal nature of pilgrimages is not accidental. Holy Mary fulfilled the function of a medium between the temporal world and the transcendent world, while also between the sacred and the profane. Attention was drawn to this by Victor and Edith Turner by distinguishing the Marian pilgrimage among all other types of pilgrimages (1978: 203-230).

As an introduction to the herein analysis, it is necessary to set forth the question as to what characteristics of a pilgrimage favour the attainment of the phase of liminality to the greatest extent? With this aim in mind, Victor Turner introduces the notion of *communitas* (1978: 231-371; 1969: 94-113). One of the features distinguishing *communitas* is that of its anti-structure. This signifies the fact that in *communitas* the social structure functioning on an everyday basis ceases to function. In a pilgrimage, everybody is equal, which is evidenced by the manner in which pilgrims relate to each other as brother and sister. This aspect is regardless of age, sex type, or social status, although the pilgrimage community itself is featured by a highly functional variation.

---

2 The concept *rites de passage* is introduced by Arnold van Gennep (1909/2006) Obrzędy przejścia [Les rites de passage]. Warszawa, PIW.

Jasna Góra sanctuary – its location, history, statistics

Częstochowa is a city of almost 240,000 inhabitants that is located in the southern regions of Poland, in the province of Silesia (Kersten 2007: 576). The city rights were acquired in 1377 (Kersten: 2002: 127). Shortly afterwards, the monastery belonging to The Order of Saint Paul the First Hermit was founded in 1382 (Kersten: 2002: 149). It is necessary to emphasize the fact that there are places of cult and pilgrimage centres of non-Catholic religions in Poland too. In the case of the Orthodox church, the most significant sanctuary is The Holy Mountain of Grabarka (Marciniak 1996), whereas for the believers of Judaism this is the district of Cracow called Kazimierz (Matlak 1996) and the tomb of the tsaddik in Leżajsk (Gładyś and Górecki 2005).

The monastery of Jasna Góra was built slightly to the west of the city on a limestone hill, which due to its bright colour received its name that translated directly as "Bright Hill". This was the origin of the name of the monastery and the sanctuary itself. In subsequent centuries, the Icon of the Mother of God which was brought from Byzantium and known in Poland as the Mother of God of Częstochowa, and as the Black Madonna around the world, became an object of cult worship. This icon was probably painted in the 13th century (Kersten 2002: 249). This type of icon is termed Hodegetria, which in the Greek language signifies the following: "the one who shows the way". The symbolics of this icon plays a significant role in this location, which is the centre of pilgrimages and additionally, foot pilgrimages.

Figure 1: The holy icon of the Black Madonna of Częstochowa. (The Press Office of Jasna Góra Monastery)

Jasna Góra is a large international centre of pilgrimages. In 2012, approximately 3.5 million pilgrims visited this centre[3]. With relation to the numbers of pilgrims visiting Częstochowa it holds third place in Europe, after Rome and Lourdes. The location of Jasna Góra in Europe as well as the locations from where the pilgrims come from are illustrated in Figure 2.

Figure 2: The direction of arrivals of the inhabitants of European countries at Jasna Góra. (Jackowski and Kaszewski 1996: 180)

Foot pilgrimages in Jasna Góra constitutes a particular phenomenon. It is necessary to underline that Częstochowa is not the sole destination for foot pilgrims. It is possible to indicate many locations in the world, where pilgrims make their way on foot (see Appendix). However, the feature distinguishing Jasna Góra is

3 http://www.jasnagora.com/ciekawe1.php?kategoria=61

the summer season in which foot pilgrims make their way along 50 different routes (Sołjan and Jackowski 1996: 163). The majority of foot pilgrims come to Częstochowa in August, which is caused by two of the most important Marian celebrations that take place in that particular month. The oldest pilgrimage is deemed to be the Warsaw pilgrimage which has been coming to Jasna Góra for 302 years without fail[4]. During communist times, this was the only foot pilgrimage that was allowed by the authorities, thus many people from all over the country (except for Warsaw)[5] participated in it. Following the fall of communism, pilgrimages have been coming to Częstochowa from the majority of dioceses.

Figure 3: Directions of foot pilgrimages coming to Jasna Góra (only pilgrimages amounting to over 500 pilgrims). (Sołjan and Jackowski 1996: 163)

4 http://pielgrzymki.opoka.org.pl/trasy/1492.1,Trasa_Pielgrzymki_Warszawskiej.html
5 http://pielgrzymki.opoka.org.pl/trasy/1492.1,Trasa_Pielgrzymki_Warszawskiej.html

In coming to Częstochowa, pilgrims avail of many forms of physical activity. The most popular ones include foot pilgrimages, but also long distance run pilgrimages, pilgrimages on horseback and even on rollerblades. The number of the particular pilgrimages and their number of participants are presented in Figure 4.

Type of pilgrimage	Number of pilgrimages	Number of pilgrims
Foot pilgrimages	278	140,956
Pilgrimages on bicycles	83	2,000
Long distance run pilgrimages	9	192
Pilgrimages on horseback	2	44
Pilgrimages on rollerblades	1	100

Figure 4: Statistics of chosen pilgrimages to Jasna Góra monastery in 2012. (Press Centre of Jasna Góra)

A further issue which is worth drawing attention to is the dynamics of the pilgrimages in the past 12 years, which has undergone some fluctuation which is in turn, illustrated in in Figure 5 and Figure 6.

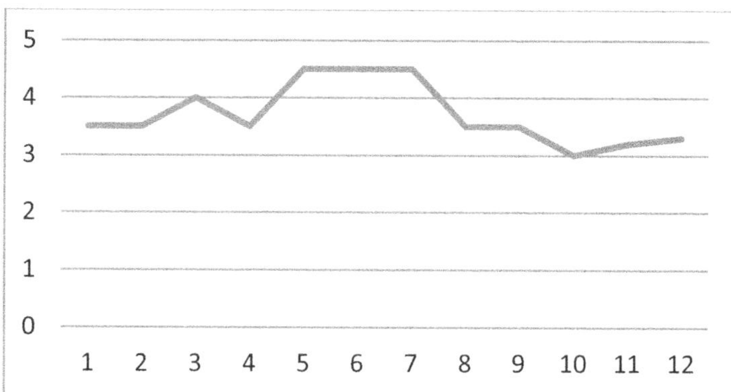

Figure 5: Total number of pilgrims arriving at Jasna Góra monastery in the period of 2001 to 2012 (in millions). (Self-analysis on the basis of data provided by the Press Centre of Jasna Góra. http://www.jasnagora.com/)

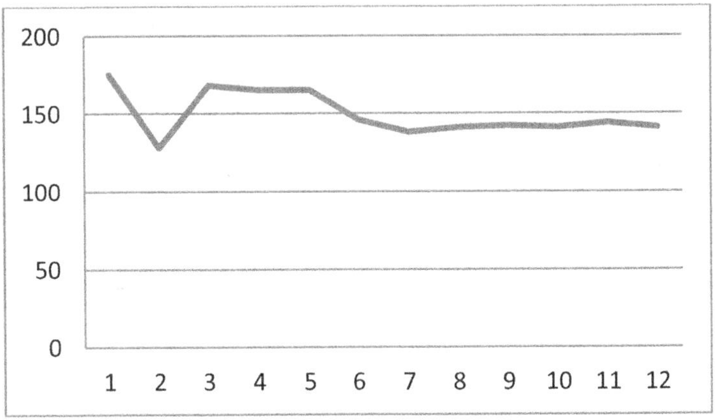

Figure 6: Number of pilgrims on foot arriving at Jasna Góra monastery in the period of 2001 to 2012. (Self-analysis on the basis of data provided by the Press Centre of Jasna Góra. http://www.jasnagora.com/)

Both of the trends relating to the total number of pilgrims arriving at Jasna Góra, as well as the one relating to pilgrims arriving in foot pilgrimages after the period of change has undergone a certain stabilization. The total number of pilgrims arriving since 2008 has stabilized between 3 and 3.5 million people, whereas the number of foot pilgrims has stabilized more or less since 2006 and oscillates around the figure of 140, 000 annually. The stability of the trend relating to foot pilgrims seems to be more evident.

Description and analysis of foot pilgrimages to Jasna Góra

Material for the herein research was collected from the 33rd foot pilgrimage from Wrocław in 2013. Observations collected during the 300th jubilee foot pilgrimage from Warsaw made in 2001 are used here as supplementary material. The basic method used in this research was participant observation, or a kind of 'disguised observation' as people who were the subject of observation were not aware that they were subjects. In-depth interviews were also used, and the results of observations and interviews were recorded by the researcher daily as part of a diary.

The Wrocław pilgrimage took place in the period between 2 and 10 August 2013, which enumerated 18 groups on a pilgrimage trail measuring 230 kilometres and was divided into 9 one-day stages. Each stage lasted 15-30 kilometres with the number of participants registered at approximately 4,000 pilgrims. In the Warsaw foot pilgrimage, the stages were set at up to 40 kilometres, while the number of participants was registered at approximately 8,000 pilgrims. This pilgrimage has to overcome a route of around 240 kilometres in a period between 6 and 15 August. Furthermore, other pilgrims also arrived from Warsaw, e.g. from the Warszawska Akademicka Pielgrzymka Metropolitalna (Warsaw Metropolitan Academic Pilgrimage) – amounting to around 3,800 pilgrims[6]. Pilgrims from abroad also participated in these pilgrimages. In the pilgrimage from Cracow there is a separate Italian group, while in turn, in the pilgrimage from Wrocław there was also a group of pilgrims from Germany.

Figure 7: Group of pilgrims from Germany in a pilgrimage from Wrocław. (Author: L. Cichobłaziński)

6 http://wapm.waw.pl/informacje, 06.2014

Pilgrimage as an institution and organization

Pilgrimage can be also considered as an institution and organization. Every pilgrim must be registered and receive a pilgrim's licence. During the course of signing up, pilgrims make a registration fee of approximately 100 PLN (the equivalent of 25 Euro), which covers the costs of materials and services essential for the functioning of a pilgrimage. Pilgrims during the course of registration also receive special materials that consist of the regulations of the pilgrimage in question, a map of the pilgrimage route with the rest points marked in, as well as the length of the particular stages and a pilgrim's badge. The regulations of a pilgrim first and foremost, determine the clothes worn i.e. pilgrims must not be excessively scantily dressed. This norm is rather important due to the summer season in which the pilgrims set forth. The second significant norm that is emphasized by the organizers is the ban on men and women sleeping in the same compartments. This principle does not relate to married couples. During the course of a pilgrimage, there is a total ban on the consumption of alcoholic drinks, as well as smoking. The regulations of a pilgrimage also recommend that a pilgrim travels in the group that he/she is signed up for. The police are notified about the route and duration of each pilgrimage, in which built-up areas are protected.

Each daily stage is divided into several parts, between which there are places of rest. Pilgrims rest in strictly marked out areas. A pilgrimage has a main guide and a quartermaster, while the guides and quartermasters in turn, have their particular groups. Each group has its own emblem apart from the registration number. A cross is carried at the front of the group. Among the pilgrimage services, which pilgrims serve in, it is possible to distinguish the protection personnel that mainly deals with directing traffic on the public roads. Members of the protection personnel are specially trained for this purpose. The functioning of the remaining services depends on the manner of organization of a given pilgrimage. Large differences in this area occur between the particular pilgrimages.

Pilgrims have merely a handbag as baggage, which they carry in small rucksacks. The main baggage, which contains for instance tents, or clothes for the entire period of the pilgrimage etc. are transported by trucks. This baggage is loaded and unloaded on these trucks every day. The problem of accommodation is solved in various ways. Some pilgrimages make use of private lodgings frequently made available by homeowners free of charge, while other pilgrims sleep in tents, as private lodgings are provided for only older people or those with health problems. Since a few years ago, pilgrims are able to receive comfortable lodgings after paying a special fee with the Piesza Pielgrzymka Warszawska [Warsaw Foot Pilgrimage][7].

Some pilgrimages have more expanded professional service facilities, whereas others are more self-sufficient, which means that some of the services are provided for by the appropriate service groups which consist of volunteer pilgrims. Much depends on the size of a pilgrimage group. For instance, the largest Warsaw Foot Pilgrimage is more professionalized. The transportation, loading and unloading of baggage, as well as collecting and disposing of waste are all carried out by professional firms. In the case of other pilgrimages, the participation of external firms is kept to a minimum. For example, baggage is transported by professional firms, but its loading and unloading takes place with the aid of the daily service groups chosen from among the pilgrims. The servicing of mobile toilets is usually carried out by professional firms.

A separate sphere of services relates to that of trade. A pilgrimage is accompanied by cars supplying the pilgrims with almost everything they need during the pilgrimage. Above all else, this relates to food and beverage, but also for instance, raincoats. All entities dealing in trade during the course of the pilgrimage receive a special permit from the organizers of the said pilgrimage. Trade only takes place during rest points of the pilgrimage. It is necessary to underline the fact that during the course of a pilgrimage, attention is paid to separating the sacred from the profane. This may be exemplified by the strict adherence to closing all mobile trading points during Holy Mass.

In Warsaw Foot Pilgrimage, it is possible to observe an interesting phenomenon of going on a pilgrimage as a way of spending a holiday. While part of the family participates in a pilgrimage, the remaining part, most frequently the father, drives the car alone thus transporting everything that is necessary for the duration of the pilgrimage. These people often drive to the location of the rest point before the pilgrimage group. They prepare the stopover points for the night (by putting up the tents or parking the caravans), as well as preparing supper for the families travelling in the pilgrimage group. These people participate in the liturgy as much as the other members of the pilgrimage group. Each accompanying car is registered by the organizers and receives an identification sticker that is stuck to the windscreen of the car.

A hugely significant role in a pilgrimage is played by the medical services. These include volunteers, doctors and nurses. They are sometimes pilgrims who have come on the pilgrimage from abroad. In the pilgrimage from Warsaw there was a doctor from Germany, while in the pilgrimage from Wrocław, a doctor from Belarus. Sanitary points are available at each rest point of the pilgrimage.

7 Information acquired from pilgrims who were participants of the Warsaw Foot Pilgrimage in 2012.

Emergency rescue cars travel with the pilgrimage that are served by volunteer rescue teams. The main problem which they have to deal with is of course injuries to feet, but also frequently sunstroke and fainting. Pilgrims who are unable to overcome the difficulties of a several hundred kilometre march, avail of the aid of nurses from the medical cars. It sometimes occurs that some people drop out of the pilgrimage. In the regulations, the pilgrim emphasizes that dropping out of the pilgrimage due to health problems or lack of energy is nothing bad. During the course of the whole pilgrimage, the leaders draw attention to protection from sunstroke and dehydration.

During the course of a pilgrimage, time discipline is strictly enforced. Groups arrive at a rest point and leave in various orders, in order for the rest time to be the same for everyone. Each group is in possession of the previously established rest points. The locations of rest points and the time of departure to continue the pilgrimage are announced over loudspeakers by the protection personnel.

Foot pilgrimage from a sociological and consumption perspective

Foot pilgrimages are organized by dioceses or orders of monks. The main guides and special guides are spiritual people – priests and nuns. Each group always consists of several priests who provide spiritual ministrations – confessions, spiritual talks, saying mass during the pilgrimage. During the course of the pilgrimage, there are conferences on spiritual issues, prayer (e.g. the Rosary) almost all the time. Some pilgrimages practice short 20-minute periods of silence to facilitate meditation. Every day mass is said at one of the rest points. Groups are equipped with loudspeaker systems. Pilgrims take turns to carry speakers which are connected with the so-called studio that consists of microphones and an amplifier. The studio serves to initiate prayer and song, as well as to run conferences. In this way, pastoral activity is carried out all along the pilgrimage route.

Analysis of the motives behind people's choice to go on a pilgrimage as opposed to other ways of spending leisure time is interesting. One of the most significant motives behind this decision was the desire to feel religious experiences. During the course of a pilgrimage lasting several days, people had time to focus on prayer, contemplation and get closer to God. Striving towards the experience of something sublime which is not an everyday experience is the feature of a multitude of foot pilgrims. During the course of the everyday periods of silence lasting several minutes the pilgrims meditated. Even those who had not done so previously subjected themselves to the influence of the others and gradually undertook meditation.

Another motive was the entrustment of a person or family with God during the course of the pilgrimage. Pilgrims by means of participation in a foot pilgrimage wanted to acquire help from God for the sick members of their families, aid in the search for employment, aid in finding a wife/husband, etc. The intentions which spurred on the pilgrims were thus varied and related to spiritual issues, as well as temporal ones associated with the profane. One of the unemployed women participating in the pilgrimage said that the most important reason for her going on the pilgrimage was to ask the Mother of God to take care of her daughter who had commenced learning at school. In her prayers she asked for help for her to learn well and gain an education that would help her to live a comfortable life – *I am going to the Mother of God of Jasna Góra to pray for God's mercy for my daughter, so that she can have a better life than me.*

Another motive which motivated pilgrims was to spend their leisure time in an interesting way. In particular, young people decided to participate in the pilgrimage in order to experience something extraordinary, meet interesting people and not only to use up their free time. In the case of many young people, this was their first pilgrimage. From the responses of one of the young participants of the Warsaw Foot Pilgrimage who was eighteen years old, it was evident that the primary goal of the pilgrimage or in other words, experiencing an interesting adventure changed with time, as while under the influence of the other participants he became actively involved in the religious services connected with the pilgrimage, e.g. prayer, song and contemplation. The greatest surprise for him was the fact that it is possible to experience something extraordinary in contacts with other people who are performing tasks together, both those connected with the sacred (prayer) and those with the profane that relate to the fulfilment of the needs of life. The pilgrimage became something extraordinary for him as for the first time in his life, he began to think not only about his own needs and ways of fulfilling them, but also first and foremost about God and his relations with him.

Another motive which stimulated the participants of the pilgrimage was the strife towards asceticism, to move away from excessive consumption. The characteristic motto of consumerism, namely, *the more pleasant, the better* is rejected by some pilgrims. During the course of walking, attention is not paid to the consumption of pleasures, but rather by means of a great physical effort they want to manifest their attachment to spiritual values associated with moderation in terms of consumption. One of the female participants of the pilgrimage, a 35 year-old woman said that she wanted to get away from making purchases in shopping malls, forget about new clothes and the necessity of paying attention to trendy clothes – *Here I can go how I want, in a way that I find most convenient. I do not have to pay attention to conventions and fashion.*

Sometimes participation in a pilgrimage becomes something of a ritual, which should be practiced every year during the summer holiday season. Some pilgrims have been participating in them for many years. For instance, in the case of a man aged 45, the annual pilgrimage constitutes an important moment in the summer season, as he has been participating in the foot pilgrimages from Warsaw to Jasna Góra in Częstochowa for 22 years. He is accompanied by his wife and two children. This is a significant time for the whole family as during the course of overcoming the distance of 220 km together in the sunshine and sometimes rain, they may mutually support each other and reinforce the family bonds. *I look forward to the beginning of August when together with my wife and kids, I can go on the pilgrimage. It is a time in which we get to know each other better and cement our family ties. We charge our 'family batteries' for the whole year.*

During the pilgrimage, a social bond is created that is characteristic of the communitas in the perception of Victor Turner. Apart from the afore-mentioned way of which the pilgrims refer to each other as sister or brother, after a few days a strong social bond is created. This is particularly visible in terms of the aid which pilgrims grant to small children, as during the course of pilgrimages families with large numbers of small children frequently participate. The bond that is created during a pilgrimage is so strong that a relatively large group of pilgrims participate in a pilgrimage, sometimes every year in the same group, which also has the same guide, or pastoral guardian. In this manner, a type of parish is formed, which is organized once a year in order to take part in the pilgrimage. Some of the members of this group remain in contact with each other during the course of the whole year. Internet websites serve this purpose, which are run by almost all pilgrimage groups. During a year, particular groups, naturally in smaller groups, meet once or even several times for one-day prayer meetings in Jasna Góra, or in the city where the pilgrimage sets off. The response of a man aged 51, who is a participant of Warsaw Foot Pilgrimage indicates that he participates in various forms of pilgrimages during the whole year, but the most significant for him is the pilgrimage to Jasna Góra in Częstochowa. What particularly attracts him to this, is the acquaintances he meets there once a year who come from many places spread out all over Poland. People from all over Poland come to Warsaw to join the pilgrimage. There is a friendly atmosphere in evidence, as well as goodwill and the desire to aid the other pilgrims. Hence, apart from the spiritual area, the relations with other pilgrims featured by friendship are significant. The collective values constitute an important element in building a community during the course of a pilgrimage. However, such a community is short-lived as following the pilgrimage people return to their local environs, in which such forms of relations do not exist. In today's society directed towards individualistic values, people feel the lack of such contacts. The pilgrimage communities do not disappear following the pilgrimage, but function in the consciousness of the people participating in them.

All of this leads to the fact that apart from the experiences that are purely religious, the participants of the pilgrimages experience particularly strong social bonds. This does not alter the fact that sometimes entire families go on a pilgrimage. Young people sometimes make acquaintances there that end in marital ties.

Figure 8: Arrival of pilgrimages at Jasna Góra monastery. (Bożena Sztajner)

The last day of the pilgrimage is particularly important for each pilgrim – the day of arrival at the sanctuary. Prayer in front of the Black Madonna is the culmination point of the whole pilgrimage, to which the participants have been preparing from a spiritual point of view the whole way. This is the most important spiritual experience of each pilgrim. The majority of pilgrims enter Jasna Góra by means of the main street of the city that is called Aleja Najświętszej Panny (the Avenue of Mary the Most Holy). The pilgrimage group is greeted from the defence walls of the fortress of Jasna Góra by the bishop of the diocese from where they came. On the grounds under the defence walls, each group approaches separately, where it is greeted and presented by the main guide of the pilgrimage group. The main guide of the group is presented, as well as the remaining priests providing pastoral services during the course of the pilgrimage, the number of the pilgrims is given and sometimes the age of the oldest or the youngest participant is also given. Subsequently, the pilgrims move in groups towards the area of the sanctuary, to the Chapel of the Mother of God. The remainder of the time is managed by the participants of the pilgrimage individually, in order to gather together again after a few hours in front of the altar on the defence walls and participate in the Holy Mass that is said with the special intention of the given pilgrimage. There is a final aspect to the pilgrimage. The pilgrims spend the rest of the day in the sanctuary and in the city, after which the majority of them return to their place of abode in the specially arranged coaches for this purpose.

There is an important problem from the viewpoint of the development of the city which the local authorities have failed to resolve up to now, namely, what to do to retain the pilgrims longer than one day in the city, thus simultaneously enabling the possibility of availing other services offered by the city and region. Indeed, this is an extraordinarily difficult problem in the case of pilgrims arriving on foot. In this area, the cooperation of the local authorities of Częstochowa with the sanctuary despite the fact that it is developing relatively rapidly (Cichobłaziński 2002; Głębocki 2006), it has not brought any effects as of yet, as in the example of Lourdes in France. In order to achieve the effective change in this field, it is necessary to undertake activities in the area of marketing and promotion of the city of Częstochowa, which should first and foremost relate to the city as a brand.

Conclusion

In analysing the phenomenon of the contemporary, post-modern consumer society, it is important to consider the categories of notions introduced by Bauman (2001: 9) in "*Consuming Life*" in which consumption serves not only the fulfilment of needs, but it is rather becoming an aim in itself. By using the metaphor of a road, it is possible to state that consuming is becoming a road, or in other words, a type of philosophy of life in which goods fulfil a symbolic function to an increasing extent and not merely utilitarian (Bylok 2005: 236-245). They do not serve to fulfil needs, but their arousal, or even the creation of new ones. In this context, consumption is taking on certain features of religion, thus becoming competition for it. The metaphor of a *road,* perceived as a philosophy of life, may thus become a common denominator in the analysis of behaviour in the field of consumption and religion. Both of these spheres may be viewed from the perspective of anthropology of the road (Wieczorkiewicz 2008: 21-25). In both cases, the main aim is to experience authenticity and self-discovery. This particularly relates to the type of consumption which tourism constitutes, as well as the particular type of religious practice that a foot pilgrimage constitutes (Wieczorkiewicz 2008: 31-42). The similarities between them may also include the liminal function of consumption. Not only religious experiences may lead to inner transformation. Sometimes these functions are fulfilled by consumption too (Cody 2012).

There are also significant differences between consumption, which also includes tourism, and the experience of the sacred, particularly during the course of foot pilgrimages. In as much as the ideology of consumerism gives rise to worshipping a multitude of Gods (each product may be a subject of cult) (Bylok 2013: 149-151), the tourist tries to expand and vary his/her experiences, whereas the pilgrim is headed in only one direction and has only one subject of cult. Consumption is integrally associated with the dispersal of attention, while pilgrimages are associated with its concentration. There is one more significant difference that is particularly important from a sociological point of view. Consumption serves the maintenance of social structures that simultaneously arouses competition and rivalry, which frequently leads to resentment. The fact of what goods an individual may afford, certifies to the position it holds in the social structure. This principle not only relates to tourism in a strict sense, but also pilgrimage tourism. Not everyone may afford to go on a pilgrimage to the Holy Land. Accommodation in typical hotels and flights are not very cheap. Nevertheless, everyone may afford a foot pilgrimage. During the course of its duration, everybody is equal, while astounding others with possessions is viewed in a negative light. This is certified by the responses of some pilgrims who emphasized that during the course of a pilgrimage they do not have to pay attention to what is fashionable. Many people participate in pilgrimages with specific intentions. Pilgrims ask for cures for serious illnesses, for success in finding employment, for resolving family and professional problems. Suffering, which in the world of consumption is directed towards immediate pleasure, is a shameful aspect that should be kept secret at all costs, whereas during a pilgrimage it becomes a natural component in the human condition. In the case of a multitude of pilgrims, this is a very important experience.

In relation to this, is participation in pilgrimages of the nature of manifesting anti-consumption attitudes, or does it have something in common with the spreading of anti-consumption movements of recent times? (Portwood-Stacer 2012). It would seem that this is not the case. Pilgrims are not alienated in the surrounding world, in which it is impossible to live without consuming multiform goods. Luxury goods are not evil either. The liminality of pilgrimages facilitates the return of the appropriate hierarchy of values, at the head of which stand transcendent values in their rightful place. From the perspective of such a hierarchy of values, an individual consumes in order to live, and does not live in order to consume, as it would appear in light of the ideology of consumerism, which was correctly noted by Bauman (2001).

References

Bauman, Z. (2001): Consuming Life. In: Journal of Consumer Culture, 1(1), 9-29.

Bauman, Z. (1996): From Pilgrim to Tourist – or a Short History of Identity. In: Hall, S. and Du Gay, P. (eds.): Questions of Cultural Identity. London: Sage, 18-36.

Bylok, F. (2005): Model społeczeństwa konsumpcyjnego i jego zastosowanie na początku XXI wieku [Model of Consumer Society and its Applications in 21th Century]. In: Jawłowska, A. and Kempny, M. (eds.): Konsumpcja – istotny wymiar globalizacji kulturowej [Consumption- a Significant Dimension of Cultural Globalization]. Warszawa: Wydawnictwo IFiS PAN, 231-255.

Bylok. F. (2013): Konsumpcja, konsument i społeczeństwo konsumpcyjne we współczesnym świecie [Consumption, the Consumer and Consumer Society in the Contemporary Word]. Katowice: Wydawnictwo Naukowe „Śląsk".

Bruner, E.M. (1986): Experience and its Expressions. In: Turner, V.W. and Bruner, E.M. (eds.): The Anthropology of Experience. Champaign, IL: University of Illinois Press, 3-30.

Cichobłaziński, L. and Wrona, T. (2002): The 6th World Youth Day in Częstochowa as an Example of a 'Big Bang' Event. Published as an accepted paper at the 38th International Congress of the International Society of City and Regional Planners (ISoCaRP), Athens, Greece, 21.-26. September 2002.

Cody, K. (2012): 'No Longer, but not Yet': Tweens and the Mediating of Thresholds Selves through Liminal Consumption. In: Journal of Consumer Culture, 12(1), 41-65.

Gładyś, B. and Górecki, J. (2005): Pielgrzymki chasydów do grobów cadyków we współczesnej Polsce [Hasidic Pilgrimages to Tzaddic Graves in Contemporary Poland]. In: Bilska-Wodecka, E. and Sołjan, E. (eds.): Pielgrzymki a sakralizacja przestrzeni [Pilgrimages and Sacralization of Space]. Peregrinus Cracoviensis, 16, 235-250.

Głębocki, K. (2006): Rola administracji publicznej w organizacji VI Światowego Dnia Młodzieży w Częstochowie [Role of Public Administration in the Organization of the VI World Youth Day in Częstochowa]. In: Peregrinus Cracoviensis, 17, 113-127.

Griffin, K.A. (2007): The Globalization of Pilgrimage Tourism: Some Thoughts from Ireland. In: Raj, R. and Morpeth, D. (eds.): Religious Tourism and Pilgrimage Management: An International Perspective. Cambridge, MA: CAB International, 15-34.

Jackowski, A. and Kaszewski, L. (1996): Jasna Góra w systemie ośrodków pielgrzymkowych świata [Jasna Góra in the World Pilgrimage Resorts System]. In: Peregrinus Cracoviensis, 3, 171-192.

Kersten, K. (2007) (ed.): Częstochowa: Dzieje miasta i Klasztoru Jasnogórksiego [Częstochowa: History of the City and the Jasna Góra Monastery], 4. Częstochowa: Urząd Miasta Częstochowy.

Kersten, K. (2002) (ed.): Częstochowa: Dzieje miasta i Klasztoru Jasnogórksiego [Częstochowa: History of the City and the Jasna Góra Monastery], 1. Częstochowa: Urząd Miasta Częstochowy.

Kowinski, W.S. (1985): The Malling of America: An Inside Look at the Great Consumer Paradise. New York: William Morrow.

Marciniak A. (1996): Święta Góra Grabarka [The Holly Mountain of Grabarka], Peregrinus Cracoviensis, 4, 179-192.

Matlak, H. (1996): Miasto żydowskie na Kazimierzu jako ośrodek ruchu turystycznego i pielgrzymkowego [The Jewish Town of Kazimierz (in Cracow) as a Centre for Tourism and Pilgrimage], Peregrinus Cracoviensis, 4, 125-142.

Portwood-Stacer, L. (2012): Anti-consumption as Tactical Resistance: Anarchist, Subculture, and Activist Strategy. In: Journal of Consumer Culture, 12(1), 87-105.

Sołjan, I. and Jackowski, A. (1996): Jasna Góra na tle innych ośrodków pielgrzymkowych w Polsce [Jasna Góra Compared to Other Pilgrimage Resorts in Poland]. In: Peregrinus Cracoviensis, 3, 153-170.

Turner, V. (1969): The Ritual Process: Structure and Anti-structure. Chicago: Aldine.

Turner, V. (1975): Dramas, Fields, and Metaphors: Symbolic Action in Human Societ. Ithaca: Cornel University Press.

Turner, V. and Turner, E. (1978): Image and Pilgrimage in Christian Culture. New York: Columbia University Press.

Urry, J. (2002): The Tourist Gaze. London: SAGE Publications.

Urry, J. (2007): Spojrzenie turysty, [The Tourist Gaze]. Warszawa: Wydawnictwo Naukowe PWN.

Wieczorkiewicz, A. (2008): Apetyt turysty. O doświadczeniu świata w podróży. Kraków [Tourist's Appetite. Experiencing the World in a Journey]. Kraków: Universitas.

Appendix:

Country	Pilgrimage Center
Lithuania	Wilnius
Spain	Santiago de Compostella
France	Paris– Chartres
Austria	Mariazell
Germany	One-day pilgrimage from Essen to Neviges,
	from Magdeburg to Klueschen Hagis in the Eichsfield / Thur-
Sweden	inga
Belgium	Sztokholm, Ecumenical Pilgrimage
Italy	Les amis Belges du pelegrinage a Chartres avec le monde du
England	travail
	from Macerary to Loreto
	Catholic National Shrine of Our Lady annual Easter Pilgrim-
	age to Walsingham in Norfolk
	to Holy Island on the Northumbrian coast of England
Scotland	from Melrose to Holy Island
	Aidan Simons
England–France	Easter Pilgrimage to Iona
USA	Pilgrims' Trail – from Hampshire to the North of France
	Chicago – Merrillville
	From Great Meadows, NJ to the American Czestochowa in
Canada	Doylestown
	Annual Pilgrimage for Restoration Shrine of Our Lady of the
Australia	North American Martyrs St. Isaac Jogues & Companions
	Auriesville, New York
	Milton – Midland oraz inna strona
	British Columbia, Prince George
	Ballarat – Bendigo in Victoria
	Subiaco – New Nursja

Figure 9: Countries in which Catholic and ecumenical foot pilgrimages take place. (http://www.fronda.pl/blogi/bliskoboga/piesze-pielgrzymki-zagraniczne,11383.html, 21.09.2013)

Facets of Mobility

Ulrich Gehmann

The scope of this contribution aims to illuminate facets of being mobile in the context of recent Western societies, together with relevant facets of socio-historical development and mythic background. The perspectives offered concentrate on those aspects of mobility which were the basis for the 'Touring Consumption' conference; focusing on phenomena related to tourism or in more general terms, on phenomena of world-consumption; which tourism is, in fact, a part of. The underlying thesis is that tourism is more than just "site-seeing" because those "sites" serve special functions and in themselves, become functionalized to a high degree by transforming them into products of consumption. These are no longer *sites*, i.e. places in the term's genuine understanding, but products, artifacts constructed to fulfill certain functionalities. This holds true even in cases where "original" sites are accessible for such consumption, e.g. places of an "original" nature like tropical forests or "wild" (i.e., original) mountain ranges visited by eco-tourists. Also in these cases, the product character of the site supersedes, and in fact replaces that site's original character: namely to be just a site, a genuine and individual *place* of own rank. In short, the world becomes a product and the meaning of the product is to be marketed.

All this presupposes mobility, either in a direct way of physically moving consumers to those (former) sites or in an indirect way, in that those sites are moving to *me*, the consumer, achieved via media devices. But being 'mobile' is not confined to travelling, to moving from one point in space to another, nor to encompassing mere technical, functional, or marketing aspects. The aim of this paper is to provide a general frame of understanding of what mobility means today, alongside our dependency towards it. This will be made apparent not only in factual terms, but also in social and especially, mental terms; terms which settle upon certain basic assumptions of a finally mythical nature and that will be outlined as follows, together with some contextual phenomena aligned to them.

The frame context

Our recent way of life can be epitomized as a *mobile* one, one that has a long tradition rooted in the 19th century, with the advent of metropolises, mass production and mass consumption (e.g. Sombart 1913: 25-41), that very epoch which paved the way for our recent state of being. It was in those times where our present conceptions of what mobility means began to emerge, before a new stage of being mobile was reached with the advent of the so-called Internet Society in the 1990s, as described by Manuel Castells (Castells 1996-98) and others.

In its factual terms, mobility began to appear on a large scale during the last quarter of the 19th century, being closely associated with modernity as such: triggered by forces of capitalist and imperialist dynamics acting in parallel (Braudel 1985; Bayly 2006: 26ff.), being mobile and being 'modern' became almost synonymous (e.g. Kaschuba 2004: 16f.) alongside fundamental changes in the social categories of time and space and its concomitant cultural codes (Kaschuba 2004: 13). One main reason for this lay embedded in the newly emerged capitalist economy of those days. Based on functional necessity, such an economy needed an economized conception of time and space, a conception turning human beings and things into objects to be moved and dislocated according to certain functionalities and in so doing, turning them into products which can be accumulated and consumed (Kaschuba 2004: 65). Without going into detail, this is the basic process – and an evolutionary tendency if you like – that underlies our prevalent understanding of mobility until today, no matter if we are aware of it or not; so the thesis is at least.

What does an "economized" conception of space and time mean, those two fundamental dimensions to which any kind of mobility is confronted with? To squeeze them, to overcome distances; both in terms of space, making accessible even the far remote, and in terms of time, in reaching a point in space (the former "site" introduced at the beginning) in shorter time than before. Given the proper technical means for doing so, such a compression of space and time can only work if a precondition is met, namely their formatting (Gehmann 2012). This is in effect a mindset, namely how reality can be approached in general before it can become "a fact", a factual force of molding that reality. In this way, the factual and mental terms work together, leading *inter alias* to the kind of mobility that is conceived as typically 'modern': to be fast, ubiquitous and individual. Applying such a mindset of formatting to space and time, they can be compressed only if they are first transformed – from concrete entities into *abstract* ones, in a literal sense[1]: I, the respective world-planning individual demiurge, refrain from a world as it is but construct a new one, one according to general, i.e. *artificial* criteria. The formerly given, the 'natural' I encounter has no value in itself (to be respected by me) but has to become annihilated, to be replaced by another kind of being. In other words, the concrete qualities of this world – the concrete sites and times it is composed of – have to be neglected in favor of new qualities imposed by me, the respective world-planning demiurge. An "economized" conception of time and space then means that new spaces, having their own (new) times, are imposed upon their original versions, with the aim of finally replacing them. Therefore, I have to *format* time and space by itemizing them, by taking modules of space and of time to become the real spaces, with their real times. An example from our everyday life (Figure 1) may visualize this:

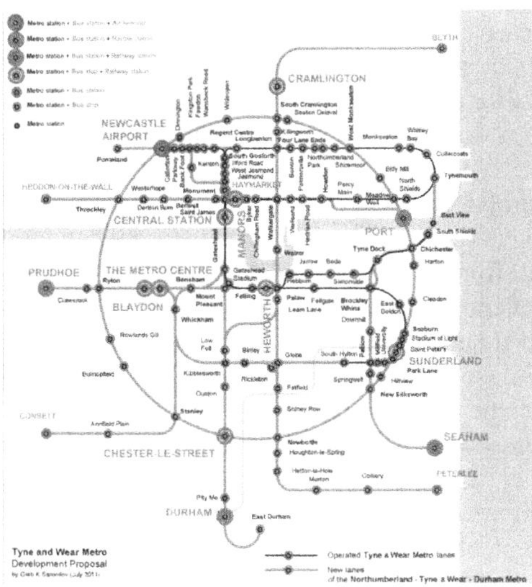

Figure 1: A functional cosmos of mobility. (Northumberland Metro System 2011[2]

1 In its literal meaning, *abstraction* stems from Latin *abstrahere*, to draw away (Heinichen 1903: 7) and, in the occidental discourse, denotes a process of refraining from the concrete, the individually given in favor of general schemes (Hoffmeister 1955: 10) which is an understanding of crucial importance in the context looked at here.

2 Drawing by Gleb K. Samoilov, http://commons.wikimedia.org/wiki/File:The_Integrated_System_of_Internal_and_External_Public_Transport_of_Tyne_and_Wear_Conurbation,_formed_by_NORTHUMBERLAND_-_TYNE_and_WEAR_-DURHAM_METRO.jpg?uselang=de

What we see here is an economized, i.e. *functionalized* space, a formatted world of its own superimposed on something originally given which has to be imagined: how the river is a straight abstract line leading to an equally abstract sea on the right, concrete sites being abstracted by dots, their *icons* of them and the individual inhabitant of this world, its *user*, appearing from nowhere. But it can also use this functional cosmos for its own individual purposes, by moving inside the terms of this cosmos (which such a world is, by its very construction). As this example should reveal, economizing space and time creates an artificial cosmos of the functional, a world as artifact laid over and superseding the originally as given. However, the original world is no longer needed (Gehmann and Reiche 2013), except as an assemblage of "tourist sites", that is, as *products*.

It leads to another aspect of importance with regards to mobility: the possibility to be mobile not just in physical, but also in virtual ways. Next to its conventional understanding of moving from one point in space to another, mobility today means living in a world of fluxes, a world which seems to be accessible at any time, in real time. That remains an illusion, of course, since the world does not exist for the purposes of the individual, no matter if the individual entity in question is a consumer or an enterprise. But after the rise of the mentioned historical caesura of an Internet Age, it is an illusion that has evolved into a strong cultural force. This makes us believe that we, the *users* of the world, have it at our disposal, via the diverse applications or *apps* we have technically derived from it. Here, too, the actual (the 'real') and the mental intermingle, by generating a new kind of reality: the so-called virtual one, consisting of world fragments – aspects of a "real" reality, e.g. a real tourist site as a concrete site in concrete space and time – which are transformed into apps the users can consume. Following Schopenhauer's (1818) World as Will and Conception (written in the times when mobility became a mass phenomenon), we, the applicants of such technical formats, can conceptualize our own worlds at any time we want in creating our own spaces.

As an emergent phenomenon, this conception triggers a paradox: as an individual user, I can stay totally immobile in physical terms whilst being virtually mobile. Moreover, I can even combine these two dimensions of mobility, the 'old' and real physical one with the 'new' and virtual one, into a new kind of the real. In this so-called Hybrid Reality (Gehmann and Reiche 2014), I can move through a physical space, e.g., an old town full of touristic sites and at the same time, *enhance* my impressions by using virtual versions of that space (Iaconesi and Persico 2013). That is, I can move also in virtual terms and "travel" in a way unknown so far in history – namely to move solely in physical space.

For us today, this might sound rather normal, perhaps even trivial. But for a more thorough understanding of the phenomena looked at here, understanding their historical dimension is crucial for gaining an impression (at least) of how non-trivial they are; if compared with that which has happened in terms of basic conditions of world perception, that which happens most of our time. In other words, it is a question about the *conditio humana*. It comprises an important, albeit unsettled additional aspect when discussing about mobility, particularly mobility today. It is not only about what these newly generated realities addressed above will trigger in terms of social and self-understanding (which already are questions about a human condition), alongside new social and cultural practices emerging as part of those realities. Important as they are, such questions are overshadowed by an even more fundamental one: If we conceive mobility in that wider meaning, sketched out in the foreground and expressed in terms of everyday culture, if being mobile is an *ontological* state intrinsically belonging to modernity and really to us, its successors, then such an ontological state – already problematic since its beginnings (Plessner 2003: 77-87; 136-217) leads to the question of what will happen when it unites with new kinds of realities (de Lange 2013). It is *When*, not *If*, since it has already happened and is continuing to happen with accelerating speed (see the discussions on man-machine interfaces, hybrid spaces, even hybrid media, and the like for a summary, Gehmann and Reiche 2014). In sum, these issues of a current, as well as, a future human condition constitute another essential domain in the framing of a context for being "mobile".

Developments

Next to mobility, *acceleration* is another phenomenon conceived as a characteristic of modernity and one closely related to mobility (Rosa 2005: 51-56). Mobility and acceleration advanced to epitomes of modernity, both in a factual and in an imagined dimension (e.g. Rapp 1994: 46-98). More specifically, it is about the mutual influences between external, "objective", and internal (or mental) "subjective" conditions that shape being mobile as an ontological state and being mobile in an accelerated manner. In the past, accelerated mobility led to a paradox effect: on the one hand, it was in need of standardized, formatted technical structures and procedures – the birth of the modern way of how to organize things – the will (and desire) to unify *masses* of entities; and on the other, it triggered an increasing fragmentation and hence, individualization. As an evolutionary movement (an additional mobility of an own kind), it finally led up to the present state, again in a factual and imagined dimension.

Some basics

The dimension labeled as an *imagined* one needs clarification. Here, it is not confined to mere phantasy or a strictly personal *ad libidum,* but owns a more common character. There are certain mindsets of how to perceive and as a consequence, of how to approach reality at all ("the world"), streaming into socially and culturally accepted practices which again form dominant conceptions of the world and out of this, into conceptions of how to *conceive* the world at all, both in interpretative ("theoretical") and practical terms. Interpreted in this way, imagination settles upon some leading ideas – being specific for a certain culture and epoch – in a very direct, almost sensitive and at the same time, encompassing sense. The term *idea* is aligned to the Greek *eidos*, denoting shape or form (Hoffmeister 1955: 186), and is an inner image I have of something; but one of a particular kind since it acts as an inner ideal model, a basic or leading idea of how to conceive and how to shape the world (Hoffmeister 1955: 317). Looking at the world presented in Figure 1, we can gain an understanding of what this means. The world presented there rests upon some basic ideas of how a *relevant world* should look like, with its essential characteristics. Its example also reveals the symbolic character of those leading ideas – the world presented *stands for* a specific mindset of how relevant worlds, and in particular, how relevant worlds devoted to mobility have to look like. In this sense, it is not just a picture, but an image – in literal terms, a world image.

If ideas and the ideal are comprehended in the way outlined here, then out of the body of ideas are ideas characterized through a particular culture or epoch, some of them constitutive for all the others. Such ideas "explain" the world "as it is" and in this sense, are narrations of origin at the same time. Out of this, also narrations about the present and the future, these ideas "reveal" the world's very nature, what it is (and therefore, evidently was and will be) that makes the world a *world* in the latter's encompassing terms. In traditional discourse, they have been termed myths, basic ideas of a literal religious character since all the others are rooted in them, being *rebound* to them (the original meaning of religion, see Heinichen 1903: 732). As one author puts it, they are certainties of faith, that is, ideas of an axiomatic character (Rappaport 1999: 293) which holds valid not only for traditional, but also for modern myths (cf. Gehmann 2003). Myths, says Blumenberg (1996), are narrations with great constancy of their narrative cores and a concomitant "marginal variability". Both features make myths suitable for tradition and thus, they gain the status of explanations that are cosmological (Blumenberg 1996: 40f.). In a literal sense, they tell the *logos* or the meaning of the world; at least of the relevant world.

It becomes apparent, those tales characterizing a particular culture or epoch are interacting by forming a system of myths, a mythology. In the figure below for instance, a world is presented, on which rests upon several myths in parallel: the myth of movement, telling that the world's essence consists in dynamics and that it belongs to a *conditio humana* which is moving. At the same time is a myth of progress aligned to that; a myth of domination believing that it is, and has to be possible to gain total control over the relevant world (which is a world of movement); a myth of modernity, as Rapp (1994) called it, the certainty of faith that a scientific interpretation of the world combined with that world's technical transformation makes a world 'as it is', or "a world that became humanities' genuine, and only place to live in" (cf. Rapp 1994: 147). In terms of such beliefs forming a system, we become aware of the interrelations between these myths, interrelations which in themselves, comprise of additional facets of mobility. Moreover, the myths of domination and of progress relate to another myth which is of crucial importance in this context, namely to the myth of the world's planneability: that it is possible to plan all processes and structures belonging to a relevant world, and that this is intrinsic to a human condition. Furthermore, the myth of a world as an ideal artifact, in all the connotations of an *idea* outlined above, *is* and must be possible in order to create a world according to our will and conception. Or in other words, it is possible to make up a model of the world (a "virtual" world) as a real world in *all* of its *relevant* components. These myths are intrinsic to a mobile world, which is a world conceived as essentially *modern*. And in particular, they intrinsically belong to our current world as the latter's outcome.

Figure 2: The aesthetics of movement. (Author)[3]

3 Lisbon, bridge over the river Tagus

Every mythology, symbolic or literal, and as long as it is a practiced, i.e. a one that is really believed in, willingly and unwillingly generates the reality suited to it. In the case of the above myths, a world has been generated that looks – as a habitable place – like the one pictured in figure 2. It is a world devoted to movement, mobility; and out of this, a deeply functional one, formatted according to the consequent and relentless application of technical criteria. In its concrete outcomes, the mythology sketched above leads to world-spaces depicted in Figure 1 and 2 and, expressed as a general morphology, to a world as a "phantom and matrix" (Anders 1987: 97-211). In its total, it is a Promethean venture to move the world (Gehmann 2004) from the 19th century onwards.

When looking at such worlds' pictorial representations, figure 1 is showing its general outlay, its principle of construction so to speak, whereas figure 2 gives an impression of its concrete shapes to live in; of how such a world looks like after it became reality. At the same time, both figures indicate another feature of the mythic: being imaginative. Mythic representation, says Boehm (1983), does generate, through the very act of representing, the conditions of its evidence. Mythical images generate a truth that will only be judged on their own and their imaginative power is the medium and guarantee of their truth at the same time (Boehm 1983: 533). Schelling, one of the founders of research on the mythic in the 19th century, the very same age that "invented" mobility, said of myths that they were tautegorical – they rest in themselves, and rely on themselves (quoted in Cassirer 1979: 235). Or posed even simpler, in the technoid diction we are acquainted with as a result of the above myths' impact, myths can be seen as self-referential, auto-logical systems of categorical character. Telling seemingly self-evident truths, they become sacrosanct in their daily practice of application, as certainties of faith. The myth is believed in because it tells the truth, and it is true because it is holy. For instance, a myth on the basis of which in its practical outcome, the myth of movement could unfold – is the myth of the free market the author experienced in its narrative core as follows (refraining from its diverse imaginative shapes, means and concretizations): free market = democracy = freedom. The latter is to be understood as the center of a human condition to be longed for: truly individuals are only liberated ones. This is not meant to be speculative, but practical since, as it has already mentioned, every myth generates its own realities. With this myth of a free market in mind, the author's equipage colonized entire territories still believing in other myths, bringing free market and hence, liberation to them.[4]

To express it in general terms, myths create meaning and the respective realities; and the latter justifies the meaning of the myth in question, thus

4 More on this myth, and on the reality-shaping powers of the mythic and its imaginative features can be found in Gehmann (2010: 19-22).

generating an entire *conceiving* – not only perception, not just comprehension – of the world in terms of the myth in question.

Some moves

Before the days of a myth of movement, but paving its way, in the Renaissance, the humanist Pico della Mirandola tells a myth about man's meaning. God put man in the midst of the newly created earth and told him that man, opposed to all the other creatures, has no definite place, no role and no meaning *eo ipso* inside the cosmic order. His meaning is to wander around, to go wherever he wants, and to build his home at any place he would like, being his own sculptor and defining by himself the form he wants to be (della Mirandola 1996: 10f.). At the dawn of a modern era already, man has to move, in an inner and outer sense: to define his place in the world, and to define himself. From now on, he is literally utopian because no definite place, no *topos* in this world is his genuine one – "utopia" stemming from the Greek *ou-topos* or non-place. Coming back to the myth's imaginative power, the mythical power of images can be characterized as the impossibility to recur to something else other than to themselves (Ammann 1983: 546f.). If the myth as such is utopian in this sense, then the myth of an essentially placeless conditio humana really is.

Mirandola's myth was published in 1496, shortly after new spaces had been opened up, the vast realms of a New World and those of the Indian Ocean. Centuries later, a researcher of such shifts discovers that there have been cultural patterns and symbolic technologies which had succeeded, starting from our occidental cultural sphere, to cover the whole world based on two major moves, the reformation[5] in the 16th century and the scientific revolution in the 17th century. And the "scientific-technocultural revolution" we underwent since then and are still undergoing, is more than just an acceleration of an industrial revolution, but an "explosive revolution of perspectives, technologies and ways of organizing" (Nelson 1984: III-IV). In terms of movement, since it requires a high degree of mobility to achieve such a state of being; a state of mind which other cultures did not have at the time of its unfolding, led to the rise of a bipolar world since the 19th century at the latest (occident vs. the others; see Kennedy 1989: 229-310).

That century was a time when a myth of progress, and connected with that, one of movement, began to fully unfold. The scientifically backed up "techno-cultural revolution" not only opened, but created new spaces, spaces which have

5 See Max Weber's famous notes about puritanism and a capitalist mindset (Weber 1992: 357-381).

been characterized as essentially technotopian, i.e. generated, managed and sustained by means of technology – a type of spatiality that became genuinely human until now (Ropohl 1979: 12f.). In a strict sense, a technotopian space is a utopian space since it is essentially faceless and non-individual. It is always constructed according to the same criteria, those of a technicality aiming at a maximum of functionality, and thus, of efficiency which embodies a specific kind of movement, heading towards the infinite. Since functionalities can be optimized, progress, growth and acceleration are embedded in them. They were rooted in technical and organizational formats operating in an algorithm-like manner, literally abstracting from the individually given. Alongside the capitalist forces through which they were enabled to occur, and fueled by the myth of the free market, it led to a myth of creative destruction (see Schumpeter 1942: 83), namely to pursue an essentially a-historical state of being where the new (the better) was in a constant move of replacing the old (the less good). And it is evident that such a process, assisted technologically, bears in itself a mighty force of acceleration.

Figure 3: Accelerated mobility, in abstract perspective. (Author)[6]

In its total, it was a movement that culminated in a global sociocultural and economical similarization (Bayly 2006: 75-78), finding its expression in "a kind of universal algebra (an algorithm), brought forward by globally ramified 'protestant' institutions, ways of life and organizational systems", an unprecedented event in human history (Nelson 1984: IV). It resulted in a myth that is "typically modern", namely a myth of movement telling us that man's destiny is to move, to forever *proceed* in constant dynamics, to avoid rest by all means (because this would equal standstill), and that this kind of progress is the meaning of the world as such and hence, of history. In its original Greek meaning, it was a utopian venture since it was no longer bound to specific

6 Giacomo Balla (1913): Abstract Velocity, Museo Agnelli, Torino

spatiality but, thanks to its formats, could be performed virtually everywhere. Since then, mobility also meant abstraction from the individually given in favor of a *world as construction,* devoted to ensure mobility as tautegorical as its myth. Of course, one needs physical substrates still, but no fixed, concrete space one is really belonging to.

Spaces for mobility

In order to unfold, a myth of movement needs the proper spaces, and a general conception of spatiality assigned to it. Starting with the 18th century, a spatial conception gained ground that conceived space as void, empty, abstract and non-sensual; according to Kant, space was an apodictic necessity, not based upon experience but a pure product of reason (Vidler 2011: 131). What began in the Renaissance as a world to wander around turned into an abstract *tabula rasa* ready for construction, paving the way for an "all-determining technological and antihumanist version of progress" (Vidler 2011: 131f.), so closely linked with movement. Because in line with a myth of the world's planneability telling that world can be *made of,* instead of being just accepted 'as it is', a constructed world was needed – a world as an ideal artifact in the above meanings of the *ideal* – that allowed for *planned movements*, i.e. for *organized* mobility, the very basic prerequisite of the capitalist forces to enter. Later on, for such a world as architecture, the architectural space of the 19th century is the endless space of the three coordinates (Kemp 2009: 120) which can be filled with a particular ideal artifact as a necessity for planned movement: the grid,[7] conceived as the net, that "encompassing container of all existences", as a French master planner of those days formulated it (Kemp 2009: 123). The mythic urge was to create a world as network allowing for free individual movement on the one hand, and on the other, for an embracing, organized mobility.

7 Although the grid, as a planning device, is very old (Kostof 1991: 95), it unfolded as an *encompassing* means for a myth of domination in the 19th century.

Figure 4: World as network. (http://memory.loc.gov/cgi-bin/query/r?ammem/gmd:@field%28NUMBER+@band%28g3904g.pm006620%29%29)[8]

Referring to the imaginative properties of the mythic, what we envisage here is a world that is the predecessor of the one portrayed in Figure 1, so to say, a world in preparation to become that one. It is a world as network, laid out for its future mobile inhabitants, covering nearly all of the visible space (the world as it was) except the empty horizon located at such a world's rim. The format of the world became a world as format.

To draw this evolutionary line to its end, later on, such an artificial world became man's second nature, up to the non-places characterizing the present human condition (Augé 1995) and the logistic landscapes of capitalism (Waldheim and Berger 2012). Still later, after the historical caesura of the Internet Age, it evolved into The Net, mythological epitome of man's liberation from physical constraints. Still even later, by using the means of a virtual mobility addressed earlier, the liberated man of della Mirandola can even use spaces without really being in need of them, by using them as *real* spaces in a *virtual* manner (Reiche and Gehmann 2012).

The movement of such a virtualizing of space and creating it anew according to certain models – of worlds as ideal artifacts for mobility – gained full sway in the 19th century, and is continuing until today. What began with a real world's geographic properties – to format them according to the functionalities they had to serve for – could also be extended to worlds not yet in existence. 'Virtual' worlds of pure functionalism could be imagined, worlds

8 Greensboro, North Carolina 1891

which could be invented and then posed upon a 'world as it is'. And since the 19th century, systems of flow also became the relevant functional worlds, each of them a cosmic structure of its own (see figures 1 and 4, in comparison). But despite their fixed structures, the morphologies depicted here were designed to enable *systems* of relevant *processes* to operate, and to do so in a continuous manner. It was about movement, not about statics. More precisely, it was about an ordered movement, organized according to the statics of fixed formats, in order to ensure the organized mobility addressed beforehand. But not only space, time was also affected. Opposed to premodern societies, these movements had to happen not only here and there, and only from time to time, but continuously, *all* the time; up to our recent Always Online-culture and its *real time*-mode, a mythic epitome receiving world fragments without delay – which at the same time, actually embodies an additional way of being mobile.

In a literal meaning of the symbolic, such worlds *stood for* certain functionalities, and even genuine human belongings could be expressed, and more importantly, actually moulded by them. For instance, in terms of traffic, work or communication flows, or in terms of distribution as a *result* of flows – of products, people, material, information, capital and so on. The common point was to establish systems of flows crucial for a larger system's viability (e.g. a society) as s*tructures* inside, in which particular *dynamics* happened, expressed as functionalized processual moves. It was about movement, dynamics and the structures as its images were those dynamics' symbolic representations. So it became possible to define a set of functionalities serving certain purposes and then – via their structuring as patterns of process flows – control them. Such worlds of functional networks became the relevant spaces of modernity. And with the rise of the Internet Age, that historical caesura that brought the process of virtualization at its logical and mythological end, evolved into spaces which are the apex of that 18th century-abstraction. They are literally utopian because they do not even need to be physical any longer.

Being mobile

Such an embracing, evolutionary process which became characteristic of modernity from the first railways onwards (Sternberger 1938: 23ff.) and which continues until today, is always in acceleration. Acceleration accelerates, and does so with accelerating speed; a very uncanny phenomenon, but as mentioned, characteristic for modernity and lasting until the present. At the end, it led to a state of being which Paul Virilio epitomized as a *running standstill*, an "absolute zero" caused by the permanent movement of the "mobility machine" constituting our age (Virilio 1997: 126f.).

As an important frame context, it gave rise to the phenomenon of *escape* mentioned in the beginning, or formulated in more neutral terms, to that of tourism. Tourism was (and still is) a peculiar form of escapism: it obeys the very same (inescapable) mechanisms of an economically triggered functionalization and formatization, as did the rest of the modern world from which escape was sought. It has been first confined to physical escape, but then after the mentioned historical cut of the Internet Age, tourism adopted other forms such as Internet gaming, visiting virtual worlds like Second Life and related phenomena; they too are forms of a recent mobility and in particular, forms of escapism from the very world the recent mobility had generated. At the end of the 19th century, the phenomenon of mass tourism gained ground, and also the first appearances of virtual worlds, adopting the form of virtual spaces. The panorama and the diorama were invented (Vidler 2011: 82f.), presenting exotic and past worlds. Moreover, resembling recent virtual spaces, they were presented in such a way that the spectator, who then became the todays' *user* of worlds of such kind, could perceive them in artificially generated perspectives impossible to achieve for the normal perception apparatus (Sternberger 1938: 12-21). It was in that time when the discussion of distinguishing the natural from the artificial began (Sternberger 1938: 23-34), precursor of the recent discussions about the boundaries between real and virtual.

Closely related to the phenomenon of acceleration was a new perception of the world also in its natural, physically given terms, pouring into a new conception of time and space. What started in the 17th and 18th centuries already, namely to conceive space not just as a void (see above), but also as a connecting element for transport and travel (Kaschuba 2004: 35), culminated into a new conception in the second half of the 19th century. It was a conception closely aligned with the social precursor of ours (so to say), the 19th century *bourgeois*. In those times, our recent concept of *landscape* had its origins, caused by mobility. The accelerated mode of bourgeois travelling generated an impression of moving *through* space, instead of moving *in* space (Kaschuba 2004: 53). On the one hand, such a technically assisted "modern travelling" was associated with a loss of authenticity and an increasing alienation. On the other, it became the favorite trope of a bourgeois understanding of the world, declaring *movement through space* as the essence of travelling, preferring velocity and the impression of 'flying' through space (see Figure 2) – both tendencies evolved into a travel culture that paved the way for modern mass tourism (Kaschuba 2004: 53).

Triggered by capitalist forces, and although it was a mass phenomenon, it gave rise to the luxury of an increased individualism, heading towards the attitude of *world consumption* addressed in the beginning. Luxury, states Werner Sombart in his description of its relation to capitalism, is every effort that exceeds the necessary, and finally aims at an *enriched* reality (1913: 71; 73), but it does so consequently, individually, i.e. driven by egoistic motives. Consumption needs the individual since in its final terms, I can *consume* only alone; and although it is marketed in an individualistic way, it needs individuals in *masses* to be profitable – and therefore, to exist at all in our world 'as it is' (to recur to that mythic term). A basic relation that applies to all phenomena of a world consuming mobility is examined here, a kind of mobility that is intrinsically connected with the myth of the free market.

As a result, mobility took place in a mental or imagined realm associated with a third phenomenon closely linked to modernity, next to being mobile and accelerated: a fundamental dissociation of time, space and the social preparing of the way for a *world as app* to come.

Figure 5: Individual masses. (Author)[9]

On the one hand, there has been the organizational drive towards abstracting, unifying, and formatting space, time and the social; on the other, there was a concomitant fragmentation, a product of the very same process.

What began in the Enlightenment as a dislocation of space, dissolving its naturally given topography and old order, also continued with time, even with historical time. Fragments of history could be placed individually, according to individual prevalence; the "medieval ruin" in a landscape park, the historical monument placed anywhere, and so on. It evolved a "simultaneity of the non-simultaneous" (Kaschuba 2004: 54f.), or in other words, even history could become the subject of mobility.

9 Tourists, Nizza 1900, Daimler Benz Museum, Stuttgart

Linked with such dislocations of both time and space, new shapes of the social also emerged. In its social terms, being mobile evolved into a social attitude and addtionally, into a social value of own rank, signifying a person's or group's social importance. It led to the prevalent recent perception that persons with restricted mobility are either handicapped in one way or the other, and/or socially unimportant. In particular after the rise of the Internet Age, being *connected* – the new, virtual form of mobility enabled by new technical means – became almost identical with being alive, first of all socially alive.

Moreover, opposed to pre-modern, even to pre-internet societies, as an individual, I can be social in my own terms, following individual guidelines as in the case of dis- and allocating time and space. In other words, I can be mobile also in social respects. Since I am no longer addicted to certain social groups, I *have* to belong to (wanted or not) just simply because I cannot *move* from my territory, my physical allocation in space, for instance my home town where I was born and now, have to stay. The same applies to my social belongings, as for instance my neighborhood in my home town. Now, after the advent of the Internet Age adding a new dimension to mobility, I can be mobile not only physically and timely, but also in social regards. I can choose the social groups I want to belong to, I can change them if I want to, even be a member of many social groups in parallel. I do not have to remain inside a pre-given physical or social space, in contrast to all the centuries before, which might look trivial but which isn't in historical terms, i.e. in terms of evolution. For *us*, it might look trivial just because we have become used to it and thus, interpret it as "normal"; but when looked at inside the frames of an entire human history, the fact of being also *socially* mobile (and not only physically) is unprecedented. Throughout occidental history so far, being social was seen as the constitutive element of a *conditio humana*: the *zoon politikon*, the social animal equaled man. Now, even this became seemingly a matter of the individual, and that means in its final terms a matter of individual moves, triggered by likings/dislikings (see the symbolical facebook sign).

Interpreted in these evolutionary terms, it leads to a paradox. Economically and technically formatted, frame conditions trigger an increased individualization, but an individualization is formatted as well. Because these frame conditions still prevail, the "individualism" they generate and allow for is a seeming one since the individual user of their products is not only a product – see above, on capitalism – but on the top of that, can only use preformatted products, in technical as well as economic terms.

As one author put it, it led to "heterotopias of consumption and illusion" which appear individualistically, but are triggered by mass-marketing strategies (Shane 2013: 307). In its overall effect, it leads to a further mobilization of the already mobile, primarily because these strategies are tuned to the virtual dimension (Shane 2013: 306f.). Connected with it, as regards mobility's mental terms – the *imagined* dimension addressed above – the real (or perceived) degree of mobility becomes not only an indicator of one's social relevance, but enables a mindset to appear. This can be seen as a new myth aligned to mobility or that a person's very *being alive* depends on that person's degree, and range of mobility; leading to the mythic belief that the more mobile I am in both these dimensions, the more alive I am. History is included next to the manifold ways of a 'virtual' mobility addressed beforehand. Envisaged in its combined outcomes and in the light of the facets of "being mobile" outlined so far, the new myth addressed above is the final fulfillment of a myth of movement since (as any 'good' myth does) it reveals man's reason to be – I am mobile, therefore I am.

References

Ammann, J.C. (1983): Zur Utopie in mythischen Bildern. In: Bohrer, K.H. (ed.): Mythos und Moderne. Frankfurt/Main: Suhrkamp, 545-571.

Anders, G. (1987): Die Antiquiertheit des Menschen (2 vol.), vol. 1: Über die Seele im Zeitalter der zweiten industriellen Revolution. München: C.H. Beck.

Augé, M. (1995): Non-places – introduction to an anthropology of supermodernity. London/New York: Verso.

Bayly, C.A. (2006): Die Geburt der modernen Welt: Eine Globalgeschichte 1780-1914. Frankfurt/New York: Campus.

Blumenberg, H. (1996): Arbeit am Mythos. Frankfurt/Main: Suhrkamp.

Boehm, G. (1983): Mythos als bildnerischer Prozeß. In: Bohrer, K.H. (ed.): Mythos und Moderne. Frankfurt/Main: Suhrkamp, 528-544.

Braudel, F. (1985): La dynamique du capitalisme. Paris: Les Editions Arthaud.

Castells, M. (1996-98): The Information age, Vol. I -III. London/Malden, MA: Blackwell Publishing.

De Lange, M. (2013): The smart city you love to hate: Exploring the role of affect in hybrid urbanism. In: Hybrid City: Subtle Revolutions, Proceedings of the International Biennal Conference, Athens, 23-25 May 2013, 77-84.

Della Mirandola, G.P. (1996) (ed.): Über die Würde des Menschen (de dignitate hominis). Zürich: Manesse.

Gehmann, U. (2003): Modern myths. In: Culture and Organization, 9(3), 105-119.

Gehmann, U. (2004): Prometheus unleashed: The quest for knowledge and the promise of salvation through technique. In: Gabriel, Y. (ed.): Myths, stories, and Organizations: Premodern Narratives for Our Times. Oxford: Oxford University Press, 165-175.

Gehmann, U. (2010): Morphologie, Mythos, und Raum: NarratMorphologien der Geschichte, Weltbildlichkeit und Raumverständnis. Karlsruhe: KIT Publishing, http://digbib.ubka.uni-karlsruhe.de/volltexte/1000021190, 30.01.2014.

Gehmann, U. (2012): Formats. In: Journal of New Frontiers in Spatial Concepts, 4, , 13-33. http://ejournal.uvka.de/spatialconcepts/archives/1494, 28.01.2014.

Gehmann, U. and Reiche, M. (2013): Advanced spatialities. In: International Journal of Art, Culture and Design Technologies, 3(1), 48-57.

Gehmann, U. and Reiche, M. (2014) (eds.): Real virtuality: About the destruction and multiplication of world. Bielefeld: transcript.

Heinichen, F.A. (1903): Lateinisch-Deutsches Schulwörterbuch. Leipzig/Berlin: B.G. Teubner.

Hoffmeister, J. (1955): Wörterbuch der philosophischen Begriffe. Hamburg: Felix Meiner.

Iaconesi, S. and Persico, O. (2013): Real-time dissent in the City: Tools and tactics for contemporary disseminated, dispersed, recombinant movements. In: Hybrid city: Subtle revolutions. Proceedings of the International Biennal Conference, Athens, 23-25 May 2013, 51-56.

Kaschuba, W. (2004): Die Überwindung der Distanz. Zeit und Raum in der europäischen Moderne. Frankfurt/Main: Fischer.

Kemp, W. (2009): Architektur analysieren. Eine Einführung in acht Kapiteln. München: Schirner/Mosel.

Kennedy, P. (1989): Aufstieg und Fall der großen Mächte. Ökonomischer Wandel und militärischer Konflikt von 1500 bis 2000. Frankfurt/Main: Fischer.

Kostof, S. (1991): The city shaped: Urban patterns and meanings through history. New York/Boston/London: Bulfinch Press.

Nelson, B. (1984): Der Ursprung der Moderne. Frankfurt/Main: Suhrkamp.

Plessner, H. (2003): Conditio humana, Gesammelte Schriften VIII. Frankfurt/Main: Suhrkamp.

Rapp, F. (1994): Die Dynamik der modernen Welt. Hamburg: Junius.

Rappaport, R.A. (1999): Ritual and religion in the making of humanity. Cambridge: Cambridge University Press.

Reiche, M. and Gehmann, U. (2012): How virtual spaces re-render the perception of reality through playful augmentation. In: IEE Xplore, Cyberworlds International Conference, Darmstadt, 25-27 Sept. 2012, 304-307. http://ieeexplore.ieee.org/xpl/login.jsp?tp=&arnumber=6337438&url=http%3A%2F%2Fieeexplore.ieee.org%2Fstamp%2Fstamp.jsp%3Ftp%3D%26arnumber%3D6337438, 31.01.2014.

Ropohl, G. (1979): Eine Systemtheorie der Technik: Zur Grundlegung der Allgemeinen Technologie. München/Wien: Hanser.

Rosa, H. (2005): Beschleunigung: Die Veränderung der Zeitstruktur in der Moderne. Frankfurt/Main: Suhrkamp.

Schumpeter, J.A. (1942): Capitalism, socialism and democracy. New York/London: Harper.

Shane, D.G. (2013): Recombinant urbanism: Conceptual modeling in architecture, urban design, and city theory. Chichester: John Wiley & Sons.

Sombart, W. (1913): Luxus und Kapitalismus. München/Leipzig: Duncker & Humblot.

Sternberger, D. (1938): Panorama, oder Ansichten vom 19. Jahrhundert. Hamburg: H. Goverts.

Verene, D.Ph. (ed.): Symbol, myth, and culture: Essays and lectures of Ernst Cassirer, 1935-1945. New Haven/London: Yale University Press.
Vidler, A. (2011): Scenes of the street and other essays. New York: The Monacelli Press.
Virilio, P. (1997): Rasender Stillstand. Frankfurt/Main: Fischer.
Waldheim, Ch. and Berger, A. (2012): Logistiklandschaften. In: arch+ 205 (März), Zeitschrift für Architektur und Städtebau, 76-83.
Weber, M. (1992) (ed.): Soziologie, Universalgeschichtliche Analysen, Politik. Stuttgart: A. Kröner.

Spectral Touring: Subject, Consumption, and the 'Wound' of the Photograph[1]

Sourav Kargupta

Introduction

This paper takes as theme the notion of 'touring consumption,' and argues its case with reference to the field of 'tourism studies.' Let me commence in the way of reflecting on this placement. It might safely be argued that 'tourism studies' have a defiantly inter-disciplinary make. As a field of knowledge it prompts a pulse of tension as it struggles to get a foothold in a realm where disciplinary boundaries are jealously kept, John Urry's founding text (Urry 1990) says as much. Tourism studies have also been a refuge for interdisciplinary travelers, for it potentially keeps a menacing force within itself, the force of asking questions that are general enough to encroach on other epistemic territories. The 'touring subject' may become a general description for the 'subject as such,' especially in the postmodern condition. But does this force of generality also not make it difficult for tourism studies to demarcate its own specificity as a discipline?

This paper tries to make some theoretical conjectures on the internal transactions between the 'postmodern subject' and the 'touring subject,' though I would prefer to use the more systematic term 'post-structuralism' instead of 'postmodernism.' Post-structuralist interventions, especially 'deconstruction' have tried to think the subject without recourse to any essentialism (in the sense of doing away with all fixed and closed notion of the 'structure' which relies on an essential subject poised to give it stability). But this is a contradictory venture since it can be argued that any predication of the subject necessarily also ontologizes a centre of consciousness and an unvarying origin of intentionality. In short, the question remains how the conscious, intending subject can be

1 I thank everyone present during my presentation at the conference 'Touring Consumption 2013'organized and hosted by the Karlshochschule International University, in Karlsruhe, Germany in 2013. I thank the organizers for supporting the trip with the 'Karlshochschule Mobilities Grant'. This is a very different paper from the one I presented at that occasion, but one that tries to incorporate a few key concerns that cropped up in the course of the conference itself. Most important of which, for me, was a need for a thorough conceptual figuring of the idea of the 'touring subject,' especially in light of postmodern and post-structuralist theory. I have tried to address the issue here.

thought without any essentialist assumption. This is the central theoretical problematic that this paper confronts. The argument further recognizes that this problem plays out at its acute in the case of the 'touring subject' and therefore tries to situate and address the problematic of the postmodern subject in the context of the act and desire of touring.

At its very basic, any act of travel or touring must have a point of reference with respect to which the 'touring' would take place. An anthropocentric account of travel takes the human subject as that poised, experiencing self who goes through the lived experience of 'touring' a place or site (the 'site of touring'). In a postmodern condition however, this situated self has to deal with experiences that might disrupt its unity, prompting for the surfacing of a more fragmentary self. How can such a divided self recover and produce a locus of perception and indeed construe a subject who organizes dispersed perceptions of the outside as experience of touring, especially if one relies on a conceptual terrain which does not takes any stable structure for granted? This would be the key post-structuralist question facing a theory of touring or of the touring subject. This articulation also clearly states the experience of a postmodern world where any subjectivity is necessarily fragmented. Does this make room for some confusion between the 'postmodern subject' and the 'touring subject,' or indicate a loss of specificity for the act of touring (if touring becomes almost synonymous with living or experiencing in a postmodern world as such)? This is an immense theoretical problem. We may further disentangle it and state that the most decisive critical problem that a tourism studies sensitive to philosophical nuances face in the contemporary world is of 'specificity,' and ironically, of authenticity. Even in the classic study of tourism by John Urry (Urry 1990) written almost twenty five years ago, this troubling problem of finding a 'specificity' for the experience of the touring subject comes up, and indeed in the very context of 'postmodernism.' "Postmodernism involves a dissolving of the boundaries," Urry reminds, "not only between high and low cultures, but also between different cultural forms, such as tourism, art, education, photography, television, music, sport, shopping and architecture" (Urry 1990: 74). Evidently then, the most immediate problem for the theoretically inclined student of tourism-studies is one of limiting the boundaries of the field, focusing on the salient features of a touring experience to resist an uncontrolled expansion of its definitions. But ironically, this can only be done at the cost of relegating such a central human experience as touring to a relatively minor subordinate position. Urry therefore rightly goes the other way, and it seems that his solution to this conundrum is to project 'touring experience' as exemplary of the postmodern experience as such. Urry famously articulates this exemplarity in term of the specular, and coins the now-much-used phrase 'tourist gaze.' He proposes that in the contemporary world (more in the "western societies"), the 'gaze' of the tourist becomes *the gaze as such*, the gaze of the average, of everyone. "The tourist gaze," Urry writes, "is intrinsically part of contemporary experience, of postmodernism" (Urry 1990: 74). But if it is already 'intrinsic' to a new way subjects experience, then what is not (a) touring (experience), would really be the key question. Can tourism studies afford such an expansion of its field? Urry's pioneering study curves out a space for 'tourism' in the specificity of its 'practices,' but even there remains a risk of generalizing the definition of a 'touring practice' too much to the widening of the field beyond the limits of a single discipline. Urry reminds that "people are much of the time 'tourists' whether they like it or not" (Urry 1990: 74)[2]. The problem of specificity for the experience of touring remains.

Urry's effort to demarcate a space of specificity for the study of tourism takes the form of a descriptive account of touristic practices. I would try the same, but in a conceptual way. The main move of this paper would be to make some tentative suggestions in theoretically thinking the complex interaction that goes on between the 'site of touring' and the 'touring subject' in making up the experience of touring. The central theme of this paper would address the following problem: how does the touring site, its objects, representations and images interrupt, resist or write the touring subject, and how the subjectivity of the tourist shapes the 'site' in question in return? What are the ways to understand this space that stays neither entirely on the side of the object nor is fully intended by the subject? I would try to argue that such problems can be understood and approached through the notion of 'spectrality,' as it comes out in the reading of Karl Marx's idea of 'commodity fetishism' by Jacques Derrida (in Derrida 2006; also see Marx 1986). The notion of spectrality thinks of a space which is neither totally authenticated or authored by the intentionality of the subject, nor by a descriptive account of its constituting objects. It also thinks of a 'life' or a survival of a representative chain through which the object and the subject may said to be writing and prompting each other. It is at the site of such a shared space of complementary otherness, I propose, that the touring subject can be best understood.

In the first section I present a focused critical account of some aspects of the Marxian critique of 'commodity fetishism.' I try to confront in brief some existing criticisms of the Marxian text, especially those coming from within the tourism or consumption studies. My account is closely punctuated by Jacques Derrida's reading of Marx, which I use in turn as the main critical tool for my

---

2 In Urry's text, this risk of a generalization of the 'tourist gaze' to the point of it becoming the *gaze as such* also comes with the alignment of the 'gaze' with the Foucauldian notion of disciplinary regimes, which itself is conceived by Michel Foucault as a *general condition* of the modern episteme (in Europe).

later discussion. It is not the Derridian deconstruction of Marx in its entirety, but only a certain movement of the Marxian scheme read by Derrida as 'spectrality' that I carry forward in studying the problem of the touring subject which is the theme of the next section. After making some preliminary arguments for a notion of a 'spectral life' in understanding the act of touring and its subject, I go on to examine an exemplary object that can empirically indicate this abstract web of subject-object transaction. Within the argument of this paper, that exemplary object would be the 'photograph' or the 'snapshot' (as an objectification of both the subject and the object in the same medium) which is studied in some detail in the penultimate section before I move onto the concluding remarks.

I should clearly state at this point the limits within which my arguments are construed. The exposition that follows, for example, does not conclusively define what constitutes the 'touristic site,' or the 'touring subject.' Such calculable demarcations can only be approached through meticulous studies of definite, located events, i.e. not by dealing in 'generalities,' but by interrupting them by the textualization of particular practices. But any such exercise would first need a conceptual groundwork, one which would study how far the general questions relevant to this field can actually be stretched. This paper does such a groundwork. Therefore, if on the one hand it stops short of fashioning precise definitions, for example of the 'touring subject,' on the other it makes the subject of touring exemplary of the postmodern subject predication, claiming for the act of touring a centrality in thinking the postmodern experience as such. This paper also does not delve into the problems of 'power' and 'law,' both key in studying the practice of touring in a world of unequal exchange and restricted mobility. However, it hopes to clear a space for such studies by going through the theoretical preliminaries. With this caveat in place, let me proceed.

Commodity-work and consumption: Derrida reads Marx

Critiques of Karl Marx's account of 'commodity fetishism' from the side of recent studies focusing on consumption follows a general pattern which states that Marx has not said much about the consumption of the commodity, that is, about what happens after the commodity is sold, or how that subject who consumes it is shaped. As a result, these criticisms point out that 'consumption' as a critical term does not adequately feature in the Marxian corpus[3]. This is a vast issue and any detailed consideration would take us away from our central con-

3 The paradigmatic critique is by Jean Baudrillard (1975), also see Appadurai in Appadurai (1986), and Hetherington (2007). A good encompassing account of this criticism is to be found in Bærenholdt (2010).

cern. But since I am trying to insert a deconstructive reading of Marx's account of commodity fetishism in understanding the touring subject, it might help if I briefly comment on some salient points of the available criticism of Marx. A good way of keeping my comment focused and short would be to approach the issue through Kevin Hetherington's summery of this discussion (and therefore avoiding a direct confrontation with someone like Jean Baudrillard, getting into a longer discussion). This would also provide us with an entry point into the Derridian reading of Marx.

Kevin Hetherington (Hetherington 2007) summarizes the existing criticisms of Marx's account of 'commodity fetishism' and singles out two main threads. The first sees Marx tied to a "productivist code created by capitalism itself" (Hetherington 2007: 70). This position is most powerfully articulated by Jean Baudrillard (1975), following whom Hetherington opines that, "Marx loses sight of his own understanding of the modern subject as a creative force in the world with a self-reflective consciousness and imagination and falls back on an earlier understanding of the pre-Romantic, pre-modern subject" (Hetherington 2007: 70). Hetherington's conclusion therefore is decisive, that Marx "certainly, and unquestioningly, essentializes the creative subject in labor" (Hetherington: 69). A possible answer to this critique would be to argue that any ontology of the human subject presupposes certain minimal essentialism, and therefore before critiquing a perceived ontologization (investing essential, intrinsic value to a term) one has to interrogate the (im-) possibilities of a fully de-essentialized version of the category 'human.' Hetherington's proposed alternative itself, the "modern subject" as "a self-reflective consciousness" can hardly sidestep the traps of essentialism (or romanticism for that matter). A consciousness reflecting on itself (intending a self-appropriation) closely tallies with the model of the Descartian subject who tries a self-validation simply by thinking about self. It can be argued therefore, following the cue provided by Gayatri Chakravorty Spivak, that Marx proposes a 'materialist ontology' based on the key concept of human labour being "super adequate" to itself which is as limited or as valid as the idealist ontology which takes human consciousness as its key central metaphor (Spivak 1987: 154). To criticize Marx for painting the human subject as only production-based would then amount to falling back on yet another ontology ('idealist' this time) which merely replaces 'labour' with 'consciousness' or 'intentionality'[4].

The second line of criticism mentioned by Hetherington is more relevant to our present discussion. In his description of commodity fetishism, Hetherington comments that Marx's "fundamental problem" is that "he does not allow that the

4 The materialist ontology is not merely a product of a specific mode of production. This might stage a confrontation with Baudrillard's central argument as stated in Baudrillard (1975).

viewing subjects he constructs within this theory of fetishism might also recognize" that in the case of the commodity "all is not what is appears" (Hetherington 2007: 69). This leads to the "central problem" in Marx's scheme where the subject is ever frozen in the moment when he encounters an object which carries the ghostly stamp of his own labor, the "alienated object." "It is as if he or she is so stunned but [sic; by?] the encounter with the ghost, an image of his or her own alienated labor power, that he or she is no longer capable of action," Hetherington concludes on the conundrum of Marx's position (Hetherington 2007: 70). It is here that I will insert the reading of Marx by Jacques Derrida, but not without a brief critical detour through Marx's central points.

Marx calls commodity a "mysterious thing," but there are two steps in this mystery clearly stated by Marx himself. Firstly, 'social labour' ("men's labour") "appears" to the workers "as an objective character stamped upon the product of that labour" (Marx 1986: 77). And secondly, "their own labour is presented to them as a social relation, existing not between themselves but between the products of their labour" (Marx 1986: 77). Therefore, whichever way one chalks the map of fetishism following Marx, what always remains at the heart of it, is the labour theory of value. In the Marxist scheme, 'value' is not something which can be empirically grasped, it is rather a differential which produces all meaning and materiality there can be within the system organized by the commodity effect. "It is value," writes Marx, "that converts every social product into a social hieroglyphic" (Marx 1986: 79). Human labour creates value, a deciphering of which is key in understanding the anthropomorphic world-making. We have already referred to this, following Spivak, as Marx's materialist ontology. Therefore, when Marx declares that one needs to "decipher" this "language," (Marx 1986: 79) we get to know something crucial, that the secret of commodities is as secret and coded *as a language*, and not merely something illusive. A language can be read (albeit with some loss of meaning), and so can the commodity form. By the deciphering of this language, Marx indicates an unwrapping of the social abstraction of 'value,' and not any true essence shrouded in mystery, or hidden behind the commodity form[5]. My contention is that it would not be possible to meaningfully gloss on the notion of commodity fetishism without a detailed engagement with the Marxian concept of value, a point Hetherington seems to miss[6].

5 I am not going here into a discussion of the notion of the 'use value' itself crucial in understanding the Marxian scheme.

6 We cannot go into Hetherington's suggestion that a way out of (what he believes to be) the Marxian stalemate on the issue of consumption can be sought by a reading of Walter Benjamin's nuanced idea of experience, as that would take us beyond the scope of this short study (see Hetherington 2007: 93-100). Hetherington's rich socio-historical account of 'phantasmagoria' does little in engaging with the key category of 'value.' He does indeed mention the Derridian reading, but his engagement with Derrida remains a bit hurried as well. For one, Der-

The most circulated and representative statement of Marx on commodity fetishism states that "it is a definite social relation between men, that assumes, in their eyes, the fantastic form of a relation between things" (Marx 1986: 77). On first reading it seems correct to assume that Marx is indicating to a realm 'beyond' the commodity form. Jacques Derrida says as much, but his astute reading also points out that the Marxist critique is focused not only on the appearance of the commodity, but on its 'form' or how it 'works,' its trail or life so to say. Only that as Marx goes on, the trail of the commodity itself seems like a mish-mash of many decipherable and indecipherable inscriptions. One remembers here that Marx starts the chapter on commodity fetishism with the famous line, "A commodity appears, *at first sight*, an extremely obvious, trivial thing," (stress added, Marx 1986: 76) and then gradually complicates this 'first sight.' Derrida's intimate deconstruction focuses on this inaugural gesture with which the commodity is introduced. What this 'first sight' shows is not merely something that guards the view, but the very artifice of 'guarding' itself. In other words, it does not show something that is merely un-true, or an illusion, but the mark of a trajectory of deviation. The commodity form consists in a 'work' (or an inscription, or *graphos* of that 'work'), through which it writes its biography, even if this biography comes through in the very act of hiding its origin (socially necessary human labour). Derrida reminds that "One must see, at first sight, what does not let itself be seen" and this is "invisibility itself" (Derrida 2006: 149). Marx, in this reading, does not merely gesture toward a much truer, more real substratum behind the flow of commodities, but he points out that the secret of commodity's biography is already written in the very body of the commodity form. One reads the 'invisible' only by giving into what Marx calls the 'first sight.' The first sight is not merely a false impression or a wrong reading, but rather as the immanent text it holds everything that is to be read. The first sight therefore "prepare us to see this invisibility, to see without seeing, thus to think the body without body of this *invisible visibility*" (stress added, Derrida 2006: 187). If I may use a rather simplified example, this 'invisible visibility' works like that often told Sherlock Holmes story, where the 'curious incident of the dog in the night-time' was that the dog did nothing during the night! The commodity tells a lot by not telling, and by registering this silence. Thus the "ghost is already taking shape" in this very first sight (Derrida 2006: 149).

Slavoj Zizek has a much similar reading where he compares the phenomenon and inscription of the commodity, which I have already called the 'commod-

rida, and for that matter, Thomas Keenan do not merely affirm that the Marxist account "remained, above all, a theory of visual illusion" (Hetherington 2007: 57). I will indicate below why this is a gross reduction of Derrida's meticulous reading. Keenan also is much more nuanced (see Keenan 1997: 99-133).

ity-work,' with Sigmund Freud's analysis of the 'dream-work.' Zizek contends that just like in the case of Freud, it would be a mistake to think that the content of dreams can be deciphered to unravel a 'hidden kernel,' the crux of the dream rather consisting in the very form in which the dream is remembered (its immanent marks which then can be read *in hindsight* as distortions and displacements), a close reading of Marx shows that the commodity-work does not hide anything, but instead lays bare, in its very form, a certain inscription of difference and displacement (Zizek 1989: 1-56). The crux of commodity fetishism then is this: it stages the possibility of a disclosure through its very mechanism of concealment. To come back to the deconstructive reading, Derrida does not have any trouble with this model of a decipherable, multilayered inscription, one that apparently indicates a beyond. He even affirms Marx in proposing that both the displaced meaning (socially necessary abstract labour), and the inscription of that very displacement (commodity-work) are always already immanent in the very 'first sight.' He only wonders why Marx would like to 'conjure' away, exorcise the inscription of the hidden, as if to reach a 'thing' without any phenomenal wrapping, or a value-form without any mark of 'exchange' on it. Derrida thinks that such a 'thing without inscription' is not possible and therefore one cannot simply take either the 'commodity form,' or 'value' as 'more' or 'less' present, as each is tied to the other in a fine correspondence of materiality and formality, in short, spectrality. Derrida typically uses the metaphor of the 'mirror' (only to break it) in explaining this spectral correspondence:

> "Men no longer recognize in it the *social* character of their *own* labor. It is as if they were becoming ghosts in their turn. The "proper" feature of specters, like vampires, is that they are deprived of a specular image [...] How do you recognize a ghost? By the fact that it does not recognize itself in a mirror. [...] These ghosts that are commodities transform human producers into ghosts. And this whole theatrical process (visual, theoretical, but also optical, optician) sets off the effect of a mysterious mirror: if the latter does not return the right reflection, if, then, it phantomalizes, this is first of all because it naturalizes." (stress in original, Derrida 2006: 195)

This, then, is also the key to the life of the 'specter' according to Derrida, a mirroring between persons and commodities, with 'labour' playing the role of the sensible (and yet) supersensible continuum between the two. The moment Marx tries to predicate the human subject through the materiality of production, he puts in motion a subject-object correspondence. But crucially this correspondence is not one of simple mirroring, the ghost cannot see itself in the mirror, and the transaction between persons and things goes on not through simple representation, but through a chain of differentials and misrecognitions. Derrida writes,

> "The "mysteriousness" of the commodity-form as presumed reflection of the social form is the incredible manner in which this mirror sends back the image (*zurück-spiegelt*) when one thinks it is reflecting for men the image of the "social characteristics of men's own labor": such an "image" objectivizes by naturalizing. Thereby, this is its truth, it shows by hiding, it reflects these "objective" (*gegenständliche*) characteristics as inscribed right on the product of labor, [...] Therefore, and here the commerce among commodities does not wait, the returned (deformed, objectified, naturalized) image becomes that of a social relation among commodities, among these inspired, autonomous, and automatic "objects" [...] The specular becomes the spectral at the threshold of this objectifying naturalization." (Derrida 2006: 196)

From 'specular' to the 'spectral,' there is a key shift. The spectral breaks the mirror and blurs the division between the levels of the fetishistic model. Spectrality therefore becomes a meaningful way not only to read Marx, but also to think of a subject-object continuum in thinking memory, meaning and most importantly, in thinking experience and survival. Following this clue, I am going to try an account of the 'touring subject.' This account is based on the 'spectral life' of the act of touring itself as it survives through the works of inscriptions both of the (touring) subject and of the object (the site of touring).

The connection of what follows to the Marxian notion of commodity fetishism is only analogical. Let me clearly state the nature of this analogy, in the way of proceeding to the next section's argument. Among many other things, commodity fetishism is also about a correspondence between a web of things (commodities) endowed with person-like qualities and a social web of persons who cannot come into transaction with each other but through the mediation of things (even if what connects them is, according to Marx, an equivalence between their labours). Both these systems or 'webs' as I have called them, are put in motion by a process of exchange and therefore 'difference,' a difference that, as if conjures a 'life' which is exchangeable freely between things and persons. For Marx, an unraveling of the inscription of this difference ('deciphering' its 'language') would exorcise that ghostly life which is both material and immaterial, organic and inorganic, or as Marx describes, "a sensuously supersensible thing" ("*sinnlich übersinnliches Ding*", see Derrida 2006: 189). The key to reading this inscription, for Marx, is the abstraction of 'value' (one may call it the 'real abstraction'). Without the key category of value, this scheme hardly remains a Marxist critique of a mode of production, but it still retains a certain movement, which I am inclined to call, after Derrida: 'spectrality.' It is this movement of spectrality that I would analogically use in commenting on the possibility of a 'touring subject,' but not before a short account of the nuances and problems of predicating a touring subject. It would also become clearer in the next sections that this exercise opens up a study of the predication of the 'subject' in the circuit of consumption and use. It should however be noted that in doing this, we are not rejecting the 'materialist critique' as such, but only selecting a nuanced version of it. Spectrality is a materiality, which albeit goes beyond the strict matter non-matter duality. An opening to this is already present in the text of Marx, and in that sense we are making a Marxist Deconstructionist argument.

Spectral touring I: Subject interrupted

I have already indicated the difficulties of identifying the specificities of the touring experience in the context of postmodernism. In Urry's inaugural study, it is clear that what postmodernism has blurred is not merely the importance, but also the very understanding and meaning of the practice of touring, and the kind of experience it produces. To be more precise, following questions are prompted by this blurring of the field. Does 'touring' necessarily involve physical travel[7], can the activities of browsing the television or surfing the internet qualify as 'touring'? But these are not ours to answer in this paper. We reverse the question and ask, what constitutes a 'touring body,' is it a certain body which travels through different experiences, if yes, then why life itself (taken to be an embodied duration through which the consciousness travels) is not the best example of touring at its most blurry general? These are the exciting logical risks involved in thinking 'tourism' conceptually to its limit. Urry confronts this problem and writes that, "what is required is a range of concepts and arguments which capture both what is specific to tourism and what is common to tourist and certain non-tourist social *practices*" (stress added, Urry 1990: 124). 'Practice' then, is the critical watchword that might still make a difference between the 'touristic' and 'non-touristic' even in the context of a postmodern blurring. I would try a different path, one of a conceptual understanding of the touring subject, and the act of touring as representative of a general condition of subject predication.

Let me now delineate this different approach in light of the discussion of spectrality that was pursued in the previous section. Production of the act of touring always assumes something unchanging, something that remains the same, something which as if plays the role of a 'surface' on which the experience of 'touring' is inscribed. Most of the time, this role is played by the subject. 'Touring,' by definition assumes a subject of touring, who remains fixed even as 'he' (it can be argued that the promiscuous, mobile, typical subject of tourism

7 A less risky question would be, can one actually compare the old way of travelling by foot with the modern way, where one sits in the same place for hours, inside an aero-plane cabin for instance, tucked within a ridiculously limited space and still 'travels' thousands of miles?

acts as metaphor of a certain maleness[8]) goes through different experiences (or, to make a slight change to this assumption, he might himself change and yet he would retain something unchanged in his system to be the same subject of experience *who travels*). It would then be interesting to ask, who is this subject, and how does he retain the unity of the gaze, which would amount to retaining a self with negligible deviation. Or does he also change, in which case, we may ask, what then is the 'reference frame' in respect of which the 'touring' takes place? I would propose that it is a certain 'life' given to the touristic site which plays the role of that unchanging reference field, on which the touring subject inscribes his memory. Let me elaborate. In the act of 'touring,' the subject tries to live through and consume a place (the site of touring) by using, buying, exchanging, recording different representations of moments, emotions, objects. In short, the touring subject tries to construe a memory for himself as touring also becomes a way of self-reflection and self appropriation. In weaving such a sutured memory through the consumption of the touristic site and its objects, the touring subject desires to give his self a unity. The subject tries to situate himself at the unflinching centre of a 'site in flux,' the touring site, which, for him, changes, passes by and therefore has a life. In this reflects the basic structural desire of the subject of propriation, who tries to re-appropriate his own varied experience and life to the surety of a unified self-presence (so much for the 'self-reflective' subject). The touring subject lives through the fragments which he gathers up in the process of consuming a place, inscribing his own memory in those objects. But this process is not unidirectional. For one, those objects have a life of their own socially, a life full of memories of different usage. This is the life that the individual tourist must both affirm (to become the lawful tourist in the first place, in being able to read the site as touristic) and resist (in individualizing his use and consumption of the place). This proposition, however, is not entirely novel. Jonathan Culler has reminded quite some time ago that "it is as signs that our practices have reality," and when specific ways of consuming a place through the practice of tourism becomes social signs, "modern quest for experience" becomes "a quest for an experience of signs" (Culler 1988: 165). But I differ from Culler via Derrida in thinking 'signs' not merely as deferred representations of 'real referents' (that exist somewhere in the world), but rather as the very nodes of materiality. Signs, in a deconstructive sense, are the partial anchorages of meaning and materiality, the nodes through which a life relates to its memory and therefore to a continuous self. In plotting such a life, signs, in effect, prompt the chains of spectral experience blurring subject-object divisions. These chains are therefore inscriptions of materiality; they are the trails not of signs, but of their differences.

8 The female tourist or the female *flâneur* would need a very different trajectory of argument.

That is why I have talked about 'inscriptions,' rather than of 'signs.' What is the difference? If signs are like knots of meaning in a shifting chain of signification, then inscriptions record the trail of that very shifting, the space which stays between the knots. Inscriptions show the differential drifts that exist *between the signs*, and therefore are not merely ideal, or discursive, but that which bridge the gap between idea and matter. Inscriptions, in this (Derridian) sense are both 'mechanical' and 'organic,' made both of non-life and life[9].

Because of its difficulty, let me once again summarize exactly how the movement of spectrality is extracted from the Marxian scheme. What differentiates Marx's approach from an idealist approach based on the consciousness of the subject is his 'materialist predication' of the subject. To quote Spivak, if in the idealist scheme 'consciousness' is not merely 'thought' or 'intention' but "the subject's irreducible intendedness towards the object," then in the materialist predication, labour-power is not merely 'work,' or an ability to produce, but "rather the irreducible possibility that the subject be more than adequate — super-adequate— to itself" (Spivak 1987: 154). Once Marx has activated this surplus possibility of human labour, a subject object mish-mash is inevitable. The reach of human labour-power actually extends to the 'things,' transforming them into commodities, which, in the process animate human-like qualities. Human labour-power, exchanged with itself and with other objects alike, becomes as if a force of repeatability and survival (code name: 'value'). This process endows objects with quasi-human life. By exchanging them as commodities, it makes them part of human memory, body and life, and in the process de-centers the locus of the (human) subject. The curious revelation of this process is not that the objects behave like human beings, or that they get a human-like life, but the very fact that now humans also can only have a human-like life, humans can now *only share this semblance with the human form.* It is no longer the case that objects mirror persons, but *both objects and persons* mirror a quasi-humanlike form. Jacques Derrida extracts the basic movement of this de-centered intentionality which is both within and beyond the senses of the human and weaves his scheme of 'spectrality.' I think it might be proposed, with the Derridian hindsight, that it is Marx's 'materialist predication' that actually also makes a 'spectral reformulation' of the 'idealist predication' (based on consciousness instead of labour-power) possible. This is a key proposition, so let me repeat it. Marx's 'materialist predication' of the subject does share a semblance with the basic philosophical predication which is 'idealist,' but its intervention lies in shifting the focus on 'materiality,' a shift that ensures not another idea-matter division, but instead a confusion between the two. It is with that curious matter non-matter, subject

9 I have discussed this notion of the 'inscription' with reference to deconstruction in my doctoral dissertation (submitted to the Arts faculty, Jadavpur University in 2013).

object, life non life mix that we are proposing to read the touring subject. In this model, the touring subject has a shared space of memory with the objects that 'he' encounters in the touring site. The touring site, which is already socially constructed as a series of images, is a site which facilitates a writing of (the touring) self, as well as resists such writing and *writes* the (touring) subject in return. This, then, is our argument in a nutshell.

We may now articulate the touring subject with the spectral structure in mind. The touring subject tries to organize and consume the objects, images, experiences related to the site of touring in thinking life as an externality. By writing his own memory on the objects that he encounters in the site, the touring subject tries to reassure himself of his unchanging observing consciousness, as if it is he, the subject, who authenticates and normalizes the objects around. In doing so, the subject forces the objects to tell his own story. This is a propriation of self at its very basic. The self tries to externalize his memories, experiences, bodies, and then in the process tries to recover and gather them back as objects he can fully intend, consume or posses (socially or individually). But contrary to this desire of propriation, the self and the body of the subject also are haunted in the process by externality, i.e. by objects and by the site of touring. The spectral life put in motion by the act of touring is therefore written on a surface which the subject cannot *fully* intend (he indeed can intend up to a point). This surface which also is a memory of the objects, of the non-human, is neither written on the side of the subject nor on the side of the object, and therefore always holds the possibility of disrupting the self-presence of the touring subject. We have just proposed that the 'external' (objects and the site) *writes* the subject as well. But how can one think about such points of break when the touring site shapes and eats into the touring subject in return, or activates an experience which is alien to the subject and yet one that he shares with the objects (or with the touring site)? Can there be a metaphor of such sensible super-sensible space that both makes and breaks the unity of the touring subject? In the final section, I propose that the 'photograph' (snapshot) can be studied as metaphoric of such interruptions. This, however, is a tentative proposition and I would only refer to some possible arguments in setting in motion a larger conceptual study beyond the scope of this paper. The choice of the photograph depends solely on the kind of argument I am making, and not on any necessity of its internal form.

Spectral touring II: 'Wound' of the photograph

John Urry marks the year '1840' as the crucial year when "tourism and photography could be said to commence in the west in their modern form" (Urry 1990:

148). This clearly shows the central position Urry gives to 'photography' in his thesis of the 'tourist gaze,' as camera was officially "invented" on that year. In a later study of the same theme with Jonas Larsen, Urry takes another step and christens 1840 as the year when the tourist gaze was 'born' in "the west" (Urry and Larsen 2011: 14). But why this centrality given to the camera? Does the 'tourist gaze' then consist of the images that flash through the mechanical eye of the photographic machine? This question deserves a longer and different discussion (and a much closer engagement with Urry's text) than the one I am trying here. The focus of this study however, lies in interrogating the force of the 'photograph' (the photograph as such, in abstract) in representing the physical space of touring and the memory associated with that space. In the previous section I have already proposed that the experience of touring, as if, constitutes its life as a spectral chain which is neither fully on the side of the subject not entirely invested in objects. But why the photograph, of all objects, is said to be exemplary of the spectral life of touring?

Geoffrey Batchen writes that "Photography is privileged within modern culture because, unlike other systems of representation, the camera does more than just see the world; it is also touched by it. Photographs are designated as indexical signs, images produced as a consequence of being directly affected by the objects to which they refer" (Batchen 2004: 31). In the last section, I have discussed a further possibility of this 'affection,' which is to be seen not as merely one-way, but as cutting both ways. I have proposed that objects representative of human memory can activate, indeed can weave memories and lives of their own, blurring any strict subject-object division (specifically in the case of 'touring'). The photograph, by being synonymous with the 'movement-image' becomes representative of this subversive mobility. The term 'movement-image' is a coinage of Gilles Deleuze (2003). In making a distinction between the 'snapshot' (the still photograph) and the individual film (one unit of the film-strip) that makes up the cinematic movement, or the 'movie,' Deleuze proposes that within the cinematic flow, the individual images are always already endowed with movement; they are "movement-images" or "mobile sections" (Deleuze 2003: 2). These movement-images act together like mechanical "assemblage" to make up the cinematic montage, "an indirect image of time" (Deleuze 2003: 30). One might conjecture following Deleuze that once the cinematic form is in place (around 1900), the nature of the photograph, at least the way one views it, and the very possibility of its representative force is also dramatically changed. The photograph always already comes to view as a mobile section, not an inert snapshot, but a slice of life.

The photograph, let me now propose, becomes representative of what I have called the 'spectral movement' chiefly because of two reasons. One, because it is also 'movement-image' which always already presupposes a motion and a movement of time, and therefore is able to stand as part of a signifying chain which constructs a site, or a 'life' that survives through a train of iterable images. This chain, like language, is both repeating and open to new variations, but always woven according to a rhythm or logic of continuation and recognition (and thus is an iterable chain). The photograph therefore, is *also* spectral; it literally is the 'writing of light.' It is a physical mark of time which has the curious power of objectifying life. The photograph most crucially catches a past life, the life of the person becoming as objectified as life of every other object which are within the frame. Roland Barthes writes that the "photograph (the one I *intend*) represents that very subtle moment when, to tell the truth, I am neither subject nor object but a subject who feels he is becoming an object" (stress in original, Barthes 1981: 14). This is the precarious feeling that the photograph prompts in the subject. The photograph has something like a democratic evenness about it, for it objectifies the life of both the object and the subject and puts them literally *on the same page*. The key to Barthes' proposition is inserted cunningly inside the parenthesis with which the quoted segment starts. Barthes is talking only about that part of the photograph (or that part of its affect) which is 'intended' by the self, what he calls the 'studium.' The photograph however has another constitutive element which Barthes christens the 'punctum,' that which is beyond the purview of the subject's intentionality. The 'punctum' thus indicates a state which is beyond life itself, or is becoming death (Barthes 1981: 94-100). One might call the Barthesian 'punctum' a work of the 'non-intentional' in the photograph, that which is not under the sway of the will of either the producer or the consumer of the photograph, and which disturbs and subverts the orderly, intended form ('studium') of its constitution. If the ego or the self invests the 'studium' with "sovereign consciousness," then the 'punctum,' Barthes says, "shoots out of it like an arrow, and pierces me," working much like a "wound," a "prick" (Barthes 1981: 26). Within our argument, this wound signifying the rupture of the non-intentional within the intentional web of life also signifies the wound that the 'touring self' inevitably invites by trying to order the objects and representations that make up the 'touring experience.' This wound, then, refers to that which the photograph inscribes on the subject (as an authenticating document of his memory, a memory that he tries to gather only by externalizing it in objects). It is a wound which the touring self shares and suffers with the 'touring site,' with the 'outside' so to say.

The possessive tourist is also possessed by the life of the site, the very life he himself extends through his camera-work. This inscription happens, as if, behind his back. The desire to travel, to see life as changing witnessed by an unchanging self makes him force his own memories on the objects outside. But what he misses is the very fact that he himself is not only changing in the process, but also that he is investing his own body into the site, into the objects which make up the site. This is risky, as the site can easily tamper with the 'body' of the tourist by breaking its expected sequence, by marking that point of a sudden unexpected frame which surprises the subject. Once the tourist is inscribed thus onto the surface of an object-life, he is open to new threats and unintended inscriptions that the object can have in store for him. If we half-affirm Jonathan Culler in saying that for the tourist in search of signs, the "*authentic* is a usage perceived as a sign of that usage, and tourism is in large measure a quest for such signs," (stress in original, Culler 1988: 155) then we are also adding that from the side of the tourist, this process also exemplifies a desire to produce the self as a meta-sign which can remain unchanged by consuming those signs outside, even if the touring subject makes himself vulnerable by that very process of consumption. Somehow, behind the back of the touring self, the signs which he intends to gather and organize his experience with, shoots back at him, like the Barthesian 'punctum,' and he sees a 'flowing wound' at the limit of the self and the photograph, a 'wound' that writes the life of the tourist in spite of and beyond the pale of his intention. The unintended 'punctum', as I have indicated, is the place where the object tries to interrupt and *write* the subject, a curious process that plays the subject's intention in reverse, the object writes back, a monstrous process. It is where the object eats the subject.

The metaphor of the 'wound' is important. It stops desire and life (for Barthes, it may represent a mourning for the loss of a 'fully intentional photograph,' and therefore a death of the self fully possessed by itself), but at the same time it also is an opening through which new desire can gush forth. As Cadava and Cortés-Rocca correctly writes, Barthes "identifies the ontological violence that characterizes photographic technology and translates it into a kind of grammar that names the effects of the image on the body of the observed subject and of the subject observing: it pierces, pricks, scans, and tears a hole" (Cadava and Cortés-Rocca 2006: 20). But the problem with Barthes is that no discernible transaction between the 'studium' and the 'punctum,' and therefore between the intentional and the non-intentional is proposed through which one might think of a logic of this pricking, piercing, wounding, in short of this writing that may include both the subject and the object. This is where the notion of spectrality comes in. As Derrida correctly points out, Barthes does not focus enough on the continuity between the studium and the punctum, or between the intentional and the non-intentional, "as soon as the punctum ceases to oppose the studium, all the while remaining heterogeneous to it, as soon as we can no longer distinguish here between two places, contents, or things, it is not entirely subjugated to a concept" (Derrida quoted in Cadava and Cortés-Rocca 2006: 12). Following the

Derridian gloss then, I am trying to think of the photograph as a sensuous materiality which is also capable of sharing a space with the subject, a space that reproduces both the objects (that are within the frame) and the subject (either clicking, posing or viewing, in one word, consuming), and sublate them to a realm beyond the senses (if the sensible is tied to a subject-object division), to the plane of the spectral life.

Let me now briefly go over the arguments made in this section. By inscribing the subject on the same surface as other objects, the photograph opens up a space that is within the reach of the senses but one that has a feel of uncanny. It is in this sense that the photograph becomes metaphoric of that spectral space which stays shared by both the touring subject and the objects that make up the touring site. The photograph does not only objectify the fleeting moves of the subject and the objects within its frame, it also does place them within the same temporal representation, forcing each point within the frame to be part of a single 'movement-image' that activates the spectral chain of the (touring) experience. It is exemplary of an overdetermined site of memory that the touring subject both desires and secretly dreads. The subject desires this site because it may help the unified subject of experience to survive and have a life; but it may also resist that same process of self re-appropriation. The site also undercuts that self-reflective subject who wants to be the sole authenticator of the objects that he desires. The photograph therefore, represents a dilemma, or a much larger '*aporia*' that haunts and constitutes the *subject as such* at the cutting edge of materiality and non-materiality, of the machine and the event, the organic and the inorganic. Within the limited space of this paper I can only highlight the need for a longer and conceptually more meticulous study of the spectral notion of 'touring' in these lines.

Conclusion

In this paper I have basically tried to do one key thing, - a study of the 'touring subject' in relation to the notion of 'touring consumption.' This conceptual study has taken the form of a deconstructive reading of the very process of 'touring,' which I have called, following Jacques Derrida, the spectral life of touring, or simply, spectral touring. If the notion of a stable subject is questioned in the process, through a fissuring of its unity with inscriptions of objects (or the 'site of touring'), then the inevitability of a subject-predication is also stressed. The concept of spectrality is crucial because it tries to understand how the 'subject' is to be thought within the corpus of Marx, who is generally seen as an astute thinker who albeit misses any discernable figuring of the 'subject,' or of the subject of consumption. Jacques Derrida does underline the importance of thinking the subject, but he also shows that this predication can only be thought as a quasi-mechanical (and quasi-intentional) inscription, and not as fully intentional. Can this inscription, which is neither fully of the object, nor entirely of the subject, be put in motion in understanding the experience of touring? This is the question I study.

In the second half of this paper, I try to think of the spectral space of touring through the exemplary case of the photograph. Why does the photograph play as an instantiation of the spectral objectification? Not merely because of its indexical nature, but because it works as a (Deleuzian) 'movement-image' putting in motion a chain which is referential, which can refer back and forth just like a memory, or like a life. I show how such a chain can be studied to speculate more on the touring experience and the way it interrupts the unified subject of desire and experience. I have called this the 'wound' of the photograph, in underlining the life-like nature of it. The wound is a rupture and yet, it remains open and flowing, which is metaphoric of the production of new memories as well as of a pain that is ever fresh, of an interruption that the subject might always feel.

The nature of this paper is purely speculative, but it tries to speculate on something which is the very crux of materiality and meaning. As the quasi-machine which produces memory, experience, and therefore 'life,' the 'spectral touring' lies at the very heart of a materialist understanding of the touring subject and of touring practices. This 'materiality' however is very different from a materialism that takes 'matter' for granted, or as fully intended/produced by the subject, a topic whose full stock-taking would take us beyond the limits of this paper. The purpose of this paper is focused and limited, an examination of the possibilities of a more conceptual study of the touring subject as well as of the act of touring itself. In all these exercises I have tried to underline repeatedly the necessity of subject predication. Without subject predication it would simply be impossible to think of any materiality of any practice, let alone of touring, and perhaps more importantly of thinking 'responsibility' and ethics of touring. 'Responsibility' is one key theme that this paper has not touched upon, but one that can be approached, I believe, through the notion of the spectral touring which does not leave everything either to the intentionality of the appropriating subject, or to the inert passivity of the objects.

It would be worthwhile to reiterate here that this paper only claims to approach the necessary groundwork prompting and enabling studies of located touristic practices, particular instances of touring consumption, stopping short of actually doing such a work The basic argument behind this exercise is the following, one cannot demand to 'know' definite, calculable definitions of a restricted subject ('touring subject') or a specific object or commodity ('site of touring' or the 'touristic commodity') without first checking how far these restricted generalities can be pursued and stretched. As I hope to have indicated in this paper, the 'touring subject' can actually be thought as exemplary of the (postmodern) subject as such, just as the commodity-form itself can be meaningfully interrogated with the notion of 'spectral touring.' These are points of radical openings as well as of risks. 'Opening' to a central theoretical positioning for the tourism studies in thinking the postmodern predicament, and the 'risk' of losing grip on the specificities of the field. But one cannot be approached without the other, and the limited aim of this paper has been to stage that dilemma, and also clear a space for studies of located practices of touring, of the touring subject and the images that fall between the two. Such works would have to take into consideration the internal fissures that run through the touristic commodities, the inevitable differences that are marks of a world of unequal exchange and restricted mobility. But those are the trajectories of a very different study.

References

Appadurai, A. (1986): Introduction: Commodities and the Politics of Value. In: Appadurai, A. (ed.): The Social Life of Things: Commodities in Cultural Perspective. Cambridge: Cambridge University Press, 3-63.

Bærenholdt, J.O. (2010): Enactment and Enchantment in Experience Economies: Presence, Place, Performance. http://rudar.ruc.dk/bitstream/1800/5604/4/Enactment_and_Enchantment_in_Experience_Economies.pdf, 12.12.2013.

Batchen, G. (2004): Forget Me Not: Photography and Remembrance. New York: Princeton Archetctural Press.

Barthes, R. (1981): Camera Lucida: Reflections of Photography. Richard Howard (Tr.). New York: Hill and Wang.

Baudrillard, J. (1975): The Mirror of Production. Mark Poster (Tr.). St. Loius: Telos Press.

Cadava, E. and Cortés-Rocca, P. (2006): Notes on Love and Photography. In: October, 116, Spring, 3-34.

Culler, J. (1988): Framing the Sign: Criticism and its Institutions. Oxford: Blackwell.

Deleuze, G. (2003): Cinema 1: The Movement-Image. Huge Tomlinson and Barbara Habberjam (Tr.). Minneapolis: University of Minnesota Press.

Derrida, J. (2006): Specters of Marx: The State of the Debt, the Work of Mourning and the New International. Peggy Kamuf (Tr.). New York and London: Routledge.

Hetherington, K. (2007): Capitalism's Eye: Cultural Spaces of the Commodity. London: Routledge.

Keenan, T. (1997): Fables of Responsibility: Aberrations and Predicaments in Ethics and Politics. Stanford: Stanford University Press.

Marx, K. (1986): Capital: A Critique of Political Economy, Volume I. Samuel Moore and Edward Aveling (Tr.). Moscow: Progress Publishers.

Spivak, G.C. (1987): In Other Worlds. London: Methuen.

Urry, J. (1990): The Tourist Gaze. London, Thousand Oaks, New Delhi: Sage Publications.
Urry, J. and Larsen, J. (2011): The Tourist Gaze 3.0. London, Thousand Oaks, New Delhi, Singapore, Washington D.C.: Sage Publications.

Fashion and the Mobile Body: The Value of Clothing and Fashion for Merleau-Ponty's Concept of Chiasm

Ian W. King

Introduction

The potential of clothing and fashion is rarely appreciated in mainstream academic literature; often it is relegated to the margins with labels such as '*ephemeral*' or '*frivolous*'. Yet, clothing (and fashion in particular) provides one of the most explicit examples of global consumerism. The significance of this form of consumerism can be amplified through the writings of German philosopher Hans Jonas in his discussion of *metabolism of life* (Jonas 1992). This concept explores the temporal means of replenishing people's desire to resist decay and death by means other than food, drink, sleep, etc. These claims are situated further in my second section where I introduce aesthetics. My understanding of aesthetics does not confine itself to traditional understandings, rather I am persuaded by the writings of US pragmatist Mark Johnson (2007) who suggests that the body together with the mind and its interaction with the environment are relational essentials in our meaning-making processes. In my third section I continue drawing from philosophy when I turn to one of French phenomenologist Maurice Merleau-Ponty's final concepts – *chiasm*. The introduction of this concept was one of Merleau-Ponty's ways of shifting attention in his later writings away from *perception* to the realisation of *being*. A realisation, discussed in the last section of this paper, that suggests there is an ontological relatedness to the arguments made in the preceding sections; one that realises the clothed body (and in particular its facility for mobility) as one of the most important research tools in meaning-making.

Fashion and clothing: The metabolism of life

Clothing, we can immediately appreciate, is important for warmth, to protect us from natural weather conditions, and not forgetting, preserving our modesty. Of course, there might be a number of circumstances where we choose either not to wear clothes (for example, in the bathroom or bedroom) or adapt our choice because of the weather (for example, rain or sun etc.) or perhaps to protect us from possible harm (from a dangerous substance or event) or even perhaps to depict status (i.e. a doctor, a nurse, a priest etc.). Furthermore, an extensive empirical study conducted by Johnson and Levy (1990) concluded that, in particular for women, a man's attractiveness and status was associated with the clothes he wears. Therefore, regardless of circumstance, the wearing of clothes is important. For as popular American author Mark Twain once wrote "clothes make the man (sic). Naked people have little or almost no influence in society" (Twain 1927).

In 2010, the fashion and clothing industry was the 2nd largest creative industry (following tourism) in the World. In terms of turnover, this industry exceeded $1710 billion during that year and employed approximately 75 million people across the globe (Fashion United 2014). In the UK, clothing and fashion is the largest employer in the creative industries, directly employing 816,000 people. The industry is similar in size to food and drink services and generates more jobs than telecommunications, car manufacturing and publishing added together. Furthermore, its impact on tourism for the UK is immense, attracting visitors to the UK to shop or visit fashion exhibitions. A minimum estimate puts this tourism impact at a value of £98 million (approx. $160 million) in 2009 (see British Fashion Council report 2010).

However, in academic terms, clothing and fashion does not invite this same degree of status – in fact, often the opposite is true – in that, it can attract a certain degree of scorn. Certainly questions such as: 'is being *in-fashion* important?' is not seen by many parts of academia as a serious question. Yet, behind this question lies an influence that is broad and extensive, for example, fashion is significant when we start to explore cultural studies or issues associated with identity or self-identity (Bartlett 2010; Entwistle 2000; Lewis 2004; Wilson 2004) or if we examined aspects of historical studies (Breward 2003; Laver and de la Haye 2002; Mendes and de la Haye 2010) or aspects of business and management studies (in particular, the areas of branding and marketing, for example Jackson and Shaw 2009) or even studies of technology (Hannelore et al. 2008) or Science (in particular I am thinking of Cosmetic Science, see Reed et al. 1986). I could continue with this listing but this is not my purpose here – rather I will suggest that clothing and fashion are valuable for elaborating some of German philosopher Hans Jonas' arguments.

Hans Jonas (1992) argues that 'replenishment' is an inherent need for all living creatures – whether it is through food and drink, sleep, leisure etc. Yet, Jonas observes, people living in our contemporary age need more than simply satisfying these basic forms of replenishment and he labels this: *metabolism of life*.

A metabolism of life, Jonas (1992) claims, is a temporal condition bound up in the continued reclaiming of life. The matter which composes people is "forever vanishing downstream" ...and yet to be alive we must constantly take in new matter to replace this" (Jonas 1992: 34), we age, we need to eat, sleep etc. but for many people in contemporary life these basic needs are insufficient to fulfill our expectations of being *alive* – accordingly we look to satisfy additional requirements. Uppermost for so many people, and this traverses over many forms of divisions globally (from culture to gender), is the desire to wear nice, contemporary clothing. For some people what we wear is as important (and for others more) as eating (Shoff and Thompson 2006)! At the core of many eating disorders are attempts to lose weight and/or 'fit' into certain forms of clothing and this is prevalent across the globe, class, religion, gender etc. This observation might open a series of important issues related to health etc., however, this is not the direction that I intend to take this examination, rather, the point I want to make here is that we can widely appreciate that in this *consumptive-driven* world that first impressions of what we wear (including recognition of specific labels/brands) are very important to many of us on a daily basis as we engage in the world.

For Jonas (1992), replenishment is a form of resistance to decay and death. Jonas (1992) elaborates that a living entity has a future insofar as its being is its doing, i.e., stretches beyond the now of its organic state to what comes next. That is, who we are and how we live, is constituted by us moving forward and grasping the new. Jonas (1992) suggests that the "will be" (the intake of new material) determines the "is", as represented by its present activity; and it is the accumulation of these collective comments that suggest fashion and clothing provides a legitimate (and central) contribution to how we live our lives in this contemporary world. In the modern world, for many of us, we no longer see clothing merely as a function of warmth or modesty. It is now more about the signs we need to express our own identity, both to ourselves and externally to others. Personal vanity, attractiveness have long been identified as key features to mask decay (aging) and ultimately delaying death (for example Eicher et al. 2008). Our clothes (and the manner we wear them) provide evidence of our identity (our wealth, status, etc), attractiveness and our on-going response to aging. The psychological need to 'look good' and to 'feel right' is a significant want to many people across different contexts, and importantly, persists throughout the whole of our lives.

Renaud Barbaras (2003: 165) argues that the essence of being alive lies outside of itself, that is, our expectations of life is characterized by the pursuit of our own essence, that is, our own significance. Barbaras labels this *desire* in a specific sense and something quite different to our understanding of the term:

'need'. Unlike need, desire cannot ultimately be fulfilled; thus if we are to satisfy our desire – this is a temporary relief – for soon after feeling fulfilled (for many of us) we turn to another for its replenishment. Fashion exemplifies this desire. Many of us have more than one coat or one dress. In fact many of us have many sets of clothes, many dresses, multiple pairs of shoes etc. Do we buy these items to satisfy our basic needs or in accordance with desire? For many people the desire for additional clothes is greater than simply wanting to look attractive or stylish. It exceeds this type of feeling and includes additional emotions, including wanting to feel confident, and/or to appear contemporary, or to represent good taste, wealth, status etc., and of course, not forgetting wanting to wear something different from last time! The pleasure of purchasing that extra pair of shoes is not confined to wearing them but seeps over to the pleasure of possession. Do we expect that purchasing this extra pair of shoes will satisfy (and therefore nullify) this desire – the answer is unlikely, perhaps only temporarily, that is, until the next opportunity arises? In our modern contemporary consumerist society, replenishment is fulfilled by a combination of needs and desires. Certainly we can appreciate the necessity to fulfill needs – and perhaps purchasing clothes for warmth, for safety, for work etc meets this? Whereas, wanting to remain in fashion is not a need - rather it is a desire, and yet in contemporary society for many of us, it is vital. The buying of shoes for some is not restricted to need (after all we can only wear one pair of shoes at a time!) but rather (for some) reflects the desire to have a variety of shoes – perhaps for different occasions, or to match certain colors of clothing etc.

Of course, not all people would characterize clothing and fashion in these categories. What is interesting about the character of desire (unlike need) is that replenishment varies across people and circumstance – it extends to status, wealth, fame, power, leisure etc. Furthermore, the character of these desires does not remain stable over time; it evolves as our own circumstances and focus changes over the course of our lives. A final point is that replenishment does not confine itself to exact replacements; it evolves and adjusts in its quest for the reclaiming of life.

The approach I have introduced here regarding the relationships between clothing, fashion and philosophy inevitably concentrates its attention around the body and in the next section I develop this further to amplify its significance in our meaning-making processes.

Aesthetics and the body

For me, my understanding of aesthetics concerns itself with the conditions of experience, that is, a breadth (and depth) of assessment that exceeds traditional descriptors of art, beauty and taste. I support the view presented by US Philosopher Mark Johnson (2007a) that aesthetics is more persuasively about how people construct and experience meaning in everyday contexts. This includes a rich variety of assessments that start from assessing the form and structure of a situation, together with its qualities, our felt sense of it, our rhythmic engagement with its context, and also our emotional interactions with the situation (if appropriate). Johnson (2007a) rejects both the cognitive view which suggests that meaning is only a linguistic phenomenon and likewise he does not support the Kantian view that Aesthetics is primarily subjective, connected to feelings and therefore non-conceptual and incapable of producing knowledge. In these circumstances, I am persuaded by a relationship that appreciates the relationship between our own body, our mind and how these are shaped and interact with everyday events.

Thus, the body in its interaction with the environment generates a dialogue of examinations and interactions that do not limit themselves to assessments of the beautiful, but rather, also acknowledges other types of appreciation. Thus, an engagement in this way draws on our sensual potential as a means of uncovering multiple layers of meaning – many of which would remain hidden unless we approach and engage with events in this way.

Eugene Gendlin (1991) suggests that meaning (in everyday life) is relational, that is, it is about how one thing, quality or event relates to, or connects with, other things. Meaning emerges through an often unconscious negotiation between the structural, formal and conceptual dimensions associated with traditional forms of knowledge intertwined with the pre-conceptual, the non-formal and felt dimensions of experience. The 'meaning' emerges from this interaction, from what we think, feel and do, and it lies in recurring qualities, patterns and feelings all blended together. In this way, Gendlin (1991) argues meaning is already there before we actually experience meaning reflexively. The words, symbols, representations are not independently existing entities that capture or express the felt sense of a situation. Nor does the felt sense exist entirely independent of the words we are speaking. Instead, they are interwoven and developed together. Traditionally, western thinking has cast *felt sense* as something that does not possess any lasting value, and that only through words does their power emerge (Gendlin, 1991). Whilst, in many circumstances this may be true, closer reflection suggests we can all point to certain emotive situations that possess power and meaning in ways that precede, if not reduces the need for, words. For example I still remember the fear of a hot iron many years after accidently touching it as a child. For me this is a memory that has less to do with articulating words and more to do with the power of a specific memory caused by pain and hurt!

Therefore, modes of thinking that only privileges traditional forms of knowledge will miss large parts of the embodied situational experiences unless we open ourselves to what constitutes these forms as being meaningful in the first place. In the ontological position I am advocating, when engaging with everyday situations, our minds need the vehicles of our bodies to interact with our environment and it is through this relational contact we are able to grasp, extract and generate multiple layers of meaning able to exceed traditional forms of knowledge. Traditionally academia has privileged the mind as governing our knowledge-making processes but in everyday situations we need our bodies, its facility for movement to work in harmony with the mind. To deny or privilege only part of this harmonious relationship produces only partial realisation of its potential and meaning.

We can start to demonstrate the potential of this engagement in multiple ways. For the sake of clarity let me amplify further, in that I am drawn to Johnson's (2007b) example that employs gestures as bodily enactments of meaning. They are not uses of bodily motions to express some pre-conceived thought, rather, here the gesture itself brings meaning into existence. In that, a gesture can be the very incarnation of meaning-making. Johnson (2007b: 93) elaborates further: "They can be 'beat' gestures, which might give emphasis to, or provide the rhythm of our thinking and speaking. They can be 'iconic', when their structure is isomorphic with some pattern or contour of our experience or perception (e.g., when you tell a motorist to turn right up ahead, while simultaneously gesturing with a right-turn curve of your hand). Or they can be 'metaphoric', where our bodily movement can be used to present some abstract domain (e.g., when you hold your arms out to the side, palms up, alternately raising first the right and then the left hand, as if measuring two weights, while saying, 'I couldn't decide whether to go out on a date with her'). But, in every case, the gesture is the realization of the meaning" (Johnson 2007b: 93).

For me, clothing and fashion provide a valuable addition to these understandings. The mobile body in developing its relational potential in the world is normally clothed. It is important to appreciate that what is worn is not a neutral activity. In addition to deciding what we want to wear to reflect our own self-identity, we hope that such choices are interpreted in accordance with the quasi-language that our clothing means to our audience (see Davis 1992 for a more detailed explanation of the quasi-language for fashion). Davis (1992) argues that audiences form assessments of others through dressing and appearance. For example, if a person is wearing a particular piece of clothing that intimidates, or attracts, or suggest a certain status this may affect our choice as we employ our bodies' facility for movement. We might either move toward or alternatively away from possible engagement based upon these initial assessments.

Traditionally, developing meaning has relied heavily on vision. Science has privileged vision; ocular-centric traditions (see Jay 1993) have dominated our knowledge-gathering approach in academia for hundreds of years. It was built upon an ontological position attempting to minimalize and control the influence of people. Accordingly, the observer adopted detached, one-way process whereby he/she identified the subject and developed various tools to acquire robust, rigorous, rational, and objective knowledge. Yet, by suggesting an embodied aesthetics approach (amongst others), this position is revoked to become one whereby the observer is no longer detached and following a one-way approach to gathering knowledge but rather one built upon a two-way, relational process whereby the traditional ocular-centric approach is complemented by our facility for movement and our other senses. Thus, there is a reciprocal potential for all of our senses, for example, our ability to listen then is no longer just a focus on what the observer can hear, but also how others listen (and respond) to them.

I could at this point proceed in a variety of directions to amplify this potential but in keeping with the principle aim of clothing and fashion and, in order to introduce the next section, I will concentrate on 'touch'. The traditional privileging of sight at the expense of our other senses has not always been greeted with universal support. Certainly in terms of touch, some philosophers (and others across other academic areas) have lamented lost opportunities. For example, Luce Irigaray (1985) claims that a woman takes more pleasure from touching than from looking. For Irigaray, touch possesses a richness that surpasses vision in that whilst we can look at an object and see its shape, size, texture etc. It is not until we are able to move ourselves towards the object/event – touch it, feel it and engage with it – that we can appreciate the deeper qualities of the object/event. For example, when we go shopping, how important is touch? Perhaps in a supermarket as we proceed down the aisles and pick up groceries wrapped in mass-produced packaging, here touch is less significant. But once we reach the vegetables and fruit sections, here we are able to still employ our vision, but it is through olfaction and touch that we can feel the texture and perhaps smell the ripeness of the produce. With regard to clothing here we can appreciate that our ability to view what people are wearing but also complement this with the experience of touching and feeling the cloth, not only as an object hanging or placed in a cupboard, but also as an object that clothes our bodies and rests on our skin. Its texture, weight and how it allows our bodies to move oscillates with other layers of meaning, for example, our expectations of what we feel wearing this item will mean something to observers. That is, are we attempting to depict style, sophistication, wealth, identity etc. Of course, whether this meaning is (or will be perceived as) the same for all members of an audience goes to the core of the discussion and it is here that we might conclude that meaning therefore is individualistic – 'that which works for me'.

It is this oscillating relationship that brings forward certain senses and allows others to temporarily retire that is important – not least, that in the next moment, as other situations emerge, this challenges a different mix of senses to come together to complement our knowing. It is the complexity of this and other relationships that we start to explore in the next section.

Chiasm and being

The claims made in the previous section suggest that body is an inter-subjective, mobile and sensitive tool capable of engaging with the most complex and demanding contexts. In other words, the body possesses a sophistication that is able to extract layers of meaning that surpass a reliance on vision. In this way, the complementarity of these various attributes is a vital feature of this approach in producing rich perceptive understandings.

In this section, I attempt to go further and employ the final writings of Maurice Merleau-Ponty to amplify his claim (and need) for something that exceeds perception. In this section I discuss one of Merleau-Ponty's (1968) more obtuse concepts: *chiasm*. Often this concept suffers from inaccessibility not least that finding accessible practical examples are limited. However, for me, clothing and fashion might offer one such possibility.

My understanding of Merleau-Ponty's notion of chiasm is based upon a basic assumption that as the body is in the world and is actively perceiving events, that he or she is also being perceived (see for further elaboration Merleau-Ponty 1964 and 1968). In other words, this role is a reversible one and this forms the basis of his introduction of the Greek letter chi or χ Merleau-Ponty (1968) labelled chiasm as a form of dehiscence – a splitting open, a form of reflexivity that allows us to occupy the position of both perceiver and perceived.

Normally, I can appreciate occupying one of these positions. I can adopt a position where I can either perceive or be perceived by others. But chiasm raises the possibility that as I actively participate in the world that I can blur these distinct boundaries and am able to occupy both positions concurrently.

Merleau-Ponty (1968) illustrates the potential of chiasm with the example of the exchange of our two hands. In that we can use our left hand to grasp our right hand – thus, the left is holding the right hand, which is being held. The experience of holding and being held can therefore be appreciated. Both experiences are different and yet related. Using this same situation we can also appreciate the potential of it being perfectly reversible in that I can swap my hands to adopt the opposite role – that is, my right hand can reverse its role to one that holds the left. If it is a perfect transfer between my hands, does this suggest a simple reversing of felt with touch? Perhaps so, yet if the situation were not perfectly reversible, then the question arises, were I able to reverse my situation would this then produce quite different forms of meaning?

Certainly, it is rare that such a perfect symmetrical relationships exists, rather, normally reversing roles and adopting the alternate position never entirely coincides in the same way as this hands swapping example suggests (see Merleau-Ponty 1968: 194f.). Yet, the point he makes is that whether perceiver (or perceived) can both draw meaning from these experiences. But he is clear that it is likely that the meaning drawn from holding, and the experience of being held, will be different, and yet from these divergent positions they can collaborate together in contributing to our understandings.

As Merleau-Ponty (1968: 123) amplifies: *"(this) does not mean that there was a fusion or coinciding of me with it: on the contrary, this occurs because a sort of dehiscence opens my body in two, and because between my body looked at and my body looking, my body touched and my body touching, there is overlapping or encroachment, so that we may say that the things pass into us, as well as we into the things"*. David Morris (2010), amongst others, extends the notion of chiasm in terms of reversibility. For Morris (2010), in elaborating his argument, returns to the traditional academic privileging of sight in meaning-making and suggests that simply reversing our roles and assuming that our being seen is a condition of seeing is a relatively basic level of perception and not what Merleau-Ponty was attempting to achieve with chiasm.

Morris suggests that Merleau-Ponty in his various later writings was attempting to develop a deeper and more penetrative means of meaning-making; one that exceeds reliance upon perception. To amplify his claim he cites a number of Merleau-Ponty foundational propositions: "the world is made of the same stuff as the body" (Merleau-Ponty 1964: 163), things and I are made of the same "element" (Merleau-Ponty 1968: 139) and "[t]hings have an internal equivalent in me" (Merleau-Ponty 1964: 164). Morris (2010) argues that the introduction of chiasm is a tool for Merleau-Ponty to shift attention away from perception to the realisation of being. A realisation that understanding our being-in-the-world exceeds the visual and basic forms of perception and encompasses the full range of our senses in developing meaning. So the relationship between perceiver and perceived are not two different *appearances* of one being, but should be appreciated as two (at least) divergent ways in which being *is* (Morris 2010).

Merleau-Ponty's (1964 and 1968) latter writings seem all to converge to this understanding that *being* encompasses and exceeds perception. That is, our understandings are not confined to vision, but extend to, what we can uncover from within the convolutions of our bodies as they move, shift and employ various senses in engaging with the object/event. In ways that are not just complementary but emerge from divergent perspectives. This, in effect, is amplifying the relationship that Merleau-Ponty labels in the title of his posthumous text: *Visible and invisible* – a title that more accurately written as (and this may suffer from translation from its original, *Le Visible et l'invisible*): *Visible and in-the-visible*. That is, what we may see in an object/event is its appearance but what really constitutes it, are layers of attributes that lie beyond the visual, that is, in-the-visible.

Finding suitable exemplars to capture this potential is difficult – yet for me clothing does possess the potential to amplify *being*. Let me enlarge, in choosing a garment from the shop/store, I employ my vision and identify something that I think I would like to wear, accordingly I move my body towards it and then complement my visual by touching the garment and feeling its texture with my fingers and hand. For many of us, intuitively we will want to go to the next stage if we are considering its purchase, and this is by deciding to try it on (rehearse its feel) in the changing room. As we can appreciate from our respective experiences, trying a garment on in this way is not restricted to test if it fits – although this may vary if the garment is being considered as a replacement (a need) or a desire (fashion). It is also about gathering other experiences to form an overall assessment. As Morris (2010: 145) observes, these might be "two inflections of being that at once line-up and follow one another: they are ever so close, yet in that very closeness they are irreducibly divergent".

Let me further amplify my understanding of this chiasmic relationship as I wear the garment. I can feel the cloth against my skin and if I were to place and press my hand on top of this same garment (acting as a mediator) whilst wearing it, then I can both touch and feel concurrently. This enriched experience is no longer confined to the one-way process of looking and touching the garment that hangs on the rack but now is one that reflects the growing potential of converging both complementary and divergent routes to my assessment of the garment. Let me elaborate a little further. I cannot rely on how it looks as I hold it up in front of a mirror – this is not enough - I need to complement my assessment with wearing the garment – but as I wear it, I don't just rely on the mirror, I brush my hand over its surface and feel its weight on my skin. Do I feel comfortable as I move my body in wearing this garment – does its weight, flow and fit meet my need/desire? These are the types of feelings and questions that bombard my assessment.

A further layer to appreciate in understanding this complex collection of signs is that as I touch and feel this garment on my skin, I also am aware (in my reflexive way) that I am exercising (a form of) oscillation between activity and passivity. Activity in the sense as I press down on the cloth/garment I am focusing my attention to privilege this sensation – however, very soon if not immediately afterwards, because I feel pressure of the cloth, I can feel its texture and the weight of touch against my skin. As such, this feeling emerges as active and the touch recedes to a passive state. Whilst at that initial moment of touching my feeling was passive – which does not necessarily mean inactive – yet as soon as pressure is placed on my skin this creates a type of transfer resulting in my feeling of the fabric to emerge and come to the fore of my attention. Can we feel both touch and feel concurrently? Or is this active and passive oscillation (between touch and felt) in practice? What does this suggest?

Of course, returning to Morris's (2010) initial propositions drawn from Merleau-Ponty's writings, at one level, someone might observe that the garment is not made of the same stuff as I am – it is a textured material and not made of flesh and blood etc. This is true, but for me, its manufacture, its feel (is it itchy, stiff or too elastic etc.), its styling, how it moves on my body, its contribution to my self-identity, and its facility to convey meaning to others who look at me wearing this garment are wrapped up in a complex web of contributions for both my own assessment and what I expect from my social experience.

A final layer already mentioned above but deserving of a little more attention is the observation that in most changing rooms there exists a mirror and inevitably as we wear the garment we look into the mirror to gain an idea how we think the garment will look on us as we wear it. There has been a long tradition of the impact and value of the mirror (see for example, Derrida (1986), Lacan (1966), and in particular Rorty (1979) and whilst this is an interesting collection of literature, for me I wish to confine my attention here to a few short observations relating to chiasm and the mirror. Not least, looking in the mirror now is quite different from my initial look when perceiving it hanging on the rack. Now, I can touch/press my garment against my skin, feel its texture and concurrently look at my image of this experience in a mirror. This combined set of sensual experiences is no longer confined to complementary but also captures and includes divergence. Thus, this is no longer a duality between touch and feel but a *plethora* of signs and signals that amplify the overall experience. The image of my body in the mirror objectifies it and yet I am also aware that it is me. However, whilst one might argue that what the image depicts is what external audiences see, my understanding of this image from the position of the wearer/actor can never be fully reduced to the same experience as the external viewer. The external audience relies only on the visual and forms their understanding from this relatively superficial assessment. An assessment that compares to what we all share every day - as we too gaze at others.

Finally I can conclude that in looking at the image of myself in the mirror (and perhaps this is especially pertinent for someone trying/rehearsing wearing specific clothing) I am now able to appreciate the layers of understanding that is emerging and how this experience is producing a blurring of relationships in the manner suggested by chiasm; one that has opened my reflexive attention to a position beyond perception towards a space for being.

Ontological relatedness and concluding comments

In looking to demonstrate the value of clothing and fashion this reminds us again of the ontological significance of the body. Traditional ontological claims refer to matters of 'real' existence – that is appreciating the distinction between a realist ontology which assumes that a social and natural reality exists independently of people's cognitive structures, as compared to a subjective ontology that appreciates that the external social and natural reality is a creation of our consciousness and cognitions. For Merleau-Ponty (1968) these are the wrong claims. He argued that we should not be concerned with issues relating to subjectivity or objectivity rather, he suggests, we need to ask – what is the status of the inquirer in relation to 'reality'? Merleau-Ponty rarely explored ontology – only mentioning it rather than expressly devoting significant attention to its examination, but with regards to the discussion presented in this paper, this lies at the core of our understandings.

Merleau-Ponty spent most of his writings advocating that the 'real' in people-based contexts requires the inquirer to be physically involved. In other words, if the inquirer is not physically involved, then who and how is an assessment being made of what is real? And perhaps most pertinently, is it legitimate for anyone to claim (as in the scientific method) that they are somehow removed or detached from the real when in fact pragmatically each person is in the world making contributions that have cause and effect! Of course, in contexts that do not focus on people (for example Science) this type of defence is likely to produce a weaker claim to knowledge (but still one that in some circumstances is contestable!).

The ontological position presented here is that being is determinate, that is, this is how we exercise our orientations, senses, meanings, differences that make a difference, rather than remaining detached and viewing ourselves as being an indifferent blank, void of all sensible determinations.

In these circumstances, Mark Johnson's (2007) embodied aesthetics-led approach emerges from the belief that perception is not an isolated activity but one that results from a network of interwoven sensual-led series of relational engagements. Fashion and its central place in consumerism provide a means of synthesising the mind (metabolism of life), with the body (appearance, movement etc) and the environment (its impact and facility to communicate). The very nature of our involvement in consumerism demands that through our fashionable clothed bodies that we actively engage; whereas an unclothed body would likely reduce (and distract) these opportunities. Yet, in clothing the body and using the experience of wearing clothes, this also enables deeper opportunities for self-reflection in ways that simply surpass ontological accounts that rely on visual observation. In other circumstances, for different academic audiences, we might have explored this potential from alternative perspectives, one example might be the potential and experience of wearing clothing and fashion that are art objects in their own right (see Kim 1998)?

Finally, clothing does provide a rare opportunity to reveal Merleau-Ponty's later ontological shift from perception to being (see Merleau-Ponty 1968). Layers of examination that penetrate beyond developing additional complementary perspectives to the positive utilisation of the body as a form of hinge (or fold), exploiting what might be described as, divergent contributions ' for itself and for the other' (Merleau-Ponty, 1968:189).

In people-based contexts, the body is a hinge because it is the agent and intermediary for attracting and enabling emerging signs. My understanding of the use of divergence in this way includes and exceeds complementary contributions to meaning. That is, a realisation that contributions not only add to each other from the similar – for example, as I actively touch the fabric I can also complement this through my vision – yet also from the divergent; in that I can surpass the passive feel of the weight and texture on my skin so that it becomes an active contributor. The result is multiple layers of sensual meaning built from a plethora of signs that I argue generate vital ingredients to aid and assist me for the future.

Merleau-Ponty's (1968) aim was to exceed perception and his appreciation of the significance of the body and the potential of chiasm has been realised through the contribution of clothing and fashion. What other contributions clothing and fashion might make to core theories remains a quest for the future.

References

Barbaras, R. (2003): Life and Perceptual Intentionality. In: Research in Phenomenology, 33(1), 157-166.

Bartlett, D. (2010): Fashion East: The Spectre That Haunted Socialism. Cambridge, Massachusetts: The MIT press.

Breward, C. (2003): Fashion (Oxford History of Art). Oxford: Oxford University Press.

British Fashion Council (2010): The Value of Fashion: Report produced by Oxford Economics group. Oxford.

Davis, F. (1992): Fashion, Culture and Identity. Chicago: Chicago University Press.

Derrida, J. (1986): The Tain of the Mirror: Derrida and the Philosophy of Reflection, Trans. Harvard: Rodolphe Gasché, Harvard University Press.

Eicher, J., S. Evenson and H. Lutz (2008): The Visible Self: Global Perspectives of Dress, Culture, and Society', (3rd Edition). New York: Fairchild Publications.

Entwistle, J. (2000): The Fashioned Body: Fashion, Dress and Modern Social Theory. Cambridge: Polity Press in association with Blackwell.

Fashion United. http://www.fashionunited.com/global-fashion-industry-statistics-international -apparel, 29.06.2014.

Gendln, E. (1991): Thinking Beyond Patterns: Body, Language, and Situations. Chicago: University of Chicago.

Hannelore, H., Hermeling, E., Hornberger, M. and R. Kilgus (2008): Clothing Technology: From Fibre to Fashion', 5th edition. Haan-Gruiten: Verlag Europa-Lehrmittel Nourney, Vollmer GmbHVollmer GmbH & Co.

Irigaray, L. (1985): This Sex Which Is Not One, Trans. Catherine Porter. New York, Ithaca: Cornell University Press.

Jackson, T. and D. Shaw (2009): Mastering Fashion Marketing. Basingstoke: Palgrave Macmillan.

Jay, M. (1993): Downcast Eyes: The Denigration of Vision in Twentieth-Century French Thought. Los Angeles: University of California Press.

Jonas, H. (1992): The Burden and Blessing of Mortality. In: The Hastings Center Report, 22(Jan.), 34-40.

Johnson, M. (2007a): The Meaning of the Body: Aesthetics of Human Understanding. Chicago: University of Chicago Press.

Johnson, M. (2007b): The Stone that Was Cast out Shall Become the Cornerstone: The bodily Aesthetics of Meaning. In: Journal of Visual Art Practice, 6(2), 89-103.

Kim, S.B. (1998): Is Fashion Art? , Fashion Theory: The Journal of Dress, Body & Culture, 2(1), 51-71.

Lacan, J. (1966): The Mirror Stage as Formative of the Function of the I as Revealed in Psychoanalytic Experience. Paris: Écrits, Éditions du Seuil.

Layer, J. and De La Haye, A. (2002): Costume and Fashion: A Concise History, World of Art. London: Thames and Hudson.

Lewis, R. (2004): Rethinking Orientalism: Women, Travel, and the Ottoman Harem. London: I B Tauris & Co Ltd.

Mendes, V. and De la Haye, A. (2010): Fashion Since 1900, World of Art. London: Thames and Hudson.

Merleau-Ponty, M. (1964): Eye and Mind. Reproduced in: Edie, J.M. (ed.): The Primacy of Perception. Evanston, Illinois: Northwestern University Press, 159-190.

Merleau-Ponty, M. (1968): Visible and Invisible, Trans. Alphonso Lingis. Evanston, Illinois: Northwestern University Press.

Morris, D. (2010): The Enigma of Reversibility and the Genesis of Sense in Merleau-Ponty. In: Continental Philosophy Review, 43(2), 141-165.

Reed, E., Hansen, J. and Waters, M.A (1986): Cosmetics, Fashions and the Exploitation of Women. London: Pathfinder Press.

Rorty, R. (1979): Philosophy and the Mirror of Nature. Princeton: Princeton University Press.

Shoff, H. and Thompson, J.K. (2006): The Tripartite Influence Model of Body Image and Eating Disturbance: A Replication with Adolescent Girls. In: Body Image, 3(1), 17-23.

Twain, M. (1927) as quoted in: More Maxims of Mark complied by M. Johnson. Chicago: Private Publishing.

Wilson, E. (2005): Adorned in Dreams: Fashion and Modernity, 3rd edition. London: I.B. Tauris & Co Ltd.

De-+-Touring through Embodied 'Inter-Place'

Wendelin Küpers

Abstract

Following insights of phenomenology, this paper aims to contribute to a critical understanding of embodied place in relation to touring and performative mobility. From a relational perspective, touring will be interpreted as a body-mediated movement, situated in 'inter-places'. Then a 'de-touring' is explored as an alternative metaphor and creative practice of inter-placed mobility. Subsequently 'heterotouropia' and the interplay of de- and re-touring are described as infra-reflexive re-configuring. Outlining forms of 'other-placing' and 'other-moving' then open up for a wisdom of in-direction. Related to this new understanding of interplaced mobility, the ethos of 'engaged letting-go' ('Gelassenheit') will be discussed, especially in relation to de-touring and more sustainable forms of mobility. In conclusion, some implications, open questions, problems, and perspectives on issues of de-touring and mobility are presented.

Introduction

Spaces, places and bodies are constitutive dimensions of all being and becoming, also for particular forms of 'touring' that is movements, mobilities with its patterns of consumption and performance. As constitutive milieu and lived realities, spaces, emplacement and embodiment influence or inflect how we engage, understand and move towards and in the world. Likewise, movement and mobilities shape how spacing and placing as well as bodily experiences and realities are perceived, created and unfold. Those who are touring through spaces and places find them-selves and engage in an enveloping nexus that affects all their embodied orienting, feeling, thinking, acting, relating and consuming.

While places and (im-)mobilities unfold together and are inherently political (Bærenholdt and Granås 2008; Pellegrino 2011), they are dynamic interplaying formations of materio-social relations (Massey 1998: 154; 2005). They are 'thrown-together' and interacting through bodily and net-worked mediation at particular locations and within globalized worlds. Increasingly, these worlds are characterized by complex, actual and imagined, movements of subjects, objects, capital, knowledge and power (Castells 2001; Elliott and Urry 2010; Urry 2007) These dynamic forces deeply transform contemporary socio-economic, cultural and political orders and their entwined relationships (Sheller and Urry 2006) and affect those who are touring and their mobility.

By connecting a phenomenology of place and of body, respectively, embodiment, to approaches and studies of mobility, the following contributes to a critical understanding of what it means to be mobile and to tour. The phenomenology of embodiment and motricity of the living body, as mediating sphere of meaning (Merleau-Ponty 2012: 143), helps to explore the experiential and situational processes of touring with its dynamic complexity. Furthermore, such an approach offers a critical stance on the current, often ideologically celebrated mobility-ideal in its concealment, ultimately opening up different possibilities. In particular, it allows developing and enacting other ways of performing mobility beyond sedentarist and nomadist approaches, thus broadening our metaphorical repertoire. This extended perspective includes considering contradictory and ambiguous ways in which mobilities and touring are understood, practiced and experienced in material and socio-cultural settings. Such understanding can then generate implications and alternative perspectives of what it means to tour and becoming mobile in a different way.

Recognizing touring and mobility as a dynamic, decentred event in relation to embodiment, helps to understand the role of 'inter-place'. This inter-place' or rather before process of 'embodied inter-placing', refers to a state and 'en-action' in which the being or presence of places and mobile subjects is extended and connected to multiple places simultaneously in real time (Küpers 2010).

One form of 'inter-placed' movement is to 'de-tour'. Such 'de-touring' marks a performative metaphor and specific practice. Interpreted as creative be(com)ing, it allows for otherwise unlikely encounters and unsuspecting sources of embodied, placed and inter-relational processes of experiences, knowledges and movements. In relation to this alternative form of mobility, and in face of hyper-mobile realities of life, the ethos of an 'engaged letting-go' ('*Gelasssenheit'*) is helpful.

First, basic ideas of a phenomenology of space and embodied place and mobility will be outlined. Such a phenomenological approach allows not only a consideration of the often forgotten primordial and opening realm of directly felt and lived experiences and realities of them to be rehabilitated. Building on Merleau-Ponty's (1995; 2012) advanced phenomenology, the role of the living body in relation to the embodiment of place and space of performed mobility, discloses important insights for a renewed comprehension. Based on this phenomenological outset, a more processual understanding of 'inter-place' respectively 'inter-placing' is developed. Such relational understanding allows considering multiple embodied local-cultural realities of places and mobilities as emerging events. Accordingly, embodied places and performative mobilities can then be conceived in their relationship. Specifically, they can be interpreted as media for an *in-between* of those involved, and how they are co-creating specific 'place-scapes' and 'move-scapes'. One quality of these placing and moving scapes is that they enact and process a specific responsiveness and responsibility in relation to place and movement.

De-touring will then be described as creative 'inter-placed' mobility and what will be called 'heterotouropia' as a different relationship to touring. Furthermore, the interplay of de-touring and re-touring practices are then described as infra-reflexive reconfiguring. Subsequently, outlining forms of 'other-placing' and 'other-moving' open up for the wisdom of in-direction.

The final part will discuss some implications and perspectives on research and practice of embodied places and performative mobilities as well as presenting the significance of 'engaged letting-go' ('Gelassenheit'), especially in relation to de-touring and a more sustainable form of mobility.

Phenomenology of embodied space, place and performative mobility

Embodied space and place

There is long-lasting debate (in research) about differences and relationships between space and place. In contrast to the more abstract conceptualized space, living places are perceived, felt, imagined, interpreted, understood and narrated (Soja 1996). While we are located in space, we feel, interpret, act in place, imbued with social meanings (Harrison and Dourish 1996) and in particular ways related to bodies. Mediated by the living body with its pre-reflective access to environing things, places with their meanings are not only socially and culturally constructed. Rather, they are primarily sensed and perceived or consumed during touring through embodied experiences before, at the point of visitation or practices as well as afterwards. "Places are not so much the direct objects of sight or thought or recollection as what we feel *with* and *round*, *under* and *above*, *before* and *behind* our lived bodies. They are the ad-verbial and pre-positional contents of our usually tacit corporeal awareness, at work as the pre-position of our bodily lives, underlying every determinate bodily action or position, every static posture of our corpus, every coagulation of living experience in thought or word, sensation or memory, image or gesture.... To be a sentient bodily being at all is to be place-bound, bound to be in a place, bonded and bound therein" (Casey 1993: 313).

Accordingly, as action-moving bodies gear into the world, the 'lived space' and places orient positions and movements, for example towards life and right, up and down, near and far, moving and at rest while being environed in meaningful relations (Merleau-Ponty 2012: 270). Thus they serve as means by which relations to things, people and tasks become possible (Merleau-Ponty 2012: 253-54). Giving the central role of locality as it arises through embodiment, Merleau-Ponty shows that spaces and places are themselves incorporated within and in-between life-worldly phenomena. This is because embodiment refers to our lived 'being-placed-in-the-world' that is an active and reversible process, indicating the negotiation of everyday life in relation to the material and social world (Dale and Burell 2008: 215). For example, depending on how we are placed, mobility is enacted and experienced through the body in different ways. Under certain placed conditions, the one who is touring may be tired and moving for her may be strenuous or boring. Or she moves in an adventurous spirit of exhilarating optimism, having a spring in her steps.

Embodied mobility can be experienced as freedom, when we leave an inhospitable place; or the opposite occurs when being trapped for instance in a traffic jam. It makes a difference whether a traveler is placed in a first, or connoisseur class or an economy class during a trans-continental flight. While the first placing offers more space and oxygen, nicer food and services, among other perks; the latter placed travelers are cramped, uncomfortable, oxygen starved and standing in line for the toilet and facing further frictions. These are all part of constellations of mobility with its embodied experiences of purpose, velocity, rhythm, route, and spatial scale (Cresswell, 2010).

The place occupied by the body, and the perception and experience of this placing, contracts and expands in relationship to a person's or group's emotions and state of mind, sense of self or identity, social relations, and cultural predispositions and practices. With this understanding of embodied place, bodies belong to place, that is, there are no bodies without place, but also place belongs to bodies, thus body and place are congruent counterparts (Casey 1993: 103). Living bodies mediate and navigate people into a co-orientation within place that allows the co-creation of 'place-scapes' (Casey 1993: 25) as embodied 'move-scapes', respectively other interrelated fluid, flowing and amorphous 'scapes' (Appadurai 1990). These scapes mediate, enable or channel mobility along designated routes or freer forms of conduits.

Particular places shape and are shaped by physical objects, events and causal processes that have both spatial and temporal dimensions as well as by memories, personal and communal narratives, social activities and institutions. Relating to both internal and external subjective and collective horizons, place is 'a structure comprising spatiality *and* temporality, subjectivity *and* objectivity, self *and* others' (Malpas 1999: 163) as part of the fabric of social bodies and the social becoming (Crossley 1996: 101; 2001; 2006) of embodied material and cultural realities.

Inter-relationality and mediality of spaces, places and mobility

In order to develop a deeper understanding of this intertwinement, spaces, places and mobility need to be interpreted not merely as a reified position or movement between two or more positions, but as ongoing emergencies of inter-relational processes. Lefebvre (1991) has shown that space in its multiplicity is a social product or a complex social construction based on values and the social production of meanings that affects spatial practices and perceptions. Not only are spaces socially produced, they are also made (un-)productive in social practices; which calls for exploring the contradictory, conflictual and ultimately, political character of the processes of the production of space.

As outlined before, space, place and mobility are multidimensional phenomena comprising entangled physical, environmental, personal and social dimensions. In particular they are (form-in-)-media that are intermediating milieus and movements, where the natural, material, individual and collective worlds meet, interrelate and interplay and thus develop and unfold transformatively (Küpers 2011b). Being media, they are simultaneously causes and effects, i.e. products of multiple interwoven relations. As they are relationally created, they are not only produced by and through the interrelations between the material and the cultural, but also reproduced, re-mediated and transformed. This relational constitution ranges from the immensity of the intimately tiny to the global (Massey 2005: 9) within an ongoing, dynamic simultaneity and entwinement. As emerging events, they are dispersed and inherently indeterminate processes, and continually reconfiguring. Thus places are not simple locations, but like mobilities a multilayered relational processuality (Casey 1993: 65; Küpers 2010).

With a relational intelligibility, we can shift our attention from an understanding of space and place as a container and mobility as movement between points, to a dynamic becoming that transpires *between* situated people and their placed artefacts-in-use (Küpers 2014; 2015). Correspondingly, placing and moving becomes factually based on processes that are jointly structured activities within a complex set of inter-relations as an ongoing event of responsive relating. Out of these interconnections, embodied perceptions, feelings, cognitions and meanings, and communities as well as artefacts, structures and functions of place and emplacement, in addition to touring and mobility, are continually created, performed, questioned, re-created and renegotiated. All of these relational elements are processed within and through a recursive and reversible nexus (Merleau-Ponty 1995), which allows developing an understanding of inter-placed movement.

Embodied touring – Moving through 'inter-place'

As shown before, by recognizing the primacy of embodied relational processes, places and touring or mobility can be seen as an inter-relational event that is continuously co-created and transformed. Embodied inter-placing refers then to an action and condition in which the being or presence of places and mobile subjects is extended and connected to multiple places simultaneously/in real time (Küpers 2010). This requires recognizing place, mobility and subjectivity as dynamic, de-centred meshed events. This mesh of 'inter-placing' moves and is distributed in dynamic sets of forms within powerful historical, corporeal, affective socio-cultural and structural dimensions. Moving through embodied inter-places includes the insight that wayfaring, storied touring is lived along open(ing) lines and spirals as relational fields (Ingold 2011: 69-70). These meshed fields are living con-textures of interwoven threads that constitute an inter-placed web or moving relationships. Thus, inter-placed movement and mobility is a kind of issuing, along with things and paths in the very processes of their generation: "not the trans-port (carrying across) of completed being, but the pro-duction (bringing forth) of perpetual becoming" (Ingold 2011: 12).

Forms, formations and transformations of inter-placed touring interrelate and co-create each other within an 'inter-world' (Merleau-Ponty 2012: 373). The inclusion of embodied placing and moving through this inter-worldly immanence provides renewed possibilities for developing richer, more textured, under-standings of how we are part of a lived involvement within what Merleau-Ponty (1995) calls *'flesh'* of the world.[1]

1 Merleau-Ponty's indirect and post-dualistic ontology of 'flesh' refers to a chiasmic, incorporated intertwining and reversibility of pre-personal, personal, inter- and transpersonal dimensions (Merleau-Ponty, 1995). Importantly for Merleau-Ponty ontological principle of 'flesh' is neither matter or some substance, nor mind, or only a representational construct. Rather, he designates 'flesh' as an 'element' of being, in the sense of a general thing or incarnated principle, situated in the midway between the spatio-temporal individual and the idea, functioning as the formative medium of or post-dualistic 'third being' out of which objects and subjects emerge (Merleau-Ponty 1995: 248; 302). With the later Merleau-Ponty's indirect ontology of in-between and intertwining within this chiasmic 'flesh', we can see that place and placing, particularly of human beings and their embedment, is only possible by being open to the flux of the open, ambiguous processes in which embodied, emotional and aesthetic spheres are interplaying constituents. Within this rhythmic, sometimes chaotic endless flow of continuous becoming with others, place and implacings, the fragile transitory and unpredict-

A phenomenological interpretation of dimensions of mobility as processually embodied and inter-placed can be revealing. This revelation becomes apparent even more in contrast to conventional studies and practices of place and mobility that are often following positivistic and 'practicalist' orientation by which these are construed in a limited or reductionistic way. In addition to providing a base for a critique, phenomenology also helps to develop different understandings and enactments of placed, moving, and performative practices. For such understanding, the body and embodiment are not merely physicalities or straight(ening) neutral operators, but ambiguous, over- or under-determined media for being relationally placed and moving. Such interpretation allows re-interpreting mobility as embodied inter-placed movements that are enacted in de-touring as an alternative wayfaring.

De-Tour(ing) as inter-placed mobility

> "Does not detour – which is anything but gratuitous – exert a certain power, which is all the more forceful for its discretion" (Jullien 2000: 7).
>
> "If you are in a hurry – make a detour" (Taoist Wisdom).

In the following section, de-touring will be discussed as an alternative metaphor and practice in relation to placed and embodied movement and mobility. Firstly metaphors of mobility and touring will be explored critically, followed by presenting some qualities of de-+-touring and how it is creative move and inter-placed 'heterotouropia'. Afterwards some critical perspectives and implications are offered on what the interplay of de- and retouring mean.

Metaphors of mobility

Being themselves moving, means of transferring meanings, metaphors, like stories affect how researchers and practitioners approach phenomena and the kinds of insights, realities and meanings they generate and enact (Küpers 2012),

---

able human beings and their embodied movements and organisations are always on the brink of being lost in larger cycles and turbulences with no secure metaphysical foundations. The generative immanence and nexus of mediating fluid 'flesh' serves as 'texture' and 'context' for all movements in relation to exterior and interior horizons (Merleau-Ponty, 1995: 131) and thus constitutes all experiences and meanings of mobility and touring with their specific foldings, gaps and reversibilities.

working often as unthematized background for scientific thought and categories (Blumenberg 1996) and guiding practices.

In mobility studies, metaphors of flow, fluidity, liquidity and the nomad have gained particular momentum. For instance, Urry (2000: 22) largely uses 'metaphors of network, flow and travel', Castells (2000) refers to flows and networks and Bauman (2000) to metaphors of liquidity and the nomad. The latter is also key in Deleuze and Guattari's (1987) work with their focus on deterritorialization and rhizomatic transgression. Nomadism is also used in Braidotti's "bodily" or "carnal" materialism (2006: 182) as part of her critical post-humanist ethics and politics (Braidotti 2013) in relation to moves towards sustainable alternative futures.

Metaphors of mobility can signify more than simply the movement of people or objects in space, time or social levels. They constitute root-metaphors for understanding of where and how societies and its members are moving at as well as how cultures are formed and reproduced in late modernity and late capitalism. How can we, in research and practice, move beyond the metaphors of flow, fluidity and nomadism, yet without falling back to idealize static, nostalgic, conservative reactionary or essentialistic ones? A proper understanding and re-imagination of mobility requires transcending the pitfalls of both the potentially one-sided nomadic, uncritical and compressible neo-liberal position with the potentially one-sided sedentarist, petrifying position. Accordingly, we need to cultivate a moving and resistant stance that refrain from approaching mobilities in a manner of either taking it as a recipe for emancipation from places or as threat to the stability of places.

While overly stressing a certain lightness and easiness of floating and moving, many of the currently dominant metaphors of mobility and touring cannot fully capture and address the ambiguities and frictions or costs involved in people's mobile touring, especially in their working lives. That is not to say that existing mobilities research does not discuss any tensions or take a critical stance. Instead, the point is that this is not sufficiently reflected in their metaphors. John Urry (2007) refers to contradictions involved in mobilities and questions the metaphor of flows, despite also using it. For instance, he is at pains to show mobilities' costs with respect to the environment: "[T]wentieth-century capitalism generated the most striking of contradictions. Its pervasive, mobile and promiscuous commodification involved utterly unprecedented levels of energy production and consumption, a high-carbon society whose dark legacy we are beginning to reap" (Elliott and Urry 2010: 140).

Compared to the metaphor of flow, mobility does not seem to sufficiently capture contradictions, 'flux involves tensions, struggle and conflict' (Urry 2007: 25). For example, touring among highly mobile elite workers in hasty mobile cycles can be experienced as stickiness (Costas 2013)[2]. Paradoxically expressed, this entails a 'fixed instability' or 'rushing standstill' of disruptive moves in and between ephemeral non-places, like airports. Research on these non-places in the tradition of Augé (1995) have shown how the 'everywhere', the celebrated supposed freedom of glamorously being on the move, collides with a 'nowhere', an impersonal, unnamed space, flattened out under notions of distance and remoteness, giving rise to a sense of dislocation and uncertainty, and loss of transformation. Entrapped in a compulsory logic of moving on and on, instead of being liberatory, this highly mobile 'on-goingness' may lead to alienated experiences and lonely working life as well as other impact and 'costs' of mobilities (Elliott and Urry 2010: 140).

Touring De-+-touring

Facing the outlined difficulties and challenges in the following, the metaphor of a detouring is proposed to discuss touring and mobilities in a different, potentially more fulfilling way. What does de-touring mean? Literarily, a detour (or diversion route) is a route around a planned area of prohibited or reduced access. To de-tour refers to the (embodied) act of going or traveling to a place along a way that is different from (and sometimes longer than) the usual or planned way; a deviation from a direct course or the normal procedure. To take a detour is to turn differently, to divert (from, from Old French '*destor*', from '*destorner*' to divert, from '*des-*' or '*de-*' + '*torner*'; to turn), that is to bypass, circumnavigate or circumvent. To proceed by a detour can also mean to avoid (something) by going around it, thus de-tours are roundabout ways to get somewhere in a non-linear fashion.

In short, de-touring refers to a sort of dis-location or removal from what is an intended trajectory; a temporal or/and spatial dis-placement of sorts. From a deconstructionist perspective, the '*de-*' of this touring stands for de-laying, as it "suspends the accomplishment and fulfilment of a 'desire' or a 'will' " (Derrida 1978: 8). As such it is a temporization that mediates attempting to postpone the arrival, the end, avoiding commitment to a closure. Thus, it operates as a de-layering as well as de-positioning or de-railing of lines, towards spiraling.

2 Costas (2013) discusses the Sartrean metaphor of stickiness to reveal how the group of highly mobile elite workers (consultants) experiences of 'ephemeral, interchangeable and monotonous non-spaces of mobility. He shows how their stickiness of being on the move can give rise to experiences of ambiguity, disorientation and loss as well as fixed instability, feeling stuck and that stick to one even when returning to places.

Accordingly, de-touring may be used for de-mythologizing that is de-bunking myths of linear progress and supposed efficient ways of direct touring.

To detour is de-fering difference or 'différance' in that it takes into account the fact that the meaning of touring is not only a question of synchrony with all the other terms inside a structure, but also of diachrony, with everything that was said and will be said or en-acted. Detours and postponements happen as all relationships and meanings of the present are always deferred, as they refer to another past or future element in an economy of traces.

Contradictions encountered on the de-toured way slow down, deflect, and rearrange the trajectories that mark culture also as travel (Dasgupta 2013).[3] The detour can take any shape, and it hardly knows where or when it will end – if it will. Instead of direct ways of touring, to detour leads astray towards an-other way. This critique of straight lines questions forms of a teleological and 'destinational' thinking, movements and orders. Delays and detours, as thickened, embodied, culturally complex experiences of contingency, undermine the teleological movement through space towards a known destination (Dasgupta 2013: 67).

De-touring challenges the teleological system with its logic of means and ends. Paradoxically, the more action is motivated by a direct, means-ends logic, 'the more likely it is that such calculated actions eventually work to undermine and erode their own initial success, often with devastating consequences' (Chia and Holt 2009: x), including not allowing situated, creative processes and actions to emerge (Joas 1996).

De-touring as creative move and inter-placed 'heterotouropia'

De-touring makes the body relate to and move differently in and towards space and place. Embodied de-touring mediates or implies moving towards unknown path-ways. De-touring, understood as movement through unfamiliar spheres, opens up and allows creative possibilities. Thereby bodily, spatial, temporal and

3 As Dasgupta (2013) shows, speed, transiency, fleetingness are crossed with detours and delays that prolong the arrival at a destination and slow down the rate at which intellectual desire seeks to cast culture as travel. Acknowledging and holding these contradictions together, and maintaining their tense signifying and experiential dimensions furthers a dialectical understanding of traveling cultures without rushing toward a narrative denouement whose destination is knowable in advance. De-touring reframes the figuration of culture between the binaries of fixity and movement, stasis and travel, tradition and modernity, by pausing, dwelling, and reflecting on what happens at both ends of the journey, and in the journey itself. Thus, the inclusion of, detours with its possible delays and derailments, allows to consider factors that are part of the living complexity of culture.

social dimensions and relations may be playfully connected. Detouring experiences and movement co-create realities of multiplicity and the unexpected in which distinct trajectories coexist with their heterogeneities (Massey 2005: 9). Moreover, de-toured places and movement through them are dis-continuously under construction as they are always in the process of being made (and un-made), thus never finished; never completely closed.

The trying-out-(play-)grounds that de-touring requires, manifests through curious leeways for relatively free movements und unforeseeable possibilities to emerge. In this way, the potential space and pace of de-touring is analogous to what Foucault (1984) calls 'heterotopia', refering to other spaces that have more layers of meaning or relationships to other places than immediately meet the eye. Heterotopias imply varied spatial and temporal disruptions that imaginatively interrogate, undermine and contest the spaces and places in which we live.

Related to this other(ing) movement, and applied to mobility it may be called *'hetero-touropia'*. In an inter-play of ambiguities of space, place and embodied movement, 'hetero-touropias' simultaneously refer, reflect, incur-porate and contest other tour(ing)s as well as invite to take and embody different spatial and temporal forms. In this way, the multiplicity of spaces and places through de-touring is a prerequisite for difference, otherness and transformation.

Withdrawing from the reigning order of necessity and instrumentality, detouring offers temporary tours of creative process, play and imagination. But for being effective and transformative, de-touring needs to be seen as being connected to re-touring.

De-Touring and Re-Touring practices of infra-reflexive re-configuring

One implication of de-touring is that it remains entwined and is ready to re-turn, differently, to what the tour was, as original proposed in due course. While keeping in mind that from which de-tour deviates, knowing the embedding context and direct trajectory remains important in order to diverge from it. The one who is de-touring needs to know where the placed path and orbit is situated and be able to go off it, respectively to move between de-touring and re-touring. In this way, a 'de-retour' opens up a critique of metaphysical foundations from the inside of the world of touring, while disrupting its 'orbit' (as paradigm of touring thinking in linear economics), for encompassing at once deviational and reconfigured spatial ('re-approximiting') and temporal ('re-presencing') move-ments, sensing the presence of an absence and before absence of a presence. Related to forms of practices of reflexivity (Alvesson et al 2008), we can distinguish between de- and re-touring as different, multi-perspective practices of positioning. While a de-touring refers to reflexive practices of deconstruction, defense, declaiming, destabilizing, a re-touring modus stands for reconstruction, reframing, reclaiming and re-presentation (ibid.: 494).

A de-touring reflexivity challenges orthodox understandings by pointing out the limitations of, and uncertainties behind the manufactured unity and coherence of tour(ing)s as well as the way in which conformism, institutional domination and academic and business fashion may account for the production of particular knowledge. A re-touring reflexivity is then more about developing and reorienting by bringing in issues of alternative paradigms, root metaphors, perspectives, vocabularies, lines of interpretation, political values and representations that aim for re-balancing and reframing voices. These re-orientational practices of touring can be employed to illuminate what is left out and marginalized. This includes all those almost missed opportunities, premature framing, reproduction of received wisdom, re-enforcement of power relations and unimaginative labeling in order "to open up new avenues, paths, and lines of interpretation to produce 'better' research ethically, politically, empirically and theoretically" (ibd.: 494-5).

As importantly, both de-touring and re-touring reflexivities need to be connected to embodied performative enactments. For example, when workplaces become stages for enacted narratives and embodied performances, they move beyond being only fixed work-stations. Rather, they are also milieus for movement, rhythms and even dance as media 'that allows the human body to play with space – seeking a concretization of spatial possibilities' (Atkinson 2008: 1089) as they emerge as a localized form of aesthetics of co-presence and aesthetic organizing (Küpers 2002).

Thresholding towards 'other-placing' and 'other-moving': The wisdom of in-direction

By recognizing the interplay between de- and re-touring, we may then form a transitional dance on thresholds (Küpers 2011) of an 'other-placing' and 'other-moving', receding into othering experiences of place and movement. In this way, de- and re-touring become transitional moves through liminal spaces and times that awaken the possible. While de- and re-touring time-spaces are unspecific, 'useless' and 'superfluous', they open up possibilities beyond the usual, returning differently to ordinary every-day life. In the liminal moments and spaces of de- and re-touring as transitions, a host of possible events and experiences unfolds transformatively.

Part of the bodily constituted and mediated de- and re-touring process of temporal-spatial transitions are rhythmic processes. In contrast to a metronomic beat that knows no pauses and transitions, rhythmicity is characterized by inter-mediated times and moves, something in-between or happening on the way. Temporal and spatial transitions are inter-ruptions from the point of view of an invariable beat of clock time, interruptions of the non-stop principle, ruptures that lead to other routes. It is precisely in the de- and re-touring time and space of 'neither-nor' that the opportunities for the 'both-and' of other connections are abundant.

A 'de-re-tour' creates the quality of transition as a connecting element and as a hinge between times, spaces and places. By disrupting the linear course of time and flattened space, re-oriented inter-placed de- and re-touring transitions that are not predetermined by direct touring purposes allow one to experience, while oscillating with different ties and patterns as they enable other and 'othering' connections.

These qualities are related to the wisdom of 'in-direction' (Jullien 1999) as process-based, self-organized, continual and immanent transformation. Being indirect and meandering, turning and returning makes de- and re-touring a circuitous, but efficacious journey and makes 'materio-socio-cultural' differences to eventual 'out-comes'. According to Jullien (1999), the 'active inaction' as part of this in-direction, allows the structural potential of convenient occurrences. Action here means not taking action in the sense of punctually touring that is, following a fixed plan or enforcing, but becoming part of the (whole) unfolding de- and re-touring course of realities. The effectiveness of this in-directional active non-doing activates potentials within the very situation of de- and re-touring. This 'non-action' is one that is inconspicuous and hence unnoticed action that goes with the fluxed flow, hence relating to latent energy and momentum of situations. This then allows attaining one's end by letting things follow their course and hence ripen for picking as an entrenched attitude and practice in its dealings in the world of affairs. Such an attitude derives from an appreciation of the presence of 'unowned' forces that are always already at work in every human situation.

Strategic indirection refers to a collectively internalized disposition whether societal or organizational that favors indirect, circuitous and non-confrontational modes of engagement in dealing with human affairs (Chia 2014) and has its specific efficacy, compared to navigational courses and interventional causes. "Where navigational routines suggest strategy to be the pre-planned, efficient movement between previously identified points, way-finding initiatives are animated by an ever open environmental sensitivity that allows for detours, lingerings and directional changes. This is the strategic skill of the bricoleur."

(Chia and Holt 2009: 173). Forcibly imposing a pre-determined, rational plan on a pre-existing and coherent world through (heroic or rational) direct touring, navigation or interventions in quick and 'decisive' manner often implies a certain amount of importunity and incompatibility. It 'tears at the tissue of things and upsets their coherence' (Jullien 2004: 54), thereby provoking reticence or even internal resistance, that gnaws away quietly at the unwelcome imposition, eventually undermining or annulling its intended efficacy (Chia 2014).

De-touring offers one to notice the effects of small, cumulative changes on the way and over time by a different, flexible movement that is in contrast to following determined forms and moving towards supposed stable end states, which tend to neglect the inexorable nature of perpetual change. Sustainable success does not come from directly seeking it, but instead arises on a 'rebound', predicated upon an implicit acknowledgement of the presence of unseen situational forces, effective on de-touring routes that have a hand in shaping eventual outcomes, regardless of human intentions. The priority shifts from one of actively intervening to one of learning, in how to be patient and allow things to take shape, then learning to mobilize the inherent tendency of the situation and to realize one's own possibilities (Chia 2014). Notions of 'actively waiting for the fruit to ripen', 'letting things happen', 'testing the ground', 'alluding to' rather than stating, using 'quotations as a proxy' (Jullien 2000: 76-78) and indeed of embracing 'strategic ambiguity', better encapsulates this more nuanced and indirect way of engaging with the world of practical affairs. It is one that implicitly acknowledges the ever-changing and transient nature of social reality. It is this celebration of the engaged passive, the understated, the circuitous and the allusive which differentiates strategic indirection from the heroic, rational-calculative approaches championed in the management literature and practice.

A cunning, metistic and practically wise knowledge and practice of de-touring is 'enamoured' with emerging circumstances on the way, while negotiating its passage ways (Chia and Holt 2009: 195). Such knowledge is an economy of force, an ability to use the present of what exists and unfolds. What is experienced on de-touring is not integrated into a pre-existing whole of a planned tour, but continually modifies the path and its way-faring as an ongoing process of 'folding, unfolding, refolding' (Deleuze 2006: 158). Instead of coming to full circle of touring, the 'de-re-touring' moves are opening de-centralising spirals.[4]

4 While revolving around a centre the circle encloses and thereby guarantees a "fundamental immobility and a reassuring certitude" (Derrida 1978: 279), hence preventing the possibility of play. Circles are stable but paralyzing grounding, for all concepts within a structure, that gives meaning and coherence to its elements. Spiraling de-touring moves are rupture in this structured order, that play with moving around centres that are not taken as a "fixed locus, but

All these musings on de-touring are connected to the seemingly trivial wisdom of knowing and enacting that the path itself is the 'goal'. Once a de-touring move is on the path, this very 'pathing' *is* the goal, with all its bliss and blisters. A poietic and poetic wandering by getting onwards in a de-touring way, is more important than arriving, nor finding a complete resolution at an end-point, in the spirit of Machado's (1912) poetic expression that there is no road, but the road is made by walking. However, this process-wisdom implies a critical twist! Not only do de- and re-touring result in a propensity to act or non-act in a manner co-responding with the demands of its shifting, ambiguous and polyvalent situation. Rather, they are qualified as moving with vigilance, alertness and sensitivity, remaining alive to vague and diverse and seemingly minor occurrence that may lead to somewhere else. The furtive quality of enacting de-touring becomes evident in that it is versed in obliquity, imaginative leaps and hence subversive moves. Thereby, the foldings of de- and re-touring are de-(con)structuring the very structures of tour(ing)s.

In this way, de- and re-touring may bring into be(com)ing what has not yet appeared, what is yet invisible, dormant, latent yet un-sensed, un-felt, un-thought and un-said or not done. Accordingly, the de-ranging of de- and re-touring may mediate a different re-arranging that e-merges into presence. Like strategy without design, de-touring "is about embracing the uncertain, the ambiguous and the unknown… making room, the limits of which are not boundaries, but the edges, where things begin their essential unfolding" (Chia and Holt 2009: 210-11). De-tours move towards and then temporarily 'dwell' in clearings as places of encounters of and with things on the way, disclosing what a foreclosing touring oversees or disregards. While touring is moving on pre-organized surfaces on flattened ordered streets, de- and re-touring is capable of moving deeper, vertical, higher and in-between in the spirit of letting-go.

[as] a function" [ibd. 208] to allow for the play of infinite signification in language and, in a post-Derridarian way, somantic meanings in embodied material expressions to avoid falling into a linguistic idealism or mentalism. Having no circularly closed perimeter and no centre or deviating from a teleological pattern that are implying a spatial and temporal displacement, detouring distorts centered circles by forming elliptical moves. These moves are creating a gap that is an in-between-sphere in the circle's perimeter that it is leaving the circle open instead of deadly circularities of closures. Ellipsis is including voluntary omission of something that is supposed to be there, providing a play of absence and presence: what is not there and what is there; and re-touring differently eternal returning towards (dis-)continuous 're-de-re-de-touring' etc. as an ongoingly refined, negotiated, social interpretative process.

Ethos of engaged letting-go or 'Gelassenheit' as relational inter-p(l)acing practice and mobility

In considering the outlined entwinement of place, embodiment, movement and mobility as well as for dealing with a world that increasingly seems to become hypermobile, forms of engaged releasement or 'Gelassenheit' might be helpful. This 'Gelassenheit' translated as releasement, letting-go, serenity, composure, detachment refers to a non-objectifying ethos of active and ongoing passivity, to an accepting by letting-go, implying an abandonment of habitual, representational and appropriating orientations.

In this letting-be of things, the de-touring being does not attempt to manipulate, master or compel things, but instead let things be in their vital nature. More importantly, 'Gelassenheit' is not about the indifference or lack of interest in things, but rather an 'engaged letting'. Entering a modus of letting-be is realized through a receptive waiting and listening, thus more an active non-doing, rather than a willing and controlling business of mastering. It moves specifically from representational and calculative modes, via presencing, meditative thinking towards more poetic relations.[5]

By resisting the seductive tendency to be overly active and instrumental via direct touring, de-touring in the spirit of 'Gelassenheit' invites a cultivation of an attitude of 'wise active passiveness' by allowing the one de-touring to be immersed in his moves and in this way, gradually absorb the lessons this

5 Heidegger (1993) problematized the technological-scientific-industrial modes and what he calls "calculative thinking," – in contrast to a meditative one – restless thinking directed toward manipulation, toward obtaining some specific result. Meditative thinking, however, requires patience and silence, being as well as doing. It requires that we somehow stop and recollect ourselves. It requires conditions in which we can practice innocent looking and listening, the kind of awareness that we experience when we truly, unselfishly love someone or something – when we love the truth. For real thinking depends on openness, openness to whatever is in front of us. And it must start with what is closest – our own being. It is only then, when we are truly open to ourselves, that what is true can enter our perception and reveal itself fully to us. It is only then that we can go beyond the "stimulus-response" mode of living; a mode of living that is suited to machines not people. Through Gelassenheit it may be possible to suspend (or silence) habitual and calculative modes of thinking and open to the promptings that come from the ontological depth of other beings. This openness clears a space for the Being of the other to emerge as it is in itself. In preserving the other's irreducible otherness, we preserve our own integrity and deepen our experience of self and other. A phenomenological analysis leads us to step back away from customary and habitual representations of beings within the ontological horizon of objective presence to the prior and more fundamental manner in which they appear in terms of worldly handiness. Gelassenheit means to step back out of representational thinking into a kind of thinking that is not in a hurry to impose its ordering and calculations on things – it is not on a mission to follow the modernist project of putting questions to nature and forcing her to answer or being used or exploited.

immersion has to offer. Such wise active passiveness is a state of calm, contemplative receptivity in which the rational touring mind is temporarily put to sleep, thereby allowing the body to absorb the impulses from the external world and be enlightened by it. Instead of directly walking fast from position A to B from a defined beginning towards a determined end without distractions, neglecting the scenery, detouring takes its time to go on a stroll including into the midst of what is between or outside of A and B. The detouring mover goes on relaxed ex-cursions in the curious and curving forests of an embodied, perceiving, feeling, thinking and acting being.

Mobility as an embodied and relational event of de- and re-touring guided by 'Gelassenheit' allows gaining access to new experiential possibilities and different orientations. Touring that follows an ethos of 'Gelassenheit' would mean remaining present, responsive and ethically responsible to the people and places encountered, thus positively contributing to reconfigured relationships to place, emplacement, time and identity. Rather than drifting out of or disconnecting from the present moment, subjects remain awake and more responsibly connected to the 'materio-socio-cultural' practices and worlds they participate in and co-constitute (Küpers 2015). As a genuine relationship to mobility and de-touring, 'Gelassenheit' is open to the presencing as it emerges while inter-placed in their touring and living.

With this orientation, embodied and emplaced temporalities of slowness, waiting and 'active non-doing' need to be seen as elements of a wider sensuous 'geo-bio-socio-graphy' of movement and dwelling. In such a broader sense, human navigation of and through embodied, kinesthetic and sensory environments are vital (Dant 2004; Jensen 2010). Following a Merleau-Pontyian relational ontology, such approaches can per- and conceive the *in-between* and liminal places at which movement is inter-rupted, paused, slowed, or stopped. Moreover, cultivating engaged releasement and released engagement towards things and phenomena allows a "yes" and "no" to what happens during de-touring, and to view things not only in an appropriating way. Hence, it discourages mindless organizing, easy consumption or exploitive orientations. Developing a relatively free relationship to what appears during de-touring does not mean aspiring for a life free from usages, for example of mobility technologies and mobile machines' like mobile phones and computer connections in the 'digital matrix' (Howard and Küpers 2015) in their ubiquiousness impacting varied time-space compressing mobilities and immobilities.

Instead, it is cultivating and leading a life that is not pervasively ordered by them, but making sustainable sense of them (Conway and Timms 2010; 2012). Orienting towards enacting, 'Gelassenheit' contributes to a more qualitative development of travelling (Hall 2010) and sustainable tourism futures (Gössling et al. 2009). Concretely, in the spirit of engaged releasement, slowed tourism then involves shorter trips (distance) and longer stays (time), where air-transport is rejected in favor of less environmentally damaging forms of overland-transport, which become incorporated as part of the experience (Dickinson 2009). This can then be an experience of 'dwelling-mobility' as part of a new form of well-being (Todres and Galvin 2010) and sustainable travelling. For example, slow tourism aims to counter negative externalities with an 'identity' that promotes sustainability and conviviality and focuses upon countering the loss of local distinctiveness as it relates to leisure, sense of place, hospitality and rest and recuperation (Woehler 2004). A correspondingly changed consumption pattern can then lead to a more eco-efficient, as well as, energy- and carbon-conscious traveler. Such a traveler is more aware of their usage of products and services and critically reflexive about the ambivalences of mobility.

By enacting an ethos of Gelassenheit, hypermobility could be refashioned as unstylish or anti-social, and contribute to redefining notions of 'good' citizenship. Slowness, stillness, stopping and proximity as well as an eco-local focus might then be up-valued or even 'glamorised' amongst cultural intermediaries. In this way, a mode of 'Gelassenheit' can become part of creating alternative markers of status and style that work in opposition to the cultural elevation of mobility and the consumption of distance.

However, the potential to activate such resistive performative movements is still relatively unexplored, as is the power that celebrity endorsement may have in channeling societies towards different social norms (Higham 2013: 7). Furthermore, being implicilty political[6], enacting an ethos of 'Gelassenheit' in

6 Gelassenheit is a political in that it implies concerns and an ethical responsiveness towards 'Others' in a different way. As such it is not a tranquilized withdrawal or quietist harmony, but a proto-anarchic condition of openness in which the relation to the singularity or non-identity of Others, including embodied inter-placed relationship and movements towards them, can take place or can go, including a freedom of (non-)choice and (non-)availability. Instead of separating from anything negative or rationally organizing scarcity with regard to homogenized mobility resources, it refers to a kind of generosity or 'prodigality' of being and becoming. Thereby the singular experienced is allowed to exist, independent of exploitative utilisation or rational justification. Accordingly, sensing, thinking and acting in modes of 'Gelassenheit' is one of responsive responsibility, rather than ratiocination; while being in situated mindfully within the political situation of our historical time and its crisis. In this way 'Gelassenheit' challenges or decenters the customary focus of mobilizing and mobility-oriented desires, wills' or deliberate intentionalities. Thereby, it is shifting towards an ontological participation in which, for example mobility and its hyper-activities are released at least partially from the dictates of an instrumental pursuit of objectives. This shift does not cancel actions of mobility or remove moral-political responsibility, but it does highlight the complex preconditions of mobile action beyond the confines of purposive goal attainment and mobility-fixated technologization of all areas of life. Far from promoting an in-different uncaring attitude 'away", Gelassenheit is a way of releasement of beings *for* their being, of letting beings be in

relation to involved tensions, struggles and conflicts of mobility, includes also 'interrogating who and what is demobilized and remobilized across many different scales, and in what situations mobility or immobility might be desired options, coerced, or paradoxically interconnected (Urry 2007: 25).

As we have seen, developing a poetics of de-touring as a form of 'bounded mobility' requires going beyond both sedentarist petrifying and nomadic liquidizing metaphors and metaphysics of fixity and flow (Cresswell 2006: 25). For approaching such orientation an 'engaged letting-go' might be a proper mediating inter-placing practice for life-worldly experiences and realities. In particular, it might be meaningful to explore how inter-placed movements in the spirit of 'Gelassenheit' give rise to rhythms, forces, atmospheres, affects and materialities (Merriman, 2012). Qualities and findings related to these phenomena may then be better expressed in poetic-narrative forms as embodied apprehensions of events of mobile inter-placing (Brewer and Dourish 2008).

Moving through embodied inter-places in the mode of 'Gelassenheit' recognizes that performative wayfaring and way-finding, as discovering, storied travelling that 'knows as it goes', is lived along open(ing) de-touring lines that are part of an unfolding meshwork (Ingold 2011: 69-70).

Conclusion: Implications, problems and perspectives

This paper has tried to open up and move through an analytical space, taking a conceptual place and movement for exploring a different more processual understanding of mobility. On our journey, we learned about a phenomenology of embodied dimensions and qualities of spacing, placing and moving. Following a relational understanding, place and mobility were interpreted as inter-place and relational movements, thus as media for an in-between towards more responsive and responsible practices in relation to mobility. Finally, de-touring was presented as an alternative concept metaphor and concept for inter-placed

---

their being that is not framed in regimes of hyper-mobility. As a comportment it is not an obscure mystic state, but a form of qualifying a nexus of knowing-doing that renders a different relationship to things and mobilities than the appropriating and perfectionising logic of calculation, super-conductivity, measurement, and quantification and its enframing. Similar like the art of practical wisdom (Küpers 2013), 'Gelassenheit' challenges the neo-liberal notion of the hyper-mobile functioning of business, organization and management, while inviting for a proto-ethical culture of 'poietic praxis' and artistry of living more sustainable. As such 'Gelassenheit' is not only an individual suspension of activity, but as a moratorium it can contribute to an agreed postponement, a collective and legally authorized period to reflective delay or active waiting, increasingly important as the emergency and urgency of the socio-ecological crises will amplify.

mobility and an ethos of engaged' letting-go' as 'Gelassenheit' was presented that may contribute to more responsive and responsible orientations of touring and forms of sustainable mobility.

By way of conclusion, some open questions and perspectives will now be raised, in particular with regard to the possibilities of replacing and 're-locating' research and its conventional focus and epistemological locations in relation to space and mobility. This will be followed by a critical discussion of emerging problems and implications.

If a discipline organizes an analytical space (Foucault 1977: 143), a more multi-, inter- and transdisciplinary as well as meta-paradigmatic journey will be important. Through such cross-disciplinary journeys, research can break the largely univocal narrative and open up to multiple and innovative knowledge and methodological places. This also implies approaching spaces and places, as well as, corresponding mobilities from first, second and third-person perspectives with its singular and plural modes of action-inquiry (Torbert et al. 2004).

Methodologically, for investigating spaces, inter-places and movements, there is a need for shifting from a way of knowing by 'looking at' to a way of knowing by being placed, that is, 'in contact, or in touch with... the adoption of an involved rather than an external uninvolved standpoint' (Shotter 1993: 20). This also implies focusing on the relationally placed social and systemic environment of touring and what this 'allows' or 'permits'. Furthermore, instead of taking isolated observational stances, starting points of reflection emphasizing negotiated procedures and local embedment in everyday-life and locally constituted situations or circumstances of touring becomes vital. From a broader perspective, the very nature of increased touring would probably generate simultaneously, a greater need for specific embodied meeting places and personal contacts (Thrift 1996). In other words, the expectable rising preoccupation of touring and its implications will most likely bring about longings for re-embodied emplacement and moves.

However, there are possible dangers involved in 're-idealising' embodied place and touring movement. One problem of re-embodied place and movement is the menace of falling into a kind of retro-romantic holism, that is, longing for an idyllic pre-personal place and way of life or pre-modern forms of moving. Narrowly restricted in scope or outlook, provincial, retrogressive and nostalgic re-enchantments, revived pastoral myths and provincial attitudes revert into pre-modern parochial place and moves. These forms of organizing are subject to historical regression. The yearning for a simplified tribal life in closer proximity to and slowed moves cannot be an adequate response to the complexities in modern and postmodern worlds or generate critical options for other ways of organizing and living. Therefore, it will be important not to substantialize or essentialize space, place and the body or (de-)touring movement, as this would lead to an abstraction of subtleties and dynamics involved. Instead of looking for metaphysical centers or positions as unified entities of embodied places and movements, a more suitable orientation would be to focus on relationality and the processual relationships between them.

The following list includes open questions and issues that are relevant in this vast research field.

How do we describe adequately the dynamic, embodied placing of post-industrial mobile touring that is situated and moving between closeness and distance, immediacy and tele-presences? Accordingly, research is called to explore touring practices that require them to be able to oscillate between locating and dislocating, placement and displacement while shifting boundaries of meanings?

How could we deconstruct this inter-placed movement of touring in a way that offers a housing habitation that is orientating and organizing for stable and secure-settling and at the same time, a disturbing 'dis-habitualization' that is disorientating or dis-organizing; which invites flexible practices while unsettles creatively?

For approaching this orientation, research needs to consider not only physical movement of objects, embodied touring and mobility of people, but also imaginative, virtual and communicative forms (Urry 2007) that are enabling or coercing them to live more 'mobile lives' (Elliott and Urry 2010). It is also important to consider: how we could develop an understanding of inter-spheres of touring, where 'pleasures of space' (Tschumi 1994: 84) and movements can be experienced, without which these become forms of unsustainable consumption.

How do we organize these 'inter-worlds' in a way to ensure responsive and responsible forms that not only satisfy consumption and economical viable, but are also at the same time environmentally and socially sustainable?

How can we consider not only corporeal travel of people and the physical movement of objects, but also imaginative travel, virtual travel and communicative travel (Urry 2007), enabling and coercing (some) people to live more 'mobile lives' (Elliott and Urry 2010)?

What about intermediaries and hybrid 'inter-embodiments' involved in touring, those sociotechnical assemblages or human/material hybrids that perform or are 'actants' as mobile systems and support specific mobility regimes (Dodge and Kitchin 2011)? What are possible effects of 'intersecting mobilities' on professional relations, commitments, attachments and (dis)identifications, for example, service providers and consumers or other stakeholders? What would 'bounded mobilities' and issues of in- and exclusions, inequalities and power-asymmetries that are accompanying demands of societal mobility imply?

Overall, what is needed is a political economy of touring that reflects critically the relation between local and global 'power-geometries' (Massey 1993), that is a politics and poetics of mobility (Adey 2013; Creswell 2012; Cresswell and Merriman 2011). As mobility is a resource to which not everyone has an equal relationship' (Skeggs 2004: 49), we need to explore power relations and dynamics of discourses and practices of mobility in creating effects of both movement and stasis, and uneven distribution of 'network capital' (Elliott and Urry 2010) or different capacities for socio-spatial motility (Kaufmann et al, 2004: 750).

Finally, how can the outlined ethos of mindfully engaged 'Gelassenheit' be enacted in our high-paced world, a world that seems unable to find time for the same? Even more so, how can engaged releasement be connected to a practical wisdom of touring and de-touring? If places and mobilities are the very contexts for embodied participation with the phenomenal, ecological, social and cultural world, then what we know and do is also shaped by the kinds of places and moves which we are experiencing or are mediated by. Therefore, the quality of a reawakened attention given to places and a mindful reengagement with them by a sensuous and body-conscious orientation and like-wise, a focus on more mindful movements becomes vital. Considering the 'political life of embodied sensation' (Panagia 2009) and reconfiguration of the share of the sensible (Rancière 2004; 2010) that defines emplacement, mobilities can contest hierarchical and exclusionary distributions, while being allowed to imagine other forms of arrangements of movement and performative practices (Spicer et al. 2009: 545-554). Not integrating socio-ethico-political dimensions enfleshed (Beasley and Bacchi 2007) and a lack of a more mindful mobility does not only impoverish human and non-human life with its materio-socio-cultural and ecological realities. It also conceals from viewing the correspondence between ideology and politics in relation to body, place and mobility, and potentially leads to biological and cultural extinctions (Gruenewald 2003).

As we have seen, reconsidering places, bodies and movement as performative mobility as well as forms of de- and re-touring, and what is happening in-between them are full of possibilities and calls for different practices. Hopefully, the ideas and discussions 'placed' here would inspire some affective and thinking moves for further exploring territories of the unknown by entering and de-+-touring into realms of embodied, movements through inter-places in a well-understood and enacted spirit of 'Gelassenheit'.

References

Adey, P. (2010): Mobility. London: Routledge.

Adey, P. (2013): Mobilities: Politics, practices, places. In: Cloke, P., Crang, P. and Goodwin, M. (eds.): Introducing human geographies. New York: Routledge, 791-805.

Alvesson, M., Hardy, C. and Harley, B. (2008): Reflecting on reflexivity: Reflexive textual practices in organization and management theory. In: Journal of Management Studies, 45(3), 480-501.

Atkinson, D. (2008): Dancing 'the management': On social presence, rhythm and finding common purpose. In: Management Decision, 46(7), 1081-1095.

Augé, M. (1995): Non-Places: Introduction to an anthropology of supermodernity. London and New York: Verso.

Bærenholdt, J. and Granås, B. (2008): Introduction, places and mobilities beyond the periphery. In: Bærenholdt, J. and Granås, B. (eds.): Mobility and place: Enacting Northern European peripheries. Farnham, Surrey: Ashgate, 18-28.

Beasley, C. and Bacchi, C. (2007): Envisaging a new politics for an ethical future: Beyond trust, care and generosity – towards an ethic of 'social flesh'. In: Feminist Theory, 8, 279-298.

Blumenberg, H. (1996): Shipwreck with spectator: Paradigm of a metaphor for existence. Cambridge: MIT Press.

Braidotti, R (2013): The Posthuman. Cambridge: Polity Press.

Braidotti, R. (2006): Transpositions: On nomadic ethics. Cambridge: Polity Press.

Brewer, J. and Dourish, P. (2008): Storied spaces: Cultural accounts of mobility, technology, and environmental knowing. In: International Journal of Human-Computer Studies, 66, 963-976.

Burrell, G. and Dale, K. (2003): Building better worlds? Architecture, space and organisation, M. Alvesson and H. Willmott (Eds.): Critical management studies, London: Sage, 177-96.

Casey, E. (1993): Getting back into place: Toward a renewed understanding of the place-world. Bloomington, IN: University of Indiana Press.

Casey, E.S. (1996): How to get from space to place in a fairly short stretch of time. In Feld, S and Basso, K.H. (eds.): Senses of place. Santa Fé: School of American Research Press, 13-52.

Castells, M. (2000): The rise of the network society. New York: Blackwell Publishing.

Chaney, D. (1996): Lifestyles. London: Routledge.

Chanlat, J.F. (2006): Space, organization and management thinking: A socio-historical perspective. Clegg, S. and Kornberger, M. (eds): Space, organization and management theory. Copenhagen: Copenhagen Business School Press, 17-43.

Chia, R. (2014): Reflections: In praise of silent transformation: Allowing change through 'letting happen'. In: Journal of Change Management, 14(1), 8-27.

Chia, R., and Holt, R. (2009): Strategy without design: The silent efficacy of indirect action. Cambridge: Cambridge University Press.

Chia, R., Holt, R. and Li, Y. (2013): In praise of strategic indirection: Towards a non-instrumental understanding of phronésis as practical wisdom. In: Thompson, M. and

Bevan, D. (eds.): Wise management in organizational complexity. Houndmills, Basingstoke: Palgrave Macmillan, 53-67.
Conway, D. and Timms, B. (2010): Re-branding alternative tourism in the Caribbean: The case for 'slow tourism'. In: Journal of Tourism and Hospitality Research, 12, 1-16.
Conway, D. and Timms, B. (2012): Are slow travel and slow tourism misfits, compadres or different genres? In: Tourism Recreation Research, 37(1), 71-76.
Costas, J. (2013): Problematizing mobility: A metaphor of stickiness, non-places and the kinetic elite. In: Organization Studies, 34(10), 1467-1485.
Crampton, C. (2001): The mutual knowledge problem and its consequences for dispersed collaboration. In: Organisation Science, 12(3), 346-71.
Cresswell, T. (2006): On the move: Mobility in the modern Western World. London: Routledge.
Cresswell, T. (2010): 'Towards a politics of mobility. In: Environment and Planning D: Society and Space 28(1): 17-31.
Cresswell, T. (2012): Towards a politics of mobility. In: Hvattum, M. and Larsen, J. (eds.), Routes, Roads and Landscapes. Farnham: Ashgate. 163-178.
Cresswell, T. and Merriman, P. (2011): Introduction: Geographies of mobilities – practices, spaces, subjects. In: Cresswell, T. and Merriman, P. (eds.): Geographies of mobilities: Practices, spaces, subjects. Farnham: Ashgate Publishing Limited, 1-15.
Crossley, N. (1996): Intersubjectivity: The fabric of social becoming. London: Sage.
Crossley, N. (2001): The social body: Habit, identity, and desire. London: Sage.
Crossley, N. (2006): Reflexive embodiment in contemporary society. Buckingham: Open University Press.
Dale, K. and Burrell, G. (2008): The spaces of organization and the organisation of space: Power, identity and materiality at work. Houndmills, Basingstoke: Palgrave Macmillan.
Dale, K. (2005): Building a social materiality: spatial and embodied politics in organizational control. In: Organization, 12(5), 649-678.
Dalle Pezze, B. (2006): Heidegger on Gelassenheit Minerva – An Internet Journal of Philosophy 10, 94-122.
Dasgupta, S. (2013): Detours, delays, derailments: La Petite Jérusalem and slow training in culture. In: C. Lindner and A. Hussey (eds.), Paris-Amsterdam underground: essays on cultural resistance, subversion, and diversion. Amsterdam: Amsterdam University Press, 65-75.
de Certeau, M. (1984): The practice of everyday life. Berkeley: University of California Press.
Deleuze, G. (2006): The Fold: Leibniz and the Baroque, trans. T Conley. London: Continuum.
Deleuze, G. and Guattari, F. (1987): A Thousand Plateaus: Capitalism and schizophrenia, trans. Massumi, B. London: Athlone Press.
Derrida, J. (1978): Writing and difference, tr. A. Bass. London: Routledge.
Dumreicher, H. and Kolb, B. (2008): Place as a social space: Fields of encounter relating to the local sustainability process. In: Journal of Environmental Management 87, 317-328.
Elliott, A. and Urry, J. (2010): Mobile lives. New York, NY: Routledge.

Etlin R.A. (1997): Space, stone, and spirit: The meaning of place. In. Golding, S. (ed.): The eight technologies of otherness. London: Routledge, 306-19.

Foucault, M. (1977): Discipline and punish. London: Allen Lane.

Foucault, M. (1984): 'Des espaces autres' [Different Spaces]. In: Architecture, Mouvement, Continuité, 5, 46-49.

Foucault, M. (1986): Of other spaces. In: Diacritics, 16, 22-27.

Gendlin, E.T. (1997): The responsive order: A new empiricism. In: Man and World, 30(3), 383-411.

Geser, H. (2004): Towards a sociological theory of the mobile phone. Swiss Online Publications. http://socio.ch/mobile/t_geser1.htm.

Gieryn, T.F. (2000): A space for place in sociology. In: Annual Review of Sociology, 26, 463-496.

Gössling, S., Hall, C.M. and Weaver, D. (eds): (2009): Sustainable tourism futures: Perspectives on systems, restructuring and innovations. New York: Routledge.

Gruenewald, D.A. (2003): Foundations of place: A multidisciplinary framework for place-conscious education source. In: American Educational Research Journal, 40(3) 619-654.

Hall, C.M. (2009): Degrowing tourism: Décroissance, sustainable consumption and steady-state tourism. In: Anatolia: An International Journal of Tourism and Hospitality Research, 20(1), 46-61.

Hall, C.M. (2010): Changing paradigms and global change: From sustainable to steady-state tourism. In: Tourism Recreation Research, 35(2), 131-145.

Hansen, H., Ropo, A. and Sauer, E. (2007): Aesthetic leadership. In: The Leadership Quarterly, 18(6), 544-560.

Hansen, N.V. (2004): Where do spacing and timing happen? Two movements in the loss of cosmological innocence. In: Organization, 11(6), 759-72.

Harvey, D, (1996): Justice, nature and the geography of difference. Cambridge: Blackwell.

Heidegger, M. (1993): The question concerning technology. In: Heidegger, M. (ed.): Basic Writings. New York: Harper Collins, 307-342.

Higham, J., Cohen, S.A., Peeters, P. and Gössling, S. (2013): Psychological and behavioural approaches to understanding and governing sustainable mobility. In: Journal of Sustainable Tourism, 21(7), 949-967.

Hillier, B. and Hanson, J. (1984): The social logic of space. Cambridge: Cambridge University Press.

Hopkins, N. and Dixon, J.A. (2006): Space, place and political psychology. In: Political Psychology, 27, 173-185.

Howard, C. and Küpers, W. (2014): Somewhere between everywhere and no-where – Traveling as Embodied and Inter-Placed 'Be(com)ing' in the age of digital Ge-stell, In: Special issue Nomadism and Organising, Scripta Nova (Spanish translation, forthcoming).

Ingold, T. (2000): The perception of the environment: Essays on livelihood, dwelling and skill. London: Routledge.

Ingold, T. (2011): Being alive: Essays on movement, knowledge and description. London: Routledge.

Jensen, O.B. (2012): Flows of meaning, cultures of movement: Urban mobility as meaningful everyday life practice. In: Mobilities, 4(1), 139-158.

Joas, H. (1996): The creativity of action. Chicago: The University of Chicago Press.

Johnston, L. (2001): (Other): bodies and tourism studies. In: Annals of Tourism Research, 28(1), 180-201.

Jones, G., McLean, C. and Quattrone, P. (2004): spacing and timing. In: Organization, 11(6), 723-741.

Jullien, F. (2000): Detour and access: Strategies of meaning in China and Greece. New York: Zone Books.

Kaufmann, V., Bergman, M.M. and Joye, D. (2004): Motility: Mobility as capital. In: International Journal of Urban and Regional Research, 28(4), 745-756.

Kirkman, B., Rosen, B. Gibson, C., Tesluk, P. and McPherson, S. (2002): Five challenges to virtual team success. In: Academy of Management Executive, 16, 67-79.

Knights, D. (1992): Changing spaces: The disruptive impact of a new epistemological location for the study of management. In: Academy of Management Review, 17, 514-536.

Küpers, W. (2002): Phenomenology of aesthetic organising: Ways towards aesthetically responsive organisations. In: Consumption, Markets & Cultures, 5(1) 31-68.

Küpers, W. (2010): Inter-Places – Embodied spaces and places of and for leader-/followership: Phenomenological perspectives on relational localities and tele-presences of leading and following. In: Environment, Space, Place , 2(1), 79-121.

Küpers, W. (2011): Dancing on the limen – Embodied and creative inter-place as thresholds of be(com)ing: Phenomenological perspectives on liminality and transitional spaces in organisations. In: Tamara, Journal for Critical Organization Inquiry, 9(3-4), 45-59.

Küpers, W. (2011a): Integral responsibilities for a responsive and sustainable practice in organizations and management. In: Corporate Social Responsibility and Environmental Management Journal, 18(3), 137-150.

Küpers, W. (2011b): Trans-+-Form – Transforming transformational leadership for a creative change practice. In: Leadership and Organization Development Journal, 32(1), 20-40.

Küpers, W. (2012): Embodied transformative metaphors and narratives in organisational life-worlds of change. In: Journal of Organizational Change Management, 26(3), 494-528.

Küpers, W. (2013): The art of practical wisdom: Phenomenology of an embodied, wise inter-practice in organisation and leadership. In: Küpers, W. and Pauleen, D. (2013): A handbook of practical wisdom: Leadership, organization and integral business practice. Imprint: London: Ashgate Gower, 19-45.

Küpers, W. (2014): To be physical is to 'inter-be-come': Beyond empiricism and idealism towards embodied leadership that matters. In: Ladkin, D. and Taylor, S. (2014): 'Physicality of leadership' gesture, entanglement, taboo, possibilities. London: Emerald.

Küpers, W. (2015): Returning forward to Embodied 'non-+-human' 'and materio~socio~cultural intra- and inter-practices in and beyond organization. In:

Michaelis, B. and Zierold, M. (eds): The re/turn of the nonhuman in the study of culture concepts – concerns – challenges, (forthcoming).
Lefebvre, H. (1991): The production of space. Oxford: Basil Blackwell.
Levett, R., Christie, I., Jacobs, M., Therivel, R. and Fabian Society (2003): A better Choice of Choice: Quality of Life, Consumption and Economic Growth. London: Fabian Society.
Malpas, J.E. (1999): Place and experience: A philosophical topography. Cambridge: Cambridge University Press.
Massey, D. (1993): Power-geometry and a progressive sense of place. In: Bird, J., Curtis, B., Putnam, T., Robertson, G. and Tickner, L. (eds.): Mapping the futures: Local cultures, global change. London: Routledge, 59-69.
Massey, D. (1998): A global sense of place. In: Massey, D. (ed.): Space, place and gender. Oxford: Oxford University Press, 146-156.
Massey, D. (2005): For space. London: Sage.
Merleau-Ponty, M. (1995): The visible and the invisible. Evanston: Northwestern University Press.
Merleau-Ponty, M. (2012): Phenomenology of perception. London: Routledge.
Merriman, P. (2012): Mobility, space and culture. London: Routledge.
Panagia, D. (2009): The political life of sensation. Durham, NC: Duke University Press.
Pellegrino, G. (2011): Introduction: Studying (im)mobility through a politics of proxymity. In: Pellegrino, G. (ed.): The politics of proximity mobility and immobility in practice. Aldershot: Ashgate, 1-14
Rancière, J. (2004): The politics of aesthetics: The distribution of the sensible. London: Continuum.
Rancière, J. (2010): Dissensus: On politics and aesthetics. London: Continuum.
Roya, S. and Hannam, K. (2013): Embodying the mobilities of the Darjeeling Himalayan Railway. In: Mobilities, 1-15.
Sack, R. (1997): Homo Geographicus: A framework for action, awareness, and moral concern. Baltimore: The Johns Hopkins University Press.
Skeggs, B. (2004): Class, self, culture. London: Routledge.
Sheller, M. and Urry, J. (2006): The new mobilities paradigm. In: Environment and Planning, 38(2), 207- 226.
Shotter, J. (1993): Cultural politics of everyday life: Social constructionism, rhetoric, and knowing of the third kind. Milton Keynes: Open University Press.
Soja, E.W. (1996): Thirdspace: Journeys to Los Angeles and other real-and-imagined places. Oxford: Blackwell.
Spicer, A., Alvesson, M. and Kärreman, D. (2009): Critical performativity: The unfinished business of critical management studies. In: Human Relations. 62(4), 537-560.
Thrift, N. (1996): Spatial formations. London: Sage.
Todres, L and Galvin, K.T. (2010): Dwelling-mobility: An existential theory of well-being. In: International Journal of Qualitative Studies on Health and Well-being, 5(3), 1-65
Tschumi, B. (1994): Architecture and disjunction. Cambridge: MIT Press.

Tuan, Y.F. (1977): Space and place: The perspective of experience. Minneapolis, MN: University of Minnesota Press.

Urry, J. (2007): Mobilities. Cambridge: Polity Press.

Woehler, K. (2004): The rediscovery of slowness, or leisure time as one's own and as self-aggrandizement? In: Weiermair, K. and Mathies, C. (eds.): The tourism and leisure industry: Shaping the future. New York, London, and Oxford: The Haworth Hospitality Press, 83-92.

Developing Branding Strategies based on Automatic Behavioural System for Mega Event Tourism, The Olympics

Erica Liu

Introduction

When planning for mega event tourism such as the Olympics, cities reorder public spaces and arenas often with a long term vision, legacy. This vision expresses the role of the event in achieving the desired future and goals of the hosting city. The planning process involves not only animating the city for staged spectacles; but also rebranding the city and managing how tourism is consumed - the planned and unplanned experience of consumption. Leisure motivated event tourists are seeking unique, personal and socially rewarding experiences (Getz 2010). These experiences may be managed through the context in which people act. By altering the context, people's experience of the event changes; hence the perception of the host city may also change.

This paper aims to explore branding design strategies for mega events that were based on the behavioural pattern of audiences and the contexts surround it. MINDSPACE theory (an acronym of nine influences - messenger, incentive, norms, default, salience, priming, affect, commitment and ego) was used as a tool to understand how people may react to different influences. Each influence will be explored with precedent studies. Branding strategies was then developed and proposed to a case study. The motivation of the branding strategies was to focus on creating experience that was coherent with the expectation of people. It was not intended to change people's behaviour, nor to question the moral aspect of the practice.

People do not act solely on rational factors such as facts and figures; but on a mixture of rational and irrational factors such as personal experience, emotion, and other fallible reasons (Ariely 2008). People react to surroundings with two thinking systems – reflective and automatic; usually a mix of both (Thaler and Sunstein 2008: 22). We tend to believe that people behave in a certain way because of conscious decisions or habits. However, research has shown that at least 80% of the factors influencing behaviour do not result from knowledge or awareness (Kollmuss and Agyeman 2002). The context or the environmental impact on people's behaviour is far stronger than expected. There is a direct link between habits and environmental context. Habits are "behavioural dispositions to repeat well-practiced actions given recurring circumstances" (Wood et al. 2005: 918). Generally speaking, habits can be developed through taking the same action repeatedly when encountering the same context. Hence, by presenting a similar context, habits could be triggered into action without the person's knowledge or awareness, i.e. automatic system. With a basic understanding of this logic, habits hypothetically could be influenced through altering the context; this 'automatic system' could then be harnessed and developed into different brand experience for mega events.

This paper will focus on the automatic system because it is applicable to most people regardless of their background. Although there is a strong connection between people's view and their behaviour, an automatic behavioural system operates according to the context of events rather than the backgrounds of people. Developing branding strategies that only deal with automatic behaviour system is particularly important when a city is hosting mega events, when audiences usually come from a multitude of backgrounds. MINDSPACE theory was chosen because it operates solely on the automatic behavioural system. It is a checklist of influences on people's behaviour for use when making policy (Dolan et al. 2009); it has been tested and applied in governmental policy making. The theory will be used as a basis of developing a set of branding strategies for mega events. It provides a tool for enhancement and assessment. Precedents such as the previous Olympic Games will be used as examples of how the branding strategies may work and what risks the strategies may carry.

The problems of hosting mega events

Mega events with global audiences and high expectations put tremendous pressure on their host cities. The city has to come up with compelling narratives to win the bid to host the event. It takes years and considerable resources to materialize these narratives. The New York Times reported that the 1992 Barcelona Games left Spain with a $6.1 billion debt; Athens estimated that the 2004 Games would cost $1.6 billion, but in the end it was $16 billion; it took Montreal nearly 30 years to pay off the $2.7 billion it owed after the 1976 Summer Games (Lyall 2012: B10). And London 2012 was more than $10 billion over its original estimate (Clark 2012). There seemed to be a repeated pattern of inflated financial projection on potential profit as a result of hosting mega events; under-estimation of the cost and huge public debt occurred. After the excitement and global attention of the events are over, many host cities are then faced with largely redundant mega structures, high maintenance costs, inefficient urban space and transport system, pollution to natural scenic sites and wild life. The financial and environmental benefit of hosting mega events remains debatable. On a social level, hosting mega events often involved urban cleansing. Removing the underprivileged people from and around the event sites criminalized marginal communities (Kumar 2012). These communities are usually ethnic minorities, homeless, prostitutes, small businesses and the poor. Rising real estate prices and monopolies of commercial activities further deepen social inequalities. Civil freedom and democracy tend to be suspended during mega events. Demoralisation and a reduction in confidence of local governance could be a risk to the host cities.

Although the unique opportunities of political, social and cultural benefits are irresistible to many cities, the fundamental issue faced by host cities as pointed out by Perryman (2012:65): "the Games are designed to serve the interests of the IOC (International Olympic Committee) in maintaining and defending their very particular model of the Olympics and not the needs of the host city and nation." The IOC is rarely if ever concerned to find "the most effective methods for integrating Olympic infrastructure needs with the present economy and a vision of its future." Hosting cities of mega events need to be realistic about managing resources and expectations, especially from local communities. Branding strategies may not provide solutions for all the above problems; however, they enable effective communication and promote long term positive impacts in the host cities after the events. They also help designers and planners to make better decisions and provide a cost effective, yet powerful way of implementing the visions or narratives set by the event organiser.

MINDSPACE Theory and precedent studies

The Institute for Government in the UK reviewed behavioural theory and policy making, and developed MINDSPACE theory in 2009 (Dolan et al. 2009). The theory provides a supplemental tool to existing legislation and regulations. The review concluded that there are mainly nine influences (*Figure 1*) that shape people's behaviour, and designed outcomes could be achieved by understanding and creating context around them, in order to trigger the 'automatic system' of people. Based on the nine influences, initial branding strategies have been proposed (*Figure 2*). These strategies were then applied to precedent studies in order to test their strength and weakness.

MINDSPACE	INFLUENCES THAT SHAPE PEOPLE'S BEHAVIOUR
Messenger	We are heavily influenced by who communicates information
Incentive	Our responses to incentives are shaped by predictable mental shortcuts such as strongly avoiding losses
Norms	We are strongly influenced by what others do
Default	We 'go with the flow' of pre-set options
Salience	Our attention is drawn to what is novel and seems relevant to us
Priming	Our acts are often influenced by sub-conscious cues
Affect	Our emotional associations can powerfully shape our actions
Commitment	We seek to be consistent with our public promises, and reciprocate acts
Ego	We act in ways that make us feel better about ourselves

Figure 1: Nine influences of MINDSPACE theory that shape people's behaviour. (Source: Dolan, Hallsworth, Halpern, King, and Vlaev: 2009)

INFLUENCES	PROPOSED INITIAL BRANDING DESIGN STRATEGIES	PRECEDENT STUDIES
Messenger	Employ national heroes	FIFA World Cup, Beijing Olympics 2008
Incentive	Schedule of reusing & opening event facilities to public	London Olympics 2012
Norms	Trendsetting, take leadership role	Sydney Olympics 2000
Default	Provide alternatives	London Olympics 2012
Salience	Create positive memorable highlights	Beijing Olympics 2008, Rio Olympics 2016
Priming	New USPs, promote unfamiliar parts of the city	London Olympics 2012
Affect	Emotional connection with audience through addressing current or recent affairs	FIFA World Cup 2010
Commitment	Highlight sponsors & institution in marketing campaigns	Beijing Olympics 2008
Ego	Promote leadership in global agenda	Beijing Olympics 2008, London Olympics 2012

Figure 2: A summary of proposed branding strategies by the author based on the nine influences that shape people's behavior and precedent studies. (Author)

Messenger

People believe and respond positively with public figures whom they respect, personalities who they can relate to, and certain groups that they are attached to. All of them are very effective as a 'messenger'. Mega event organisers have often attached themselves with local heroes in the hosting countries; not only to promote the events, but also to help improve upon negative aspects of the organiser's image. For example, the 2010 World Cup linked the FIFA figures to iconic South African heroes such as Nelson Mandela and Desmond Tutu. These were very powerful messages and appealed to mass international audiences. Choosing the right figures to represent an event can enhance the occasion; because they symbolise the spirit and the inspiration of the host city and the organisers. Beijing took a different approach in the Olympic Games 2008. The messenger was the authority; the message was that the city was a modern cosmopolitan with a strong culture and people that were able to impact on the world; and the city was comparable to other international Asian cities such as Tokyo, Singapore and Hong Kong. This top down approach was not well received. The branding strategy of the Beijing 2008 Olympic Games has been criticised as "selective story telling", which aimed to highlight accomplishments, and to change or minimize negative images and controversial issues that the international community had voiced (Eckstein and Throgmorton 2003). The key point of using a 'messenger' is to build an instant rapport with audiences. Communicated messages need to be consistent and not contradict to observable reality.

Incentives

Host cities often publicise the vision of long term benefit for hosting mega events, such as advancing the position of the host city in the global city hierarchical system (Brownell 2008); through improvement of international relations, enhancement of economic and social capacities, upgrading of international gateway status, and the speeding up of urban redevelopment (Derudder et al. 2003); and creating, publicizing, and consolidating the city's identity through media coverage, tourist visits, public participation and community support (Gold and Gold 2008). However, these visions do not necessarily represent the expectation and perception of citizens. During the Beijing Olympics, "the city government tended to interpret the city's identity and values in accordance with the government's vision and motivation of development. The top down city branding tried to convey the goals that the city authority intended. Nonetheless, the general public often viewed the city with the city's utility functions and their expectations of personal prosperity." (Zhang and Zhao 2009: 253). London and Partners' plans for the 2012 Olympics were to bring in an extra 1.1 million visitors over the period of the Games and subsequent five years, and contribute around £650m to the capital (Jones 2012). Grand long term visions are good but do not necessary amass support from citizens. In economics, "hyperbolic discounting" means people will discount future gains heavily when they are facing immediate sacrifice. There is evidence that the immediacy of reward has an impact on the success of the event (Green et al. 1994). Planners need to acknowledge how the event may benefit the citizen personally within a short period of time, for example, job opportunities, access to better infrastructures and public spaces, reuse of post event facilities and building, etc. Through the 2012 Olympics, London successfully regenerated the east part of the city; there are plans to build 8000 homes around the Olympic Park in addition to the 2800 houses in the athletes' village (Moore 2012); the Stadium has a new tenant, West Ham football club; the thousands of seats in the wings on both sides of the Zaha Hadid designed swimming pool will be reused by schools and other institutions (Dyckhoff and Barrett 2012); the swimming pool will be opened to the public in 2014. The key incentive to win the audiences over was the immediate rewards.

Norms

Planning for mega events can be a two way process. Studying current social norms and network groups provide insight of what may be more appealing to target audiences and end users, design around these social norms enhance the success of the events. At the same time, mega events could also be used as a channel to influence current social norms; and even behavioural changes in organisations. Instead of building in a location with natural scenic spots, Sydney introduced the trend to locate Olympic venues in former toxic sites such as landfills. The city took the opportunity to clear the land for development and to enable rehabilitation of the environmental hazardous locations (Preuss 2004).

Attempts to create norms as a strategy alone may not be effective. Combining norms with the right messenger, such as social media and popular network groups, as well as ego – nation pride, could influence the behaviour of a community, although the longevity of such influence still needs further research. In anticipation of the 2008 Beijing Olympics and the Shanghai World Expo 2010, the Chinese Government launched a campaign "calling for increased levels of culture and civilization." (Yardley 2007). The Chinese authorities tried to change some of the negative social norms such as spitting, swearing, and inappropriate attire in public places. Similar campaigns were launched before the London Olympics. These campaigns were a combination of norms, incentive (fines and rewards) and messenger (celebrities). The campaign has yet to prove its effectiveness; its success depends on the continued efforts and persistence of the authorities.

Salience

Unusual and unforgettable experiences have a strong impact on people's memory in comparison with consistent experiences; because memory tends to be made up of important and intense moments, as well as self-reflection on a series of events. Mega events are a mass mobilisation exercise, involving public and private sectors, volunteers and community involvement in preparation and supporting the events. These activities are a collection of individual and group memorable moments; a collective memory that can be combined with 'messenger' to leave a stronger impact to host cities. Mega events are full of unforgettable positive experience; which can be accumulated into a lasting positive collective memory. However, there are also likely negative outcomes; staging mega events involves reordering public spaces and transportation routes; in some case, relocating communities (Kumar 2012). These changes cause inconvenience, traumatisation or even public upheaval among citizens. Introducing new elements in built environments can cause distress and negative experience. Although in hosting mega events such as the Olympics, democratic systems tend to give way temporarily to enable authorities to orchestrate the event, planners need to consider the long-term impact of the Games on the collective memory of citizens. How would they like the Games to be remembered? Will the citizens understand the Games as an occasion of celebration and national pride; or as an opportunity for the authorities to pursue the gentrification of the city and to expand the terrain of profitable activities (Harvey 2008).

Take 1992 Barcelona Olympics as an example, the city went through significant urban restructuring to host the mega event. A two-mile beachfront and marina were created by demolishing industrial buildings on the waterfront before the games. The city had little media attention prior to the event. Through hosting the event, its culture, people and architecture impressed and changed how people thought about the city and the country as a whole. Between 1990 and 2001 Spain went from being the 11th "best country" in Europe to the 6th; and Barcelona is now the 12th most popular city destination for tourists in the world, and 5th in Europe (IOC 2012: 5). Nevertheless, the cost was high - between the period from 1986, when the city won the bid to host the Games, to 1993, 2,500 citizens were evicted from homes, housing prices rose 139% for sale and 145% for rentals, the availability of public housing was decreased by 76%, and over 90% of Roma population was displaced in areas surrounding the Olympic Village site (COHRE 2007; 2008: 2).

The choices offered in terms of compensation and spatial arrangement may relieve part of the negative experience; for example, alternative relocation and supports for affected communities, financial compensation, novelty in design (green building, sustainability), clarity in spatial order (accessibility), and effective project management (site management, financial management, provision of temporary public transport routes and structures during construction). These proposed solutions may be insufficient to solve the vast problem. Urban cleansing of the working class, social displacement and unjustified public spending will leave a negative imprint in the citizen's long term memory of the event. Planners need to ask an important question – how would they like the event to be remembered?

Priming

London being already a well-known international city is different from Barcelona; when hosting the Olympics in 2012 the city needed to employ different tactics. All the unique selling points and major landmarks were already familiar to the international media and tourist, how else could the city brand itself for the mega event? Through imagination, feelings and judgement, people translate their perceptions into their own understandable identity of a city. Priming the audiences in a different way could provide a new perspective on a familiar subject. Priming means people's subsequent behaviour can be manipulated by exposing them to certain cues; these cues could be certain sights, words etc. Priming is different from memory and experience; it leads people to act outside their conscious awareness. By using priming, host cities of mega events can prepare the audiences mind to accept interpretation of the city vision and identity that may be different from their conscious perception. A city usually has certain identifiable images or core values. For example, Paris is perceived for romance, Milan for style, New York for diversity and dynamics, Washington for power, and Tokyo for modernity (Smidt-Jensen 2006). London, with its previous failed city branding as the "Cool Britannia" in the 1990s, marketed itself carefully as an inclusive multi-faceted society that encourages adventure, contradictions and juxtaposition. The city mayor Boris Johnson described London as "a cacophony of noise"; and Ritterband explained: "people go to New York to become a New Yorker; people come here to be themselves. Anything can blossom in London and everything is encouraged in London." (quoted in Jones 2012). With this vision, the city engaged audiences with over five hundred social, cultural, business and entertainment events, hoping to expose the media and audiences to different parts of the city which they were not familiar with; and to experience a "different" London. Developing a formerly deprived location, East London, which was unfamiliar to the media and tourist, provided opportunities for them to discover and to experience London in a different context.

Affect

Emotional branding is about creating a connection between the brand and the audience emotionally; which could turn a mega event into a lasting legacy. Affect as the act of experiencing emotion is a powerful element in the automatic system. It can be rapid and intuitive, sometimes people can react based on an emotion before they realise what they are reacting to. Words, images and events can trigger emotional responses. Mega events provide an opportunity to generate emotional responses and engagement with global communities. The emotional response of global audiences and media is usually high immediately after historical events, including traumatic ones such as wars. Capturing the momentum of this emotion and presenting audiences with a positive hope for the future is the key to creating a legacy. Former Axis power countries had hosted the Olympics to signify conciliation and rehabilitation – Rome 1960, Tokyo 1964, Munich 1972. The 1995 Rugby World Cup in South Africa and the 1998 FIFA World Cup in France signified social changes and a symbolic unity in dividing communities. Generating and capturing the public emotion, then applying it to the branding and planning of mega events required a subtle but clear approach. Combining salience and messenger with affect will provide a more effective strategy. The Rugby World Cup 1995 in South Africa took place one year after the democratic government set up in the racially divided country. President Nelson Mandela wore a Springbok team jersey with white Captain Francois Pienaar's number six on it and presented him with the champion trophy; which was perceived as the beginning of reconciliation and breaking down of discrimination (Baade and Matheson 2004).

Commitments

Planning a mega event needs active support and involvement from government officials and citizens. The making of public commitments increases the likelihood of them being fulfilled; because breaking the commitment will lead to reputational damage. During the FIFA World Cup 1995, South Africa launched event ambassador programmes when prominent city officials, high profiled business leaders committed publicly to lead various committees and initiatives for the event. The event enjoyed great success and was well received by the public. The Chinese Government made a public commitment to make Beijing 2008 the "Green Olympic", with the air in Beijing city as clean and fresh as that of Paris by 2008. In the months running up to the event, all factories in the city were ordered to stop production; private transportation was restricted; scientists tried to force rain through technological intervention and conducted many experiments in order to clean up one of the most polluted cities in the world. The promise was fulfilled with the air quality of Beijing improved by 30%. Although studies showed the longevity of the commitments varies with the political context in which they were made (Chen et al. 2011), the delivery of them was likely to happen when these commitments were made in public.

Ego

People tend to behave in a way that gives the impression of a positive self-image. It is even more important when a host city is under intense attention from international media and other countries. Many developing countries have used mega events to announce their "coming of age"; and to make a statement of national identity. This egotistic approach has often led to iconic buildings, gigantism and high costs. However, this ego approach could be turned into something positive when managed properly. Mega events can be used to promote global citizenship. Being good global citizens means considering the impact on the environment when building for mega events. Appealing to the citizen's self-image and national pride, and providing physical structures that citizens are proud of, brings out the best impact on the events. Planning for mega events is no longer about gigantism and excessiveness; but being unique, special and memorable. When the 2008 Beijing Olympics overwhelmed global audiences in terms of scales; the 2012 London Olympics did not attempt to overdo Beijing, but to promote a more responsible attitude. The principles of planning design were to build responsibly and sustainably. The London Olympics created affordable and adaptable structures that minimised waste. The main stadium was a compact lightweight structure that was designed for dismantling; it used a quarter of the steel used in Beijing's stadium; 98% of the materials from building demolished in the Olympic Park have been reused and recycled (Smith 2012). The economic and the wise use of resources for the mega event has been widely praised by the media and supported by the citizens and environmental groups. This responsible approach also set a positive example for future hosts of mega events. A successful event needs not to be bigger and better than others; intelligent use of limited resources and modern building methods and technologies are more desirable under current environmental and economic context.

Branding strategies re-think

From the precedent studies, each of the nine influences carried potential weakness. For instance, employing national heros to promote the event may build a relation with the audience; however, the strategy on its own may not be sufficient. By supplementing the strategy with other influences such as affect – selecting a national hero who has connection with recent social issues; and norms – to set a positive example or even a new trend; will maximise the impact of the combined strategies. (*Figure 3*)

INFLUENCES	PROS	CONS	SUPPLEMENT
Messenger	Build a relation with audience	Insufficient on its own	Affect
Incentive	Effective mass mobilisation	Risk of unable to materialise	Commitment
Norms	Challenge existing norms, start new ones	Accept bad practice without judgement	Ego, priming, messenger
Default	A quick way to control result	Top down approach	Non applicable
Salience	Create memorable snapshots	Negative experience impacts on overall perception	Priming
Priming	Accept new perspective	Ethical issue	Salience
Affect	Emotional connection	Risk of contradiction to observable reality	Messenger, ego
Commitment	High probability of promises being fulfilled	Risk of reputational damage	Ego
Ego	Promote nation pride, global citizenship	Prejudice, discrimination	Salience

Figure 3: The strength and weakness of the proposed strategies based on the nine influences. And the proposed supplement strategies from the author. (Author)

Cognitive dissonance theory states that if people experience a contradiction between their attitudes and their behaviour, they change their attitudes so they are consistent with their behaviour (Festinger 1957). In other words, to change people's behaviour, it is their attitudes that should be changed first. Nevertheless, the branding strategies proposed work the other way round. They seek to create experiences that would make subtle influences to behaviour; and a collection of such experience would lead to subsequent change in attitudes and perception without conscious awareness. Through the branded experience, visitors and audiences of the mega event may develop a more positive perception of the Olympic brand and with the host cities. The proposed strategies are a generic place branding model developed from the study of automatic human behaviour triggered by contexts. The model will be further optimised into a more coherent and user-friendly version. Also it needs to be tested on a case study with consideration of the regional context.

Case Study

Tokyo has been chosen as a case study because it successfully won the bid for the 2020 Olympic Games; also the city's historical relationship with the Games provides an interesting study of the changes in the city's branding direction. Tokyo was the first non-Western city to win a bid for the Olympic Games. In fact, the city had won the bid twice previously but only hosted the Games once. The city withdrew from hosting the Games in 1937, because of the breakout of the Sino-Japanese War; the Games never happened and was later suspended due to the breakout of Second World War. Tokyo, however, was the first to host the Olympic Games in Asia in 1964. Twenty years after the Second World War, Japan was keen to rebuild its image as a peaceful and friendly nation. Through hosting the summer Olympic Games, Japan successfully rebranded itself and re-established its diplomatic position in the global arena. Winning the bid to host the summer Games for the second time in 2020 has increased Japan's soft power; a survey showed its global ranking moved up from sixth in 2012 to fifth place in 2013 (Albert 2013). With a renewed sense of possibilities and a reinvigorated economy, Japan needs to show a positive image that is steadily recovering from the recent tsunami and nuclear plant disasters.

The branding of Tokyo for the Olympic Games from the 1930s to 2014 showed a progression of cultural development and changes in attitude of the nation. The graphic representation of the Games promotional materials for Tokyo Olympics 1940 revealed its military ambition before the Wars. A giant samurai standing in front of the Japanese flag and dwarfing Mount Fuji in one poster; another one showed an angular sculpture of an abstracted soldier behind the text Olympiad Tokyo 1940, and another showed an athlete shadowed by a giant samurai both with raised arm to hail victory; the Olympic logo was discreetly displayed in a corner or on the athlete's vest. The graphic materials were similar to the style of Stenberg's constructivism, which used little colour and sometimes monotone; the portrait was austere and patriotic; the messages were about domination and victory. There was a strong sense of national pride, almost an attitude of aggression. Although the promotional materials showed very basic design skills, the message of the brand was clearly communicated. To Japan, the Games was a symbolic channel to announce to the world that a new power was rising.

In contrast, the marketing materials for the 1964 Tokyo Games were very different. Japan was ready to emerge with a new identity twenty years after being defeated in the Second World War. Post war Japan needed to expand its economy and to do so, it needed the world to regard it as a friend and not a threat. Hosting a sport mega event with intense international attention such as the Olympics gave the country an ideal platform to re-launch itself as a capitalist and democratic country. Much effort was dedicated to the design and branding of the event. The graphic design by Hara Hiromu and Kamekura Yusaku subtly deciphered a continuity of the Japanese traditional visual composition of medieval crests and the geometrical abstraction of modernism. The same approach was also articulated in the architectural design of the Olympic structures. The National Gymnasium by architect Kenzo Tange was a contemporary structure with contemporary materials and building methods, the structure's proportions were wide and flat with giant roofs. The two main spatial masses were connected by wide bridges and well defined open spaces. The spiral-shaped roofs were constructed from two giant sweeping arcs with different radii. Although it was a modernist design; it was also reminiscent of a traditional Japanese pagoda and the shape of Mount Fuji. The Japanese designers found a way to express a harmonious coexistence between past and future; nationalism and internationalism. The juxtaposition of tradition and modernity has continued to be the essence of Japanese culture and design today. The 1964 Tokyo Olympics was a spectacle and set a standard for future hosts of the Games in Asia.

Tokyo is preparing to host the summer Olympic Games for the second time in 2020. Japan is no longer a developing country as it was in 1964. Fifty years have passed and Japan has moved on substantially in both culture and economy. Tokyo has bid for the Olympic Games five times in the past and won three. It is estimated that the city will spend \$5-6 billion for the 2020 Olympics; constructing from new twenty two out of thirty seven venues. The marketing strategies show an enthusiastic and optimistic attitude that focus on the future. The Tokyo

2020 logo was made up of a colourful ring of sakura flower; the slogan was 'Discover Tomorrow'; the mascot has yet to be decided but presumably it will be something similar to the ambassador mascot of the bidding stage, Doraemon the space cat, which has a pocket full of gadgets that provides technological solutions to every problem that its owner encountered. The architecture of main stadium designed by Zaha Hadid also focuses on the futuristic fantasy, although it has little reference to the regional and cultural characteristic. The Japanese public response to hosting the 2020 Games has been a mixed one and mostly negative. An online survey done by the Japan Today website in 2013 showed that 62.5% of respondents opposed hosting the Games. Below are quoted from respondents:

> "most of the investment will be wasted. plus 2020 itself will be a tourist hell."
>
> "the community will end up with a few high maintenance empty facilities to maintain and decades of debts to repay on tax money."
>
> "The homeless will be moved to different areas, people near the venues will have their lives and land disturbed."
>
> "run-down places the Oyaji in charge think nobody wants to visit will continue to decay."
>
> "Tokyo is very unfriendly towards disabled people by means of infrastructure even though they will also host the Paralympics. They will get criticized and, of course, brush it off with something along the lines of 'you do not understand us'."
>
> "They should host the game permanently in Athens."

This opposing sentiment has been unchanged since the bid for the 2016 Games. A survey done by Kietlinski in 2008 (Kietlinski 2011) revealed a split of opinion on hosting the Olympic Games among the Japanese public. The survey concluded that there were three overarching patterns in the attitude of the Japanese people. Firstly, those who object to host the event focus on the pragmatic problems such as financial burden and soaring house prices; and those who support the Games focusing on the symbolic meanings and intangible benefit of the Games such as national pride. Secondly, those who support the Games recognising the potential financial problems; they believe hosting the Games will bring financial benefit in a long run, but they cannot explain how the financial benefit will happen. The vocabulary they used to justify their opinion was very similar to the intensive marketing campaign used in promoting the Games. Those who object to hosting the Games, on the other hand, tended to ignore the intangible benefit. Thirdly, the rhetoric memories of the 1964 Olympics played a part in affecting the opinion of some citizens. Those who supported the Games tended to be over the age of 50 and had experienced the 1964 Games; hosting the Games brought back positive memories and they wished to experience the excitement again. However, the Olympics memories have little effect on the younger Japanese whom most objections came from. Hosting the 2020 Olympic Games in Tokyo continues to generate controversial debates, from whether to build from scratch or renovate old structures for the Games' venues (Kurtenbach 2014), to the social cleansing of Tokyo streets to make way for the Games (Guyatt 2014).

For a successful 2020 Tokyo Olympics, the city not only needs to navigate through many controversial debates; but also uphold the Olympic Charter in promoting 'a peaceful society concerned with the preservation of human dignity', which 'requires mutual understanding with a spirit of friendship, solidarity and fair play' (IOC 2013). Based on the research findings above, the author proposes five branding directions for the event (Figure 4).

Proposed Strategies	Impact 1	Impact 2	Impact 3
Diversity	Accept new perspective (Priming)	A quick way to control result (Default)	Effective mass mobilisation (Incentive)
Redefine Perception	Challenge existing norms, start new ones (Norm)	Create memorable snapshots (Salience)	Accept new perspective (Priming)
Emotional Connection	Emotional Connection (Affect)	Build a relation with audiences (Messenger)	High probability of promises being fulfilled (Commitment)
Global Citizenship	Promote nation pride, global citizenship (Ego)	A quick way to control result (Default)	High probability of promises being fulfilled (Commitment)
Trendsetting	Accept new perspective (Priming)	Create memorable snapshots (Salience)	Challenge existing norms, start new ones (Norm)

Figure 4: Proposed branding directions and the potential impacts based on automatic behavioural responses. (Author)

Diversity

As part of the requirement to host the Olympic Games, host cities need to put in place specific legislation to protect the Games' branding right. For example, London Olympic Games and Paralympic Games Act in 2006 were set up to protect the 2012 Games. The Act aimed to protect the exclusive rights of sponsors, preventing ambush marketing from rival companies, and stop any unauthorised use of any image, footage, graphic, words, etc. that may associate the Olympic brand with any organisations, communities and individuals, for both profit and non-profit purposes. This requirement of the IOC imposed a monopoly on all commercial activities associated with the Games. The sponsors of the Games are usually international giants such as Coca Cola, Adidas and VISA. The monopoly rights allow the visitors no other option but to use the official sponsors in the Olympic venues, whilst also excluding the marketing of local businesses and communities. Local shops and even charities may face prosecution if they use the brand in their commercials and fund raising activities. The civic rights of democracy and freedom of choice of local businesses, communities and consumers are temporarily suspended (Lazzari 2012). Moreover, the exploitation of workers by Olympic sponsors and contractors contradicts the Olympic spirit of respecting human dignity and fair play; such as Coca Cola in India (Mathiason 2006); Adidas in Bangladesh (Chamberlain 2012); toy mascot manufacturers in China for London 2012 (BBC News 2012); and the construction companies for Sochi 2014 (Vasovic and Zuvela 2014). Monopoly sponsorship deals for mega events have done harm to hosting cities. It makes little sense to allow such exclusive dealings on public investment; and protect the monopoly with legislation at the expense of public interest. Monopoly dealings can also be seen as damaging the Olympic brand as they contradict its Charter.

Hosting cities need to make commitments to protect not only the Olympic brand but also the civic rights of the people who work for and consume the brand. Monopoly exclusive rights should be avoided (Default). Diversifying the supply chain and expanding the competition to include minority suppliers and local businesses will ensure that financial dealings for the event are conducted in an unbiased manner. The demographic of local suppliers could be researched and attention paid to minorities and historically under-represented suppliers, to make sure they are justly represented in the procurement process. Financial incentives such as guaranteed bank loans and start-up funds (Incentive) would help smaller businesses to find the necessary capital investment. Tokyo is after all a diverse metropolitan city where both smaller family businesses and global giants thrive in harmony. Visitors to the 2020 Tokyo Games would expect to be able to consume a variety of products supplied by a variety of outlets in the event venues

(Priming), not the exclusive chips from McDonalds as was the case with the London 2012 Games. Suppliers should also have a record of ethical practice, any brands with a history of violation of human rights and causing environmental damage in their operations should be banned from associating with the Olympics. Scrutinizing the suppliers' code of conduct will protect both the Olympics and the Tokyo brands.

Redefine perception

Tokyo is perceived as a global city (Sassen 1991) and a rich city with the highest number of millionaires (Sedghi 2013). However, the problems of social inequality and poverty are increasing. The New York Times reported that "After years of economic stagnation and widening income disparities, this once proudly egalitarian nation is belatedly waking up to the fact that it has a large and growing number of poor people. The Labour Ministry's disclosure in October (2009) that almost one in six Japanese, or 20 million people, lived in poverty in 2007 stunned the nation and ignited a debate over possible remedies that has raged ever since." (Fackler 2010: A6). Hosting a mega event may add strain to the existing problem and further alienate the under-privileged citizen; alternatively, the city could take advantage of this opportunity to alleviate parts of the problems. The event committee decided to spend 31.3% of the $5-6 billion dollars total budget on buildings and venues, it would benefit the city in a long run to channel some of the budget into regenerating economic destitute areas such as Sanya, Adachi and Katsushika, and also promoting the less known parts of Tokyo such as Shimotakaido, Asagaya, Shoto, Jindai and Minowabashi. By doing so, Tokyo 2020 could introduce new narratives and new experiences to the city (Salience, Norm); for example, citizens who previously were unlikely to visit Sanya will have reasons to go there. Encouraging the integration of destitute locations with the rest of the city would change the perception of the citizen towards these areas (Priming); for they will no longer be a 'burden' to the city.

Emotional connection

Public emotion and media response are usually high immediately after a disaster or a traumatic event. The Japanese public are concerned about the appropriateness of hosting a mega event within such a short space of time after the disaster of the 2011 tsunami and subsequent meltdown of the Fukushima nuclear plant; for the Olympic Games may potentially direct vital resources away from the disaster sites in the northeast, Tōhoku and Kantō regions. To plan for a lasting legacy of the event, it is crucial to build an emotional connection with the public (Affect). The Japanese government and the Tokyo Olympic 2020 organisers need to work together to address the recent disasters, by showing commitment to rebuild the disaster sites and to support the displaced communities (Commitment). The Olympic spirit of bringing a peaceful and better society may be spread towards the disaster sites through profit sharing and knowledge transfer. Ideally, part of the profit/ revenue generated from the Games could be used to rebuild the disaster sites. However, precedent studies show that there is no guarantee the host city will make a profit from the Games. Suppliers and contractors of the event may be made to commit part of their gross income to the disaster sites as part of the deal; this can be done through taxation. A contribution could also be gained from ticket sales and broadcast rights for the event. Moreover, the future income generation from tourism and usage of the event venues after the Games could be dedicated to a disaster relief fund. Furthermore, all broadcasters may allocate air-time to charity appeals for the disasters as part of their contract. National and international sporting heroes who are participating in the Games may also address the issue in public, whether through appeal in media or by wearing a subtle logo or tagline on their clothing (Messenger). Commitment to disaster relief from both macro and micro levels of the Olympic Games would gain support from the public, enhance the brand image and reinforce the Olympic Charter.

Global citizenship

Being a global city, Tokyo has the obligation of global citizenry; an identity that transcends geographical and political boundaries. This obligation means being responsible for the well-being of global communities and the environment. Parekh (2003) further defined this identity as global oriented citizenship, one that bears strong ties within the immediate community; at the same time recognising and acting towards obligations in other communities in the world. Tokyo prides itself in leading cutting edge technologies in many areas. This national pride could be optimised in the construction and operation of the 2020 Olympic Games (Ego, Commitment). A responsible approach to construction could be adopted by employing sustainable technologies and methods, for example, minimizing the number of newly built structures and reusing / renovating existing structures. Multi-functional and flexible building design could allow building structures and components to be resold and recycled after the Games. The green credentials of the supply and contracting companies could also be one of the main selection criteria in the tendering processes, so that all suppliers and contractors involved with the Games are environmental responsible by default (Default).

Trendsetting

Although Japan has experienced economic stagnation for more than a decade since the 90s, its cultural influence in areas such as fashion, technologies, architecture, attitudes, etc. has grown since the 80s (McGray 2002). However, the unsuccessful branding of 'Cool Japan' in 2000s failed to capitalise on the country's youth culture in the international market (Kelts 2010). At the same time, a strong rivalry of 'Korean Wave' dominates the Asian markets and is fast gaining popularity in other countries (Nip and Choi 2012). It is not just the cultural market that Korea is competing with Japan, but also the technology and manufacturing markets (Japan Today 2012). To remain competitive in its soft power, Japan needs to rethink its relevant strategies. During the last 15 years, when Korea invested heavily in its cultural industry, Japan could have provided more support for its struggling cultural industry. Japan spent 0.12 percent of it national budget on the arts in 2008, compared with 0.79 percent by Korea (Grunebaum 2012). Moreover, the Japanese cultural industry is more insulated when compared to that of the Korean, with the Korean cultural industry being more proactive in optimising internet and social media to brand itself.

The 2020 Tokyo Olympics provides an opportunity for Japan to rebrand itself. 'Cool Japan' echoed the failure of 'Cool Britannia'. The brand needs to reconnect with its audiences. The new brand should emphasise the parity between tradition and modernity, which is the strength of Tokyo; not attempt to copy and to please American and Western European counterparts. Korean pop culture retained a degree of conservatism and traditional values, which made it uniquely attractive to Asian audiences. Tokyo 2020 branding should avoid their J-pop elements such as anime, manga, cosplay, cuteness and spare the international audiences from a Hello Kitty Olympics. Instead, the city may remind global audiences of its status as a trend leader in design and technologies, whilst at the same time holding onto its traditional values and characters. This parity should be expressed throughout the branding of the event.

Summary

The fundamental objective of branding is to promote brand loyalty, which is to build a long-term relationship between the brand and the audiences. Branding for a mega event such as the Olympics poses many problems for host cities and ultimately the Olympics brand itself. An understanding of automatic human behaviours enables designers to create contexts in which audiences will react in a predictable manner; and achieve brand loyalty. The MINDSPACE theory was used to systematically categorize the reaction of people to different influences; and as a tool to review precedent studies. The strengths and weakness of the strategies were identified through these studies. Alternative strategies were then proposed and developed, with consideration of regional characteristics, and social and economic factors of the host city. The 2020 Tokyo Olympics was used as a case study to apply the alternative branding strategies; it would be interesting to continue reviewing how the event develops and make comparisons to the proposed strategies. Areas that may need further research are the social factors that shape people's perception of the Olympics brand. The social factors of a city are influenced by many factors such as media campaigns, political and economic events, natural and man-made disasters, social media and peer opinion, many of which could be unpredictable. An unplanned experience may impact on the brand perception and provide another angle to study branding practice.

References

Albert, H. (2013) (ed.): Soft Power Survey 2013, http://monocle.com/film/affairs/soft-power-survey-2013/, 15.06.2014.

Ariely, D. (2008): Predictably Irrational: The Hidden Forces that Shape our Decisions. London: HarperCollins.

Baade, R. and Matheson, V. (2002): Bidding for the Olympics: Fool's Gold. In: Transatlantic Sport: The Comparative Economics of North American and European Sports. Massachusetts: Edward Elgar, 127-151.

Baade, R. and Matheson, V. (2004): Mega-Sporting Events in Developing Countries: Playing the Way to Prosperity? In: South African Journal of Economics, 72(5), 1084-1095.

BBC News (2012): London 2012: Golden Bear probes Chinese Games mascot factory. In: BBC News, 21.01.2012, http://www.bbc.co.uk/news/uk-england-shropshire-16666262, 16.06.2014.

Bem, D. (1967): Self-perception: An Alternative Interpretation of Cognitive Dissonance Phenomena. In: Psychological Review, 74(3), 183-200.

Brownell, S. (2008): Beijing's Games: What the Olympics Mean to China. Lanham, MD: Rowman & Littlefield.

Chamberlain, G. (2012): Olympic Brands Caught up in Abuse Scandal. In: The Guardian, 03.03.2012.

Chen, Y., Jin, G.J., Kumar, N. and Shi, G. (2011): The Promise of Beijing: Evaluating the Impact of the 2008 Olympic Games on Air Quality. Published as an accepted paper at the conference of NBER, working paper no. 16907.

Clark, J. (2012): How Much Will The London Olympics Cost? Too Much. In: Forbes, 28/03/2012, http://www.forbes.com/sites/johnclarke/2012/ 03/28/how-much-will-the-london-olympics-cost-too-much/, 21.08.2013.

COHRE (2007, 2008): The Olympic Games Have Displaced More Than Two Million People in the Last 20 Years, http://tenant.net/alerts/mega-events/Olympics_Media_Release.pdf, 13.10.2013.

Derudder, B., Taylor, P.J., Witlox, F. and Catalano, G. (2003): Hierarchical Tendencies and Regional Patterns in the World Cities Network: A Global Urban Analysis of 234 Cities. In: Regional Studies, 37(9), 875-886.

Dolan, P., Hallsworth, M., Halpern, D., King, D. and Vlaev, I. (2009): MINDSPACE, Influencing Behaviour through Public Policy. London: Cabinet Office.

Dyckhoff, T. and Barrett, C. (2012): The Architecture of London 2012. Chichester: Wiley.

Eckstein, B. and Throgmorton, J.A. (2003) (eds.): Story and Sustainability: Planning, Practice and Possibility for American Cities. Cambridge, Mass: MIT Press.

Fackler, M. (2010): Japan Tries to Face Up to Growing Poverty Problem. In: New York Times, 21.04.2010.

Festinger, I. (1957): A Theory of Cognitive Dissonance. Stanford, CA: Stanford University Press.

Getz, D. (2010): Event to Tourism: Pathways to Competitive Advantage. In: University of Lincoln press, http://www.lincoln.ac.nz/documents/leap/2010-don-getz-christ church-event-tourism.pdf, 21.06.2013

Gold, J.R. and Gold, M. (2008): Olympic Cities: Regeneration, City Branding and Changing Urban Agendas. In: Geography Compass, 2(1), 300-318.

Green, L., Fry, A.F. and Myerson, J. (1994): Discounting of Delayed Rewards: A Life Span Comparison. In: Psychological Science, 5(1), 33-36.

Grunebaum, D. (2012): Is Japan Losing its Cool? In: The CSMonitor, 08.12.2012, http://www.csmonitor.com/World/Asia-Pacific/2012/1208/Is-Japan-losing-its-cool/(page)/3, 19.06.2014.

Guyatt, R. (2014): There Are Groups in Japan Protesting against the 2020 Tokyo Olympics. In: Planet Ivy, 28.03.2014, http://planetivy.com/dogma/91626/japanese-groups-protesting-2020-tokyo-olympics/, 16.06.2014.

Harvey, D. (Sep-Oct 2008): The Right to the City. In: New Left Review, 53: 23-40. In which David Harvey named the process of cleansing the city for profitable purposes as 'accumulation by dispossession'.

International Olympic Committee (2012): Fact Sheet, Legacies of the Game, 07/2012, http://www.olympic.org/Documents/Reference_documents_Factsheets/Legacy.pdf, 20.08.2013.

International Olympic Committee (2013): Olympic Charter. Lausanne, Switzerland: DidWeDo S.à.r.l., 11.

Japan Today (2012): Japan Losing its Manufacturing Edge to South Korea. In: Japan Today, 27.01.2012, http://www.japantoday.com/category/kuchikomi/view/japan-losing-its-manufacturing-edge-to-south-korea, 19.06.2014.

Japan Today (2014): How do you think Tokyo will change for the 2020 Olympics? In: Japan Today, 07.01.2014, http://www.japantoday.com/category/have-your-say/view/how-do-you-think-tokyo-will-change-for-the-2020-olympics/comments/popular/id/3923721, 15.06.2014.

Jones, S. (2012): Branding London: Selling an Olympic City of Contradictions, In: The Guardian, 16/07/2012, http://www.theguardian.com/uk/2012/ jul/16/london-2012-olympics-marketing-capital, 15.08. 2013.

Kelts, R. (2010): Japanamerica: Why "Cool Japan" is over. In: 3:AM Magazine. 17.05.2010, http://www.3ammagazine.com/3am/japanamerica-why-cool-japan-is-over/, 18.06.2014.

Kietlinski, R. (2011): One World One Dream? Twenty-first Century Japanese Perspectives on Hosting the Olympic Games. In: Sport in Society, 14(4), 454-465.

Kirby, K.N. (1997): Bidding on the Future: Evidence against Normative Discounting of Delayed Rewards. In: Journal of Experimental Psychology: General, 126(1), 54-70.

Kollmuss, A. and Agyeman, J. (2002): Mind the Gap. In: Environmental Education Research, 8(3), 239-260.

Kumar, A. (2012): Want to Cleanse your City of its Poor? Host the Olympics. In: Cease Fire Magazine, 12/04/2012, http://ceasefiremagazine.co.uk/ olympics-opportunity-cleanse-city/, 13.10.2013.

Kurtenbach, E. (2014): To Demolish or Design: Japan Split on 2020 Stadium. In: AP Sport, 05.06.2014, http://wintergames.ap.org/article/demolish-or-design-japan-split-2020-stadium, 16.06.2014.

Lazzari, A. (2012): Do Olympic Branding Rules Go too far? In: EDP24, 25.06.2014, http://www.edp24.co.uk/news/special_report_do_olympic_branding_rules_go_too_far_1_1421430, 16.06.2014.

Lyall, S. (2012): Cost Complaints, an Olympic Rite, Voiced in Britain. In: New York Times, 27.03.2012.

Mathiason, N. (2006): Coke 'Drinks India Dry'. In: The Guardian, 19.03.2006.

McGray, D. (2002): Japan's Gross National Cool. In: Foreign Policy. 1 May 2002, http://www.foreignpolicy.com/articles/2002/05/01/japans_gross_national_cool, 18.06.2014.

Moore, R. (2012): How the Olympics Will Shape the Future of East London. In: The Observer, 19/08/2012, http://www.theguardian.com/artanddesign/2012/aug/19/olympic-park-regeneration-rowan-moore, 15.08.2013.

Nip, A. and Choi, C. (2012): How Korean Culture Stormed the World. In: South China Morning Post, 01.12.2012.

Parekh, B. (2003): Cosmopolitanism and Global Citizenship. In: Review of International Studies, 29(1), 3-17.

Perryman, M. (2012): Why the Olympics Aren't Good for Us, and How They Can Be. New York: OR Books.

Preuss, H. (2004): The Economics of Staging the Olympics: A Comparison of the Games, 1972-2008. Cheltenham, UK: E. Elgar.

Sandercock, L. (2003): Cosmopolis II. Mongrel Cities for the 21st Century. London: Continum.
Sassen, S. (1991): The Global City: New York, London, Tokyo. Princeton: Princeton University Press.
Sedghi, A. (2013): Which Cities Do the World's Millionaires and Billionaires Live in? In: The Guardian, 08.05.2013.
Smidt-Jensen, S. (2006): City Branding: Lessons from Medium Sized Cities in the Baltic Sea Region. In: Medium Sized Cities in Dialogue around the Baltic Sea (ed.). Danish Centre for Forest, Landscape and Planning, KVL.
Smith, T. (2012): London 2012 Olympics: A Story of Sustainable Architecture. In: Responding To Climate Change, http://ww.rtcc.org/2012/07/23/london-2012-olympics-a-story-of-sustainable-architecture/#sthash.3EGQdkLD.dpuf, 22.06.2014.
Thaler, R. and Sunstein, C. (2008): Nudge, New Haven: Yale University Press.
Traganou, J. (2011): Tokyo's 1964 Olympic Design as a 'Realm of [Design] Memory'. In: Sport in Society: Cultures, Commerce, Media, Politics, 14(4), 466-481.
Vasovic, A. and Zuvela, M. (2014): For Migrant Workers, Olympic Dream Turns to Nightmare in Sochi. In: Reuters, 05.02.2014, http://www.reuters.com/article/2014/02/05/us-olympics-migrants-idUSBREA140HW20140205, 16.06.2014.
Wood, W. and Neal, D. (2007): A New Look at Habits and the Habit–Goal Interface. In: Psychological Review, 114(4), 843-863.
Wood, W., Tam, L. and Witt, M. (2005): Changing Circumstances, Disrupting Habits. In: Journal of Personality and Social Psychology, 88(6), 918-933.
Yardley, J. (2007): No Spitting on the Road to Olympic Glory, Beijing Says. In: New York Times, 17.04.2007. http://www.nytimes.com/2007/04/17/world/asia/17iht-web-0417china.5314587.html?pagewanted=all
Zhang, L. and Zhao, S.X. (2009): City Branding and the Olympic Effect: A Case Study of Beijing. In: Cities 26(5), 245-254.

Protecting the European Medical Tourist: A New Challenge for the E.U. Law?

Fernando Peña López

Introduction

Medical tourism is currently an emerging issue that will probably have to be tackled by the European Union law, as well as by the member states' internal legal systems in the near future (Pai 2007: 567). This issue has been treated for several years in the US scholarly papers, anticipating a discussion that we could have in Europe soon (Fabbrini 2011: 51, regarding medical tourism linked to access to services). That anticipation was due to certain features of the American health care system that make it clearly different from those of the EU countries. Essentially, I am talking about the lack of a socialized health care in the U.S. equivalent to the European standards, and the high level of prices in the American medical services market. Nowadays, however, there are some reasons to think that we could see a similar development of this question in Europe.

Medical tourism, as a phenomenon, has many faces. Some of the problems surrounding this topic are quite new and still developing. Those new issues still need to be discussed and analysed by scholars in Europe. Many of them will be treated later on in this paper. Others, like the traditional stream of medical tourists coming from underdeveloped nations to developed countries are linked to very old practices that clearly reveal that medical tourism is not new. On the contrary, there have been people practising something that we could call «medical tourism» since ancient times (Cohen 2010: 1471). Therefore, medical tourism is not a new phenomenon. What is new is the importance of the phenomenon, and the new causes and trends that feature medical tourism currently.

Before going into the intricacies of this multi-faceted problem, it would be better to start with a broad definition of the phenomenon we are discussing. Medical tourism could be defined, from a law perspective, as travelling across jurisdictions for the purpose of receiving medical care (Cortez 2008: 76).

1) This short definition highlights, in the first place, that being provided with a service related to health care has to be the real motive of the mobility when

we talk about medical tourism (Terry 2007: 422). Thus, it is not enough that the surgery or medical treatment involved in the mobility must have been planned and hired in advance. It has also to be planned as the main part of a travel package that, on the other hand, might include other complimentary leisure or cultural activities.

2) The second element that could be derived from the definition is that medical tourism implies necessarily a change of jurisdiction as a result of the mobility. It is not just travelling for medical purposes; it is travelling across jurisdictions for getting medical care (Cortez 2008: 76; Williams 2011: 611). A change of the law rules applicable to the planned services is essential for being in front of a case of medical tourism. Naturally, changing the jurisdiction does not always mean going abroad. In decentralized states like the US, Germany or Spain it could also mean travelling to another *land*, federal state or region. The only condition for this is that the different regions or '*länder*' involved must have competence on health care or, at least, some different rules regarding the medical service that is the objective of the trip.

I will try to demonstrate along this paper that the phenomenon we have just defined is, from a legal point of view, multidimensional. It is a relevant matter for consumer protection law, but also for international administrative law and even for such a sensitive branch of law as human rights legislation. Connected with this statement is the related assumption that consuming medical services abroad has very important social, moral and economic consequences in the patients' home country, as well as in the nation that receives them. We will see how medical tourism is able to produce transcendental changes in the way that ethically relevant medical treatments and surgeries are regulated in the country that provides patients to other nations. Other risks, dangers and opportunities (regarding population welfare, internal health care policy, international legal private conflicts, etc.) for the sending countries and his nationals will be described in this work as well. At the same time, it will be exposed how medical tourism is also considered to be challenging the health care systems of the destination countries, with negative effects in the fields of equality, population and quality of life.

Thus, medical tourism shows the strong and direct connections between a certain type or aspect of tourism and the social and economic behaviour of all the agents involved in it: consumers and providers, but also states and populations. Therefore, it is not a simple question to be contemplated from a "supply side perspective reviewing economic value within market segments" as the outlines of the conference claim about touring consumption in general. On the contrary, medical tourism is a topic that should be addressed taking into account its multidimensional character and the important effects that could be derived from it.

Until now, medical tourism has been addressed only partially by the EU and the different European national legislators. Since medical tourism is a reality that seems to be here to stay, all these legislatures will have to confront its existence and effects whether they like it or not. The aim of this paper is to review which aspects of medical tourism have been tackled properly by the EU and its member states and which have not. Therefore, I do not mean to assess if medical tourism is positive or the contrary. My only intention is to expose its alleged causes and effects and the legal problems that could arise from its presence, considering basically the U.S. experience. Bearing that in mind, in the following pages, I will try to set forth systematically the challenges that medical tourism pose nowadays to European legislators. As I have said, some of them have been tackled not so long ago. Others still require being discussed and evaluated in their possible impact and future development.

Why do patients travel abroad for health care services nowadays?

As it has already said, medical tourism is not a new issue. Patients have been travelling abroad to receive health services ever since Roman times and beyond (Howze 2007: 1015-1016, Cohen 2010: 1471). Every city named Spa or Bath is a living evidence of a health resort of the ancient world. This kind of health holiday obviously still exists, but that is not the medical tourism that worries the U.S. scholars who are currently addressing the issue. Nor is the old and well-known phenomenon of people from less developed nations travelling to Europe or the U.S. to obtain high quality health care services not available in their own countries a consideration. In fact, neither create any relevant social problem, at least not in the US or in other western countries.

Medical tourism as a matter of law and economic research is currently linked to trends quite different from these old versions of going abroad for medical treatment (Howze 2007: 1016, Terry 2007: 421, Cohen 2010: 1471). Nowadays medical tourism research is studied as a phenomenon that investigates how people from more developed nations travel abroad in search of treatments or surgeries they cannot access in their own countries: a) for public policy reasons (the treatments are forbidden or legally limited), b) for reasons related to malfunctioning of their national socialized public health care systems (waiting lists) or c) because either they cannot afford to pay for a service or treatment in their own country, or they just want to save a big amount of money (there is a big cost discrepancy between the price of the service at home and abroad).

All these motives underlying medical tourism worldwide are also present in the European context. Some of them are old concerns of the European legislators and some are quite recent. In the European Union context, where twenty-five different national health care legislations coexist, questions related to access to medical treatments or procedures forbidden or more limited in a member state than in others have been a permanent challenge (Fabbrini 2010: 2-25). Classical controversial law matters like abortion, sperm and egg donation, embryo cryopreservation or assisted suicide have different legal solutions throughout the different EU countries. Women visiting a neighbouring country to practice an abortion not permitted in their own nation, or to be implanted with a cryopreserved embryo in the same situation are issues that the EU has dealt with. Other questions, like the possibility of visiting another EU member state to avoid the national waiting lists for certain treatments or surgeries, have also been tackled from a legal point of view long ago (Pai 2007: 556-567).

However, those causes related to medical services costs (medical tourism with the purpose of saving money, or getting services out of consumer's pocket in his/her own country) are new concerns that, so far, have been out of the European legislator list of priorities (see the "Whereas" of the Directive 2011/24/EU of 9 March 2011 *on the application of patients' rights in cross-border health care*, where it is impossible not to realize that the only concern of the EU legislator regarding the cost of medical services is the economic relationship between the socialized public health care systems of the EU countries). Nevertheless, it is safe to say that, taking into account the current evolution of the different European health care systems and the austerity policies developed by the EU and national governments, these are questions that should probably start being considered as new challenges for the immediate future. The US experience demonstrates clearly that when the state reduces the level of health care provided to population, there is room for this type of medical tourism as long as there are medical services expensive enough to make worthwhile staying in a foreign country in order to acquire them.

The reasons behind medical tourism that were mentioned in the previous paragraphs, however, would never have brought about this phenomenon, only by themselves. These last years' medical tourism boost has been only possible because of the presence of Internet and the information global traffic that came along with it (Cortez 2008: 85) Without the omnipresent development of information technology, providers of health care services in developing countries would never have reached so many prospective customers in the US or Europe (see Terry 2007: 438-439, about the consequences medical tourism internet advertising in Europe and the U.S.). Figures would never be so high without these new information technologies. A study in 2007 made by Deloite estimated that 750 000 American citizens went abroad to get medical services and that in 2013 it will be five or six million (Williams 2011: 610). Therefore, even if we do not insist any more on this factor underlying the current development of medical tourism, the reader has to take it into account that this will be a major cause for investigation from now on.

EU concerns about medical tourism I: The problem of accessing medical services

In the previous section, we saw that there are several different reasons that determine a patient's decision to go abroad for medical services. As it has been exposed, according to Cortez (2008: 77, see also Howze 2007: 1016), those causes could really be reduced to two fundamental reasons. The first was related to access to medical services. The main problems posed by this first cause, as we will see, have been addressed, at least partially, by the EU some time ago.

Difficulties related to access to medical services, as a cause of medical tourism, could be defined as those legal or administrative obstacles that prevent a patient from getting the treatment or the surgery needed or wanted in his/her own country. In many European countries, certain medical services or treatments have limited access or they are forbidden or not allowed. Sometimes the access is not possible because of the country's moral or ethics (e.g. abortion, cryopreservation, human cloning), other times because of the veto of the national health care authorities, or just because the medical product or procedure is being tested (e.g. laetrile, stem cells treatment). Finally, in many occasions, the access is prevented by internal problems (linked with a lack of resources or inefficient allocation of resources) of the national health care system that obliges the patients to wait by including them in a never-ending waiting list.

Those treatments, surgeries, drugs or products forbidden by some member states of the EU, but permitted by other member states, pose a problem related to the contradiction between state's sovereignty and freedom of movement within the Union. On the contrary, when the reason for travelling abroad is to avoid the waiting lists, the issue that the European authorities have to deal with is about the right of European citizens to receive health care from a socialized system other than the patient's national system. In the following paragraphs we will address both problems separately.

Freedom of movement vs. state's sovereignty

The problem posed by the prohibition or limitation of certain medical products, treatments or surgeries in a member state has challenged European legislation since free movement of people was enshrined as one of the four basic European freedoms (Fabbrini 2011: 24).

Currently the problem of travelling abroad to acquire services forbidden in the citizen's own state is linked to different medical activities, most of them included in the so-called «reproductive tourism». This concept refers to any travel outside a jurisdiction to access reproductive technologies (Ikemoto 2009: 281), and covers a lot of medical services, from assisted conception technologies (such as in vitro fertilization, assisted insemination, intracytoplasmic sperm injection) to cryopreservation and storage of sperm, eggs and embryos, and even surrogate motherhood. Many of these practices and treatments are allowed in some countries and forbidden or limited in other EU members. This obviously determines why a number of people take the decision to travel abroad to get those services not available in their own countries. For example, Sweden, Norway and the Netherlands permit only known sperm donors, so citizens from these countries usually go to Denmark for sperm (Ikemoto 2009: 296). On the other hand, Spain and Romania have been very popular destinations for in vitro fertilization and donor eggs, as long as these nations allow payment to donors and anonymity (Ikemoto 2009: 297).

However, the European case law that regulates this matter was created regarding abortion. This issue is for sure the most controversial due to the moral questions at the core of it. During the last twenty years, important cases surrounding abortion have reached the European courts. The court's decisions settling those cases compound today what we could call the European abortion law.

The first of those cases is the so-called *Grogan* case (ECJ Case C-159/90, Society for the Protection of Unborn Children vs. Grogan, 1991, ECR I.4685). In this case, a pro-life Irish association (SPUC) sued three activists, representatives of students' unions that were informing in Ireland about overseas abortion providers. SPUC argued that the Irish constitution banned such type of advertising. The Irish High Court asked the European Court of Justice (ECJ) whether a ban on information about abortion providers could be considered contrary to the EU law or not. ECJ decided, in the first place, the fundamental question about abortion being considered or not a service under the EU law: "medical termination of pregnancy, performed in accordance with the law of the State in which it is carried out, constitutes a service, within the meaning of the EECT". This was a decisive statement and its consequences were not hard to predict: according to the EU principle of freedom to provide services, a prohibition of advertising services lawfully provided in a EU country would be incompatible with the EU law. Nevertheless, this conclusion was only implicit in the ECJ decision because, in the end, the students' unions were not allowed to continue advertising abortion services because they were not directly connected to the service provision. The ECJ made clear that: "should a party directly connected to providing abortion become involved, the outcome could be different".

Years later, in the *Open Door* case (Open Door Counselling vs. Ireland, App. No. 14234/88 & 14235/88, May 15, 1990), the European Court of Human Rights (ECHR) addressed the abortion advertising issue in another case similar to *Grogan*. This time two family counselling clinics based in Dublin were prohibited to provide information about abortion services overseas. The main issue arising from this case addressed by the ECHR was the consistency of the restraint imposed to the clinics with the freedom of information of Article 10 of the European Convention on Human Rights (ECoHR). The ECHR decided that, though the prohibition of giving information about abortion could be justified in the legitimate aim of the Irish state to protect the life of the unborn, the absolute prohibition imposed to the applicants "from receiving or imparting information was disproportionate to the aims pursued" and, thus, contrary to the right to freedom of information.

Finally, in the *Tysiac* (Tysiac vs. Poland, App. No. 5410/03, 2007-I, Eur. Ct. H.R.) and *A,B,C* cases (A,B and C vs. Ireland, App. No. 25579/05, 2010, Eur. Ct. H.R., 2032) the ECHR tackled directly the question of the limits of any member state's law about abortion imposed by the EU membership. These decisions have not really gone too far in establishing a minimum standard for any European abortion regulation (such as what happens in the U.S. law since Roe vs. Wade – 410, US 113, 1973-, Fabbrini 2011: 27) but they have stated that there are some basic assumptions that every state has to respect when legislating for abortion. Abortion is not this paper's topic, so it will be enough to say that in these cases the ECHR settled that, once abortion is allowed in certain cases, there must be "effective mechanisms...under domestic law to ensure an abortion in such...situations" (A,B and C vs. Ireland, App. No. 25579/05, 2010, Eur. Ct. H.R., 2032, 250). With regard to our issue, these ECHR decisions made clear that there could be no legal impediment in any EU country for "travelling for an abortion abroad". As a matter of fact, this was one of the basic assumptions in all these cases regarding abortion from the beginning. Even in the *Grogan* case, AG Van Gerven stated in his report that it could never be in accordance to the EU law "a ban on pregnant women going abroad or a rule under which they would be subjected to unsolicited examinations upon their return from abroad" (Adv. Gen. Van Gerven opinion on SPUC vs. Grogan C 159-90, ECR I-4703, 29).

As a result of these cases, the current EU case law clearly protects any patient travelling to another EU country seeking medical services forbidden or limited in his/her own country. In addition, any health care service provider based in a member state is protected from any attempt of other member states to forbid or restrict advertising of those services that are lawful in the place of provision. Moreover, some additional restrictions could be imposed to eventual state's bans, even regarding people not directly involved in the service provision, on the basis of freedom of information. In a world where information flows easily through the Internet, the door to medical tourism for reasons of access to health is fully open within the EU. State sovereignty cannot prevent medical tourism on the grounds of national moral or ethics in any way.

This situation has been deemed positive in the scholarly papers on medical tourism (Cortez 2008: 112; Williams 2011: 619). It has been said that it enhances patient autonomy allowing people to «vote with their feet» when they disagree with their country's policies (ibid.). In modern democratic countries medical tourism permits a minority of dissident citizens to act according to their own convictions regardless of the national rules about the object of those convictions. On the other hand, from a European point of view, it could be also argued that voting with the feet prevents an EU citizen from being denied access to a service available to other EU citizens. Both arguments have effects (or at least could have) in the internal policy of the EU member states making some of them reconsider or change their own decisions by taking into account the EU environment (Cortez 2008: 112-113). Also they could be of help in order to build and promote a European common position around basic issues directly linked to human rights and human health care.

Despite of all its benefits, some important equality concerns arise from the possibility of voting with their feet recognised by the EU law to all European citizens. Those concerns are usually remarked in several scholarly papers on this issue (i.e. Ikemoto 2009: 301-309; Fabbrini 2011: 50). Fabrinni (2011:50) explains the reasoning for abortion: "a legal regime that discriminates between women by making abortion possible and lawful only for women that can financially afford it and making it impossible and unlawful for the poor, conflicts with the principle of equality that should govern any liberal democratic constitutional system". For these reasons, though it seems clearly unlikely to happen soon, Fabbrini (2011: 51) argues that some measures should be adopted at the European level to prevent national abortion legislations from producing the effect of discriminating low-income women.

This discriminatory effect obviously exists wherever people are permitted to vote with their feet. It happens in the US as well, insofar as the constitution prohibits any restriction on travelling from one state to another. In the US, as well as in the EU, only people with enough economic resources to travel can benefit from this aspect of the freedom of movement. Nevertheless, the US Supreme Court, at least regarding abortion, has a consolidated doctrine establishing minimum requirements on its regulation on the grounds of human rights protection. Those minimum requirements are binding to all states and ensure a basic equal protection to all American citizens. This still has not happened in Europe and it is undoubtedly one of the challenges for the EU providing that it has an interest in making the European Charter of Human Rights something more than a mere declaration.

The «waiting list» problem

The other fundamental problem that the EU had to confront in the field of access to health care services was linked to the relations between the national health care systems of the EU countries. The starting point of this problem is again the freedom to go to another EU member state seeking medical services. This right was recognised by the EUCJ to any service recipient within the Union, as a derivative of the freedom to provide services (i.e. in Luisi, Carbone vs. Ministry of the Treasury of Italy, Joined Cases 286/82 & 26/83, 1984, ECR 377). The right to seek medical treatment in other EU country combined with the principle of non discrimination between EU citizens creates a legal environment where patients could seek and receive medical care all over the Union in the same conditions awarded to each country nationals.

The above situation, however, has to be confronted in the presence of a national health care system that ensures universal access to comprehensive health care to its recipients (putting aside prohibitions based on moral or ethics grounds such as those examined in the last section). Each EU worker is attached to one of those national systems, normally the state where he works (according to Regulation EEC No. 1408/71 of the Council of 14 June 1971 on the application of social security schemes to employed persons and their families moving within the Community). The problem of people, insured or covered by one of these systems, moving abroad temporarily (i.e. for studies or on holidays) is currently resolved by the so-called European Health Insurance Card. The card allows its beneficiary to get medical care from any EU national system under the same conditions and at the same cost (free or not) as people insured in that country. But the right to medical care granted to card-holders is expressly excluded when the patient is travelling with the direct aim of obtaining medical treatment, that is, in the cases of what we have called medical tourism.

Understandably, most of the EU national health care systems are reluctant to provide medical services (equivalent and at the same cost to those provided to nationals) to patients from abroad directly seeking those services (*Fundación EOI, Ministerio de Industria, Energía y Turismo* 2013: 15,16). The fear of an excessive burden to national health care budgets, the aim of preventing a possible reduction of national medical services' quality due to a growing demand, as well as the will to avoid foreign attempts to alleviate their own national systems by sending their patients to other countries are some influential factors for that reluctance. The question was so relevant that it was easily predictable that the EU would have to deal with it sooner or later.

The only statutory rule regarding the problem of medical tourism from this point of view for more than thirty years was article 22 of Regulation EEC No. 1408/71. This rule established that a patient has the right to be sent to be medically treated by another member state from his own EU country only when the treatment is needed and «*cannot be provided for the person concerned within the territory of the Member State in which he resides*» (art. 22.2). The patient's right to go abroad to be treated for an illness, in any case, was conditioned to a previous authorisation of the national health care service. This authorisation would be rejected whenever the health authorities for the patient's member state found that the medical service is available at home. Therefore, the notion of service availability (art. 22 requires that the service «cannot be provided» at home) was crucial since the neccessary previous authorisation depended on it.

The expression «service that cannot be provided» was interpreted by the ECJ in several cases (i.e. C-157/99 Geraets-Smits vs. Stichting Ziekenfonds VGZ, 2001, ECR I-5473, §.103; Müller-Fauré vs. Van Riet, 2003, ECR I-4509, §.89) as including the right to be sent abroad to get a service when it cannot be provided without «*undue delay*». More recently, in *Watts vs. Bedford Primary Care Trust* (case C-372/04, 2006, ECR I-04325), the ECJ established that the meaning of «undue delay» has to be determined case by case with regard to the individual's state of health and probable cause of the disease. So the existence of waiting lists in the home country for a specific treatment cannot be a valid ground for refusing reimbursement when it is asked by a patient that has gone abroad seeking medical services. On the contrary, if the specific service in question could not be provided at home within an acceptable delay considering the patient's condition (clinical history and probable course of the illness, degree of pain, etc.), authorisation must be granted to the patient (see Pai 2007: 560-564). Even more so, the patient has the right to reimbursement whenever he/she was unduly denied the required prior authorization, but went abroad getting the treatment needed at his/her own expense.

Directive 2011/24/EU of the European Parliament and the Council of 9 March 2011 on the application of patient's rights in cross border healthcare, has recently transformed in statutory rules the ECJ decisions exposed in the previous paragraphs. It establishes, as a general rule, that any patient can seek and receive treatment in any EU country and ask for reimbursement when he had paid for the services. As a principle, reimbursement will be made providing that the service is «among the benefits to which the ... person is entitled in the ... state of affiliation» (art. 8.1), and according to the level of costs that «would have been assumed by the Member State of affiliation» (art. 8.4).

However, this right to seek medical services abroad can be subject to prior authorisation in so many cases (most of them related to the cost of services, see art. 9) that, at the end of the day, any serious treatment is conditioned to it (and so was it, for example, in Spain, where the regulation transposing the Directive - *Real Decreto 81/2014 de 7 de febrero, por el que se establecen normas para garantizar la asistencia sanitaria transfronteriza*- establishes that reimbursement for any overnight service is conditioned to prior authorisation). Following the doctrine of *Watts vs. Bedford*, prior authorisation can be denied by national authorities only if «the healthcare can be provided on its territory within a time limit which is medically justifiable, taking into account the current state of health and the probably cause of the illness of each patient concerned» (8.6.d).

It has been said that the European legislation applicable to reimbursement of medical services provided in other health care systems all over the Union is a step forward (Pai 2007: 564). According to Pai's view, it facilitates cross-border medical access for EU citizens (Pai 2007: 565). This author also states that, though there are some risks to the balance between the coexisting social security systems, European citizens benefit from a better access to high quality health care services that could not be available at home (Pai 2007: 565). Moreover, the right to reimbursement we are analyzing could even be useful to enhance the standards of health care at the patient's home country (Pai 2007: 565).

In my opinion, if the EU is really interested in achieving those goals for all Europeans, there are some important steps forward to be taken. First, once again, the present rules regarding this issue produce inequality in health care between citizens. Only those patients with enough money to pay in advance are able to take advantage of this right to get reimbursement for the payment of medical services provided abroad. These differences between patients depending on their means could be avoided by changing the rules regarding reimbursement. A possible step forward in this matter could be to establish that EU national systems are obliged to provide services to authorised foreign patients and to obtain direct reimbursement from their national social security systems. But even without a rule like this, if we really want to make real and effective the right to obtain medical services abroad when there is an excessive waiting list, it would be of help to lay down another rule related to the situation described in article 8.6.d. A rule establishing that a patient can get any treatment or surgery abroad, with or without prior authorisation, provided that conditions under article 8.6.d concur. Otherwise, national health care systems will keep on preventing patients from going abroad seeking treatment by delaying the authorisation procedures.

EU concerns about medical tourism II: The cost-based medical tourism

It was explained in the first part of this paper that the second reason for medical tourism is related to the price of medical services. The difference between the cost of medical treatments and surgeries in Europe, the US, Canada, Japan or other highly-developed countries and the cost of the same medical services in the so-called emergent economies or in quick developing countries is huge. According to recent studies, a western country citizen can save up to ninety percent of the total cost of fifteen common surgeries going the get them in one of these countries (Terry 2007: 426, Williams 2011: 613-614).

However, it is clear that there have always been differences in price level between developed, developing or under-developed countries. Since cost-saving medical tourism is a phenomenon that has recently appeared in some countries (especially the U.S.), there has to be some other motives that underlie the boom of this kind of medical tourism. Those other motives are linked to the improvement of health care quality as well as to the current patient economic conditions in the developed nations and the quality of services available there for them. Therefore, what we have called cost-based medical tourism is not just related to costs. It is also linked to the quality of the medical services provided nowadays in developing countries.

Today, high-quality medical services can be provided in an important group of developing countries. It is easy to find hospitals accredited by the Joint International Commission (the international branch of the institution that accredits US hospitals) in these countries, advertising services provided by a staff with plenty of American or European top universities degree holders (Gluck 2008: 478-485, Cortez 2008: 83-86). Some of these hospitals have even US or European subsidiaries. Those reasons explain why many people from Europe go to Latin America or Asia to have an affordable access to high quality medical services not provided in their home countries by their social security systems (see Gluck 2008: 478-488; Cortez 2008: 82-85).

An important number of American people and a much lower number of European patients are not insured or underinsured (this situation keeps on in the US despite the Obama administration legislation on Health Care "PPACA", see Williams 2011: 608-613). For those patients going abroad to get the treatment they need, medical tourism could be, in the worst case, a life or death situation. For other patients it is just a question of saving a huge amount of money for attending other basic life necessities. An example should be enough to prove this statement: A US citizen could save in 2008 up to $ 26.000 if he goes to India or Hungary for a coronary artery bypass graft, and up to $ 8.500 in an in-patient knee surgery (from Cortez 2008: 80). There are even other patients for whom this sort of medical tourism is a luxury experience that they would never be able to feel in their own country hospitals (in those facilities they usually have access to, of course). Williams told us how American patients "are often astonished by the quality of services they receive and the personal attention with which it is rendered" (Williams 2011: 623).

Moreover, considering the differences between countries in terms of cost, a logical decision for some private insurance companies in Europe or the US would be to include medical services abroad in some of their insurance contracts in order to offer them at better prices than the only at home services insurance. Some companies are just starting to do that in the US offering discounts if the insured goes to Mexico to get dental care (e.g. Williams 2011: 616).

All these circumstances and the on-line accessibility of the worldwide offer of health care services suggest that medical tourism still has a lot of room to grow. In Europe, where this phenomenon had less impact in the last decades than in the US, the aftermath of the economic crisis could have an influence in this eventual growth. Many countries have reduced their social security budget, especially those countries more affected by the so-called austerity policies imposed by the European authorities. Hence, it is not hard to predict that there will be more people under-insured in Europe in the near future. As we have seen, this is one of the factors that led the US citizens to seek medical services abroad more and more frequently. Therefore, maybe it is time for the European scholars and legislatures, both national and of the EU, to start discussing about this kind of medical tourism. The range of issues arising from cost-related medical tourism is varied. It is not possible to treat them all properly in a paper like this. Therefore, I shall confine myself to make a brief reference to the most important questions it poses from a legal point of view.

Safety of patients (concerns on service quality)

One of the most important questions posed by medical tourism to the authorities of developed nations is how to protect patients from low quality services offered abroad (Williams 2011: 628). Today, the existence of facilities according to the western standards on health care quality in many developing countries is commonly recognized. Despite this fact, there is not available data about the quality and conditions of a great percentage of the health services offered overseas to Western patients. In the US scholarly papers, the necessity of an information system (or other equivalent mean of control) for the patients to rely on when seeking medical services abroad has been pointed out, i.e. a public site fed with information provided by international accreditation entities databases, or other reliable sources. In any case, scholars (e.g. Cortez 2008: 103; Williams 2011: 628-637) have stated that measuring quality is a very difficult task, and that some statistics used with this aim like mortality rates are a «crude proxy for quality».

Legal remedies against malpractice

Another concern arising from cost-based medical tourism is related to access to legal remedies when a medical negligence causes damages to a patient. Although health care facilities in developing countries could be as good as in the US or the EU, this similarity could not be extended to legal systems (Cortez 2010: 4-5, Cohen 2010: 1494). As far as there is nothing such as an international legal framework to be applied to damages resulting from medical malpractices all over the world, medical tourists are unable to find legal remedies different from those available in destination countries when malpractice happens. The only option to get some legal relief in the patient's nation is to find enough links to the home country to let the national court exercise jurisdiction against the negligent physician or hospital. This is normally quite difficult when the treatment is provided in other continent. Looking for compensation in developing countries is considered a difficult endeavour, which seldom ends up with good results, that is to say, an outcome comparable to the compensations ordinarily awarded in the patient's home country (Cohen 2010: 1504, Williams 2011: 646). Warning eventual medical tourists about legal risks of seeking treatment abroad is undoubtedly something that home countries should do. At the same time, scholars have considered several options to confront these risks with legal measures. Among other measures, it has been proposed with this objective to act against brokers with residence in the patient's home country, to include the legal protection offered in health care facilities accreditation when they are overseas, to promote international agreements between developed nations and the most common medical tourism destination countries, or to make the «*forum non conveniens*» doctrine more flexible (Cortez 2010: 2-89; Cohen, 2010: 1501-1511)

Surgery or treatment follow-up back at home

A more specific but also crucial question, derived, in a sense, from the previous posed by cost-based medical tourism is related to the follow-up of the treatment received abroad. Many patients coming back from medical tourism destinations need some kind of follow-up after being discharged, and sometimes to be treated again due to medical complications regarding the treatment or surgery (Cortez 2008: 103-104). These patients should be informed of the limits of their health care insurance at home, either it is private or public. Surprisingly, in the US experience, many patients are not informed about those limits or, even worse, they are obliged to sign release forms absolving the sending company from liability for any negligence committed by foreign hospitals or physicians (Cortez 2008: 121-123). Again, sending countries should begin to take medical tourism seriously in order to protect their citizens from terrible and unknown consequences of a phenomenon of increasing importance.

Effects of medical tourism in developing nations

Finally, one of the major concerns about medical tourism is linked to its effects in destination countries (Cohen 2011: 9-15). It has emerged as a big and profitable industry in developing countries. The new health care facilities built to attend to patients from highly developed countries have bloomed in the last decade (i.e. Cortez 2008: 84, Gluck 2008: 462-473, Cohen 2010: 1492). These hospitals with high quality services consume a great amount of resources. Besides, the best staff available in each country are attracted by a position in those facilities. This situation has been considered dangerous to health care systems in medical tourism destination countries, and, therefore, to their own populations (see, discussing this issue, Cohen 2011: 9-10). It is clear that the new technology and high quality services brought about by medical tourism remain out of reach for most of the destination country citizens. Even worse, there is evidence that could prove that the quality of services for local population is reduced because of medical tourism (see recently, Chen & Flood 2013: 286-

298). Certainly, there is still a lot of research to be done in this area. Even though it is difficult to grasp the big picture of medical tourism, and see its impacts in low and middle income countries, this issue becomes increasingly relevant and needs to be considered in terms of European legislation committed to health and human rights protection at home and abroad.

References

Chen, Y.Y.B and Plood, C.M. (2013): Medical tourism impact on health care equity and access in low and middle-income countries: Making the case for regulation. In: 41 J.L. Med. & Ethics, 286.

Cohen, G.I. (2010): Protecting patients with passports: medical tourism and the patient-protective argument. In: 95 Iowa L. Rev., 1467.

Cohen, G.I. (2011): Medical tourism, access to health care and global justice. In: 52 Va. J. Int'l L., 1.

Cortez, N. (2008): Patients without borders: The emerging global market for patients and the evolution of modern health care. In: 83 Ind. L.J., 71.

Cortez, N. (2010): Recalibrating the legal risks of cross-border health care. In: 10 Yale J. Health Pol'y L. & Ethics, 1.

Fabbrini, F. (2011): The European Court of Human Rights, The EU Charter of Fundamental Rights and the right to abortion: Roe vs. Wade on the other side of the Altlantic?. In: 18 Colum. J. Eur. L., 1.

Fundación EOI, Ministerio de Industria, Energía y Turismo (2013): Turismo de Salud en España. http://www.minetur.gob.es/turismo/es-ES/PNIT/Eje3/Documents/turismo_salud_espana.pdf

Gluck, E. (2008): Incredible accreditable India: Trends in hospital accreditation coexistent with the growth of medical tourism in India. In: 1 St. Louis U.J. Health L. & Pol'y, 459.

Howze, K.S. (2007): Medical tourism: Symptom or cure? In: 41 Ga. L. Rev., 1013.

Ikemoto, L.C. (2009): Reproductive tourism: Equality concerns in the global market for fertility services. In: 27 Law & Ineq., 277.

Pai, H. (2007): Watts v. Bedford Primary Health Care Trust: The uncertain prognosis for health tourism in the European Union. In: 29 Loy. L. A. Intl & Comp. L. Rev., 553.

Terry, N.P. (2007): Symposium: The politics of health law: Under-regulated health care phenomena in a flat world: Medical tourism and outsourcing. In: 29 West New Eng. L. Rev., 421.

Williams, H.T. (2011): Fighting fire with fire: Reforming the health care system through a market based approach to medical tourism. In: 89 N.C.L. Rev, 607.

How Tall Can the Acacia Grow? Cityscapes between Conviviality and Mass Invasion

Florin Mureşanu / Monica Mureşanu

With more than 1 billion cross-border tourists worldwide during the latest years, the tourism industry is responsible for a considerable segment of the global cash flow (US$2.1 trillion in 2012, of US$6.6 trillion total in combined direct, indirect and induced impacts[1]). However, most of the capital tends to concentrate towards established destinations. Even if customary leisure destinations are still preferred for relaxation, the contemporary tourist's interests are widened to encompass more activities, usually to be found within anthropic environments. The big cities of the world rise as well in the hierarchy of the traveller's preferences. Higher demand for well-known places is explained by the behaviour of the contemporary vacationer, with the intent to acquire the highest degree of gratification over the short span of yearly holidays. Urban tourism is a growing global trend that targets places not only for their recreational attributes, but also for complementary entertainment assets of the local culture. Economy wise, this symbiosis works excellently, but often to the extent that existing resources are repurposed to become touristic capital. Deprived of their former use to the benefit of the local communities, these resources are becoming subject to ongoing negotiation that, sometimes, ends in conflictual situations. Between the "natives" and the "invaders", how much goes to whose benefit is a matter of usually unplanned market trends and spontaneous reaction towards them. However willing and stretch appropriate to accommodate tourism the cities would be, saturation does not go without losses. How much tourism the cities can take does not involve the tourism economy alone, but also the usually ungagged figures, of which the general contentment of the local communities might make the difference between a convivial state and a mass invasion conflictual one.

1 Official numbers, according to World Travel & Tourism Council's report, *Economic impact of travel & tourism 2013: Annual update,* http://www.wttc.org/site_media/uploads/downloads/Economic_Impact_of_TT_2013_Annual_Update_-_Summary.pdf, 28.08.2013.

Intertwined evolution

What's the acacia got to do with tourism? Aside from the fact that it probably sets the perfect background for a safari picture, practically they do not have much in common. But as an analogy, it makes good sense. A personal study conducted amongst first year students in urban planning and landscape architecture over several years indicated that a considerable percentage identified traveling as their preferred activity. The students were asked to prepare a Pecha Kucha presentation about a favourite activity or subject, with no constrains on the selection. Consistently, whether they had to choose the subject for themselves or blind, for their peers to perform, 70-85% chose traveling in general or a city that they previously visited or wished to visit and wanted to know more about.

The fact that individuals engaged in lucrative activities increasingly positions tourism as a necessary leisure activity, complementary to their compulsory occupations (Richter 1991; Vanhove 2005: 55; Frangialli 2005), was already explained through cognitive-normative models (Cohen 1972; 1974; 1979; Pearce 1982; Plog 1987; 2005). However, the stress associated with work, urban agglomeration or household problems is not generally present amongst youths; therefore, this could not explain their predilection. Instead, we can take a look at the very evolution of tourism. We see tourism now as such a common experience that, although some of its facets do involve luxury, it is no longer something that one indulges in as, perhaps, a hundred years ago. Furthermore, tourism as a global industry is no longer associated exclusively with leisure (Garnham 1996). Although intentionally shaped for leisure, places are continuously shaping the tourism geography. Leisure travellers outnumber travellers with other interests by a ratio of two to one (Lew et al. 2008: 23). One can tour for relaxation and simultaneously address other interests. The range of adjectival tourism is becoming ever extended along with certain demands gaining popularity.

Thus, the students' choice is more likely a predictable one and based on their personal pursuit than, perhaps as it was first assumed, a generic pick that would mask the lack of pastimes. It is even not uncommon presently for students to travel abroad for educational purposes in international student exchanges or scholarships. Usually, students in architecture, urban planning and landscape architecture do travel abroad for field trips and there is a high incidence of diploma projects in locations chosen abroad. Although the mobility programs do not render them "proper tourists"[2], they are motivated also by interests complementary to their academic pursuits. They are also indirect consumers of typical touristic commodities: hospitality services, culture, cuisine etc. Likewise, the

2 The commonly established definition of the tourist refers to a person that travels to a place pleasure (Merriam-Webster, Oxford dictionaries, Collins).

tourism industry seems to poach on some human activities that have nothing in common with the seeking of pleasure, other than the fact that they make use of the same conveniences. Traveling for medical purposes and on pilgrimage routes, for instance, can exist outside the field and are even much older activities than tourism itself (Lam and Lei 2002). It is even highly probable that the individuals taking part in these voyages do not see themselves as tourists. Yet, they are often considered by the industry, because of their similar form of consumption, as speciality forms of tourism.

Whether just for pleasure or following interests of other nature, the contemporary individual enjoys traveling. The need for the activity itself has produced an entire industry, and one that by now has become so intertwined with the other fields of the global economy, that its hypothetical sudden disappearance is perhaps inconceivable. The economic and social damage would have an immeasurable effect for those directly and indirectly involved. There are regions on earth, mostly underdeveloped and developing countries that are dependent entirely or almost entirely on tourism, and that otherwise would probably be in decline if not returned to an incipient stage of evolution (IUOTO 1975; Britton 1979; Hiller 1977; Britton 1989). For example, Greece, which is not even a developing economy but whose 85% of the private employment is in the service sector (EC 2013), took a tremendous blow with the last global crisis, because of the diminished inflow of tourists (Kapiki 2012; Kollewe 2012; Lowen 2012). This gets us back to the acacia that, along with the giraffe, form an odd symbiosis. The two occupy the same areal – the savannah. Even if, apparently, the acacia developed protection against browsing by getting taller, growing thorns and producing tannin, it is dependent on the animals that feed on its leafs and fruits and, by doing this, they spread the acacia's seeds. Without them the acacia would not be able to achieve the status of the widest spread tree in the savannah. Amongst acacia's suitors, by far, the most dependent is the giraffe. Without the acacia, the giraffe would not be able to feed, because all the other supplies are outside its neck's span, whether too high or too low. This dependency reveals a capitalization of individual features that ensures a reciprocal advantage in common survival. Much like the way tourism manifests itself. It is not a painless relation, neither in nature, nor in life, but it seems to be efficient, since it is assumed to be more a gain, then a loss on both parts.

Is it a bird? Is it a plane? The tourist's "chemistry" dilemma

Tourism as a human activity was neither recognized nor defined as such until early to mid-20th century, although even before people were traveling to specific destinations for recreational or leisure purposes. The activity itself was defined in 1941: 79 by Walter Hunziker, founder of one of the first institutes dedicated to tourism, together with Kurt Krapf: "Tourism is the sum of the phenomena and relationships arising from the travel and stay of non-residents, in so far as they do not lead to permanent residence and are not connected with any earning activity". Tourism was recognized as an essential activity by the Manila Declaration on World Tourism of 1980 for its effects on the culture, economy and international relations of all nations and has become one of the fastest growing industries ever since.

It was pointed out that tourism in its modern form started as a customary itinerary amongst young people from the landed gentry, serving as a rite of passage in their education[3] (Towner 1985). However, tourism as a mass movement developed *ad hoc* with more and more upper-class urbanites searching for certain resources that lacked quality within the cities. Especially during the Industrial Revolution, tourism found its purpose in complementing the negative side of the city with recreational and leisure activities whether as trips to the countryside or to selected destinations (Kerr-Jarrett 1993: 125-126; Spirou 2011: xvi; Cloke 2013). The mid-18th century not only reinvented tourism as a remedy to the downsides of the industrial life, but through technology, allowed its further development. The ascending industrial elite provided the iron and the power of steam on rails and water to an increasing middle class (Butcher 2003: 34).

Generally, the purpose of tourism did not change over time, but as leisure time grew along with the quality of life, so did the variety of touristic interests (Uysal et al. 2012; Hall and Rath 2007). The ever extending "adjectival tourism" list points out to the wide addressable touristic resources that suit the consumer needs of the average tourist and, just as well, those of the niche enthusiasts. The lack of boundaries between tourism and other entangled tourist-like traveling experiences have led critics to argue the existence of an "industry" as a foundation (Leiper 2008: 237) and production system (d'Hauteserre 2006) for all the related activities. The tourism industry is rather a vehicle for capitalist and non-capitalist pursuits that, conjecturally, encompasses leisure, leisure related or leisure complementary activities.

What then would be a good, modern definition of the tourist? Since the current definition only refers to the individual's action of traveling to a place for

3 The custom of the *Grand Tour* changed over the years and, while it is still remembered in the *GT* name of the cars able to withstand the London-Paris-Geneva-Milan-Rome trip in comfort and style, the coming of age Britons targeted a more familial land mass destination – Ibiza. However, started during the 1960-70s, the "gap year" closely resembles the practice of the Grand Tour for the young persons to carry it out all over the globe.

pleasure[4], maybe we should revisit it. Tourism is no longer a spontaneous phenomenon conditioned by the same action performed independently by unrelated individuals. Modern tourism is organized up to the point that it is universally recognized as an organizational construction. After all, we do refer to tourism as an industry and treat it as such. Thus, the modern tourist is less and less the explorer or the offbeat and more a pack member. Tourism would be, if so, the action of organized individuals traveling to more or less remote locations in order to experience their riches. If no belligerent action is mentioned, then this might resemble an invasion. It happened all over history and they didn't call it tourism, so let's assume misconduct is kept to a minimum.

Tourists bring back souvenirs. It happened through the 18th and 19th century and nobody noticed their displacement until their display in the west European museums. The modern tourist does not indulge in unconcealed vandalism, although at the time the concept emerged it was not considered as such. Modern souvenirs are more of a benign nature, either made in China or shot with something made in China. Let's not forget that money is exchanged, even if one may think that colonialism fits as well up to this point. The global free market and the fair trade actions are now in place, so the modern tourist has to negotiate his potential touristic satisfaction based on affordability. No longer is he traveling for pleasure alone, regardless of other factors. Therefore, a proper definition of the tourist would be: "an individual, commonly prepared in advance, that travels to a place that regularly requires mediation between the will to compensate for pleasure and need to adapt to local conditions". This definition leaves us with a larger variety of tourists, one that would properly suit the contemporary circulating typologies, such as those of Smith (1989) and Plog (2001).

It is not uncommon, even amongst tourists, to make differentiations, as if one could be a "better tourist" than somebody else. These differences come naturally to satisfy the tourist's need of accomplishment and the recognition of his adventurousness. If we would rank the level of satisfaction that each destination could offer and add the numbers, this would probably satisfy the human need to compete with palpable results. One could then be a more experienced tourist than his peers with the same amount of travels, but with more rewarding destinations. It is obviously easier to "stick more flags" in Rome than in Borneo, although the jungle flag would potentially have more "scars" than the ones left by the poor

---

4 Just before Hunziker and Krapf, the League of Nations, concerned with the cross-border extent of the tourism phenomenon, defined it in 1936 as the "traveling abroad for at least twenty-four hours". It was later, in 1976, when the Tourism Society of England detailed the purposes of tourism: "Tourism is the temporary, short-term movement of people to destination outside the places where they normally live and work and their activities during the stay at each destination. It includes movements for all purposes" (Allan 2002: 313).

service and fake city guides. But let's admit that if the conditions in tourism would be like "at home" everywhere, one would no longer seek to satisfy other needs than the one to relax. So let's assume that the vacationers do search for adventure and for the unusual, but in different proportions, according to their personal degree of handling the unexpected. There is still a chance that the touring satisfaction is not met, independent of the tourist's preparation. Unaccounted local factors or inaccurate marketing have the potential of ruining the hypothetical "chemistry". Thus, choosing beaten tracks or traveling in large groups seems a more viable alternative that would ensure either a certified familiar journey or the adaptation to the destination by having at least a pack experience. A mass is thus being formed either at the terminus from unrelated individuals that share the same pattern of vacationing, usually defined by local conditions being applied to all incoming tourists, or from interrelated parties that would follow a planned pattern of their common choosing and applied to all.

<table>
<tr><th colspan="3">Type of Tourist</th><th rowspan="2">Number of tourists</th><th rowspan="2">Adaptation to local customs</th></tr>
<tr><th>Cohen</th><th>Smith</th><th>Plog</th></tr>
<tr><td rowspan="8">Existential, experimental and experiential</td><td>Explorer</td><td>"Venturer"</td><td>Very limited</td><td>Accepts altogether</td></tr>
<tr><td colspan="4">Behaviour: Explorers in a "quest for discovery and knowledge" (Smith 1989: 11).</td></tr>
<tr><td>Elite</td><td>Near "venturer"</td><td>Rarely seen</td><td>Adapts fully</td></tr>
<tr><td colspan="4">Behaviour: Elite tourists, "usually include individuals who have been almost everywhere" (Smith 1989: 12) and tour to uncommon places using pre-arranged indigenous services.</td></tr>
<tr><td>Off-beat</td><td>Mid centric</td><td>Uncommon but present</td><td>Adapts well</td></tr>
<tr><td colspan="4">Behaviour: Off-beat travellers avoid tourist crowds or "heighten the excitement of their vacation by doing something beyond the norm" (Smith 1989: 12).</td></tr>
<tr><td>Unusual</td><td>Mid centric</td><td>Occasional</td><td>Adapts to some extent</td></tr>
<tr><td colspan="4">Behaviour: Tourists that sometimes participate on prearranged excursions to remote destinations, in addition to their main objective.</td></tr>
<tr><td rowspan="4">Diversionary and recreational</td><td>Incipient mass</td><td>Near dependable</td><td>Steady flow</td><td>Seeks western amenities</td></tr>
<tr><td>Mass</td><td rowspan="2">Dependable</td><td>Constant entries</td><td>Expects western amenities</td></tr>
<tr><td>Charter</td><td>Massive arrivals</td><td>Demands western amenities</td></tr>
<tr><td colspan="4">Behaviour: Mass tourism - as the numbers of tourists expands from a steady flow to massive chartered arrivals, the interaction with the locals gradually diminishes, while the tourist services head towards Western norms.</td></tr>
</table>

Figure 1: The table exemplifies the relation between the frequency of tourists and their adaptation to local customs (Cohen 1979; Smith 1989: 12; Plog 2001). The typology points also towards the broadening of tourist behaviour in regard to its adjustment to the experience's qualities. (Authors)

For the inhabitants of their destinations, it makes no difference, and they would perceive the same mass, regardless of its point of aggregation. They have to adapt just the same and maybe the "chemistry" is just as important for them. The locals usually make the difference between incoming visitors, based on their cultural and behavioural profiles that are generally acknowledged worldwide. Aside from the seasonal patterns, something they would be prepared for, cultural values are amounted according to shared regional and historical commonalities. For example loud Italians are tolerated in Spain, but loud Americans are not; camera-face Japanese are noticeable all over the western world as well as money spending Germans are appreciated everywhere they go, except for the places their forerunners visited previously with less than amiable intent. Shared ancestry is considered at both ends and it usually sets the parameters of this "chemistry".

There is one more factor to take into account. Global forces are changing the world. The global migration and tolerance policies are transforming more and more places into a blend of local and international cultural characteristics (Satin 1968: 58; Norton et al. 1991: 67). There is no Indian-British conflict in London, not even Indian-Pakistani, nor aversion towards the French in northern Africa, as long as there are millions of Maghrebis living and working in France. The big cities are different. They even take pride in their multiculturalism. Restoring Chinatowns in the US or black people riding bicycles in Amsterdam are far from newspaper headlines now. One can presume that the world's big cities are prepared for visitors.

Vedi Napoli e poi muori: Remedial traveling, cliché mapping and bucket-list tourism

With Paris, London and New York leading the top of the most popular tourist destinations, we can only assume that the high concentration of landmarks within the cities is attracting tourists with both the quality and the quantity of their resources. The urban tissue of the big cities, rich in overlaid tourist attractions, continues to attract the consumers by guaranteeing a predictable satisfaction. In contrast with the early tendencies of tourism to target the healthier countryside or perhaps the slow paced life of the Mediterranean towns, the average contemporary vacationer turned towards a more condensed offer (Hall and Rath 2007). No longer is leisure exclusive to the well-off's spare time, but also to the blue collar's furlough. Furthermore, the wage earner's short leave angled the traveling experience towards "shorter breaks", rather than towards long vacations (Misiura 2006: 87). The big cities do not only accept tourism *per se*, as a consequence of their spontaneous development which accidentally led to the creation of unique cultural attractions, but due to a higher concentration of their touristic highlights, they already began to steer the process of capital accumulation. They are becoming the hotspots of the global tourist flows, no longer spontaneous, but concertedly organized, with the active involvement of all actors.

Naples, May 5th, 1841 – the English painter, sculptor and traveller Arthur John Strutt writes in his journal: "Eccoci finalmente qui. Un proverbio italiano dice: Vedi Napoli e poi muori!, ma io dico: Vedi Napoli e vivi, perché c'è molto qui degno di essere vissuto"[5]. (Strutt 1970: 91). Strutt could have not anticipated this, but he accidentally stumbled upon a local saying that would mark the birth of tourism as a universally recognized human activity for both its leisure and economic rewards. At its origins, the expression might have had a more limited significance, such as for the region's inhabitants to see the big city of Naples before their passing away. The melancholic desire for the Neapolitan experience, the so-called *napolitudine*[6], can be encountered in late 18th to mid-19th century art, especially in the Neapolitan filmography[7]. But, it seems that across Europe it attained yet another meaning, the one that every traveller must absolutely get to Naples too.

In the context of 18th to early 19th century, the Mediterranean seashores, of which Italy had plenty, in the absence of penicillin, were extensively advised as a remedy for the rising respiratory symptoms of the heavily industrialized Europe. Statistics conducted at the turn of the century shown an extreme incidence of the tuberculosis, in some cases the bacteria being present amongst more than half the urban population (Mc Carthy 2001; Fletcher et al. 2003). The tuberculosis was so widespread that it offered a familiar subject for literature's Romantic Movement. It was documented in the writings of Sand, Dumas, Murger, Hugo and many other less famous authors, as well as in operatic depictions, for instance those of Puccini and Verdi. With such a high frequency it was inevitable that some ended in causalities and it is probably not so far-fetched to assume that few

5 Tr. *Here we are, finally. An Italian proverb sais: See Naples and then you can die!, but I say: See Naples and then live, because there's a lot here worth seeing.*

6 "E mor pe' 'sta smania 'e turnà a Napule" (tr. "I die because of this madness to return to Naples") catches in Michele Galdieri's 1945 poem *Munastero 'e Santa Chiara* a post-WWII changed, but still surviving, Naples (Cavallo: 2005).

7 Eugenio Perego directs the movie *Vedi Napoli e poi muori* in 1924. Several other films with the same title or on the same subject, such as Riccardo Freda's 1951 *Vedi Napoli e poi muori*, and Eduardo de Filippo's 1945 *Napoli milionaria*, followed over time. The Neapolitan atmosphere is best pictured during the late 30s – mid 60s period by Totò (Antonio de Curtis Gagliardi Griffo Focas Comneno) and Peppino De Filippo, two of Naples's most prolific actors, as well as in Vittorio de Sica's filmography.

of them occurred during their Italian alleviation[8] (Flick 1891), from Anthony Ashley-Cooper, 3rd Earl of Shaftesbury to John Keats. Where the Italian proverb caught amongst the recuperating community is not known, but its use, previously encountered only in travel journals (Kelly & Hook 1826: I 35; Reynolds 1826: I 24; Stendhal 1829: II 328; Thompson 1835: 184; Brown 1942: 89), started to show in novels such as Robert Hichens's 1980 *A Spirit in Prison*, Joseph Conrad's 1908 *Il Conde: A Pathetic Tale* or in Goethe's famous *Faust*, which premiered in 1829 in Brunswick. Of course the saying gave birth to countless paraphrases, as for example those of Fanny Parkes or George Dennis[9], meant for competitive comparisons amongst places worth to be seen.

Already spread through Italy at the beginning of the 19th century, in its original Neapolitan form "Vide Napule e po' more.", "Vedi Napoli e poi muori!" was commonly misspelled as "Vedi Napoli e poi mori!"[10], which although enigmatic, is not implausible. One of the sources is related to the Naples 18th century synod, which forcefully repressed the unholy and heretics with the excommunication and, at times, with the capital punishment (Rey-Mermet 1983: 219)[11]. The second version relates to the former settlement of Mori (Bell 1962: 16) that, first recorded in the 9th century, situated near Naples, it gave sense to a Latin expression saying "Videre Neapolim et Mori" with the meaning that one should consider big and small equally. With reasonable doubts, there is another version that indicates Mori as being an island in the Gulf of Naples[12]. Thirdly and perhaps more factual, the origin of the proverb is attributed to an inhabitant of Mori, a small village in Trentino, who so proud of his hamlet reacted to a tourist's prais-

8 Flick cites De Renzi, a local Physician: "Out of 5,285 admissions to one of the hospitals of the city of Naples during the year 1828, 1,108 were consumptives; and out of 1,366 deaths which occurred in the same institution during that year, 699 were due to that disease".

9 In *Wanderings of a Pilgrim in Search of the Picturesque* (1850) Parkes writes "With the Neapolitan saying 'Vedi Napoli, e poi mori' I beg leave to differ entirely, and would rather offer this advice – 'See the Taj Mahal, and then – see the Ruins of Delhi.'" Dennis induces in its 1839 *Summer in Andalucia* (153) the similitude between the Neapolitans and the Sevillanos by making use of the same proverb.

10 Since there is little phonetic difference between "muori" and "mori", the declination of the Italian verb "morire" (to die) is so commonly misspelled by foreigners that the altered form is as much present in writing as the correct one. The Merriam-Webster dictionary, for example, offers the misuse with the correct explanation, www.merriam-webster.com/dictionary/vedi napoli e poi mori.

11 Regardless of this, in the 18th century the expression already had its entrenched sense of praising the beauty of Naples, since it appears as such in Carlo Goldoni's 1751 play *La bottega del caffè*.

12 William White expresses his suspicion upon the existence of the island in his *Notes and Queries* (1900: 449), since he had no confirmation of such a place.

ing of the beauties of Naples, "Vedi Napoli eppoi Mori"[13], with the implication of Naples not being quite the ultimate traveling experience.

Still eloquent presently, the "old" Italian proverb might refer to any geographic cliché produced by the traveling culture, whether through the readings of the 19th century, or the more prolific media of the 20th century. A considerable part of these clichés have their origin in the European Romanticism that overlapped the peak of the European colonial empires. The romantic writers and artists travelled the globe in search of the original and the authentic, an attempt to escape the urban growth and sprawl accompanying the Industrial Revolution. In an ironic twist, the industry, often subject to Romantic negative reactions towards modernity, provided just the means for the Romantic spirit to get to the, until then out of reach, landscape sought by poets and painters (Butcher 2003: 34-35). Their Counter-Enlightenment imagination soon embraced the exotic and unfamiliar far-lands, with the direct consequence of publicising their "worth to be shared" cultural treasures. Experienced previously only by the great explorers and cartographers of the Age of Discovery, such as Vasco da Gama, Marco Polo, Magellan and Jacques Cartier, the Orient as well as the Americas were still concealed by unbelievable legends.

The rational mind of the enlightened scientists was struggling to contain the expanding paradigms within the limits of the conventional logic. For example, before the modern times, the giraffe was not present on the European continent but as a gift for the occasional eccentric monarchs, from 15th century Lorenzo de Medici, to Charles X of France or George IV of England (Williams 2010: 59, 76). The 19th century exemplars that caused stir and "giraffanalias"[14] throughout Europe (Williams 2010: 81) were still seen as incredible creatures. Therefore, the name attributed to the giraffe by the scientific community, *Giraffa camelopardalis*, went along with the ancient Latin belief that the giraffe is an unnatural crossbreed of a camel and a leopard. Meanwhile, their contemporary romanticists were busy retracing the routes of the caravels and caravans not in search for fundamental answers, but for the wonders of distant China, India or Siam. Of course the outposts of civilization were the pinnacle of the exotic, but equally, the railroads laid all across Europe during the 19th century (Ingle 1991) were a

13 The Evening Post 8 June 1915, vol. LXXXIX, Issue 134: 8.

14 A "giraffanalia" was a memorabilia frenzy accompanying the parade of giraffes through the European cities. "Camelopard yellow" and "camel's hair" became trendy colours and fabrics (Frohman 1923; *La Belle Assembleé* 1827a; b, 1828a; Palmantier 1995: 61). Considering that "*Zerafa*, meaning *the elegant*, is the Arabic term for the Camelopard" (*La Belle Assembleé* 1828b) "'à la giraffe' was the fashion from towering bonnets to dappled gloves; gowns, necklaces, and waistcoats were fashioned in the color of her spots" (Dagg and Foster 1976: 6).

good excuse[15] for the noble rediscovery of the forgotten marvels of the Old continent and, maybe, reason to bring back a few. Ancient relics along with artistic representations and travel stories endorsed the new "leisure time" in its metamorphosis to fashionable and, then to stereotypical.

What the clichés from the Romantic period brought is a parallel mapping of the world. While the conventional understanding of the globe followed geographical boundaries and political vectors, its cultural perception was sketched with images worth a thousand words. Long before any intention of marketing for tourism, certain places began to acquire international reputation as their intrinsic cultural substance was advertised through the symbolic actions of storytelling and writing. Conventional mapping has the shortcoming of offering data and not information. The geographical coordinates are able to indicate the global position of a place and even induce a feel of its identity based on further cultural association, but they do not detect its identity. On the other hand, the semiotic mapping defies the conventional processes of mapping and point towards more immaterial characteristics of the place, even when describing the material.

How certain places got their postcard-perfect image imprinted upon the collective consciousness of the worldwide travellers is less important, the reality of their desirability is what matters to most. After all, Columbus himself was convinced that he was sailing towards India; in fact so convinced that he identified the native inhabitants of the Caribbean islands as Indians. While relying on conventional geography, Columbus was also charting instincts on unconventional basis. Often, the ideal nature of stereotypes is taken into consideration more than their symbolic significance. One would take action, at least when choosing a destination, not only based on quantifiable factors such as expenses, hospitality reviews, availability of certain services, but also bridging on empathy towards an ideal standard, commonly universally embraced. Palm tree beaches, white lime houses crowded on narrow streets, spice markets, *tiki* umbrellas, are just a few of the mandatory inputs of any potential travel for pleasure.

The ideal place stereotypes do not find their way on the "to do lists" of the dedicated vacationer which has more oriented travel plans. The scrupulous tourist is particular on choosing destinations based on other factors than just the pleasure of vacationing. Some travel for or in addition to business, are gourmand eager to experience the world's cuisine, feel attraction to cultural particularities or peculiarities or just enjoy bird watching.

15 Thomas Cook was responsible for the first chartered excursion train to be advertised for the general public, in 1841. In 1845 he scheduled a train fare from Leicester to Calais for the Paris Exhibition. His enterprise grew during the following years with planned trips to European countries, as well as to Egypt and the United States.

Rob Reiner's (2007) *The Bucket List* depicts what everybody else's top spots on the list are. With no hidden sarcasm, they typically follow the same patterns: something old, Greece for example, something new – Dubai would fit excellently, something borrowed such as Las Vegas's Venetian, and something blue, warm and clear. In short, the action involves Edward Cole and Carter Chambers, a billionaire health-care magnate and a blue-collar mechanic, played by Jack Nicholson and Morgan Freeman, both diagnosed with terminal lung cancer. As they wait to "kick the bucket" in a hospital ward, Carter's "bucket list" appeals to Edward's more adventurous nature. After his offering to finance the entire operation, the two flee the hospital with the help of Edward's assistant, in order to engage themselves in an around-the-world vacation that doesn't miss Paris, the Taj Mahal, The Great Wall of China, Mount Everest or Giza.

Vedi Venezia e poi discori[16]: floating city, "floating cities" and body snatchers

Dating back, allegedly, to the victory of the *Serenissima Repubblica* against Ulrico de Treven (1162) that ended in street celebrations, the Carnival of Venice takes place in February, forty days before Easter. Perhaps the oldest on-going tradition of celebrating the beginning of the Lent, this carnival is a celebrated event, acknowledged probably worldwide. After a long period of inactivity, the Carnival of Venice was resumed in the 70s. Coinciding with the aftermath of the 1966 floods, many Venetians recall the early carnivals as collective goodbye parties of those leaving the city. The floods rendered unusable many of the ground floors, thus affecting businesses, as well as in some cases, the integrity of the structures.

In time the carnival gained prominence, but in 2012, confusion followed what seemed to be a second carnival taking place in Venice. The city's posts and fences were peppered with not only the posters announcing the yearly event, but also with ones containing the following announcement: "Venerdi 17 Febbraio 2012 / Carnevale No Grande Navi / Fuori la MSC Magnifica da Venezia! / Le grandi navi non le Vogliamo! / Dalle 14.30 in poi alle zattere/ Musica, vin brule e… sorprese!"[17]. Piggybacking on the Venice's real carnival, the *No Big Ships*

16 In full, "Vedi Napoli e poi mori, vedi Venetia e poi discori" is a Venetian saying with unknown origins. Obviously, a paraphrase to the famous Neapolitan proverb, to "see Venice and then prattle" about it is the expression of the Venetians taking equal, if not greater pride in their own city (Vidulli: 2009: 24).

17 Tr. "Friday, February 17th, 2012 / No Big Ships Carnival / Out with the MSC Magnifica from Venice / We don't want no big ships! / From 14:30 to the rafts / Music, mulled wine and… surprises".

Committee (*Comitato No Grandi Navi*) was seeking to get extended exposure from the media prepared to cover the few days of carnival. The organized protest was calling the Venetians to demonstrate against the ever-bigger cruisers entering Venice's canals. The biggest to that date was the *MSC Magnifica*, operated by the Mediterranean Shipping Company Cruises. With a length of 293.8 m and a tonnage of 95,128 GT, the *MSC Magnifica* carried a total of 1,027 crew members and up to a maximum of 3,605 passengers[18] on cruises in the eastern Mediterranean, visiting ports in Italy, Greece, Turkey and Croatia[19]. But most impressive of all, its 13 passenger decks passing through *Canale della Giudecca* cast a shadow over Venice's 3-4 stories buildings. With the MSC's new *Divina* cruise ship (139,400 tons) entering service on the same route as *Magnifica*, beginning March 2012, the Venetians feared further potential hazards on Venice's already frail underpinnings, not to mention the added stress on the city's infrastructure and residents. However, following the protests, the *MSC Magnifica* changed course to operate a transatlantic route between Western Europe and Brazil[20].

Figure 2: MS Queen Victoria's superstructure dwarfs Venice's old buildings. Returning to its birth place, Marghera's Fincanteri shipyard, Queen Victoria is no longer allowed to traverse *Canale della Giudecca*, due to new legislation. (Andreas Pichler: *Das Venedig Prinzip*, 2013)

18 MSC Cruises – MSC Magnifica's technical sheet, http://www.msccruisesusa.com/flotta/technical/Magnifica_ENG.pdf, 16.02.2014.

19 Ship Parade, http://www.shipparade.com/az/MSC_Magnifica/MSC_Magnifica.htm, 16.02.2014.

20 Ibid.

Although aimed at the dissonant image of the big ships, the protests, which continued throughout 2012 and 2013, were essentially addressing the growing unrest of Venice's community. The continuous visitor's inflow, that exceeds 20 million each year (Kington 2009), is after all the main contributor to Venice's economy and to its population decay just as well. Although much of the tourists, such as those brought by the "big ships" are day-trippers that only bring congestion and litter, the interest for Venice has also a real estate facet. Even if the residents that own a property do not face this problem directly, the local tenants are forced to compete with the romance seekers keen to rent flats in the Mediterranean's utmost romantic city. Reaching 174,000 in 1951, and keeping close to 120,000 even after the 1966 floods, Venice's resident population recently dropped under 60,000 (Newman 2009; Squires 2009). The rest moved inland, to Mestre or other Italian cities, not able to keep up with the climbing expenses. This sad reality was best portrayed in Andreas Pichler's 2013 documentary – *Das Venedig Prinzip* (*The Venice Paradox*). Born in Bolzano, northern Italy, not far from Venice, Pichler was well aware of the process of population swap. As one of the films' subjects laments: "Venice has become nothing but a dormitory" while taxying along with his belongings towards the mainland part of the city. Most of the properties in Venice are now sold to wealthy Italians and foreigners on the look for a profitable investment. They rent them out year-round as temporary vacation units. "The entire architectural heritage of Venice will be damaged" declares a real estate agent, thinking of all the transformed buildings to better suit the tourist's requirements. "I'm a defeated man. This great bitterness takes hold of you and doesn't let go."

The *No Big Ships Carnival* was not the first attempt to scare off some of its tourists. In 1999, the former mayor of Venice, Massimo Cacciari, turned to Oliviero Toscani, the photographer behind the notorious Benetton campaigns, to produce a negative publicity campaign, which he did in a series of billboards. The goal of the campaign was to arouse interest towards preservation amongst the complacent residents, as well as to discourage low spending day-trippers, in order to cut down on associated costs. In the opinion of a Venetian: "People used to come here for a proper two week vacation. Now they fly in, take a quick look and fly out" (Pichler 2013). Unluckily, the campaign had quite the opposite effect by marketing the very thing the tourists sought – the aristocratic death on a dying city (O'Reilly 1999), so a more durable solution was finally adopted, by implementing a "booking with benefits" system (Russo 1999). Attracting more willing to spend tourists would, in Cacciari's opinion, if not stop the migration, at least cover the budget needed to preserve and clean the city.

Figure 3: Leaflet announces the 2012 "alternative" carnival. (Living Venice: livingveniceblog.com/wp-content/uploads/Out-Out-Big-Ships.jpeg, 2013.10.18)

Figure 4: The cover of Pichler's *Venice Paradox* shows *MSC Magnifica* passing by Venice's *Santa Maria de la Salute* church. (© FILM-TANK 2012)

Another protest was organised by Matteo Secchi, the leader of *Venessia.com*, a resident's action group. Secchi updates regularly his electronic board set in a shop window, close to the Rialto Bridge, with the latest statistics. "The number of locals has dropped 600 since we started counting last March and we are set to go under the psychological 60,000 barrier in May" (Kington 2009). A third of Venice's peak population are now competing in the rights to the city with an average 55,000 tourists a day. Considering the grim foresight of Venice not having one single authentic resident by 2030 (Pichler 2012), things are getting alarmingly out of anybody's control. But the remaining residents are still able to indulge in a little humour. "Where do they all pee? They're going to make the water level rise" said an old man, one of Pichler's interviewed, facing the tourists swarming on *Molo Riva dei Schiavoni*, Venice's promenade on *Canale di San*

Marco. In 2009, Secchi organized a protest party on the Rialto Bridge during the carnival and along with a few hundred other residents, dressed up as American Indians, distributed leaflets throughout the city, with the following message written in five languages: "Our cultural identity is at risk of dissolving if Venice becomes a theme park. We Venetians will not surrender!"

Figure 5: The scribbling on the box “stuff from the kitchen and the room” announces another Venetian’s moving out of the city. (Andreas Pichler: *Das Venedig Prinzip*, 2013)

The activist movements in Venice intensified during the late years, a sort of late countermeasure to their diminishing number. As if the massive exodus of Venice’s population on the mainland in the aftermath of the 60s floods was not enough, the downward spiral of closing businesses that are being replaced by the exponents of the global economy is a continuous toll on the residents, which currently are left with fewer options of employment. Most of the remaining ones are forced to turn to the very same cause of their discontent, the tourism industry and, thus, to service the very people they want out.

In the end, the perseverance of the relentless optimists did have some positive outcome. The Clini-Passera decree issued in March 2012 put a ban on ships heavier than 40.000 tons to cross the *Canale della Giudeca*, with the mention that alternative routes are found[21]. Benetton has bought properties in the historic Venice and has offered to build new theatres and restaurants and Cacciari believes that this will encourage other investors, but until now the new projects are reluctant to leave the drawing board. The *40x Venetia* forum, founded in October 2008, has more than 1.500 members involved in sustaining Venice's public life that has to continue even with the drawbacks caused by mass tourism. Promoting the participatory planning, the forum acts as a buffer between the tourist oriented actions, the administration's policies and the community's own interests.

Currently Venice is still sinking slowly in the lagoon's waters and gets flooded with every heavy rain. It sells a contrasting image of garbage next to luxury shops, of picturesque passageways that reveal the smouldering discontent of the enduring residents in anti-tourist graffiti. How come this image still sells? Minus the waste and mould, Venice's touristic success is even replicated, gondoliers and pigeons included, in Las Vegas. Its theme-park potential was, ironically, envisioned by no other then Walt Disney, who was just about to build a Floridian Venice resort on Seven Seas Lagoon by 1976, but the project was scrapped due to the 1973 oil crisis. The cloning of Venice worldwide inspired its mayor to make an approach towards copyrighting the name. Venice spends about 32 million dollars a year on sanitation, public safety and transportation of its annual 76 million dollars budget[22]. But with 65% of its budget coming from tourism associated services, Venice is irreversibly dependent on the income the tourists bring. With not much room to steer its development towards community sustainability, considering that only about 3 million dollars were spent last year on culture and recreation, the only other alternative that Venice has is to consider tourism as the proverbial "necessary evil". To cite another of Pichler's interviewed inhabitants of Venice: "We all must kneel before the god of money. This isn't a democracy, it's a dictatorship."

---

21 Since the only other alternative route for entering Venice through *Bocca del Lido* is through *Bocca di Malamocco*, the big ships are usually stalled outside the lagoon. They can proceed then to their usual landing – Statione Maritima – through Marghera's *Porto Merci* and then the newly deepened *Canale Cotorda – San Angelo*. Still, more than 600 big ships traverse annually the traditional route through the city of Venice.

22 According to City of Venice's Adopted Budget for the Fiscal Year 2012-2013: "The FY budget has a General Fund allocation of $20,930,600. The total compares to last year's General Fund of $20,659,696. The city's total budget is $74,792,310, compared to last year's total of $80,159,386." (www.venicegov.com\Files\Finance\2012-13_ADOPTED_BUDGET.pdf, 15.01.2014).

Barcelona és bona si la bossa sona[23]: If you can't bite the hand, at least growl at it

Barcelona is another city facing a similar problem. The tourists in large groups and the Americans are often greeted with bad looks and irritated Castilian expressions. Anti-Americanism is common throughout the whole of Spain due to the mutual history that encompasses the 1898 Spanish-American War, Washington's support of Franco after the 1936-1939 Civil War, the 1953 Pact of Madrid that allowed the installation of US military bases in Spain and sparsely because of the American administration's support of South-American dictatorships, especially amongst Spain's numerous Latin immigrants.

As for the other tourists, the Spaniards' attitude might have something to do with their exacerbated nationalism. Poor, underdeveloped and in social unrest until the 1960s, Spain was isolated from the rest of Europe. Kept even out of the United Nations due to its fascist past, its economic lag came to an end only with the US's interest in the Iberian Peninsula, during the Cold War. During the 1959-1974 economic boom, known as "the Spanish miracle", Franco's technocrats, under the guidance of the IMF, implemented the development plans (*Planes de desarrollo*) that opened Spain to foreign investments and unveiled it as a tourist destination (Martin 1998). In little over a decade, Spanish economy experienced a growth from 12 to 76 billion dollars[24], of which tourism accounted for 10% (Martin 1998). The Spanish bet on tourism was, nevertheless, a synchronized success. With the population's exodus towards the industrial cities, many rural areas were struggling with demographic and economic loss, which fortunately was balanced by vacationers' moving in. Spain's Mediterranean and Atlantic coasts represented an attractive investment for retreat residencies or houses rented to other tourists. The frenzy of buying in Spain met a controversial attitude from the Spaniards. On the one hand they were no less than keen to take the US's and EU's money while, on the other hand, are resentful of the fact that they are selling off their country. This inconsistency is best felt in Barcelona, Spain's number one tourist destination.

Barcelona is a tourist trap, Europe's fourth destination after London, Paris and Rome[25]. Ever capitalising on Antonio Gaudi's avant-gardist spirit, the city is

23 In full, "Barcelona és bona si la bossa sona, però tant si sona com si no sona, Barcelona sempre és bona" ("Barcelona is good if you have money in your pocket, but even if you have or you don't, Barcelona is always good") is a Catalan saying that best represents the locals enterprising spirit.

24 According to Countryeconomy.com, http://countryeconomy.com/gdp/spain, 15.01.2014.

25 Based on Euromonitor International's top city destinations ranking, http://blog.euromonitor.com/2011/01/euromonitor-internationals-top-city-destinations-ranking.html, 15.01.2014.

bursting with touristic attractions. With eight UNESCO World Heritage Sites and yearly events, especially in culture and fashion[26], Barcelona can be considered the honey pot of the Mediterranean coast of Spain. The tourism in the province of Catalonia alone accounts for about 25% of the Spain's tourism market[27]. In its peak year, 2013, Barcelona was visited by 7.5 million vacationers and over 16 million "overnighters"[28]. With an income of 3,069 million Euros just from the tourism industry, Barcelona cannot complain of bad business[29]. The Catalan enterprising spirit, meaningfully illustrated in the local saying "Barcelona is good if you have money in your pocket", placed Barcelona on the 9th position in the top of the growing European cities, with the best of all sustained growth year after year (2.7%)[30].

Still, Barcelona is not enjoying the attention all the time. On a rooftop facing the hill of *El Carmel*, a message greeted the visitors: "Why call it tourist season, if we can't shoot them." The message received an extended audience since on the same hill, *Park Güell*, Gaudi's masterpiece, lures in visitors day after day. Even if more on the amusing side, the message discloses a parallel "hospitality" standpoint. Same as in Venice and other tourist urban hotspots, Barcelona faces the downsides of its celebrity: streets crowded with puzzled map-readers or just aimless "passerbuyers" sensing the pulse of the city.

Barcelonans fall into three categories. On the one hand, there are those embracing the "social exchange" (Homans 1961: 31, 31) and willingly participating in tourist related exchanges (Pizam 1978; Ap 1990; Allen et al. 1993; Jurowski et al. 1997; Gursoy et al. 2002). They understand tourism as a substantial source of income for the city; not only business owners, but regular people as well. The second category is represented by the indifferent, unsympathetic, but otherwise not action oriented either. Usually they avoid La Rambla's central walkway, populated by tourists, street vendors, living statues, magicians and pickpockets. The last category is the most vocal, typically living in Barcelona for generations. It was pointed (Besculides et al. 2002) that the inhabitants' concern about the negative effects of tourism differs even within the same community, the ones

26 Since 2009, Barcelona dropped two spots from its third position in the top of world cultural capitals, according to Global Language Monitor's ranking, http://www.languagemonitor.com/category/fashion/fashion-capitals/, 15.01.2014.

27 Catalan News Agency citing figures released by the Spanish Ministry of Industry, Energy and Tourism, http://www.catalannewsagency.com/business/item/catalonia-welcomed-15-6-million-foreign-tourists-in-2013, 15.01.2014.

28 According to the *Tourism Statistics for Barcelona and province*, http://professional.barcelonaturisme.com/imgfiles/estad/Est2013.pdf, 15.01.2014.

29 Ibid.

30 According to Price Waterhouse Cooper's *European cities hotel forecast 2013* report, www.pwc.com/en_GX/gx/hospitality-leisure/assets/pwc-european-cities-hotel-forecast.pdf, 15.01.2014.

with stronger community ties worrying the most. They occupy the old quarters, obviously the most targeted by tourists' curiosity, as well as all the associated motives of dissatisfaction, such as inflation, littering, traffic and parking problems (Pearce 1980). Typically, they are the Catalan "extremists" who would complain even of the fact that things are written in Spanish and not in the local dialect. The discontent towards tourists is, however on the rise in Barcelona. Stencils, graffiti artwork and blog comments appear periodically to give it a voice.

One action, taken in 2010 copied an initiative that took place in New York two weeks before (Goldsmith 2010; Sutherland 2010). In New York, a group of improvisation artists divided a stretch of sidewalk on the east side of Fifth Avenue with chalk-sprayed stencils into two lanes, one for New Yorkers and one for tourists. "*Improv Everywhere* is a New York City-based prank collective that causes scenes of chaos and joy in public places", as Charlie Todd, the representative of the group declares on their Internet blog. Posing as Department of Transportation employees, they enforced a fictive new regulation that would supposedly improve the pedestrian traffic in New York by separating the slower moving tourists from the faster walking residents going about their business. Residents and tourists alike were interviewed about the action (Greenspan 2010) with the outcome of the first being generally approving of such an original and thoughtful action coming from a "government agency" and the latter complying willingly with the "new regulation". New York Magazine classified the project in their Approval Matrix graphic as both "brilliant" and "highbrow", even if its short life was interrupted four days later by the real Department of Transportation. Asked in a press conference about the idea, Michael Bloomberg, mayor of New York responded: "When I saw it I said, 'Oh, that's a nice thing to do.' I thought it was very cute" (Greenspan 2010).

The division of lanes in Barcelona took place overnight in one of its most frequented quarters, the *Barrio Gotico*. The New York initiative received positive critics about addressing a pressing issue – that of coping with the rising number of tourists on top of an already busy traffic. The Barcelona City Council immediately declined any part in this action, but Maria Mas, the president of the Association of the Historic City Quarters declared that it is nowhere near being discriminatory, but a good subject for future debates (LV 2010).

There are, however, differences between the two. The only thing that separates the tourists from the inhabitants in the city of New York is the behaviour, and perhaps the obvious tells of a tourist. Otherwise New Yorkers, many of them recent immigrants, feel no hostility towards visitors to the New Continent. Barcelona, on the other hand, offers a different setting. The marginalization of other activities, unrelated to tourism, in some of Barcelona's areas is something that happens in many European old cities that receive exaggerated touristic attention. The issue of coping harmoniously with both the bringers of additional income and the residents that, without a doubt, have rights to their own city is a sensible one that is often ignored until something bursts. The case of Barcelona presents a situation on the verge of conflict. Not all messages that concern tourism are, even if in their apparent irony, friendly.

In its book *Carcelona*, published in 2011, the cultural activist Marc Caellas, gets to be the voice behind the anti-system anarchic attitude of the Barcelonans. As he declares, Barcelona is not Catalunia anymore; it's a trademark - "BCNothing but tourism!" In one of his stories in the book, a well-oiled tourist got into a gang alley night argument with a resident who was angry at how he was behaving. The foreigner, however, was surprised by the fact that "people lived there", for in his opinion, only tourists came into *Barrio Gotico*. Displeased with the fact that the officials and the Catalan bourgeoisie are not taking an active stand against the foreign conquest of Barcelona's historic centre, Caellas nostalgically recalls the Spanish Civil War. Barcelona is "the best shop in the world", "cool only for tourists", "a mountain of spam advertising" are just a few opinions of people cited in the book.

Figure 6: Anti-tourist graffiti on a retaining wall in Barcelona. (Authors)

Conclusions: "it's a bit like getting pregnant"[31]

The recognition of our stereotypes makes us conscious of the hegemonic significance of our own worldviews and cultural meanings (Hallett and Kaplan-Weinger 2010: 101; Smith 1989: 12). Venice and Barcelona are facing challenges encountered worldwide, where historic sites are transformed into modern theme parks for the tourism industry. The contemporary will to reclaim history has equally to do with the past and with the future. The mapping of the future in strategic plans and development measures in order to ensure an on-going social and economic stability has, at times, an edgy path. The idea of a convivial "business as usual" tourism industry, free of conflicting situations, might just be a utopia. Aside from the cases of tourism facilities developed in "no preservation needed" locations, the natural as well as the built environment are subject to opposing evolutionist and protectionist vectors that limit or, on the contrary, promote development.

As much as protecting the existing environment comes as a necessity towards safeguarding cultural markers, the fear of shrinkage of local economies as well as the communities, along with the lure of potential incomes, steers the development more often towards overdevelopment then towards a sustainable one. It might be that because of the tourism characteristic of creating seasonal flows, the amenities for tourists are calibrated to satisfy the peak demand, which in turn, creates a dependency on tourism with the need to maintain and run the infrastructure off-season too. The development of niche or speciality forms of tourism in order to take advantage of the unused amenities seems to be the next logical step. Fashion shows, conferences, local celebrations, the local cuisine become handy artifices in the support of the otherwise off-season resources consuming amenities. A vicious circle of dependency on tourism is, thus, created, as the substitution affects more and more local businesses and inhabitants as well. Their place is taken by tourist related amenities. The public life of communities starts by being affected until at some point, it is almost totally replaced by the swarm behaviour of "passerbuyers". The experience of place is altered along with its transformation into a museum. The pace of life, the customary activities of the communities, even the spoken language are gradually replaced by protection ropes, glass cases, flashes and local cuisine prepared by international chefs in carefully staged restaurants that even resemble an original setting.

31 According to Richard Butler, in an interview to ABC's *Wish you were here: Australian Tourism Studies* program, tourism "…if you're not careful it's a bit like getting pregnant - it can be great fun getting pregnant, but once you're pregnant it grows and it gets a life of its own and it takes over", www.abc.net.au/ola/tourism/transcripts/tran8.htm, 02.05.2014.

There is the risk that communities would no longer benefit from tourism, as in, for example, the case of Venice, where the revenue from tourism activities is directed exclusively towards sanitation and the maintenance of landmarks. As proved in many cases, tourism is a slippery slope as even the most intensive tourism cannot support the "museification" of an entire site. The expectations of many "paying customers" have to be and are effectively met by local actions. In most cases traveling is accompanied by a paradoxical incongruence: that of what tourists expect to see and what they expect to get as associated services. Old and new don't always go along well, so much of the "old" must make room for the "new". Beijing's picturesque *hutongs* are disappearing along with their inhabitants, to be replaced by glass and concrete structure hosting offices, hotels and international franchises. If sarcastic, one could say that this is evolution and it happened before, otherwise we would have entire ancient and medieval sites and would not have to call for archaeologists to dig them up. But they were lost in wars, fires and earthquakes, and later replaced by something newer, that perhaps would not have existed otherwise, but we now appreciate just as well. Renaissance's architecture was met with suspicion and disapproval, not to mention the Rococo. Baron Haussmann is responsible for Paris's medieval building's mass extinction, but then again we would not have the same Paris today, if not for his restructuring plan. What's to say modern architecture that enjoys now the same critiques will not be something to receive the traveller's interest? Even today it is.

City branding and marketing becomes more and more important since attractiveness translates into incomes. Since the 1990s and rise of the *Four Dragons* when the *sogo shoshas* needed to have a global impact and have done this by appealing to daring projects like Pelli's *Petronas Towers*, Foster's *Hong Kong and Shanghai Bank* or Taiwan's *Taipei 101*, public and private commissioned urban image "starchitect" signed (Hornstein 2011: 107) flagships are invading the travel offers in order to attract the modern tourist (van der Borg and Russo 2008: 1; Hornstein 2011: 103-106). Dubai's *Burj al-Arab* and the newer *Khalifa*, Valencia's *Ciutat de les Arts i les Ciències*, Bilbao's *Guggenheim Museum* and countless others are beginning to alter the disproportioned presence of Europe and the US's traditional destinations.

After all, is mass tourism just another calamity endangering our global legacy, or is it a natural process in the human evolution, that ensures the preservation of the successful genes, while letting the other genetic markers of our cities evolve and not be an obstruction to the path of development? Maybe it is for the future generations to say. Maybe it is just human vanity that tries to protect and propagate something we consider to be our essential values now for the progenies to regard later. Whatever the case, it is probably worst before it gets better.

The world came just recently to accept global migration as a natural process with even beneficial outcomes. The interest towards touristic destination is also a doubled edged sword. It brings certain devastation but, equally, raises the flag on what is of greater meaning, perhaps exactly those things that would otherwise be forgotten and buried by history.

References

Allan, B. (2002): A Dictionary of Travel and Tourism Terminology. Wallingford: CAB International.

Allen, L.R., Hafer, H.R., Long, R. and Perdue, R.R. (1993): Rural Residents' Attitudes toward Recreation and Tourism Development. In: Journal of Travel Research, 31(4), 27-33.

Ap, J. (1990): Residents Perceptions Research on the Social Impacts of Tourism. In: Annals of Tourism Research, 17(4), 610-616.

Bell, R. (1962): By Road to Naples and Sicily. London: Robert Hill.

Besculides, A., Lee, M.E. and McCormick, P.J. (2002): Resident's Perceptions of the Cultural Benefits of Tourism. In: Annals of Tourism Research, 29(2), 303-319.

Van der Borg, J. and Russo, A.P. (2008): Regeneration and Tourism Development, Evidence from Three European Cities, Working Paper No.21/WP/2008. Venice: Ca' Foscari University of Venice, Department of Economics.

Britton, R. (1979): The Image of the Third World in Tourism Marketing. In: Annals of Tourism Research, 6(3), 318-329.

Britton, S. (1989): Tourism, Dependency and Development: A Mode of Analysis. In: Singh, T.V., Theuns, H.L. and Go, F.M. (eds.): Towards Appropriate Tourism: The Case of Developing Countries. Frankfurt am Main: Peter Lang, 93-116.

Brown T. (1942): The Reminiscences of an Old Traveler through Different Parts of Europe, including Historical Details of the Russian Empire, and Anecdotes of the Court. Edinburgh: Bell & Bradfute.

Butcher, J. (2003): The Moralisation of Tourism: Sun, Sand... and Saving the World? London: Routledge.

Caellas, M. (2011): Carcelona. Santa Cruz de Tenerife: Editorial Melucina.

Cavallo, P. (2005): La fine di un mondo: Atteggiamenti mentali e sentimentali degli italiani nella seconda guerra mondiale (1940-1943). In: L. Parente, F. Gentile and R.M. Grillo (eds.): Giovanni preziosi e la questione della razza in Italia. Salerno: Rubbettino, 371-390.

Cloke, P (2013): Rural Landscapes. In: Johnson, N.C., Schein, R.H. and Widers, J. (eds.): The Wiley-Blackwell Companion to Cultural Geography. Malden: Wiley-Blackwell, 225-237.

Cohen, E. (1972): Towards a Sociology of International Tourism. In: Social Research, 39(1), 164-182.

Cohen, E. (1974): Who is a Tourist? A Conceptual Clarification. In: Sociological Review, 22(4), 527-555.

Cohen, E. (1979): Rethinking the Sociology of Tourism. In: Annals of Tourism Research, Jan/Mar, 18-35.

Dagg, A.I. and Foster, J.B. (1976): The Giraffe: Its Biology, Behavior, and Ecology. New York: Van Nostrand Reinhold Co.

Dennis, G. (1839): Summer in Andalucía. London: Richard Bentley.

Fletcher, H.A., Donoghue, H.D., Holton, J., Pap, I. and Spigelman, M. (2003): Widespread Occurrence of Mycobacterium Tuberculosis DNA from 18th-19th Century Hungarians. In: American Journal of Physical Anthropology, 120(2), 144-52.

Flick, L.F. (1890): The Prevention of Tuberculosis – A Century's Experience in Italy under the Influence of the Preventive Laws of the Kingdom of Naples, Enacted in 1782. In: Public Health: Papers and Reports, Volume XVI, 60-70. Concord: Irving A. Watson, American Public Health Association.

Frangialli, F. (2005) (Secretary-General, World Tourism Organization): Foreword. In: W.F. Theobald (ed.): Global Tourism (3rd ed.). Burlington, MA: Elsevier, ix.

Frohman, L.H. (1923): The Romance of Camel Hair Cloth. New York: S. Stroock & Co.

Garnham, R.W. (1996): Alliances and Liaisons in Tourism: Concepts and implications. In: Tourism Economics, 2(1), 61-77.

Goldsmith, S. (2010) Artists Divide Fifth Ave. Sidewalk into Separate Walking Lanes for New Yorkers Tourists. In: New York Daily News, May 19, 2010, http://www.nydailynews.com/new-york/artists-divide-ave-sidewalk-separate-walking-lanes-new-yorkers-tourists-article-1.448158, 28.08.2013.

Greenspan, J. (2010): The Tourist Lane. In: Improv Everywhere, June 8, 2010, http://improveverywhere.com/2010/06/08/the-tourist-lane/, 28.08.2013.

Gursoy, D., Jurowski, C. and Uysal, M. (2002): Resident Attitudes: A Structural Modeling Approach. In: Annals of Tourism Research, 29(1), 79-105.

Hall, C.M. and Rath, J. (2007): Tourism, Migration and Place Advantage in the Global Cultural Economy. In: Rath, J. (ed.): Tourism, Ethnic Diversity and the City. New York: Routledge, 1-24.

Hallett, R.W. and Kaplan-Weinger, J. (2010): Official Tourism Websites: A Discourse Analysis. Bristol: Channel View Publications.

D'Hauteserre, A.-M. (2006): A Response to 'Tracing the Commodity Chain of Global Tourism' by Dennis Judd. In: Tourism Geographies, 8(4), 337-342.

Hiller, H.O. (1977): Industrialism, Tourism and Island Nations, and Changing Values. In: Farrell, B.H. (ed.): Social and Economic Consequences of Tourism in the South Pacific. Santa Cruz: University of California Centre for South Pacific Studies, 115-121.

Homans, G. (1961): Social Behavior: Its Elementary Forms. New York: Harcourt Brace Jovanovich.

Hornstein, S. (2011): Architecture, Memory and Place. Farnham: Ashgate Publishing.

Hunziker, W and Krapf, K (1941): Beiträge zur Fremdenverkehrslehre und Fremdenverkehrsgeschichte. Bern: Buchdruckerei AG Berner Tagblatt.

Ingle, R. (1991): Thomas Cook of Leicester. Bangor: Headstart History.

Jurowski, C., Uysal, M., Williams, R.D. (1997): A Theoretical Analysis of Host Community Resident Reactions to Tourism. In: Journal of Travel Research, 36(2), 3-11.

Kapiki, S.T. (2012): The Impact of Economic Crisis on Tourism and Hospitality: Results from a Study in Greece. In: Central European Review of Economics and Finance, 2(1), 19-30.

Kelly, M. and Hook T.E. (1826): Reminiscences of Michael Kelly of the King's Theatre and Theatre Royal Drury Lane, Including a Period of Nearly Half a Century, Vol. I. London: Henry Colburn.

Kerr-Jarrett, A. (1993): Journeys into the Past: Daily Life in the Victorian Age. New York: Reader's Digest.

Kington, T. (2009): Who Now Can Stop the Slow Death of Venice? In: The Observer, March 1, http://www.theguardian.com/world/2009/mar/01/venice-population-exodus-tourism, 28.08.2013.

Klymkiw, G. (2013): The Venice Syndrome – Historic City Destroyed: Dumb Tourists, Stupid Rich People. In: The Film Corner with Greg Klymwik, 20/07/2013, http://klymkiwfilmcorner.blogspot.ro/2013/07/the-venice-syndrome-review-by-greg.html, 28.08.2013.

Kollewe, J. (2012): Eurozone Crisis Knocks Greek Tourist Trade. The Guardian, 29 July, www.theguardian.com/world/2012/jul/29/eurozone-crisis-greece-tourist-trade, 16.02.2014.

Lam, C., and Lei, C. (2002): City Brands and Special Interest Tourism: Macau. In: Morgan, N., Pritchard, A. and Pride, R. (eds.): Destination Brands: Managing Place Reputation. Oxford: Elsevier, 213-223.

Leiper, N. (2008): Why 'the Tourism Industry' Is Misleading as a Generic Expression: The Case for the Plural Variation, 'Tourism Industries'. In: Tourism Management, 29(2), 237-251.

Lew, A, Hall, C.M. and Timothy D. (2008): World Geography of Travel and Tourism: A Regional Approach. Oxford: Elsevier.

Lowen, M. (2012): Journey across Crisis-hit Greece. BBC News Europe, 6 June, www.bbc.com/news/world-europe-18332793, 16.02.2014.

Martin, B. (1988): The Franco Era, 1939-75. In: Solsten, E. and Meditz, S.W. (eds.): Spain: A Country Study. Washington: GPO for the Library of Congress, 139-143.

McCarthy, O.R. (2001): The Key to Sanatoria. In: Journal of the Royal Society of Medicine, 94(8), 413-417.

Misiura, S. (2006): Heritage Marketing. Oxford: Elsevier.

Newman, C. (2009): Vanishing Venice. In: National Geographic, August 2009, http://ngm.nationalgeographic.com/2009/08/venice/newman-text, 28.08.2013.

Norton, M.B., Katzman, D.M., Blight, D.W., Chudacoff, H., and Logevall, F. (1991): A People and a Nation: A History of the United States. Andover: Cengage Learning.

O'Reilly, J. (1999): Death of Venice. In: The Observer, July 18, http://www.theguardian.com/theobserver/1999/jul/18/life1.lifemagazine1, 28.08.2013.

Palmantier, R.A. (1995): Speaking of Animals: A Dictionary of Animal Metaphors. Westport: Greenwood Press.

Parkes, F. (2002): Begums, Thugs and White Mughals (first published in 1850 as Wanderings of a Pilgrim in Search of the Picturesque, during four-and-twenty years in the East; with Revelations of Life in the Zenana). London: Sickle Moon Books.

Pearce, J. (1980): Host Community Acceptance of Foreign Tourists: Strategic Considerations. In: Annals of Tourism Research, 7(2), 224-235.

Pearce, P. (1982): The Social Psychology of Tourist Behavior. Oxford: Pergamon.

Pizam, A., (1978): Tourism's Impacts: The Social Costs to the Destination Community as Perceived by its Residents. In: Journal of Travel Research, 16(4), 8-12.

Plog, S.C. (1987): Understanding Psychographics in Tourism Research. In: Ritchie, J. and Goelder, C. (eds.) Travel Tourism and Hospitality Research. New York: Wiley, 203-213.

Plog, S.C. (2001): Why Destination Areas Rise and Fall in Popularity: An Update of a Cornell Quarterly Classic. In: Cornell Hotel and Restaurant Administration Quarterly, 42(3), 13-24.

Plog, S.C. (2005): Targeting Segments: More Important than Ever in the Travel Industry. In: Theobald, W.F. (ed.): Global Tourism (3rd ed.). Burlington, MA: Elsevier.

Rey-Mermet, T. (1983): Il santo del secolo dei lumi: Alfonso De Liguori (1696-1787). Roma: Città Nuova Editrice.

Reynolds, F. (1826): The Life and Times of Frederick Reynolds, written by Himself, Vol. I. London: Henry Colburn.

Richter, L.K. (1991): Political Issues in Tourism Policy: A Forecast. In: Hawkins, D. and Ritchie, J. B. (eds.): World Travel and Tourism Review. Wallinford, OX: CAB International, 189-193.

Roberts, L. (2010): World in One City: Surrealist Geography and Time-Space Compression in Alex Cox's Liverpool. In: Burns, P.M., Palmer, C. and Lester, J-A. (eds.): Tourism and Visual Culture, Volume I: Theories and Concepts. Wallingford, OX: CAB International, 200-215.

Rosaspina, E. (2010): A Barcellona pedoni divisi: corsie per residenti e turisti. In: Corriere della Sera, May 10, 2010, 29.

Russo, A.P. (1999): Venice: Coping with Culture Vultures. In: The UNESCO Courier, July/August, 1999, 42-43.

Satin, M. (1968): Manual for Draft-age Immigrants to Canada. Toronto: House of Anansi.

Smith, V.L. (1989): Hosts and Guest: The Anthropology of Tourism (2nd ed.). Philadelphia: University of Pennsylvania Press.

Spirou, C. (2011): Urban Tourism and Urban Change. New York: Routledge.

Squires, N. (2009): Venice Population Falls to Lowest Level in Centuries. In: The Telegraph, October 26, http://www.telegraph.co.uk/news/worldnews/europe/italy/6440198/Venice-population-falls-to-lowest-level-in-centuries.html, 28.08.2013.

De Stendhal, M. (1829): Promenades dans Rome, Tome Seconde. Paris: Delaunay.

Strutt, A.J. (1970): Calabria Sicilia 1840: Avventure di un inglese nel Mezzogiorno borbonico, a cura di Guido Puccio. Napoli: Edizioni Scientifiche Italiane.

Sutherland, S. (2010): Walk this Way, NYers. In: New York Post, May 20, 2010, http://nypost.com/2010/05/20/walk-this-way-nyers/, 28.08.2013.

Towner, J. (1985): The Grand Tour: A Key Phrase in the History of Tourism. In: Annals of Tourism Research, 12(2), 297-333.

Thompson, W. (1835): Two Journeys through Italy and Switzerland. London: John Macrone.

Uysal, M., Woo, E. and Singal, M. (2012): The Tourist Area Life Cycle and Its Effect on the Quality-of-Life of Destination Community. In: Uysal, M., Perdue, R.R. and Sirgy, M.J. (eds.): Handbook of Tourism and Quality-of-Life Research: Enhancing the Lives of Tourists and Residents of Host Communities. Dordrecht: Springer, 423-444.

Vanhove, N. (2005): The Economics of Tourism Destinations. Oxford: Elsevier.

Vidulli, M. (2009): Antichi proverbi e detti veneti. Milano: Lampa di stampa.

White, W. (1900): Notes and Queries. Oxford: Oxford University Press.

Williams, E. (2010): Giraffe. London: Reaktion Books.

*** (1827a; b): Cabinet of Taste, or Monthly Compedium of Foreign Costume: Costume of Paris. In: La Belle Assembleé, or Court and Fashionable Magazine; Containing Interesting and Original Literature, and Records of the Beau-Monde. London: Geo. B. Whittaker. Vol. XXXIII, September, 124-125; Vol. XXXVI, December, 260-261.

*** (1828a): Cabinet of Taste, or Monthly Compedium of Foreign Costume: Costume of Paris. In: La Belle Assembleé, or Court and Fashionable Magazine; Containing Interesting and Original Literature, and Records of the Beau-Monde, Vol. XXXVII, January. London: Geo. B. Whittaker, 30-32.

*** (1828b): Literary and Scientific Intelligence. In: La Belle Assembleé, or Court and Fashionable Magazine; Containing Interesting and Original Literature, and Records of the Beau-Monde, Vol. XXXVII, January. London: Geo. B. Whittaker, 44-45.

*** (1975): The Impact of International Tourism on the Economic Development of the Developing Countries. Geneva: International Union of Official Travel Organizations (IUOTO).

*** (2010): La línea que separa a los turistas de los barceloneses. In: La Vanguardia, June 8, 2010. http://www.lavanguardia.com/vida/20100608/53942648263/la-linea-que-separa-a-los-turistas-de-los-barceloneses.html, 28.08.2013.

*** (2013): European Commission (EC): Enterprise and Industry 2013 SBA Fact Sheet – Greece,http://ec.europa.eu/enterprise/policies/sme/facts-figures-analysis/performance-review/files/countries-sheets/2013/greece_en.pdf, 16.02.2014.

Filmography

Das Venedig Prinzip. Dir. Andreas Pichler, 2012.

Napoli milionaria. Dir. Eduardo de Filippo, Italy, 1954.

The Bucket List. Dir. Rob Reiner, 2007.

Vedi Napoli e poi muori. Dir. Eugenio Perego, Italy, 1934.

Vedi Napoli e poi muori. Dir. Riccardo Freda, Italy, 1951.

The ACACIA Paradox: Built Heritage Conservation versus Increasing Tourism

Florin Mureşanu / Monica Mureşanu

> "But I am in the hopes that I shall see more of you at Castle Dracula" (Stoker 1897: 75)
>
> "It was almost impossible to believe that things which we had seen with our own eyes and heard with our own ears were living truths. Every trace of all that had been was blotted out. The castle stood as before…" (Stoker 1897: 600)

A superficial view over the tourism industry, which is not neglectful by any means, but something the average tourist usually does, can only reveal the obvious consumption relation created between the particular resources and their specialist consumer. Not taken very often into account, the tourist–destination interaction is an essential variable that can "make or break" the experience because of the diverging interests of the two. While the tourist mandates the interaction to be authentic, intense and gratifying, the "destination" usually trusts fewer traces of the passage, some that would not alter its integrity. Where the two meet is the universally commended ideal, but the interaction rarely happens without leaving traces on either side. Long established touristic destinations, whether they are confronted and solved by this impasse in their past, or found through a sustainable way to cope with the impact, do not reveal the background processes behind the regular consumption of touristic resources. The emerging destinations, on the other hand, struggle, all good practices given, with their individual evil-good tourism dilemma.

The paper aims to analytically reveal the problems arising for the heritage sites ascending as touristic opportunities. The cause of their acknowledgement can be equally traced to their inward discovery or outward marketing. While preparing for the reciprocal advantageous symbiosis, the heritage sites are yet to discover that "being", in tourism, usually means "being available" and that, sometimes, having the "perfect guests" has to be coerced in order to secure their sustainable consumption. Rather of late availability for tourism, three heritage sites, two qualified and one aspiring UNESCO site, were selected for the purpose of this paper. Voroneţ is an iconic Moldavian monastery fallen into oblivion for several decades for not providing the state with the appropriate ideology. Sighişoara was a medieval Saxon citadel that gathered recent fame due to one of its former residents, which stands as a contemporary icon for the dark fiction genre. Sibiu is the farthest eastern German outpost that, through its multi-ethnic inheritance, aims to set the pace for cultural tourism in a former communist country on the path to rediscover its past. The three provide a range of cultural centres case studies, peripheral to the global established touristic paths that are developed as focal travel landmarks.

The ACACIA concept, acronym for "Asserting the Centre as Consumer Interest Area", deals with the urban milieu no longer perceived as the original and unique product of a specific culture, but with the redefinition of notions such as place, boundary and identity, as products of and for the global culture. The better part of the human settlements – their "centres" have become marketable commodities for the benefit of traveling consumers, that hyperlink between disparate destinations, usually of acknowledged significance.

The ACACIA

The original, the variation, and the conservation paradigm

Society tends to reject or, at least, not favour what does not comply with its expectations or established norms. Usually, the strange, the unfamiliar, the harmful are pushed out by these norms, in order to protect the usual, familiar and safe path of the slow change that we refer to as "natural evolution". The tendency to protect a norm operated environment from external interferences, over the evolution of humanity, has led to a wide variation of unique cultural features that, even combined with neighbouring characteristics in regional similarities, still identify places as inimitable. Overlapping temporal layers are responsible for peerless local mutations, at least until the coming of the Industrial Revolution. The standardization it brought had every intention of replacing the unique. Also, the slow paced cultural adjustments turned into a rushed alteration of the traditional milieu. Yet, paradoxically, what is known as the Second Industrial Revolution because of the production line and mass production, coincided with the first actions towards the preservation of the pre-existing setting[1].

1 The Second Industrial Revolution is identified with the second half of the 19th century, until the beginning of World War I. The first attempt to apply the Ruskian theory of conservation in

Whether because the built heritage was too affected by the growing urban pollution or because the rapid changes were leading to an equally fast replacement of what reminded of a glorious past, historic buildings and sites were tagged as irreplaceable, if somehow lost. Hence, even if the global trend was pushing the settlements' development towards the standardization of urban life, whatever was erected up to that time was relatively frozen to their latest stage of development. Europe, for example, arrested its city centres to the stylistic variation of the turn of the century Eclecticism and whatever survived from earlier periods. Thus, later currents only left their mark due to accidental events[2], and further contributed to the individualization of the urban cultural DNA.

There is little need to motivate the conservation attempts on heritage sites, yet their arrested development is not universal. Although the doctrines of conservation are acknowledged worldwide by now and the variation of the supporting legislation is minimal from country to country, there is one other phenomenon that keeps the real from being the ideal. Rarely what conservation tries to achieve is the original in all its aesthetic features. Generally the archetype of a heritage site is the highest degree of accepted compromise between the original and all the successive adaptations to suit contemporary needs. Sometimes even the recreation *in integrum* of the original would raise suspicions of overdoing.

The temptation

Developed over time, the regulations regarding the built heritage were created in order to stem the space-time oxymora incidental to the urban evolution. Paradoxically, this seems to negatively affect the residents more than the visitors. While the first should have an empathic relation with their native environment and a direct interest in preserving it, the latter are expected to show respect towards the display of local values, which usually happens. However sometimes conflict arises and generally its source is associated with the newcomers. The contemporary tourist is no longer the off-beat traveller willing to adapt and fully

Europe was through the actions of the *Society for the Protection of Ancient Buildings*, founded in 1877 by William Morris and Philip Webb.

2 WWII bombings cleared part of the buildings from the big European cities, leaving the emptied plots to be occupied by Modernist and Functionalist architecture. Later currents, such as Postmodernism only took advantage of real estate ventures and the early stage development of the conservation regulations. Worth to be mention that, until the 1970s, much of the restoration on old buildings involved the large scale use of concrete.

immerse in the direct, unmediated experience of a new place (Cohen 1979; Smith 1989: 12). If not demanding, the tourist is at least expecting certain standards of hospitality which, by now, are universal[3].

Nevertheless, the education and the tolerance towards "the other" are increasingly becoming the mediators that alter the differences, based on cross-cultural exchange (Smith and Hall 2006; D'Amore 1983; Severiades 2001: 38). The tourist destinations, in particular, incline to no longer just represent a local identity. They are becoming eclectic spaces of cultural diversity, collecting bits and pieces of global culture on top of a local foundation. However, even if tolerance towards tourists is present, sometimes, if the carrying capacity of the site is exceeded (Williams and Alison 2005; Archer et al. 2005), congestion might suppress the positive attitude towards the tourists (Long et al. 1990; Prentice 1993; Soutar and McLeod 1993) and even disregard the economic benefits of being "in the spotlight" (Davis and Cosenza 1988).

Just as much as the tourist is expecting to find "friendly locals", bearing a tolerance towards incongruent habits, the natives are anticipating a "look, but don't touch" visitor behaviour, with limited impact of their passage. But the contemporary tourist has western claims of comfort, with the risk of his future absence, if they are not met. Somehow, he is the unconscious missionary of the contemporary lifestyle, which the locals are keen to adopt even at the expense of altering the authenticity of their characteristic environment.

Amongst the tourist destinations, cities are the most resilient to cultural collision (Lew et al. 2008: 101), perhaps because of their size and already present heterogeneity of the resident population. The boundaries of tolerance are more flexible and might be breached only in extreme adverse cases, let's say by mass tourism (Doxey 1975). Equally, the big cities in particular are expected to evolve and change towards a global representation, thus towards an assisted compulsory transformation, both from socio-economical and physical perspectives. The changes that come with tourism are often insignificant, something that cannot be said about smaller settlements. The desire to attract tourists, for them, is eventually bound to come with consequences that, on a smaller scale, are sure to produce substantial alterations. On the one hand, the local communities are bound to follow local, national and sometimes international rules that protect

3 For example, according to the 2012 *Water Equity in Tourism* report, tourism development threatens in some areas the livelihood and food security of the local population, just by offering standards otherwise considered "decent". While tourists expect not only fresh drinking water, but also water for sanitation amenities and even pools wherever they travel, regions with economies highly dependent on tourism, such as Bali, Kerala and Goa, Zanzibar or The Gambia are confronted with critical depletion and inequitable appropriation of freshwater supplies (Noble at al. 2012).

their milieu. On the other hand, the desire to take part in the tourism industry by tapping into a latent touristic potential stirs the commercial development at the expense of other components. Attracting tourists sometimes has a different outcome than what is expected: culture clash and commodification, and community collapse may occur. Paradoxically, the tourist is involuntarily responsible for the actions taken to lure him in.

The ACACIA paradox

The ideal of public space as a place for social life is continuously altered by the focused attention mainly on the aesthetic and, often, the formal values of the space. In a not so far-fetched analogy one might compare the city as touristic destination with the African *Acacia* and in the same manner, the contemporary tourist with the acacia's nemesis, the giraffe. It seems that the evolution affected both of them, in looks and behaviour, in order to complete a peculiar symbiosis. As the acacia is the widest spread tree in the African savannah, so is the urban environment- the most common contemporary touristic destination. The acacia would not be so common if not for the interest its fruits present to the giraffe. But the fruits are not enough to satisfy the appetite of a one-ton mammal all year-round, so branches are devoured too. The same goes for the traveling consumer whose leisure experience is not way-in – way-out, but expends on all additional services.

The acacia is on to protect its heritage not only by raising its branches, but also by growing thorns and secreting tannin. Much the same, the city employs rules, regulations and specific legislation in order to protect its built heritage from the trampling souvenir collectors, as well as their services suppliers. Some acacia species, such as the whistling thorn (*Acacia drepanolobium*) host ant defenders (*Pseudomyrmex*). The correspondent urban occurrence is found in the recent public space activism advocating the social diversity and civic use of space.

Growing higher does for the giraffe just the same as regulating and rising prices does for the consumer – creates the need to adapt – a process of natural selection similar to Darwin's "competing browsers hypothesis". The symbiotic relationship forces the two partners – acacia-giraffe or tourist-destination to an adapting negotiation of that which is offered and compensated in order for them both to achieve a similar degree of gratification. In tourism, the gratification scale leans towards either of the associated partners according to their ability to withstand the other's "abuse", physical or pecuniary.

"And Jesus went into the temple of God, and cast out all them that sold and bought in the temple"[4]

The lucrative side of tourism is looked for to sustain the conservation of cultural heritage. Raising money from touristic activities helps to maintain and repair historical buildings or entire sites. However, as demonstrated by some researchers (Garrod and Fyall 2000), money from admission fees covers only a fragment of the total costs of maintenance and running of a heritage site. That is partly because the admission fees are usually symbolic in order to make the sites more accessible for the general public (Pearce 1981). On the other hand, the heritage benefits from national or local subsidies – a fee, let's say, from the community or, in some cases, *maecenates* from patrons of the arts. Built heritage represents the cultural asset of previous generations, a symbol of their achievements and ambitions, left for the current generations to experience and pass on to the next ones[5]. Unfortunately the cultural inheritance from the previous generations has a geographical distribution that does not always overlap the contemporary spread of economic leads. However, the relatively recent recognition of a common universal legacy ensured at least the survival of what is considered to be irreplaceable heritage[6]. While heritage sites in developed economies have already undergone all the necessary steps for their rehabilitation, those in developing or underdeveloped economies are struggling with shortages in funding their conservation operations. And not all global heritage is benefiting from the international attention of a World Heritage Sites list. The means we choose to transmit cultural values from one generation to another, sometimes include measures that have secondary effects such as mass tourism, overuse and constant transformation of heritage sites. It seems that tourism, in many cases, is the guarantee of a surviving endowment in the hope that, at some point, the capitalised interest of the touring individuals will arise the concern upon heritage's cultural significance. However, tourism, especially if spontaneous and combined with a potential lack of conservation measures, can lead to negative outcomes and the concern not upon heritage's significance, but its integrity and identity.

4 Matthew 21:12

5 According to the 1987 Brundtland Report and the 1964 Venice Charter.

6 UNESCO's heritage preservation activities started in 1960 with the salvage of the Great Temple of Abu Simbel from the effects of the Aswan Dam. The organization's following campaigns on heritage led to the adoption of the Convention concerning the Protection of the World Cultural and Natural Heritage, in 1972. The World Heritage Committee was established in 1976 and the first sites were enlisted on the World Heritage List in 1978. The Convention for the Safeguarding of the Intangible Cultural Heritage was adopted by UNESCO in 2003.

UNESCO raised the question that addresses the importance of control and regulations by underlining the paradigm of tourism and sites conservation, as tourism can attract awareness and public interest towards the traditions and local culture, as well as, it can endanger and erode them at the same time (The UNESCO Courier 1999: 21). Since then "heritage has become a familiar, easily accessible commodity providing surprises, relaxation and enjoyment" (Patin 1999: 35) leading to the development of the tourism infrastructure, sometimes a little too fast and a little too loose. Such a situation, of uncontrolled development is ongoing in Voroneţ.

Voroneţ used to be a medieval village in Suceava County, in the Eastern part of Romania, geographically known as Moldavia. Now on the outskirts of Gura Humorului, Voroneţ still preserves what occasionally is referred to as the "Sistine Chapel of the East" (Sandberg-Diment 1998; Gillmore 1999; Brockman 2011: 408), a XV century monastery, included in the UNESCO World Heritage Sites, along with seven other Moldavian monasteries. It is considered, a masterpiece in Byzantine influenced art, unique in Europe (World Heritage Sites list, September 1990). It has exceptionally well preserved exterior frescoes, famous for their intense azure colour. They are known as "Voroneţ Blue", a vivid[7] cerulean of an up-to-date unknown recipe (USDC 1971; Prina 2008: 309), but believed to have a base of crushed lapis lazuli.

Closed for a long period[8], Voroneţ was considered for the World Heritage List in 1993. Although, during the Communist Era the monastic life was persecuted as unproductive for the society, the state ideology could not entirely ban the functioning of the church. It remained the focal point of the local community that tried to make the most of the situation. Since, during communism, the centralised economy allowed no private lucrative operations, the site of the monastery and its surroundings remained untouched. However, this changed with the attention that accompanied the qualification for UNESCO's World Heritage Sites list. The growing tourist arrivals and the area's lack of hospitality infrastructure happened to be the perfect opportunity for the soon to mushroom inns and guesthouses. Unfortunately, during the communist years there was no need or will for conservation strategies. Even if benign for this case in particular, the lack of conservationist concerns was to show its

7 Considered unique in the world, the blue pigment used in the 1547 frescoes are still unaffected by the weather and the passing of time. The impervious "Voroneţ Blue" is the more mysterious since the monastery was deserted for two centuries.

8 Following the 18th century (1775) Habsburg annexation of northern Moldavia, the monastic community left the monastery, to return only in 1991.

effects later. Especially during the 1990s, the construction industry, now privatized, had no special regulations to comply to.

Figure 1: The Voroneţ Monastery. (Ionescu 1937: 256)

Figure 2: *Popasul Domnesc* guesthouse. (www.booking.com)

Thus, piggybacking on the monument's potential to draw the cash flow from tourism, new spontaneous erections crowded the area. With no intended regard for the time-honoured landscape, the new touristic amenities are rather oriented towards the consumer's physical needs than those of a more spiritual nature. Along with the inns, the locals' houses were extended and transformed in order to accommodate a few rooms for tourists. These also, in most of the cases, have no regard for the vernacular architecture of the traditional landscape. The general appearance of the monastery's surroundings are now a peculiar mix of old and new, with a diminishing identity, paced with the on-going transformation. The sole promoter of the place's history is the monastery itself, even if its legendary blue is masked by the adjacent contemporary dye, PVC and other finishes alike.

The heritage site, the monastery and the monastic household, occupies 3.27 hectares. There is also a recently defined buffer zone that extends the protection regulations on 37.71 hectares around the site. A 2013 report to UNESCO authored by the Romanian government incorporated information regarding the measures undergone for consolidation works, the protection of the frescoes and the management of tourists and visitors. Also "General Town Plans and Urban Plans for protected areas have been developed and implemented in order to enhance the control of all works within the property and its buffer zone" (State of Conservation Churches of Moldavia C 598bis, 2013). However, these measures were not able to reverse the real estate damage, even if some of the contemporary conceptions were obviously covered by the buffer zone (Figure 2 and 3).

Figure 3: The image shows the heritage site (continuous) as well as its protected area (dotted line). The circle marks the location of the guesthouse illustrated in Figure 2. (UNESCO 2010, http://whc.unesco.org/download.cfm?id_document=105235, 02.02.2014)

Going back to the acacia-giraffe analogy, the exposure of Voroneţ, as well as the other seven Moldavian Byzantine churches, was minimal until their labelling as World Heritage Sites. In order for a touristic site to achieve notoriety, if not already established, it has to get into the spotlight. For certain, UNESCO added no cultural value to the site itself, but by certifying its relevance for the universal heritage, disclosed its location for the specialist consumer. The touristic trail of the eight Moldavian monasteries is considered mostly a pilgrimage on a spiritual road that takes the tourists back into the region's medieval history. Usually, the tourists are themselves religious individuals that seek not only an architectural satisfaction, but also the transcending experience that the monasteries might provide. Similarly, the acacia's "bitterness" does not appeal to all the herbivores. Having a taste for it implies having the right attributes to go around the thorns and poisonous leaves and, most of all, to reach its crown. How come, then, the acacia gets to maturity without being wiped out from the ground? Its shared common evolution with the giraffe made the latter unable, even in its infancy, to reach what grows close to the ground. The giraffe's anatomy limits its neck's span to a certain height. Likewise, the sites with touristic potential are virtually of no or limited interest pending their accidental emergence. In Moldavian monasteries' case, the provisional neglect, regarding their cultural significance, practically preserved their integrity until their coming out as UNESCO credited worthy touring opportunities. Even currently, they are protected by their scattering in remote locations with limited accessibility[9]. The number of tourists is increasing though, but so far, as the UNESCO reports show it, the site management was successful with the potential damage from tourist arrivals kept under control and the freeloading within the buffer zone ceased (UNESCO 2013). The site is also continuously monitored by the Romanian authorities, as well as the Orthodox Church. We might say that in this case the acacia outgrew its *nemesis* with minimal browsing impairment by appealing to a narrow market – religious tourism – and drawing on the remote location. The benefit from UNESCO's attention and the recently established conservation regulations came for Voroneţ in a rather biblical form (Matthew 21:12-13; John 2: 13-16).

"I trust that your journey ... has been a happy one, and that you will enjoy your stay in my beautiful land. -- Your friend, Dracula."[10]

One of the bestselling up-to-date icons, the forefather of all vampires, although a product of fiction, Dracula is the unofficial designated timeless ambassador of Transylvania. Even if Dracula's "lairs" are often disputed between several locations[11], the birth place of the historic character[12] that stirred a modern youth-

9 The trail of the eight Moldavian monasteries is 376 km long, with the nearest international airports at Iaşi (110 km) and Bacău (114 km). With no highway accessibility and partially on country roads, the trail is no random or unintentional experience for the spontaneous tourist.

10 Bram Stoker (1897) Dracula, page 7. In full "I trust that your journey from London has been a happy one, and that you will enjoy your stay in my beautiful land. -- Your friend, Dracula."

11 Bran Castle is the best known of Dracula's marketed lairs, although Vlad the 3rd is only tangential associated with this Saxon citadel. Other locations include Poenari Castle, built by the Basarab monarch, which has a more a reliable geographical link with the former ruler of Wallachia; Hunyad Castle, a gothic-renaissance Transylvanian castle belonging to several Hungarian ruling houses, along with other relatively obscure locations profiting from Dracula's

culture movement is the medieval town of Sighişoara, built during the 12th century over a former Roman fort known as *Castrum Sex* (Six-sided Camp). The Saxon settlement achieved its urban status in 1367 as *Civitas de Segusvar* from the Holy Roman Empire during the rule of Karl IV, due to its strategic and commercial role at the Eastern border of the empire. Heavily fortified with as many as 15 fortifications and lines of defence the town's power peaked during the exile in the city of Vlad Dracul (1431-1435), father of Vlad the Impaler. Assigned to full power by Sigismund I of Luxembourg, coins, otherwise a monopoly of the Hungarian kings, were minted in Sighişoara during his stay.

Sighişoara "is an outstanding example of a small fortified city in the border region between the Latin-oriented culture of Central Europe and the Byzantine-Orthodox culture of south-eastern Europe. The apparently unstoppable process of emigration by the Saxons, the social stratum that had formed and upheld the cultural traditions of the region, threatens the survival of their architectural heritage as well" (UNESCO 2000: 16). It was included in the World Heritage Sites list in 1999 and is monitored by UNESCO on a regular basis. Central Sighişoara, known as "the Citadel", sits on a hilltop and is one of the few medieval fortified towns still inhabited. Along with the conservation measures undergone, a revival of the medieval traditions is present, especially during summer time when the city is filled with foreign and local tourists. Started in 1992, the Sighişoara Medieval Festival is held on the last weekend of July. Along with the Crafts Fair, also organised in July since 1994, they are central events for the local craftsmen, theatre companies, music bands, as well as medieval re-enactments enthusiasts. Other events and celebrations compete each year for the attention gained with Sighişoara's recognition as a World Heritage Site and its secured tourist inflow.

The Medieval Festival was initiated before the international awareness by a few renaissance enthusiasts. In its early years it developed not only by expanding the range of reborn medieval traditions, but also by attracting spontaneous tourists. The medieval atmosphere backed up by the gothic and baroque architecture of the Citadel were the perfect setting for a media covered at large event, which in turn signalled the heritage significance of the city. Regrettably,

notoriety, as well as his ambiguous history/legend, in order to market a lucrative touristic enterprise.

12 Vlad the 3rd, also known as Vlad Ţepeş (*the Impaler* – only in use posthumously, even though *Kazikli Bey* (*Sir Impaler*) was his ottoman alias) and Vlad Dracula (derived from the Romanian *Drăculea* – son of Dracul (*Draco*, *Dragon*), surname that indicated his father's admission to the chivalric *Order of the Dragon*) due to his cruelty towards his enemies during his three reigns (1448, 1456-62, and 1476), was the inspiring character for Bram Stoker's novel.

the notoriety that followed UNESCO's listing of the site attracted the private investors to the area willing to profit (Rodwell 2007: 199).

In the early 2000s one project received intensive media exposure for its intention to build a Dracula theme park 6 km from Sighişoara, on the Breite Plateau that also hosts an oak tree nature reserve. Planned to start in March 2002 and complete by the end of 2003, the cost of Dracula Park was estimated at $31.5 million secured by a public-private partnership. The Sighişoara Township, the initiator and the major stakeholder (mainly in land value) was to attract funding from the Ministry of Tourism and several private investors. The estimated 1.1 million visitors annually were to generate an annual income of $12 million, much of which would be invested in the restoration of the Citadel (Vela 2001a, 2001b). The project was aggressively marketed and 15,000 people bought shares (Avram and Grosu 2003) in this western mimicking (Shandley et al. 2006) "100 percent Romanian" endeavour (Burtan 2001). Although the "rise" of Dracula for tourism had major supporters (Năstase 2001) and the Minister of Tourism, Dan Matei-Agathon, dismissed the initial objections to "the most spectacular tourism project of the start of this millennium" (Constantinescu 2001), protests followed nationwide. Many of the religious denominations, aside from the Romanian Orthodox Church, condemned the initiative. Sighişoara's Lutheran pastor argued that "from the point of view of the Christian religion, 'Dracula-Land' is an aberration and a grave sin in the face of God" (Frölich 2001: 14). Others joined, amongst which two NGOs – *Liga Pro-Europa* and *Sighişoara Durabilă*, complaining against the endangerment of cultural and natural resources (Leigh 2007). The UK based *Mihai Eminescu Trust*, a conservationist organisation involved in the restoration of Saxon villages, used the press to express discontent and worries (Parau 2009) in an open letter addressed to President Ion Iliescu (Leigh 2012: 136-7). The local concerns were soon to be shared by UNESCO, especially because the project was pushed forward with no notifications. Its World Heritage Congress, held in December 2001, noted the view of ICOMOS and urged Romania for an immediate environmental impact study and the consideration of alternative locations (UNESCO 2001b). The Cultural Commission of the European Parliament called for a suspension of the project until UNESCO's evaluation (Andrei 2002) and the Government temporarily halted the advance[13] until the results of a pending

13 Following the decision to halt the development of a themepark close to the World Heritage site of the „Historic Centre of Sighişoara", Tamas Fejerdy, chairman of the World Heritage Committee, addresed an oppen letter to the President of Romania, which stated: "In my capacity as Chairperson of the World Heritage Committee I would like to applaud the decision to halt the proposed development of the theme park "Draculaland" at the World Heritage site of

visit from UNESCO officials, programmed for March 2002. Following these, the Sighişoara site was dropped in July 2002 (Leigh 2007) and the total abandonment of the project was confirmed in June 2003 by Miron Mitrea, the new Miniser of Tourism, as "not a priority" (Neagu 2003).

Figure 4: Sighişoara's Citadel – view towards the main square. In front of Vlad Dracul's house (left) "the prince of the dark" draws the tourists' attention towards the restaurant inside. Hanged from the balcony, a dragon effigy signals the building's historic significance. (Authors 2014)

Escaping the lucrative shadow of the "count", Sighişoara gradually assumed its place as an intangible paragon and concentrated on conserving and marketing its resources. The aforementioned festivals are, since, the sole events that trouble the otherwise silent life of the Citadel, even with all the seasonal tourist traffic. The early editions of the Medieval Festival added to the initial renaissance enthusiasts and their associated bystanders: a colourful crowd of social misfits, scammers, vagrants, as well as street vendors that sold everything else but folk

the "Historic Centre of Sighişoara" (Romania). On behalf of the World Heritage Committee, I wish to express my appreciation for the commitment of your Government to protect this unique World Heritage property for future generations" (WHC, 6 February 2003).

art and crafted merchandise. The whole thing threatened to turn into something partly bazaar and partly Mardi Gras, since beer was plentifully involved. The supporters of the event, tired of the kitsch souvenirs and mock medieval polyester costumes, pressed the local authorities to take the necessary actions to limit the negative aspects of the festival. In 2007 the organizing committee of the festival issued a set of regulations which was to be, if not mandatory, at least informative about the expected behaviour of both the participants and vendors (Organizing Committee for the "Medieval Sighişoara" Festival 2007). After several years of lobbying, the regulations turned in 2011 into a draft through which the municipality backed up the initiative. Finally, in 2012 the regulations were made official through a decree issued by Sighişoara's Local Council[14].

Figure 5: Souvenir shop makes use of the retaining wall at the base of the *Covered Staircase* leading to the Lutheran *Church on the Hill.* Amongst the wooden swords and shields, traditional pottery and old-fashioned jewellery, the souvenir seeker can also find plastic Ninja swords, Venetian-like masks and Chinese hand fans. (Authors 2014)

However, even if the new regulations forbid the sale of "unauthentic" souvenirs during the yearly events, it seems that the shadow of Dracula is easier to cast away then the shadow of kitsch. While the street vendors are kept out, the local

14 H.C.L. nr.8/2012, www.sighisoara.org.ro/portal/portal.nsf/All/B74D34E9E359C778C2257A3A002C420C/$FILE/Regulament FSM 2012.pdf, 22.01.2014.

shops, not bound by the special regulations, continue to sell poor quality items. The pricier traditional art and objects perhaps do not make the perfect souvenir for everybody and even "tacky", at times, is a worthy token.

In Sighişoara's case, the local traditions and values suffered many changes and had to adapt to different cultures as the Saxons, Hungarians and Romanians swapped places in the resident population's proportions. The Saxon citadel was overlooked and almost fell into oblivion, especially during the communist regime when it couldn't fit into the centralized urban strategies and the foreign tourists were just a few and usually with family ties in the area. On the other side, its temporary neglect and the underdeveloped urban infrastructure might have been just the things to save the Citadel in an almost perfect conservation state. Revived by few enthusiasts and brought into the spotlight by UNESCO, its real notoriety was to come with the help of its immortal former resident. Paradoxically, the endangerment of the heritage's integrity by a rather absurd, if not silly, proposal raised the residents' awareness regarding the fragility of the traditions when coming face to face with the contemporary "idols".

With a rough start here, the acacia escaped with the giraffe only cleaning the lesser branches that were just, to paraphrase Charles Lamb[15], "cramping its style". To go further with the paraphrase, the intended use of "alternate" methods to attract tourists, other than the existing traditional potential, ended in the total rejection of what was unfit for Sighişoara's historic résumé. Even with the lagging decisions and the poor administration of the local authorities, the public *Pseudomyrmex* ants, in this case the residents, NGOs and mass media, managed to save the best of the acacia, its "Citadel".

Since "cultural tourists increasingly search for *authentic* experiences of *everyday culture*, they are more likely to avoid commercial products" (OECD 2009: 69), therefore, at some point in the process, the municipality realised the danger of not planning in detail their long term strategy for the historical centre of Sighişoara and took some action towards supporting the conservation of authentic local culture. In the case of Sighişoara, the will to attract tourists led in the end to residents pressing for a real conservation of the cultural heritage. The synergy between the local cultural development strategies, the heritage management and tourism is still a goal to be achieved on a common ground for all the actors involved. While the residents do have a direct interest in the preservation of their traditional landscape and their elected representatives will, in time, find the right path, the tourist's need to "seek instant gratification in the dreamscapes" (Burns et al. 2010: xvii) might still be confusing. The tourist is not

15 Charles Lamb to William Wordsworth (7 June 1819): "I will never write another letter with alternate inks. You cannot imagine how it cramps the flow of the style." (Lucas 1905: 524)

only part of a colourful bunch that trails diverse pursuits, but also often falls victim to trends set by a fastidious consumer oriented enterprise – the tourism industry. Even tourism is culture oriented and trend guided and it is possible that, for Sighişoara, the current Goth and youth vampire subcultures seek, aside from all the world heritage oriented conservationist actions, a more authentic setting than that of a theme park.

Capitalizing on cultural heritage

Rated 8th by Forbes in a top of Europe's most idyllic places to live[16] (Becket and Olson 2008), Sibiu was an important Saxon centre (*Cibinium*, later *Hermannstadt*) from the 12th century onward. The capital of the Principality of Transylvania for a century (from 1692 to 1791), Sibiu's influence in the region came not only with the military power of an eastern outpost of Central Europe's powers, but also through its economic and cultural reputation as the largest German town in Southeast Europe. Even with the massive loss amongst its German speaking residents, following WWII and the later Soviet influenced state policy[17], the Saxon cultural heritage is an important part of the city's urban landscape and of region's local traditions.

The municipality of Sibiu made an official request in 2004[18] for its historic centre to be considered by UNESCO for the inclusion on World Heritage Sites list. Its application for candidacy[19] was submitted in 2005, but withdrew in 2007

---

16 The top was suggested by a panel of five travel experts: Lucy White, travel editor and writer for travel guide *Lonely Planet*; Ala Osmond, director of Exeter International, a private tour company; Jan Medlycott, a senior home search coordinator for Icon Relocation; Gay Gillen, travel consultant from Brownell travel consultants; and Fiona Kingden, a representative from Savills International Estate Agents.

17 The Germans were persecuted by the Soviet army after Romania, until then an Axis member, turned to the Allied side on August 23rd, 1944. In order to escape the post-war deportations, either to East Germany or Siberia, according to their participation in the conflicts, many changed their names by marrying into Romanian, Hungarian and even gipsy families. Furthermore, the ethnic cleansing continued under the communist regime, as the exacerbated nationalist state policy "assisted" the remaining German population to move abroad. According to the Romanian censuses, their number dropped continuously from about 60% at the turn of the 20th century to 40% before WWII, 20% in early 1970s, 3,5% after the communism's collapse in the East, to finally reach just 1,5% nowadays.

18 Tentative List of UNESCO, 29.06.2004, http://whc.unesco.org/en/tentativelists/1929/, 25.01.2014.

19 The 208 pages application – *Nomination of Sibiu, The Historic Centre, for Inscription on the World Heritage List* – was submitted on behalf of the State Party by the Minister of Culture and Religious Affairs, www.sibiu.ro/ro2/pdf/2007/Documentatie_Unesco.pdf, 25.01.2014.

following an ICOMOS (International Council on Monuments and Sites) report (Toader 2008). The report pointed towards the state of conservation of the historic centre, the traffic problems, the lack of a control plan regarding the tourist inflow and the already built new hotel, present in the future buffer zone. However, in 2004 as well, along with Luxembourg, Sibiu was voted by the Commission of the European Union to be European Capital of Culture in 2007. The preservation of tradition and cultural values and, paradoxically compared to the ICOMOS report, the high degree of conservation regarding the urban tissue and architectural heritage, were key factors for its nomination. The city's personality[20] is defined by a mix of historically overlapped Gothic, Renaissance and Baroque architecture, with the focal point to the central system of public squares: Grand Square (*Großer Ring*), Lesser Square (*Kleiner Ring*) and Huet that mantle the City Council, along with the Jesuit Church and a 13th century fortification tower, known as the *Council Tower*.

For Sibiu, the preparations preceding its role in 2007 as European Capital of Culture involved a serious financial support from the Romanian State, European Union, local investors and sponsors for the restoration and rehabilitation of the urban infrastructure and the buildings within the historical centre, usually referred to as the *Upper Town* (*Oberstadt*). According to an official report, along with public buildings and important historical monuments such as churches, the City Council, the Brukenthal National Museum[21] etc. (Nistor 2008: 16), over 30 private buildings and (or) facades and 20 courtyards and passage ways were rehabilitated by the Ministry of Culture (Nistor 2008: 94). One of the most important and costly part of the preparations for the event was the improvement of the city's hospitality infrastructure, as well as the modernisation of its international airport (Nistor 2008: 15).

As it turns out, the number of tourists in 2007 doubled compared to the previous year[22], however the international tourist arrivals only recorded a 2,7% increase compared to 2006 (Nistor 2008: 105). Rising at a steady pace from year to year, the international tourist arrivals seemed to be unaffected by the special event. Nevertheless, the real gain from the preparations was the residents' awareness concerning the historic centre of Sibiu and, equally, that of other

20 According to its mayor, Klaus Johannis, in his welcome as the chairman of Sibiu 2007 Association, www.sibiu2007.ro/en3/about.htm, 25.01.2014.

21 The former residence of Samuel von Brukenthal, Governor of Transylvania between 1777 and 1787, who established its first collection around 1790, opened as a museum in 1817, making it one of the oldest in the world.

22 According to the official event site, the cultural event attracted around 800,000 tourists, double compared to 2006 and triple compared to 2005, http://www.sibiu2007.ro/ro3/bilant.htm, 25.01.2014.

Romanian cities starting to prepare and apply for the status of European Capital of Culture[23]. Other programs such as European Capital of Sport and European Youth Capital[24], are considered opportunities to widen the international footprint of the candidate cities on the tourism market.

The event was generally considered a success, even if critics pointed towards, in some cases (Toader 2008), the superficiality of the restoration works that were carried out almost exclusively (with)in the public space. Considering that the financial support, as well as the time span of the intervention were limited compared to the real rehabilitation needs of the historic architectural fund, most of the privately own buildings only received cosmetic care. As circulated (Nistor 2001), this was meant to impel the owners to continue carrying constant maintenance on their properties[25]. Additionally, amongst the large number of cultural programs and events, some (of them) targeted the sustainable development of the city and the conservation of cultural heritage. These attracted to Sibiu a large number of professionals and students, who contributed actively to outline a long term strategy for the city.

Sibiu's rehabilitation of its historical centre only relatively affected the development of the surrounding areas, as the conservation plans were limited to the inner core of Sibiu. Areas such as the *Lower Town* (*Unterstadt*), a culturally rich area with baroque architecture, inhabited by Sibiu's merchants, was not included in the 2007 plan. Superficial rehabilitation works were, however, conducted.

---

23 Romania, along with Greece, is entitled to nominate a 2021 capital and five cities (Iaşi, Cluj-Napoca, Craiova, Timişoara and Arad) have already applied, http://eur-lex.europa.eu/legal-content/EN/TXT/?uri=CELEX:52012PC0407, 25.01.2014.

24 Cluj-Napoca, the "regional capital" of Transylvania, is already considered to host the 2015 European Youth Capital, www.europeanyouthcapital.org/capitals/cluj-napoca-2015, 25.01.2014.

25 A German based NGO, GTZ, conducted during 1999-2000, in collaboration with the local authorities, an "orientation phase" that targeted to establish the responsibility of all the urban actors and to further plan actions, asses objectives, structure priorities and evaluate the progress through four workshops (Project 95.4808.2-026.00, co-ordinated by Arch. Steffen Mildner, Leipzig, FRG). One of GTZ's results pointed that even if the residents complained about the state of the buildings in the historic centre, they were (85%) willing to help to their improvement than to move. Educating the inhabitants was one of the project's priorities and the results showed improvement in the quality of the materials used and of the rehabilitation works.

Figure 6; Figure 7: Images from Sibiu's Lower City, showing the shallow cosmetic intervention outside the city's core. (Authors 2006; 2007)

Regarding the sustainability of the European Cultural Capital concept and its benefits for Sibiu, it is generally considered a success and a positive effort towards the conservation of the cultural heritage of the historic centre. Tourism's returns probably did not rise to the local authority's expectations, but the framework of the 2007 events is still followed as a sustainable development strategy for both the city and the community. The local community was the beneficiary of educational programs, and professional support, along with the financial aid, in order to understand and implement good practices in the conservation of their properties[26]. The role of the community is essential in the development of the historic centre since "historic cities are perceived not as much as static objects to be admired for their history and architecture, but as living spaces to be occupied and appropriated by local communities' identity and sense of belonging" (Rodwell 2007: 187). Sibiu's local community managed to

26 In 2000 after interviewing the home owners from the historic center, the local authorities and experts drew the *Charter for the Rehabilitation of the Historic Center* (Nistor 2001: 12).

acknowledge the cultural value of their heritage and make substantial efforts to protect it.

The education of the community was the more important as some of the owners are not the original proprietors. During the communist nationalization many buildings that used to be single-family houses became rental apartments for several families. The connection between the current home-owners and their houses is not commonly an empathic one. Therefore, learning how to use their properties and be informed of their cultural significance, beyond the market value, was an important objective in the rehabilitation of Sibiu's historic area. Gesellschaft für Technische Zusammenarbeit (GTZ)[27] and local experts conducted public seminars and campaigns in order to educate the community about the importance of traditional crafts and materials, while also offering expertise and technical support.

A combined effort from the authorities, several organisations and historical building owners made possible a real symbiosis between conservation and tourism. To conclude this third case study in the acacia-giraffe manner, Sibiu proves that the acacia is not such an unwilling food source. Its reluctance towards the leaf browsers is motivated by the potential impairment of its crown. However, if not for the herbivores, its seeds would not travel the savannah, thus perpetuating its legacy. Other cities applying for cultural programs in order to boost their importance for the tourism industry eloquently proves the case. The acacia is not in a real danger. Its crown's low profile only offers narrow margins for consumption. Correspondingly, tourists tend to concentrate usually in touristic established areas, thus only experiencing part of the *genius loci* (Norberg-Schulz 1980), which they, supposedly disseminate to the touring community. And usually, the "power of place" (Walton J. and Wood J. 2008: 1) is something they like to experience courteously. Perhaps the destination is able to match its touristic commodities with the benefits the tourists are seeking (Misiusa 2006: 130) well enough, so they don't feel the need to devour the place in search of satisfactory experiences.

Satisfaction guaranteed, yet even a cat's lives are planned

The three case studies are examples of the complex relationships created between tourism and the cultural heritage. As pointed out, all of them benefit from a turning point moment that created a consistent use framework of the local

27 GTZ was a core actor in the strategy for rehabilitation of the historic centre of Sibiu. Its involvement was concluded in 2008, after about eight years of successful activity in Sibiu.

touristic resources, as opposed to a spontaneous and potentially menacing exploitation. The threat came for Voroneţ from the local private initiatives, dammed by the recognition of its world heritage assets. Oppositely, for Sighişoara, its international acknowledgement was exactly the start off for a potentially damaging exploitation from the very structures meant to protect it. Somewhere in the middle, Sibiu is still struggling to synchronize its management of heritage and tourism, while equally receiving and asking for international recognition. From a conservationist point of view, the international acknowledgement comes with ups and downs, as the growing exposure and the pressure it generates has a sharp edge path that, if strayed from, can lead to either overuse or neglect damage. The guarantee is the most fundamental and effective strategy to cope with this potential ambivalence. Sam Walton, the founder of Wal-Mart, said "The two most important words I ever wrote were on that first Wal-Mart sign, 'Satisfaction Guaranteed'. They're still up there, and they have made all the difference" (Walton and Huey 1992: 316-317). The potential negative consequence of one's action, as the decision to choose between several options, such as touring destinations for example, usually generates a reluctance towards the lesser candidates, following a ranking based mainly on reputation. A reliable guarantee, by diminishing the reluctance towards the anticipation of negative consequences, doesn't even need any more to promote the positive, feature, since the negative ones are already removed (Knowles and Riner 2007: 100).

Already with a history of its own, the tourism industry works with established brands, certified brands and the dicey rest. Targeting "world relics" for their unique cultural values is, at least for the heritage passionate tourist, a contemporary *Grand Tour*, ratified by the numerous national and international heritage organizations. UNESCO, which is perhaps the most reputable of them, developed its World Heritage List based on a series of principles called "Operational Guidelines" that work with six main criteria for selection of cultural sites. These criteria aim for unicity, intrinsic values, outstanding buildings or type of building, traditional values and cultures, association with events or traditions etc.[28] The heritage tourist has, in many ways, an already guaranteed gratification of his planned endeavour as long as this gratification comes with the endorsement of the reputable heritage establishments.

On the other hand, certifying the heritage comes with expectations from the consumer. The tourist's experience does not resume to the consumption of heritage items, but encompasses also the rest of the iceberg, what is referred to as

28 The UNESCO Operational Guidelines 2005, available on the United Nations Educational, Scientific and Cultural Organization website, http://whc.unesco.org/en/criteria/, 03.01.2014.

"cultural diversity"[29]. It accounts as well for the cultural transfer – the trip to and from, and the encounter with the intangible cultural heritage. These are not always subject to an arbitration coming from trustworthy organizations. Of course, the touring community has its ways of transpiring relevant information in order to smooth a potential "culture clash". The tension is usually released in efforts to adapt the destination's environment so as to fit the needs of the visitors as well. The proportionality of this effort is equal to tourism's importance for the local economy. If this condition is not met, the tension ruptures in an altered touristic experience that, regardless of the heritage's quality, may result in a diminished satisfaction for the tourist. However, excessive tourism and insufficient tourist control, puts the heritage in a vulnerable position. History proves that "curiosity killed the cat" countless times[30], with the twist that it was not the cat's curiosity. What better example for this than Egypt? Parts of Egypt's "sacred cat" are, for centuries now, in Western museums and in private collections. Even if wrongfully attributed to O'Neill[31], he took the metaphor further by saying "but satisfaction brought it back" (O'Neill 1920). Let's indulge in saying that parts are returned nowadays to Egypt in an international effort, even if met by critics[32], to put back the "borrowed" artefacts to their rightful place. Tourists' curiosity and what derives from it may endanger the integrity of sites, but as more interest is concentrated towards the touristic destinations, their importance grows, their sustainability becomes mandatory, and is enforced by specific regulations. Tourists, sometimes, are possessed by the irresistible impulse to take souvenirs or to leave behind a sign of their visit behind. While the first is an understandable potential remembrance aid, the latter seems to be an ancestral urge, that we may address to as the "I was here syndrome" (Boustan et al. 2011:

29 UNESCO Convention on the Protection and Promotion of the Diversity of Cultural Expressions (2005), http://unesdoc.unesco.org/images/0014/001429/142919e.pdf, 25.01.2014.

30 The problem of the international displaced heritage restitution was largely debated during the The Conference on International Cooperation for the Protection and Repatriation of Cultural Heritage, 7-8 April 2010, held in Cairo, Egypt. The conference ended in international claims for the return of certain cultural artefacts which had been looted or stolen during former colonial interferences. Dr. Zedi Hawas, the initiator of the conference, is Egypt's top archeologist and an internationally recognized campaigner for heritage restitution.

31 Eugene O'Neil included the variation in his 1920 play, *Diff'rent*. However, the earliest reference to the saying goes to James Allan Mair, who listed it in his 1873 *A handbook of metaphors: English, Scottish, Irish, American, Shakespearean, and scriptural; and family mottoes* (Mair 1973: 34).

32 "The problem of the repatriation of cultural heritage to its country of origin is an old one, based on a 19th century doctrine enshrined in the Treaty of Vienna that scientific and artistic collections cannot be expatriated because they are destined to meet the permanent intellectual needs of the country of origin." (Eyo 1994)

152) that haunted mankind for centuries as a mark of the achievement of getting someplace (Reisner 1971: 70). Scribbling and painting on walls started long before tourism became an industry, as some of the first examples go back to the Palaeolithic Age when cave drawing recorded events and life experiences in an artistic form. Even recently, during the 19th century, it was fashionable enough for adventurers and campaigning French soldiers to substantiate their visit to Egypt in traveller's graffiti. This trend was reported by documents and testimonies of early wanderers (de Keersmaecker 2006) and, of course, by its everlasting marks.

Figure 8: *French army bivouac in Aswan* (Jean-Charles Tardieu 1812). The centrepiece of the painting shows a group of Louis Desaix's soldiers scribbling on the relics of the ancient city of Swenett during the Upper Egypt campaign, in late 1799.

Contemporary scribbling is generally considered an act of vandalism and is taboo when involving historical sites and monuments. The gesture of a young Chinese tourist who wrote his name, luckily in chalk, on a Luxor temple wall in May 2013 (Wong 2013) was internationally condemned. Reason enough for publicly assumed national shame, as a result, the Chinese government released a set of guidelines for the international traveling Chinese tourists, with an explicit code of conduct (Cripps 2013). As it turns out, coincidentally, the 112-article guide was already approved since April 2013, but was rushed to come into effect as a law in October 2013[33].

Conclusions

The question arising is: How much protection from tourists can a heritage site enforce in order to ensure its preservation? Will this protection have negative effects on the site's image and authenticity or will this impact the tourists' experience? Historical sites rely a lot on image and, consequently, "defensive" procedures may have a negative impact on the setting. Contemporary surveillance and protection measures are not always compatible with the historic ambiance of aged materials and textures. Perhaps the excessive safeguarding can lead to "museification" and alter the feel of the very elements that caused the site's consideration. The experiential nature of cultural heritage tourism makes tourists aim for as much contact as possible with the monument or site, which leads to numerous conservation problems. The need to interact and have a sensory experience, also present in the "I was here syndrome", overlapped the already present need of making the most out of the experience and satisfying one's personal curiosity.

Touching the walls of historical buildings, monuments, wood and metal works might lead to their accelerated degradation in time. Chemical substances and organic residue can harm irreversibly the original materials (Watt 2008; Carria 2004). Temperature fluctuation and humidity have a negative impact on historic enclosed perimeters. Temples in Egypt (MacDonald 1996: 113), the rock-cut temple of Petra (Luton 2007), the caves of Lascaux[34] are a few examples of world cultural heritage sites that encountered conservation management issues because of a large number of tourists modifying the parameters of the sites. Many acknowledged sites, such as Angkor (De Launey 2012), had to take drastic measures in order to safeguard their preservation. Direct tourist contact is not the only damage they suffer. Aside from their extensive use, other contemporary environmental factors, such as pollution and climate change have a massive impact on fragile artefacts and monuments. As much as we like to believe that tourism contributes substantially to historic sites

---

33 According to China's National Tourism Administration, cnta.gov.cn/html/2013-6/2013-6-4-10-1-12844.html, 02.08.2013.

34 As described in UNESCO's World Heritage Committee decision 32COM 7B.88, regarding the inscription in the World Heritage List of the "Prehistoric Sites and Decorated Caves of the Vézère Valley", http://whc.unesco.org/en/soc/930/?mode=doc, 12.09.2013.

preservation, it is also one of the main degradation factors. For the building as a living organism, in a somehow disturbing analogy, we could say that tourism is the "chemotherapy for heritage conservation", giving hope of salvation, while equally leaving profound marks in secondary effects.

Figure 9: Harry Harrison's cartoon piece covering the "Sino-Egyptian" incident. (South China Morning Post, May 27th 2013)

Adapting the sites for public use is an important and challenging part of their preservation. Safety measures, not a part of the original structure, are however necessary for public safety. But as long as contemporary interventions do not damage the hypothetical harmony of the whole and the additions are not significant (Jokilehto 1999), the cultural and artistic value of a historical site is not altered. Giving universal access to heritage sites makes perfect sense, since they represent "the common heritage of humanity" (UNESCO 2001a). The great challenge arising is balancing the historical character of sites and their contemporary additions, whether they occur for accessibility, safety or security. With technological advancement, less invasive and better integrated solutions do minimize the heritage management dilemmas (Hollinworth et al. 2012).

Some of the sites require a conversion from a previous use to another, which, in order to be accessible to the public, must be appropriated and directly linked with the context and local community (*Venice Charter* 1964). This change may alter several components of the building in order to meet the contemporary ergonomic standards. These "corrections" to the original have to be carefully designed and harmonious with the historic context (Jokilehto 1995: 73). This might be a necessary evil, due to the fact that it allows the building to survive when it no longer has an operative function, other than servicing tourism related activities. Historical buildings and sites have already survived the test of time, some by resisting to change and others by adapting to new uses and users. Maintaining the balance between the transformation and the conservation of heritage values is a difficult mission since it ultimately deals with the requirement for the authentic feel of the experience, but challenged by the norms of the contemporary society.

On a global level, maintenance, conservation regulations and good practices are applied rigorously on historical sites, in order to preserve their cultural value and authenticity. On the other hand, tourists' attraction towards heritage and historical sites is proportional with their unicity and their complementary intangible features. The authenticity is often expected by default as a compensation for the traveller's expense. Heritage is, after all, a cultural commodity for the touring consumer. Somehow paradoxically, this lucrative symbiotic relationship between heritage and tourists generates preservation and degradation at the same time.

As for Romania, the current lack of conservation practice and strategies for tourism is balanced consistently by the state of tourism amenities and mobility infrastructure which helps in keeping the heritage sites remote and thus, to limit the tourists inflow. Based on recent prediction for the next decade, Romania expects a low but steady grow in tourism[35]. As collateral victim of more than twenty years of transition towards democracy, the heritage sites are as much important for Romanians as they rediscover their cultural identity placed in a global context and not confined anymore within an ideological bubble. While still seeing tourism as a new, not experienced before, way to profit, the heritage as commodity menaces the heritage as cultural drive for community sustainable development.

References

Andrei, C. (2002): Parlamentul Europei cere oprirea lucrărilor la "Dracula Park" până la prezentarea raportului UNESCO. România Liberă, 29 April.

Archer, B., Cooper, C. and Ruhanen L. (2005): The Positive and Negative Impacts of Tourism. In: Theobald, W.F. (ed.): Global Tourism (3rd Ed.), Burlington, MA: Elsevier, 79-102.

35 According to the World Travel & Tourism Council which detailed the economic impact of tourism in Romania in 2013, and made predictions for 2023 as well: Travel & Tourism Economic Impact 2013 Romania, http://www.wttc.org/site_media/uploads/downloads/romania2013_1.pdf, 14.10.2013.

Avram, L. and Grosu, C. (2003): Dracula Park a supt miliarde de la bugetul de stat. Adevărul, 2 July.

Beauregard, R.A. (1998): Tourism and Economic Development Policy in US Urban Areas. In: Ioannides, D. and Debbage, K.G. (eds): The Economic Geography of the Tourist Industry: A Supply-side Analysis. London: Routledge, 219-234.

Becket, E., and Olson, P. (2008): In Pictures: Europe's Most Idyllic Places to Live, http://www.forbes.com/2008/11/18/europe-homes-dollar-forbeslife-cx_po_1118realestate_slide_4.html, 15.01.2014.

Boustan, R.S., Kosansky, O., and Rustow, M. (2011): Jewish Studies at the Crossroads of Anthropology and History. Philadelphia: University of Pennsylvania Press.

Brockman, N.C. (2011): Encyclopedia of Sacred Places. Santa Barbara: ABC-CLIO, LLC.

Brunet, S., Bauer, J., De Lacy, T. and Tshering, K. (2001): Tourism Development in Bhutan: Tensions between Tradition and Modernity. In: Journal of Sustainable Tourism, 9(3), 243-263.

Burns, P.M., Palmer, C., and Lester, JA. (2010): Tourism and Visual Culture, Volume 1: Theories and Concepts. Oxfordshire: CAB International

Burtan, A. (2001): Casa Groazei şi ţeapa-jet în Dracula Park. Evenimentul Zilei, 6 November, 12.

Carria, F. (2004): La conservazione delle facciate materiali e tehniche per il recupero. Milano: Tecniche nuove.

Cohen, E. (1979): Rethinking the Sociology of Tourism. In: Annals of Tourism Research, 6(1), 18-35.

Constantinescu, M. (2001): Dan Matei Agathon este gata să se întâlnească cu contestatarii "Dracula Park". Cotidianul, 6 November.

Cripps, K. (2013): China's First Tourism Law Comes into Effect, Tourists Issued Manners Guide. CNN, 4 October, http://edition.cnn.com/2013/10/03/travel/new-china-tourism-law/, 02.08.2013.

D'Amore, L. (1983): Guidelines to planning harmony with the host community. In: Murphy, P.E. (ed.) Tourism in Canada: Selected Issues and Options. Victoria: Department of Geography. Victoria: University of Victoria.

Davis, D.J.A., and Cosenza, R.M. (1988): Segmenting Local Residents, Interests, and Opinions toward Tourism. Journal of Travel Research, 27(3), 2-8.

Doxey, G.V. (1975): A Causation Theory of Visitor-Resident Irritants: Methodology and Research Inferences. San Diego, California: Proceedings of the Travel Research Association 6th Annual Conference, 195-198.

Evans, G. (2003): Hard-branding the Cultural City – From Prado to Prada. In: International Journal of Urban and Regional Research, 27(2), 417-40.

Eyo, E. (1994): Repatriation of Cultural Heritage: The African Experience. In: Kaplan F.E.S. (eds.): Museums and the Making of "Ourselves". London: Leicester University Press, 330-350.

Feilden, B. and Jokilehto J. (2005): Management Guidelines for World Cultural Heritage Sites. ICCROM, Rome.

Ficeac, B. (2001): Turism în ţara lui Dracula. România Liberă, 22 November.

Frölich, H.B. (2001): Nu avem nevoie de un Draculaland. România Liberă, 5 November.

Garrod, B. and Fyall, A. (2000): Managing Heritage Tourism. In: Annals of Tourism Research, 27(3), 682-708.

Gillmore, L. (1999): Romania: Cold Comfort and the Last Judgement; Some of the Finest Frescoes in the World Are to Be Found in the Convents and Monasteries of Romania, but Don't Expect a Warm Welcome. The Independent, November 13.

Goldman, R. and Papson, S. (1996): Sign Wars: The Cluttered Landscape of Advertising. London: Guilford Press.

Hollinworth, N., Hwang, F., Allen, K., Minnion, A., and Kwiatkowska, G. (2012): Interactive Sensory Objects for Access to Heritage, http://www.academia.edu/3196836/Interactive_Sensory_Objects_for_Access_to_Heritage, 08.02.2014.

Hornstein, B. (2011): Losing Site: Architecture, Memory and Place. Farnham: Ashgate.

Jokilehto, J. (1995): Comments on the Venice Charter with Illustrations, http://www.icomos.org/venicecharter2004/jokilehto.pdf, 13.02.2014.

Jokilehto, J. (1999): A History of Architectural Conservation. Oxford Butterworth Heinemann.

Kavaratzis, M. (2004): From City Marketing to City Branding: Towards a Theoretical Framework for Developing City Brands. In: Place Branding, 1(1), 58-73.

Kavaratzis, M. and Ashworth, G.J. (2005): City Branding: An Effective Assertion of Identity or a Transitory Marketing Trick? In: Tidschrift voor economische en sociale geographie, 96(5), 506-14.

Knowles, E.S. and Riner, D.D. (2007): Omega Approaches to Persuation: Overcoming Resistance. In: Pratkanis, A.R. (ed.): The Science of Social Influence: Advantages and Future Progress. New York: Psychology Press, 83-114.

De Keersmaecker, R. (2006): Travellers' Graffiti from Egypt and the Sudan, Volume 3. R. O. de Keersmaecker.

De Launey, G. (2012): Are There too Many Tourists at Angkor's Temples? BBC News Asia, 9 June, http://www.bbc.com/news/world-asia-18363636, 12.09.2014.

Leigh, D. (2007): Dracula Tourism in Romania: Cultural Identity and the State. In: Annals of Tourism Research, 34(3), 746-765.

Leigh, D. (2007): The Dracula Dilemma: Tourism, Identity and the State in Romania. Surrey: Ashgate Publishing.

Lew, A., Hall, C.M. and Timothy, D.J. (2008): World Geography of Travel and Tourism: A Regional Approach. Oxford: Elsevier.

Long, P.T., Perdue, R. and Allen, L. (1990): Rural Resident Tourism Perceptions and Attitudes by Community Level of Tourism. In: Journal of Travel Research, 28, 3-9.

Lucas, E.V. (1905): The Works of Charles and Mary Lamb, Volume VI: Letters, 1796 – 1820. London: Methuen & Co.

Luton, T. (2007) Preserving Petra: The Crumbling City of Stone. Discovering Stone, Issue 11. Australian Stone Advisory Association, 38-44.

MacDonald, J.K. (1996): House of Eternity: The Tomb of Nefertari. Los Angeles: The Getty Conservation Institute.

Macleod, D. (2005): Alternative Tourism: A Comparative Analysis of Meaning and Impact. In: Theobald, W.F. (ed.): Global Tourism (3rd Ed.), 123-140. Burlington, MA: Elsevier.

Metro-Roland, M.M. (2011): Tourists, Signs and the City: The Semiotics of Culture in an Urban Landscape. Surrey: Ashgate.
Misiura, S. (2006): Heritage Marketing. Oxford: Elsevier.
Năstase, G. (2001): Dracula – produs touristic. Cotidianul, 15 November.
Neagu, B. (2003): Mitrea l-a restructurat pe Dracula. Ziarul Financiar, 30 July.
Nistor, S. (2001): Romania's Urban Architectural Heritage between Neglect and Revitalization, in Proceedings of ARCCHIP Workshop A03, http://www.arcchip.cz/w03/w03_nistor.pdf, 06.02.2014.
Nistor, S. (2008): Sibiu Capitală Culturală 2007 ianuarie 2005 – decembrie 2007. Raport Sinteză. Ministerul Culturii şi Cultelor.
Noble, R., Brown, M. and Cole, S. (2012) (eds.): Water Equity in Tourism: A Human Right – A Global Responsibility, Research Report. Tourism Concern Action for Ethical Tourism.
Norberg-Schulz, C. (1980): Genius Loci: Towards a Phenomenology of Architecture. New York: Rizzoli.
Nuryanti, W. (1996): Heritage and Postmodern Tourism. In: Annals of Tourism
Research, 23(2), 249-60.
Parau, C.E. (2009): Impaling Dracula: How EU accession empowered civil society in Romania. West Europe Politics, 32(1), 119-141.
Patin, V. (1999): Safeguarding Heritage. Will market forces rule? In: UNESCO Currier 52 (July/August), 35-36.
Pearce, D. (1981): Tourist Development: Topics in Applied Geography. London: Addison-Wesley Longman Inc.
Prentice, R. (1993): Community-driven Tourism Planning and Residents' Preferences. In: Tourism Management, 14(2), 218-227.
Prina, F. (2008): Architecture: Elements, Materials, Form. Princeton: Princeton University Press.
Reisner, R. (1971): Graffiti: Two Thousand Years of Wall Writing. New York: Cowles Book Co.
Rodwell, D. (2007): Conservation and Sustainability in Historic Cities. Oxford: Blackwell.
Rojek, C. (1997): Indexing, Dragging and the Social Construction of Tourist Sights. In Rojek, C. and Urry, J. (eds.) Touring Cultures: Transformations of Travel and Theory. London: Routledge, 52-74.
Sandberg-Diment, E. (1998): Artistic Route through Romania. New York Times, June 21.
Selwyn, T. (1996): "Introduction". In: Selwyn, T. (ed.): The Tourist Image: Myths and Myth Making in Modern Tourism. Chichester: Wiley, 1-32.
Severiades, S. (2001): A Quantitative Examination of Perceptions of the Impact of Tourism upon Family Life in Cyprus, PhD dissertation. Surrey: School of Management Studies for the Service Sector, University of Surrey.
Shandley, R., Jamal, T. and Tănase, A. (2006): Location Shooting and the Filmatic Destination: Transylvanian Myths and the Postcolonial Tourism Enterprise. In: Journal of Tourism and Cultural Change, 4(3), 137-158.
Smith, M. and Hall, D. (2006): Enlargement Implications for European Tourism. In: Hall, D., Smith, M., and Marciszewska, B. (eds.) Tourism in the New Europe: The

Challenges and Opportunities of EU Enlargement. Wallingford, OX: CAB International, 32-43.

Smith, V.L. (1989): Hosts and Guest: The Anthropology of Tourism (2nd ed.). Philadelphia: University of Pennsylvania Press.

Soutar, G.N. and McLeod, P.B. (1993): Residents' Perceptions on Impact of the America's Cup. In: Annals of Tourism Research, 30, 571-581.

Spirou, C. (2011): Urban Tourism and Urban Change: Cities in a Global Economy. New York: Routledge.

Theuma, N. (2006): Malta: Re-imagining the Mediterranean Destination. In: Hall, D, Smith, M. and Marciszewska, B. (eds.) Tourism in the New Europe: The Challenges and Opportunities of EU Enlargement. Wallingford OX: CAB International, 213-223.

Toader, A (2008) Sibiul aspire la un loc pe lista Patrimoniului Mondial UNESCO. BBC Romanian, 25 March, www.bbc.co.uk/romanian/news/story/2008/03/printable/080325_arena_patrimoniu_sibiu.shtml, 25.01.2014.

Vela, A. (2001a): Lângă Sighişoara – Dracula Park. Adevărul, 6 November.

Vela, A. (2001b): Dracula Park – la 6 km de Sighişoara pe Platoul Breite. Adevărul, 21 November.

Walton, J. and Wood, J. (2008): The Future of Heritage – Changing Visions, Attitudes and Contexts in the 21st Century, in Virtual Symposium: Blackpool, http://www.semioticon.com/virtuals/blackpool/walton_wood_3.pdf, 02.02.2014.

Walton, S., and Huey, J. (1992) Made in America: My Story. New York: Doubleday.

Watt, D. (2008): Building Pathology: Principles and Practice. Oxford: Blackwell Publishing.

Williams, P.W. and Alison, G. (2005): Addressing Carrying Capacity Issues in Tourism Destinations through Growth Management. In: Theobald, W.F. (ed.): Global Tourism (3rd Ed.). Burlington, MA: Elsevier, 123-140.

Wong, H. (2013): Netizen Outrage after Chinese Tourist Defaces Egyptian Temple. CNN, 29 May, http://edition.cnn.com/2013/05/27/travel/china-egypt/, 02.08.2013.

*** (1964) Venice Charter, 2nd International Congress of Architects and Specialists of Historic Buildings, Venice, 25-31 May, www.international.icomos.org/charters/venice_e.pdf, 15.01.2014.

*** (1971): Romania, Volume 22, Issue 23. U.S. Department of Commerce, U.S. International Trade Administration.

*** (1978): UNESCO, Convention Concerning the Protection of the World Cultural and Natural Heritage. Paris, 16 November 1972. UNESCO. General Conference, 17th Session. Records of the General Conference, Paris, 17 October to 21 November 1972. Volume I: Resolutions, Recommendations. UNESDOC database, http://unesdoc.unesco.org/images/0011/001140/114044e.pdf, 30.01.2014.

*** (1978): UNESCO, Intergovernmental Committee for the Protection of the World Cultural and Natural Heritage, 2nd Session. Final Report. Washington, DC, 5–8 September 1978. CC-78/CONF.010/10 Rev. UNESDOC database, http://unesdoc.unesco.org/images/0003/000347/034793eb.pdf, 30.01.2014.

*** (1999): Tourism and Culture: Rethinking the Mix. In UNESCO Currier 52 (July/August), 21-22.

*** (1999): Tourism and Culture: Rethinking the Mix. In UNESCO Currier 52 (July/August), 21-22.

*** (2000): UNESCO, Report WHC-99/CONF.209/22, Paris, http://whc.unesco.org/archive/1999/whc-99-conf209-22e.pdf, 30.01.2014.

*** (2001a): UNESCO, Universal Declaration on Cultural Diversity, General Conference of UNESCO, 21st session, 2 November 2001, http://unesdoc.unesco.org/images/0012/001271/127160m.pdf, 30.01.2014.

*** (2001b): UNESCO, World Heritage Committee, 25th session, Helsinki, Finland, 11-16 December 2001, http://whc.unesco.org/document/1248, 30.01.2014.

*** (2003): UNESCO, Convention for the Safeguarding of the Intangible Cultural Heritage. Paris, 17 October 2003. General Conference, 32nd Session. Records of the General Conference, Thirty-second Session, Paris, 29 September to 17 October 2003. Volume I: Resolutions. UNESDOC database, http://unesdoc.unesco.org/images/0013/001331/133171e.pdf, 30.01.2014.

*** (2007): Organizing Committee for the "Medieval Sighişoara" Festival 2007: Regulament de organizare şi desfăşurare a Festivalului Sighişoara Medievală 2007, http://sighisoaraonline.com/20070620_54_prima_Regulament-de-organizare-si-desfasurare-a-Festivalului-Sighisoara-Medievala-2007.html, 22.01.2014.

*** (2009): The Impact of Culture on Tourism. OECD, http://www.tava.gov.lv/sites/tava.gov.lv/files/dokumenti/petijumi/OECD_Tourism_Culture.pdf.

*** (2013): UNESCO, Convention Concerning the Protection of the World Cultural and Natural Heritage. World Heritage Committee, 37th Session, Phnom Penh, Cambodia, 16-27 June 2013, http://whc.unesco.org/archive/2013/whc13-37com-7B-Add-en.pdf, 30.01.2014.

*** (2013): UNESCO, State of Conservation Churches of Moldavia C 598 bis, http://whc.unesco.org/en/soc/1988, 07.02.2014.

The Legally Pluralistic Tourist

Roy Andrew Partain

This article presents the idea that law can be consumed as an act of tourism and invites law to be compared with other traditional acts of culture and identification, as an act of authenticity, as an act of belonging. Yet when law is consumed as a tourist good, then it is an act of redefinition, of belonging to the other, of seeking authenticity outside of one's normal legal culture. Thus, the inquiry of this study is to ask, can law be seen as a ritual, ceremony or performance that tourists could participate in, much as they might other aspects of culture? Also, if so, what forms of touristic acts of legal consumption might be fruitful for research?

The study will proceed by answering the first question in the affirmative. Yes, ritual and ceremonies are well described in the literature. The roots of what western society deems 'law' do appear to derive directly from the magical and mystical rituals that intrigued van Gennep (1961) and Turner (1969). Roman law in particular shows substantial evidence of being intimately related to rituals both sacerdotal and social, that what was once clearly religious became secularized but never lost sight of its divine or idealistic core. Thus western law, and its extensive export of itself to many lands abroad, consists of legal ritual and ceremonies.

Next, the legal philosophy of Cover (1985) will be explored to demonstrate that the sociological character of contemporary law can be extended in useful ways to research the rituals and performances of legal acts. The jurisprudence will be included to demonstrate how Cover's (1985) legal philosophy has been applied to evidence that legal systems and acts extend far beyond the nineteenth century's positivist perspective to include recognition of the overlapping legal and normative spheres that everyone finds themselves engaged in the everyday. The context of a legally pluralistic tourist is thus developed to recognize that legal acts and rituals exist, that the tourist is faced with choices of belonging and engagement, and that the tourist acts through her or his choices of legal performance.

This article will review several areas of research within touring and consumption. It will attempt to identify key ideas and concerns from each of those areas of research and reveal how law might fit within those research areas. This article does not present a discussion from the sociology of law, rather it attempts to identify the mundane and routine acts of law as taken by tourists as moments of ritual or ceremony. Those functional acts, like other acts of viewing, performing or experience sharing, provide insights into both tourists and the cultures from which they arrive and to whence they travel. Tourists consume legal acts, performances, and choices of law as services and sometimes as abstract goods totemizing ideals. Thus, an argument is proposed that the legal acts, performances, or choices of tourists belong among the list of acts and services worthy of notice and study within the sociology of tourism.

Tourists consume law

One of the enjoyable parts of tourism for many tourists is the ability to experience the other in safe and consumerable forms. Law can be considered a good or service to be consumed by the tourist.

Law as a consumable act or ritual

Law is not limited to sets of legislative rules and judicial decrees. Law is both acts of constructive communication establishing cultural norms and acts of performance in the material world law; law entails social choices and obligations. Law is but another aspect of culture; the researcher can treat it with the same tools.

Law is a means of cultural interaction for both tourist and host. Hosts can offer legal acts differentiated from those available to the tourist at home; the tourist can then consume legal acts as an act within the broader set of tourist experiences. Various motivations have been identified for why tourists engage in tourism and travel; these motives include education, exploration, evaluation of self, facilitation of social interactions, and experiential and existential motives. (McIntyre 2007: 118). The tourist can satisfy these motivations within legal acts, performances, and choices.

For the purposes of this enquiry, the idea of a *legal act*, of a *law act,* capable of consumption, are those acts wherein tourists from a home country engage with the legal cultures, obligations, and potential castigation of a host country in a substantive manner. Law has been staidly defined as: "A rule or method according to which phenomenon or actions co-exist or follow each other. Law, in its generic sense, is a body of rules of action or conduct prescribed by controlling authority, and having binding legal force." (Black 1990: 884). The same authority defined a juristic act as "one designed to have a legal effect, and capable thereof." (Black 1990: 855). (See a more complete discussion on law and its problematic definitions, infra)

One does not consume law whole; one cannot speak of consuming the whole of German or French law. Rather, law is consumed act by act, obligation by obligation. Law is often spoken of as a whole, but it is composed of many sub-units; statutes have sections and subsections, cases have *dicta* and holdings, concurrences and dissents. The law can be atomized, *meme*-tized. One can accept a fabric of law, yet still resist a certain atom or meme of it. Ergo, one can venture on tour and consume certain atoms of law not available or contrary to the laws within one's own home jurisdiction. One can venture to the liminal edge, test the atom of law, and decide to regress or to proceed to post-liminal acceptance of the new and post-alien law. The tourist has many opportunities to engage in legal acts, but the law is foreign, it is not the law of the tourist's home.

Legal acts are those acts that legally engage and commit the tourist to a legal paradigm beyond the legal paradigms of home. It can be acts of many scale, from minor purchases of items or services not legally available at home, e.g. the purchase of a beer, to acts of life identification and characterization, e.g. the consumption of a same-sex wedding ceremony and the onset of a legal marriage.

What is it to 'consume' a wedding, especially as a legal act? First, the wedding itself is routinely a performance, with lead actors usually in front of an audience of friends and family. But also, a wedding is a legal act of obligation, to support each other in future states and to share each other's assets and liabilities. A wedding is not the marriage itself, but the transformative act that brings the post-liminal obligations and benefits of the marriage. To consume a wedding, legally speaking, is to avail oneself of the legal option to so obtain for oneself those obligations and benefits. To some people in some jurisdictions, these rights and privileges are not available. E.g., two men may not marry in many locales, two women and one man cannot marry in many locales, and two first cousins might not be able to marry in certain locales. However, by travelling, all of these parties can find locations wherein they can consume the legal act of a wedding. (e.g., in Netherlands, in Indonesia, and in 25 states of the 50 U.S. states, respectively.)

The legal ritual of a wedding can be broken down into three stages, per Van Gennep (1961) and Turner (1969) (see infra). Parties to a hoped-for wedding reach a pre-liminal state where they desire to wed but cannot due to local law. A liminal state is reached, they travel in search of an allowance to wed; they seek to consume a law not of their own home. Finally, they reach an appropriate destination and are able to cross that threshold of marriage, to get married, and begin to enjoy their post-liminal legal enjoyment of their wedding and marriage.

Law as a choice of consumption

Law generally operates within notions of time and space; these legal zones are called jurisdictions (Black 1990: 853). To travel is to move between these jurisdictional spaces, yet often we carry duties and connections to the legal spaces and jurisdictions left behind. On tour, we are liminal between home and alien, between this law and that law. This overlap of legal spaces and the choices that a tourist might make on tour is referred to as legal pluralism; legal pluralism recognizes that most actors have multiple competing legal and normative spaces within which the actors often face conflicting or competing legal options or obligations (see infra).

While the consumption of touring-facilitated events, goods or services might also be seen through other lenses, they should also be recognized as events enabled by alternative legal paradigms, the consumption of which requires tourism away from the ordinary and routine environments of the tourist. Among the primary legal goods and services, there are the epicurean legal goods; *e.g.*, the legal norms allowing the purchase of Cuban cigars, the purchase of cannabinoids in certain teashops, the purchase of medicines not available at home, and the purchase of certain otherwise taboo *viandes* and protein sources in different countries. Law can offer to certain tourists the *gekaufte Paradies*; legal havens can offer to tourists "the creative space for the consumer's aesthetic personal projects to unfold," (Trauer 2006: 183), in part due to the legal permission to undertake that project of consumption. There are also certain lifestyles that are made available under only certain legal regimes; e.g., the gambling tables of Monaco and of Las Vegas, the sexual service industries of places *divers*, the celebration of homosexual marriage in certain liberal states in America. The act of legal consumption can also tinge the divine; e.g., the *sharia*-inspired regimes of Islamic republics, the local ordinances of communes both Amish and Hasidic, and the legally sanctioned sanctity of certain shrines around the world.

Beyond those more traditional categories of touristic experiences and acts of consumption, there exists yet another range of touristic-legal experiences available for the traveler; acts of mobility. Legal goods or services are often in the support of well-established social networks or socially interactive needs. The adoption of children often occurs in conjunction with travel abroad. In the modern dispersed world, family members often need to convene for funerals and the processing of inheritances. Families may share holidays by jointly owning or leasing a vacation home. Mobility requires an engagement with law through the multiple locales traversed.

Then there are those activities, while legal acts in themselves, which are often overlooked as acts in which tourists engage but support important aspects of tourism: the leasing agreement while renting a car, the liability rules that enable social interactions to occur safely, the legal conventions on which lane to drive within, the right to record a touristic performance or the legal prohibition against, the right to enjoy privacy from photographers or the lack thereof, the right to read what one pleases or a ban thereof, and in some places the legal rights to exist and live for some travellers; or public censure and worse. Thus, there is a wide collection of legal acts, performances, and choices that consumed by tourists, both as primary and secondary targets.

Law as ritual and ceremony

Herein is presented an argument that ritual and ceremony are not only major elements of the performance of law, but in fact that law, as western society perceives it, derived from ritual and ceremony and that even modern law, divorced as it might first appear from the mystical, is still heavily engaged in what might be seen as ritual and ceremony.

In preview, rituals and ceremonies have long been identified with community building and the enablement of individuals to pass through liminal stages from one sense of identity to another. Western law derived from Roman rituals and ceremonies, acts sacerdotal, communal and interfamilial. While Roman law transitioned from cultural custom to structured practices and codes, the cultural content of performances remained. In the modern world, we oft find ourselves under multiple systems of laws, what legal scholars call legal pluralism. Legal pluralism holds that people often find themselves under multiple legal spheres, both positive and cultural in origin. Each person must then find their identity and intertwist the multiple claims on their legal identity. A choice is left to each, to choose from multiple options what legal identity to assume. A legal tourist must choose to engage with one legal community or another; that choice renders them a consumer of the legal system of the community that generated the paideic content of the legal system.

A quick sketch of what follows; first, a brief review of rituals and ceremonies is provided. The pre-liminal, liminal, and post-liminal stages of rituals and ceremonies are detailed (see Turner 1969).

Second, a review of the historical evolution of the concept of law under the Roman jurists is sketched. The close affiliation of Roman law, from which most European and also Common Law is derived, to sacerdotal rituals and the derived linguistic and cultural terms that continue to bind law to its rituals and ceremonies are explained.

Third, a review of Cover's (1983) *nomos*-matic theory of paideic and imperial law is provided, to connect the first two sections. Cover (1983) wrote of the intertwining of culture and law, of society building through both emergent and organic creative legal discourse and the acts of imperial law to provide structure, hierarchy, and delimiting definitions. The integration of Cover's (1983) philosophy into the field of legal pluralism is discussed to demonstrate both the acceptance of the paradigm and its potential use to recognize the choices of law faced by tourists.

Theories of ritual and ceremony

Rituals and ceremonies are acts of performance found in many cultures. They both create and transmit cultural ideas or obligations; such acts often bind individuals to groups and extend membership from the group to the individual. While some may distinguish rituals as more religious and ceremonies as less so, ultimately both rituals and ceremonies engage in a threshold of transformation. Such liminal or liminoid experiences will later be seen to be central to the experience of law, especially for the legally pluralistic tourist.

Turner (1957) saw rituals as performances that held societies together; they provided a means to stabilize family and interfamilial relationships. Deflem (1991: 7) stated that Turner (1969) followed Van Gennep's (1961) general statement on rituals; that rituals "accompany every change of place, state, social position and age." According to Turner (1967: 94), Van Gennep (1961) had previously defined rituals as 'processual' or procedural in form; they proceeded through three stages (i) the pre-liminal, (ii) the liminal and (iii) the post-liminal. The pre-liminal stage is when a person becomes detached from their routine or regular status (Turner 1967: 94). The liminal stage finds that person ambiguous, in consideration of alternatives states. Finally, in the post-liminal stage, that person selects and enters into a new status with its own rights and obligations (Turner 1967: 94). As such, the participants of the rites were "neither here nor there; they are betwixt and between the positions assigned and arrayed by law, custom, convention, and ceremonial" (Turner 1969: 95).

Turner (1977: 183) provided a procedural definition of rituals, that they were "a stereotyped sequence of activities involving gestures, words, and objects, performed in a sequestered place, and designed to influence preternatural entities or forces on behalf of the actors' goals and interests". For rituals to become effective for the group performing the rites, the rites must hang on to common cultural teachings "which have for their object invisible and intangible beings or powers which a human group recognizes as superior, on which it depends" (Turner and

Turner 1982: 201). But those rituals can be founded on otherwise mundane bits of human activity, such as phrases, gestures or activities (Turner 1967:19).

Akin to Cover's (1985) notions of paideic law and imperial law, Turner (1969: 96-97) provided for communitas and structure. Communitas reflected that aspect of community life that provided the sense of belonging, of comradery; communitas carried a liminal aspect. Structure provided hierarchy, reinforcement. While Turner (1969: 131-140) identified three types of communitas, i.e., existential, normative, and ideological, it is the normative communitas, those that support the organization of social system, that best corresponds to Cover's (1985) notion of a paideic community. Turner (1969: 132 or 1974: 282) saw communitas as emergent and organic, but that they would fall into "structure and law," only to potentially arise in new emergent communitas. This yin-yang of organic meaning yielding to structure, only to re-emerge from that very structure anew, is much in alignment with Cover's (1983) overall sense of *nomos*, that the emergent and jurisgenerative ("law creating") paideic laws are then structured by imperial laws, only to repeat until jurispathic ("law killing") judges are required to clear the underbrush of confusion.

Turner (1969) argued that rituals tied to tribal religion were liminal, whereas those rituals of modern life were more likely to be liminoid, limited in the spiritual context but active in the politico-social construct of a community, especially those groups below the nation-state level. As explained by Delfem (1991: 16):

> "Liminoid phenomena, on the other hand, take place in the complex industrial world; they are the products of individual or particular group efforts and are generated continuously. The liminoid originates outside the boundaries of the economic, political, and structural process, and its manifestations often challenge the wider social structure by offering social critique on, or even suggestions for, a revolutionary re-ordering of the official social order. ... ritual activity is no longer nationwide but individualized to certain specific groups."

Thus, the role of ritual activity, even if delimited to liminoidal acts, is to provide a means for potentially providing social critiques to the established order. As will be developed, infra and extensively within Sec. 3, the legally pluralistic tourist is enabled to select from alternative *nomos*-spheres which rituals of law to engage with; and by so doing, the legally pluralistic tourist is potentially enabled to transform the *nomos* of both the home and the host as interactions with their *nomos*.

Law as derived from ritual, law as ceremony

Roman law is the foundation of both the civil law systems of the world and much of the common law systems found in England and the U.S. (Schiavone 2012: *en passim*). It was founded in mystical rituals but evolved to function more transparently. In the definitions of Turner (1969), see supra, the rituals and performances of Roman law evolved from liminal to liminoid as the spirit of the law transitioned from literal gods to abstract ideals of justice. As such, the act of engaging in law is a ritual or ceremony, potentiated by a liminoidal belief in the role of law to deliver the ideals of justice.

The Roman jurists focused not on the political processes and positive foundations of law, but rather on the normative structures that provided interpretation to the prescriptive aspects of their laws (Schiavone 2012: 33). Although today one might conceive of law as bounded to rarified code structures, thus was not the original intent, at least per the Romans. Roman law, as experienced by the Romans, was "a 'living law of custom,' case-based and guided by experts: much closer to American law … than to French law after the codification under Napoleon, or to Italian law subsequent to the codification of 1865." (Schiavone 2012: 32). The phrase *ius civile*, commonly interpreted as civil law, in fact might have lain closer to civil rites or civic performances; later Roman law was wrought out "of hermeneutic paradigms lying somewhere between legal 'prudence' and religious caution, between the rigidity of the *ius civile* and the ritualistic unremittingness of the sacral prescriptions." (Schiavone 2012: 61). Roman law was not founded on codes and texts but on ritualized customs.

Nomos and *chromos*, rule and time, were seen as part of the inherent dialectic that produced law and culture (Schiavone 2012: 38). Schiavone (2012: 38-39) cites Plato as explaining that norm and rule are the "revealing of being;" that law teleologically enables a culture to provide some sort of stability against the changing facts of time's passage. In this sense, Schiavone is setting up a similar relation to Cover's (1983) paideic and imperial senses of law, that law has both creative and generative aspects and structure imposing aspects.

The words *justice*, *injury*, and *just* all descend from the Latin *ius*, which in later Latin was taken to mean law. The Romans saw *ius* as that which governed the rituals, exchanges and inter-obligations between the *patres*, leaders of the *patriafamilia*; *ius* was not seen by early Romans as related to the decrees of their kings (Schiavone 2012: 55). *Ius* appears in phrasing associated with oath giving, formula making, and consecration; in its origins with the *patres*, law was ritualized behavior (Schiavone 2012: 61).[1]

1 The then-contemporaneous Greeks had developed similar ideas, reflected in the *themis* of a priest-king and the thesmotic rules governing interfamilial relationships (Schiavone 2012: 88).

But the origins of *ius* are more divine than secular, in that *ius* is believed to be derived from **yaus*; cognates exists across both Vedic and Iranian and thus *ius* is belived to be quite ancient in origin (Schiavone 2012: 61). *Ius* was cultic; *ius* in Rome was as in Greece earlier, identified as part of the mythical and ritual-magical substrate of precepts and normative complexes spanning from archaic to classical eras (Schiavone 2012: 56). The Romans likewise saw divine aspects in their *nomos*; the terms *fas* (licit) and *nefas* (illicit) gave rise to the modern terms of festival (religious sense of holiday) and nefarious (Schiavone 2012: 60). "We can say that *ius*, then, was tradition (*mos*) in its most preceptive sense."[2] (Schiavone 2012: 75).

At the center of Roman law was the function of the ritual. "[T]he perception of a temporality marked be repetition … must have played a decisive role," (Schiavone 2012: 75) in the transformation of ancient rites into law. "The *mos* featured as the symbolic transfiguration of this experience, which became rite, rule, and *ius* ("*mos est ius*")." (Schiavone 2012: 75). The legal ritual, as it transformed from divine to secular, became known as the *responsa*, a combination of acts, utterances, and social conventions (Schiavone 2012: 76). "The *responsa* constituted the city's living rules, the crystallized and symbolic projection of its social relations." (Schiavone 2012: 76). Thus at its core, law is ritual.

As Roman law evolved alongside the development of its political processes, especially the development of public assembles and the rise of the *centuriae*, Roman law become secularized, albeit never secular in the modern sense, but the Romans did begin to distinguish civic law as *res humanae* as opposed the sacerdotal rites for *res divinae* (Schiavone 2012: 71-72). Even as late at Ulpian, (i.e. second and third century A.D.), we find reliance on the Roman paideic lesson of the intertwining of law's foundations in both matters secular and divine, but always ritualized; *iudex atque arbiter habetur rerum divinarium humanarumque*, Uplian turned a phrase once referent to priests and applied it to the Roman judges of his era (Schiavone 2012: 68).

Thus, the underlying foundations of western law, and of those countries that have imported civil code legal regimes, lay in ritual and ceremony. Law has always required acts of pre-liminal, liminal, and post-liminal performance. Perhaps the role of the robed priest in the temple has been displaced by the robed judge in the court, and the mysteries of the goddesses Iustitia and Themis dis-

---

Yet by the fifth century B.C., the Greek words of *themis* and *thesmos* had fallen out of favor for the broader *nomos* (Schiavone 2012: 89). *Nomos* contained ideas of documented rules, of secular rules, of democratically derived rules (Schiavone 2012: 89).

2 It is of note that precept itself derives from *prae* (pre) *capere* (take), and thus derives the notion of taking an order from a leader.

placed by the ideals of justice and equity, but the liminoid character of law remains central to the its function.

Law as ritual and ceremony within contemporaneous communities

We are defined by our interactions with law. By our actions within the legal *nomos,* we affect, create and communicate the law. By our acts, we both create and consume law itself; as a tourist engaging with the *other* we consume a sense of law that is otherwise inaccessible at home. The acts are ritualized, in that they both require overt communicative acts to a group and that they enable a liminal threshold to be crossed into alternative states.

The jurisprudence of Robert M. Cover (1985) provides a framework that is readily applicable within sociological settings (Berman 2007: en passim). Cover (1985) wrote that legal positivists had tried too hard to distance the definition of law from cultural materials. He held that "all collective behavior entailing systematic understandings of our commitments to future worlds" could lay equal claim to being 'law' or legal in nature (Berman 2007: 307). Thus, any rituals or ceremonies that attempt to bind people together in meaning or to reinforce obligations with regards to future or post-liminal states could and should be considered acts of law, per Cover's (1985) perspective (Berman 2007: 307).

Cover's (1983: 4) theory of jurisprudence is that no law, no set of legal instructions or prescriptions, can exist apart from the narratives that give that law its meaning and effect. Cover (1983: 4) saw 'law' as a normative universe composed of two interlocked ingredients, the law as composed of legal institutions and legal prescriptions and the law as composed of epics, scriptures, and narratives that locate the law and give it interpretative function and meaning. He called the structural and enforcement aspects imperial law, the generative and emergent aspects paideic law (Cover 1983: 12-13). That interwoven and intertwined sense of paideic narratives and imperial controls he called *nomos;* the *nomos* contains both the mythological and positive aspects of law (Cover 1983: 5). *Nomos* is law but law from a cultural perspective beyond mere statutes and regulations; *nomos* includes the narratives, markers, and social discourse that sustain a legal system's sense of justice and social cohesion.

For tourists, the mythological aspects of law contain the markers of travel destinations; the mythological content of what it will mean for the tourist to consume that law from the host's *nomos.* It is upon this mythological content, of the host's paideia, that the tourist will first turn his gaze in anticipation (Urry 1995: 132). It is in the paideic content of the host's culture that the tourist will find the motivations to travel.

Cover (1983) established three roles for law within society. First, law is a cultural force that validates the propriety of societal transactions and the extent to which violence is permitted or tolerated to effect those transactions (Cover 1983: 9). Second, law is a social field, he called it a 'force field', that binds our societal world together through a normative space, influencing and affecting behavior (Cover 1983: 10). Third, law is a set of normative rules that enable ordinary people the capacity to make socially interactive decisions and take socially interactive actions without crumpling under the eschatology of philosophies applied within a material world (Cover 1983: 9).

There are similar concepts within the sociology of tourism. Social networks are a theoretical basis for why locations are visited and revisited (Larsen et al. 2007: 259). Social networks and their corresponding obligations are motives for tourism (Larsen et al. 2007: 258). Grammars of social order, economic and political relations can be revealed by the examination of social obligations and the resultant acts of mobility (Büscher and Urry 2009: 103). Tourists are producers, producers of social relations. They do not simply consume via tourism, they engage in the active lives of disparate communities (Larsen et al. 2007: 259). The consumption of tourism can lead to the possession and telling of tall tales, of the generation of "narratives that recreate myths for and of the individual," (Trauer 2006: 185) the unfolding of experiences that determine meaning for the individual.

Each society will have its own balance and justifications of societal transactions and violence; travel forces and requires us to encounter these alternative societal fabrics. Each society has a different force field of law, its *nomos* will be unique to its sphere; once the tourist enters that sphere the tourist comes under the tug and pull of that new *nomos* of the host. (The resultant dynamic between *nomos* and tourist may be perceived as either pleasant or unpleasant; no argument is made herein of an *a priori* value for the tourist.) There is no otherness within the effective zone of the *nomos*, as the imperial aspects of power will enforce its application to the tourist as assuredly as it would to one of its own residents. Finally, the role of the *nomos* itself is to enable strangers, aliens within a common community, to gainfully interact and build meaning and social relations. The *nomos* is the calculus to which the tourist will be integrated into the host's network, enabling social interactions within the host's culture and relations. *Sans* the *nomos* and its effects, the tourist would be unable to function as a tourist; even the norms of the roles of host and guest are mediated through Cover's (1983) notion of narratives and *nomos*. The tourist consumes law in touring, and touring is enabled by that consumption.

In a deeper sense, law is a means of interactive communication on the aspirations and limitations of a community; the communal *nomos* emerges from the conflicts of the community's aspirations and limitations. Law results from a matrix of acts, acts of interactive obligations that are constantly redefined by those persons who act within the community's *nomos*, both resident and tourist. By travelling, the tourist takes on a legal adventure into *nomos incognita*; the tourist's interactions with the alien *nomos* transform both the tourist and the host, it mandates interactivity.

The field of legal pluralism has extended Cover's (1983) analysis to recognize that law extends far beyond the codified constructs of the nineteenth century. Law is now recognized to include much more than just the positive laws of codes and legislations. And jurisdiction is much more complicated than the physical zones of control exercised by nation states. As Berman (2007: 302) explained:

> "… international legal scholars (and those studying law and globalization more generally) increasingly recognize that we inhabit a world of multiple normative communities, some of which impose their norms through officially sanctioned coercive force and formal legal process, but many of which do not. These norms have varying degrees of impact, of course, but it has become clear that ignoring such normative assertions altogether as somehow not 'law' is not a useful strategy."

> "Cover argued that law is constantly constructed through the contest among various norm-generating communities. Thus, although "official" norms articulated by sovereign entities obviously count as "law," to Cover such official assertions of prescriptive or adjudicatory jurisdiction are only some of the many ways in which normative commitments arise."

Is there room for a legally pluralistic tourist within Cover's (1983) jurisprudence, a tourist that finds herself submerged under many multiple forms of legal communities, including those that advertise to her to come and enjoin them in their communitas? Yes, as Berman (2007: 313) puts it, there are micro-societies that create their own norms that at times can trump state law. A tourist in her engagement and interaction with another community than her own, can create exactly such a micro-society and thus establish a new ritual of law or she can simply enjoin in the otherwise established jurisdiction of a state other than her own and enjoy her legally pluralistic construct of law. Tourists can engage in legal pluralism, that choice to so act is an act of definition and identity, and ultimately of finding one's place, legally, in-between home and the other.

Indeed, the tourist, *cum* immigrant, *cum* work traveller, *cum* extended family member, carries legal pluralism as he relocates; mobility is what Tamanaha refers to as the "global movement of people." (Tamanaha 2008: 388). The impact of mobility on legal pluralism is seen as one of the five major threads of theoretical work within legal pluralism literature (Tamanaha 2008: 403). Tamanaha

(2008: 403) discussed how immigration waves often create communities in which laws from several homelands are operationally observed, even if in contrast to the local positive laws of the local jurisdiction.

While concerns on the exact definition of law have been raised by legal pluralists, as various modes of norm setting and enforcement range from the clearly public ordinance to the quasi-social norms of clubs; see Tamanaha's concerns on the semi-autonomous social fields of Moore (Tamanaha 2008: 392-393, citing to (Moore 1973: 719)), of Malinowski's concatenation of obligations (Tamanaha 2008: 391, citing to (Malinowski 1926: 14)), of Griffith's normative pluralism for examples of functionally awkward definitions (Tamanaha 2008: 395, citing to (Griffith 2005: 63-64)), such problems are not troubling for the present line of inquiry. This paper explores traditional acts, rituals, and performances of law; albeit it is noted that even richer investigations might await the role tourists play in less formal arrangements of laws and normative systems.

Settings for research within touring consumption

Law can be consumed by engaging in the legal rituals and performances of the host and thus enacting a choice to join the *nomos* of a host.

The legally pluralistic tourist seeks to find that which cannot be found at home; they seek experience different from those from the known frame of reference (Lauring 2011: 219). The tourist seeks to free herself from the routine of everyday life (Lauring 2011: 219). As the peasant was bound to his field and the lord took travel on his horse, the ability of the common person to, if temporarily escape their binds and pursue legal alternatives elsewhere is democratized the notion of sovereignty, *iLegislator*.

The legally pluralistic tourist navigates between legal spheres and spaces. While there are many modalities in which that tourist could seek such legal otherness, the present study presents five modes expected to be prevalent with legal tourists.

Consuming law as an act of tourism

The consumption of goods and services, even while on tour, serve as an elaborate social communication system; the significance of the goods and services' consumed provide value primarily in their ability to communicate cultural values (Snepenger et al. 2007: 311). That tourism is a subjective experience communicated through the consumption of goods and services, comports well with the observation that these cultural events all occur within a narratively structured *nomos*. As such, law and the consumption of law by tourists are a part of that activity of communication-by-consumption.

The sociology of tourism is concerned with "touristic motivations, roles, relationships, and institutions and of their impact on tourists and on the societies who receive them" (Cohen 1984: 373). Similarly, the anticipated experience is constructively built upon preconceptions fostered by images, representations and stories (Lauring 2011: 218). Even though tourism always contains objective elements, it is primarily a subjective experience (Lauring 2011: 218). The tourist's legal encounters are flush with relationships and institutions; those social forces intertwine with the paideic narratives to produce law. In both the primary and secondary consumption of legal acts, the tourist consumes subjective experiences and services.

The tourist experience of a live event, of a political, celebratory, or artistic character, generates strong feelings of co-presence (Urry 2001). The tourist amidst the peoples of the host provides the social dynamic that results in consumption of law; their interactions result in *nomos*-bound legal events. By their joint engagement in legal acts, co-presence is affirmed and provides a foundation for social practices. The law act, via the narratives underlying the *nomos*, may serve as both central elements and as markers for the tourist.

Consuming law as an act of pilgrimage

The tourist can travel to pursue visions of legal acts not accommodated at home, like a pilgrim seeking a 'promised land,' the tourist can hope to fulfill an alternate vision of his or her life by engaging in an alternate developing *nomos*. The tourist can transform the host by engagement in the host's paideic development and the tourist can return home educationally transformed and re-engage in the paideic evolutions at home.

Cover's (1983) *Nomos* includes concepts drawn from George Steiner's (1977: 222) 'alternity', that law functions to bridge our existent reality and the alternities present within our narratives and cultures. By comparing postmodernists Eco's 'hyperreality' and Baudrillard's 'simulacra and simulation', the concept of alternate visions become so infused and fundamental to basic social discourse that they no longer remain questions of truth versus falsehood, but queries as to constructive authenticity (Wang 1999: 356). Law's tension between reality and vision quest provides the cultural justification of its authenticity and its sense of authority (Cover 1983: 9). The tourist has the option to become authentic and embedded in local *nomos,* the tourist can become engaged in 'emergent authenticity.' (Wang 1999: 355).

The legal tourist seeks an alternative to the political and legal realities that they face at home in ordinary life. Yet it is not clear that the host itself generates this product, the tourist has likely formulated the tourist experience prior to the trip at home, mediated by exposures to ideas interpreted from his home frame of reference (Lauring 2011: 220).

If tourism is a modern variety of the traditional pilgrimage, then the crusade for legal commodities forbidden at home can illustrate the need for touristic consumption of legal acts. *E.g*., perhaps a homosexual finds his or her love life legally barred at home, then the pilgrimage to a host that legally permits homosexual behaviour may seem as necessary and as transformative as any search for saints or relics. But there are other aspects of persons in pilgrimatic search of legal acts. Individuals might identify certain host areas as better manifestations of their personal legal ideals that their home might not offer to them. An American might take consumptive comfort in the restrictive gun laws of a tourist destination, to walk freely without fear of gunplay. A person from a politically tense country may enjoy the legal freedoms of Hyde Park and might engage in a legal act of free speech. These parties may not seek permanent refuge from their homes, they may have many ties and affiliations too thick to cut, but that moment of pilgrimage in the land of desired legal act, might drive their tourism to the host.

Consuming law to find the self

One of the primary motives for touring in general is the pursuit of the development of self and of one's self-concept (Todd 2001: 184). By encountering and consuming the law of the host, the tourist can be transformed and the act of self-discovery enabled.

Todd quotes from William James' original definition of "Self", which stated

> "... a man's Self is the sum total of all that he can call his, not only his body and psychic powers, but his clothes and his house, his wife and his children, his ancestors and friends, his reputation and his works, his lands and horses and yacht and his bank account" (James 1890: 291 in Todd 2001: 185).

Even in this early definition, a man's Self was characterized by all of his claims, which would include obligations to him established under the performance of legal acts. Perhaps it is this very matrix of obligations that best describes the Self and its sum total.

The possession of his clothes, horses and yacht would all be governed under movable property laws, his house under immovable property. The law of inheritances would govern the manner that he held those goods, received them from ancestors, and transferred them to friends and descendants. The manner in which his marriage was bonified and recognized, and the manner in which his children were recognized or legitimized, would be bound by family law considerations. A cluster of laws, not limited to banking laws, securities laws, commercial paper laws, and laws of fiduciary duties would govern his interactions with the bank. All of these laws would and could vary substantially depending on the nation within which the said man was to find his Self. France would strongly limit his manner of asset conveyance in inheritance, whereas America would not. Some countries might recognize his marriage after an initial divorce; others might not. Some nations would provide him simple unfettered fee in his lands, other countries might limit his leasehold to 99 or 999 years.

The notions are simple and commonly held, but the exercise and authenticity of the experiences of self would vary tremendously country to country; it is long established in both fact and fiction that people journey far to obtain favorable results. Legal acts, and the interwoven obligations therefrom, have thus always fit within the notion of self and self-concept.

When the concept is extended to 'possible selves,' the notions of exploration and testing become essential to discovering one's true self-concept (Todd 2001: 186). The concept of possible selves enables one to experience through tourism alternate modes of one's self, as if trying on different clothes at a boutique. The alternate modes might include approach and avoidance selves, positive and negative selves, aspiration and avoidance selves (Todd 2001: 186).

As we are defined within a paideic and imperial matrix of law and meaning, the opportunity to explore alternative legal frames of reference through the tourist consumption of law acts enable one to invest and re-vest one's self into different sets of meanings and obligations. Tourists collect as a means of making the intangible tangible and transportable back to their home (Todd 2001: 188). The markers thus collected are "inextricably linked with one's self-concept and the role of being a tourist." (Todd 2001: 188). The collection of legal acts, and their incumbent networks of obligations, is no different from the tourist's collection of authentic experiences and their tangible markers. The very law acts consumed are means to making real the intangible, to manifest legal notions of self-concept as real world actions.

Consuming law within mobility and interconnections

The legally pluralistic tourist is on the go; beyond traditional tourism the tourist is visiting family, business connections and other members of their dispersed community. Many segments of the modern world are highly mobile; they commute not only home to job, but also travel around the world to meet friends and families scattered by the forces of modern economies (Larsen et al. 2007: 245). The production and reproduction of social relationships both near and afar, is an important aspect of tourism in the twenty-first century (Larsen et al. 2007: 245). In as much as the key focus of law is the production of social relationships, and the commitment to the resultant obligations, the overlap of tourists consuming law is only magnified by this tourist development. To the extent that social life needs to be maintained at a distance, often law is involved; either directly as an intra-personal obligation, e.g. a contract, or as a subsidiary act of the overt social activities, e.g. the lease on a beach house in Spain.

The actions of the global friend or family member will require engagement at a more substantial level than a "fun and sun" tourist; they won't be limited to schedules of sightseeing and 'facing' events (Larsen et al. 2007: 246). They will be more likely to engage in embodiment and performance (Larsen et al. 2007: 245). Acts of law fit into this concept. Law requires performance, the act of consent, the juristic act itself, the act of performance to complete and conclude the legal act. It is barely possible to engage in law, touristically, in a 'facing' or 'sightseer' sense of tourism; the act of law requires a fuller sense of intercourse with its participants.

The sociology of tourism, as experienced as a means or mode of consumption, needs to focus analysis on the obligations, social networks, and social capital required to sustain these networks of meaning and self-identity (Larsen et al. 2007: 259). That tourists engage in networks, that those networks can operate at temporal and physical removes, assumes functioning legal systems to provide for the interlocking obligations and securities that such networks need to operate. Tourists consume law in sustaining their networks.

Business travelers often visit far away destinations only to meet with friends and coworkers previously co-located. They often do not travel alone but with bundled groups, perhaps coworkers (Larsen et al. 2007: 250). Business travelers can also be seen as visiting friends, albeit mediated through a workplace environment. The touristic assumptions of business travelers can also be seen from a perspective of "producing thick embodied socialities of corporeal proximity where people are accessible, available, and subject to each other." (Larsen et al. 2007: 247).

Business travelers are strong consumers of local laws and legal alternatives. Corporate boards of directors have routinely established touristic board meetings in foreign locales in order to replace the legal reporting requirements or tax requirements of their homes with the laws of their host; indeed, the Caribbean today is awash in corporations if in few true genuine corporate employees or functions. Financial or commercial activities might be illegal in certain jurisdictions but nationally encouraged in others. A traveler can relocate to find a legal means of self-determining the moment of his or her death.

Certain legal acts can be performed at a distance, but it is still customary wisdom that nothing replaces a face-to-face encounter in business; corporeality matters, tourism is required to enable the "perform[ance] of rituals, and sustained quality time." (Larsen et al. 2007: 248). For the mobile,

> "[T]ourism enters the lives of business people and global professionals, second home owners and their friends and families, exchange students and gap-year workers abroad, migrants and (former) refugees ..." (Larsen et al. 2007: 249).

Again, many of the categories described therein are legally shaped. A homeowner in a host nation finds herself facing the property laws of the host, not of their home. Migrants and refugees are both categories of citizenship and loss thereof; they are ultimately categories of the host's *nomos*. Business people and global professionals rely on a vast matrix and nexus of hosts' laws, as they move from place to place. A tourist consumes law and acts of law on the go, even more so for the newly highly mobile denizens of the tourisphere.

The typical mobile denizen is so engaged in tourism and travel, that one can speak of tourism "as a search for home." (Larsen et al. 2007: 249). If so, then the denizens of the tourisphere may well participate in their own paideia and *nomos*. They carry aspects of their home's *nomos* and of their destinations' *nomos*; the opportunity to affect change in both locations is present.

Finding citizenship in multiple nomos

The heart of legal pluralism is that each person belongs to multiple legal spheres, complete with their own *nomos* and rituals. The concept of citizenship is more functional than definitional; citizenship is that *iota* of legal belonging that engages the imperial aspects of Cover's (1983) jurisprudence. Citizenship is enabled, jurisprudentially, through imperial systems of jurisdiction; once tourists enjoin in legal acts, they become engaged in rights and obligations, legal and political practices, and are bound by the contextual *nomos* of the host. It is in crossing that threshold that the tourist, if temporally, becomes a local citizen and obtains a sense of belonging. As a face-painted jersey-wearing Arsenal F.C. fan might *belong* once arriving at the venue of the big game, the legal tourist *arrives* at citizenship by engaging in the host's *nomos*.

Normally, most of us are born into our paideic communities and we pass through their liminal stages as youth; yet, many remain unfulfilled by those original settings. Tourism offers a second chance of exploration to learn of new communities. The notion of citizenship, as explored in many sociological studies of tourism, is quintessentially of legal character; does one belong to this society and its norms, or to that society? Destinations can market access to inclusion and acceptance to potential tourists (Coon 2012: 531). Citizenship can be viewed as another tourist activity alongside lounging on sunny beaches and touring historic locales (Coon 2012: 531).[3]

Because of its spatial and temporal components, tourism enables a different kind of access to citizenship (Coon 2012: 514). People are drawn to destinations to seek citizenships that they cannot obtain at home; those marginalized at home will seek belonging elsewhere on vacation (Coon 2012: 515). Legal engagement as a tourist is one of the most immediate means of asserting membership as a tourist. The opportunity to define one's self in a community wherein one has not been previously characterized and defined by neighbors and society is a key aspect of the motivations to develop self-concept through tourism (Todd 2001: 189).

Postmodernism enables the modern tourist to have a fragmented, if continuous sense of citizenship across locales; a tourist might need additional locations to satisfy other aspects of their full personality. The interpretive approach, under a post-modern framework, held that reality is socially constructed, multiple, holistic, and contextual (Cova et al. 2013: 215). The reality of belonging to a community is likewise socially constructed, multiple, holistic, and contextual and as such extends beyond a received patrimony or a received family context.

There is value in belonging to a group, social value as an aspect of tourism is well identified (Williams and Soutar 2009: 417). Citizenship includes belonging and participating in a group or community, the bearing of certain rights and obligations, legal and political practices, and also cultural practices and representations (Coon 2012: 514). Myths, social matrices and social obligations are central to Cover's (1983) jurisprudence. Myths place the individual within his or her own normative universe, and thus their sense of belonging to a tribe (Cover 1987: 65). The idea of citizenship can be self-constructed within one's own context of

3 Coon (2012: 528-529) reveals how potential 'citizenship and the lack of enforcement of laws against homosexual lifestyles have been used to promote tourism to gay and lesbian tourists.

meaning, within multiple *nomos-frabicant* communities. This is no less relevant for the tourist.

But being welcomed into a marketplace, such as a touristic zone of consumption, does not necessarily grant full rights of citizenship; albeit such may be initial requirements of obtaining full citizenship (Coon 2012: 514). That people seek citizenship, or the partial version by consuming another's political discourse and laws, reveals a great deal about the state of affairs for those people at home; to paraphrase, the fact of the consumption of alternate citizenships or legal cultures can be used to interrogate the 'normal' back home (Coon 2012: 515).[4] But the market is seen as responsive to dissonance and capable of being a mechanism to enable the incorporation of protest into successful products and services (Cova et al. 2013: 216). Thus, while a tourist may engage in legal tourism abroad, such tourism may ultimately enable change at home.

Modern liberal democracies provide each citizen with the potential to engage in the political process, to elect representatives and to make their voices heard on substantive legal and political matters. Tourism enables the citizen tourist to visit and view the legal results of other lands, to learn within a participatory gaze. A tourist is enabled to consume law acts or behaviors that would not pass reasonable judgment in 'everyday' life (McIntyre 2007: 126). After a successful experience has been consumed, tourists are likely to engage in additional risky acts of consumption (Williams and Soutar 2009: 429). The tourist is capable of developing a cosmopolitan legal savvy by her experiences from travelling.

Yet, the results of democracies are central frameworks to which each citizen needs to abide; there is but one system of law for each country. Democracies can handle differences of opinions and multiple political parties, but what they cannot do is to render multiple-choice politico-legal systems wherein all opinions are able to be served as they would prefer to be served. Democracies eventually decide on a singular politico-legal path. One citizen may obtain what he wants with one law, a different citizen obtains what she wants in a different law; ergo, it is likely that each citizen will be both satisfied and dissatisfied with the results. This provides the source of the lacking law that the tourist seeks to consume on vacation. Democracy, at least within the home jurisdiction, works to avoid legal plurality. A tourist can ensure access to legal pluralism by travelling outside her home to a host, seeking that other not available at home.

The engagement of tourists to seek legal events elsewhere are likely to create events back home that transform the home to offering the tourist what was once sought on travel. Yet, that transformation of the home will likely be pro-

4 Similarly, tourism, and the acts of consumption engaged in by the tourists while on vacation, can be employed by theorists to identify what the tourists want to escape from back home (Coon 2012: 531).

cessed though official institutions and applied in common across the community at large. This in turn will leave yet another citizen tourist in need of something other than the newly rendered *nomos*. Legal tourism enables the tourist to escape and enable change, but it cannot render a Shangri-La of perfect *nomos*, because each tourist has a unique combination of needs to fulfill.

Conclusion

Law is an act that can be consumed. It is a social, obligational, interactive, participatory act that has consequences for both tourist and host. Ultimately, the argument has been made that tourists seeking such adventure or survival learning experiences might not so much 'consume' touristic experiences as 'bathe' in them (McIntyre 2007: 128). The transformations thus gained as seen as not limited to the tourist but are shared with both the host's consumerist environment and other consumerist environments that the tourist comes in counter with in future periods, including the tourist's home (McIntyre 2007: 128). Law and the consumption of legal acts, performances, and legal choice making enable the tourists to bathe in the *nomos* of the host; the tourist gains the ability to choose the *nomos* and narratives that they wish to live within, if but temporarily.

Law is a collection of acts that can readily be engaged in by any tourist at any time, placing herself within the legal *nomos* of the host; the authenticity of which is limited only by additional acts of law again within the constructive discourse of the tourist and host. With acts of law, the 'gaze' is mutualized; the chance to join or merge in communal *nomos*-matic paideia offers both sides authenticity of meaning and obligation.

In review, law exists both in abstract and in performance. Law is a ritual, a magic rite that can be visited and engaged in by tourists. Visit a courtroom, see the stage set before the audience with the judges enrobed with visages reflecting a social distance. Magic papers are read, ancient languages spoken, the pomp of high mass is present. It is not unlike a visit with a shaman or to a performance of theatre.

But law does not remain in the courtroom. Law extends beyond the institutions of the sovereign. It has actors scattered throughout the town and village. Law offers, in most countries, the notion of private law. Private law is that law which we self-create and which we self-engage in as act between us and others. Private law is that which build a social relationship upon a legal act. Contracts are an instance of private law. In some states, marriage is an act of private law. Partnerships and corporations are often acts of private law. Torts are private law; the tourist's 'trip and fall' is a private legal act between the tourist and tortfeasor.

The private law does not stand alone. It remains both guided by host law and litigated within the functional legal systems of the host.

Some legal acts may not be fully volitional; a tourist might recognize the trans-liminal moment, but fail to anticipate all of the eventualities of that passage. The accidental tort may result in the tourist's engagement with the legal acts of the host; specifically the tourist's tortious act is a legal act within the host's systems of law. While not the ordinary perspective of touristic activities, tourists do seek out hosts and then proceed to act in violation of the host's law; in many cases the illegal act is a volitional act of consumption. Should one choose to engage in negative law, to break a local law, then the tourist may experience the negative legal act and the resulting imprisonment or punishment.

The tourist has the opportunity to visit the ritual and rites of law, to participate in civil acts of law, to engage in private acts of law. The tourist can seek various levels of engagement with the host and its laws. This pursuit may or may not be in full compliance of the laws of the tourist's home laws. Finally, the tourist has a unique level of control to seek different levels of authenticity in the experience of legal acts; to interactively evolve and participate in the paideic development of the host's *nomos* and perhaps reflectively on the tourist's own domestic *nomos*.

What runs through all of these events is a contrast between the routine definition of self and of local legal norms and the search to be and act beyond that self-imposed definition. The modern paradigms of law are generally grounded upon democracy and direct or indirect legislation by the citizens. The legal character of each country is generally said to reflect the national character and history through the joint assent of its people through democratic institutions of legislation. Yet, the very consumption of these legal alternatives implies that something is not quite fit, not quite *just*; that the general theory of democratic jurisprudence leaves the citizen wanting something more, something else. Even when the tourist engages in creative paideia after returning home, bringing transformations from abroad, the result is ultimately the same. The *nomos* evolves due to tourism, but it remains a collective matrix applied to each and all in similar manner. This was the original problem to be solved by tourism, the desire for a solution unique to the tourist's needs.

The citizens want their democracy; yet, they want a little something on the side, too. They want a tourism of legal destinations, a journey to consume legal alternatives to the socially constructed house of norms that they have built for themselves at home. Are these touristic acts then acts of rebellion or acts of duality, a search for a mixed strategy of law and identity? And finally, is the stability of law something that should be allowed to be escaped, once in a while, to provide more stability in the long run?

The need for such alternative legal consumables suggests a crack in the democratic means of legislation; that we all need something more than a democratic process can provide. We need legal diversity, we need both home and other. The consumption of legal diversity also implies in itself an act of rebellion, of resistance, to the norms of our domestic societies. The touristic consumption of law enables both a pressure relief for stable democratic societies but also a means of testing new legal alternatives not available at home. That could be both minor alternatives, e.g., different limits of toleration, or major, such as fundamental shifts in legal status, e.g., broad and full human rights for certain genders, races, or social strata. It could be as consequential as enabling tourists to experience societies committed to democracy and human rights.

References

Berman, P.S. (2007): A Pluralist Approach to International Law. In: Yale Journal of International Law, 301-329.

Black, H.C. (1990): Black's Law Dictionary. Saint Paul, Minnesota: West Publishing Co.

Büscher, M. and Urry, J. (2009): Mobile Methods and the Empirical. In: European Journal of Social Theory, 12(1), 99-116.

Cohen, E. (1984): The Sociology of Tourism: Approaches, Issues, and Findings. In: Annual Review of Sociology, 10, 373-392.

Coon, D.R. (2012): Sun, Sand, and Citizenship: The Marketing of Gay Tourism. In: Journal of Homosexuality, 59(4), 511-534.

Cova, B. and Maclaran, P. and Bradshaw, A. (2013): Rethinking Consumer Theory from the Postmodern to the Communist Horizon. In: Marketing Theory, 13(2), 213-225.

Cover, R.M. (1983): The Supreme Court, 1982 Term – Foreword: *Nomos* and Narrative. In: Harvard Law Review, 4-68.

Cover, R.M. (1985): The Folktales of Justice: Tales of Jurisdiction. In: Capital University Law Review, 179-203.

Cover, R.M. (1987): Obligation: A Jewish Jurisprudence of the Social Order. In: Journal of Law and Religion, 5(1), 65-74.

Deflem, M. (1991): Ritual, Anti-Structure, and Religion: A Discussion of Victor Turner's Processual Symbolic Analysis. In: Journal for the Scientific Study of Religion 30(1), 1-25.

Griffiths, J. (2006) The idea of sociology of law and its relation to law and to sociology. In: Law and Sociology. Oxford: Oxford University Press, 49–68.

James, W., (1890): The Principles of Psychology. New York: Henry Holt & Co.

Larsen, J. and Urry, J. and Axhausen, K.W. (2007): Networks and Tourism: Mobile Social Life. In: Annals of Tourism Research, 34(1), 244-262.

Lauring, J. (2011): Creating the Tourist Product in the Opposition Between Self-Actualization and Collective Consumption: The Case of Charter Tourism. In: Journal of Hospitality & Tourism Research. 37(2), 217-236.

Malinowski, B. (1926). Crime and custom in savage society. New York. Harcourt, Brace & Co.
McIntyre, C. (2007): Survival Theory: Tourist Consumption as a Beneficial Experiential Process in a Limited Risk Setting. In: International Journal of Tourism Research, 115-130.
Moore, S. F. (1973) Law and Social Change: The Semi-Autonomous Social Field as an Appropriate Subject of Study, Law & Society Review, 7(4), 719-746.
Richards, G. (2002): Tourism Attraction Systems: Exploring Cultural Behavior. In: Annals of Tourism Research, 29(4), 1048-1064.
Schiavone, A. (2012): The Invention of Law in the West. (Carden, J. and Shugaar, A., transl.) Cambridge, Massachusetts: The Belknap Press of Harvard University Press.
Snepenger, D., Snepenger, M., Dalbey, M. and Wessol, A. (2007): Meanings and Consumption Characteristics of Places at a Tourism Destination. In: Journal of Travel Research, 45(3), 310-321.
Steiner, George. After Babel. University Press, 1977.
Tamanaha, B. Z., (2008): Understanding Legal Pluralism: Past to Present, Local to Global. Sydney Law Review, 30, 375-411.
Todd, S. (2001): Self-concept: A Tourism Application. In: Journal of Consumer Behavior, 1(2), 184-196.
Trauer, B. (2006): Conceptualizing Special Interest Tourism: Frameworks for Analysis. In: Tourism Management, (27(2), 183-200.
Turner, V.W. (1957): Schism and Continuity in an African Society: A Study of Ndembu Village Life. Manchester: Manchester University Press.
Turner, V.W. (1967): The Forest of Symbols: Aspects of Ndembu Ritual Ithaca: Cornell University Press.
Turner, V.W. (1969): The Ritual Process: Structure and Anti-structure. Chicago: Aldine.
Turner, V.W. (1974): Dramas, Fields and Metaphors: Symbolic Action in Human Society. Ithaca: Cornell University Press.
Turner, V.W. (1977): Symbols in African Ritual. In: Symbolic Anthropology: A Reader in the Study of Symbols and Meanings, Edited by Dolgin J. L., Kemnitzer, D. S., and Schneider, D.M., New York: Columbia University Press, 183-194.
Turner, V.W. and Turner, E.L.B. (1982): Religious Celebrations. In: Turner, V.W. (ed.): Celebration: Studies in Festivity and Ritual. Washington, D.C.: Smithsonian Institution Press, 201-219.
Urry, J. (1995): The Consumption of Tourism. In: Consuming Places. New York, Routledge,. 129-141.
Urry, J. (2001): Globalising the Tourist Gaze: Cityscapes Conferences, Graz, Austria. As posted by the Department of Sociology, Lancaster University.
Van Gennep, A. (1961): The Rites of Passage. Chicago: University of Chicago Press.
Wang, N. (1999): Rethinking Authenticity in Tourism Experience. In: Annals of Tourism Research, 26(2), 349-370.
Williams, P. and Soutar, G.N. (2009): Value, Satisfaction, and Behavioral Intentions in an Adventure Tourism Context. In: Annals of Tourism Research, 36(3), 413-438.

The Hidden Dimensions of Cultural Consumption within the Framework of Tourism Mobility

Tamara Rátz / Viktória Kundi / Gábor Michalkó

The paper aims to explore the consumption of cultural events realised within the framework of invisible tourism mobility in Hungary, based on the assumption that a significant proportion of the Hungarian population's tourism-related cultural event consumption remains hidden as a consequence of inadequate data collection, despite the economic and social contribution of culturally motivated trips to the individuals' quality of life and the destinations' and attractions' demand and revenue characteristics.

The study presented in the paper was carried out within the framework of a 4-year-long research project, supported by the Hungarian National Research Fund, entitled "Invisible tourism in Hungary: investigation of the social, economic and environmental aspects of unconventional tourism mobility" (OTKA K100953).

Introduction

By the 21st century, tourism has become a major component of both leisure consumption and the sphere of work. The tourism industry, aiming to satisfy all the needs of the travelling population, is present in the economy of almost every nation and, in many countries, is among the main contributors to the GDP of these destinations. In 2012, UNWTO registered 1.035 billion international tourist arrivals, while revenues created by international tourism reached USD 1.3 billion (UNWTO 2013).

The dynamic evolution of the tourism phenomenon during the past decades has led to the appearance of various forms of tourism mobility beyond its conventional concept (i.e. temporary travel of not more than one consecutive year to a destination outside one's normal place of residence) (WTO 1989). At the same time, there is relatively little information available about the volume, composition, directions and duration of unconventional tourism activities and the complex relationship of their social, economic and physical impacts.

The hidden dimensions of cultural consumption in tourism

Cultural consumption may be considered a key activity in everyday life as well as in tourism (McCracken 1990; Mackay 1997): its individual characteristics help to form one's personal identity and lifestyle, may symbolise achievement and success, and may maintain social distinction (Storey 1999). Cultural consumption patterns are often shaped by gender (e.g. Bihagen and Katz-Gerro 2000), social status (e.g. Chan and Goldthorpe 2006), education, work or urban status (Richards and Queirós 2005). Although the cultural consumption of tourists is often very similar to their cultural consumption at home, i.e. it may be considered an extension of their everyday life (Thrane 2000), being a tourist is a different experience compared with one's daily routine (Harrison 2003), resulting in heightened interest in the visited destination's cultural events and attractions (Richards 1996). Focusing on specific cultural themes in the process of destination branding may also have a major impact on individuals' culture-motivated mobility, bringing about social and economic changes both at the individual and the community level. For example, those destinations that actively publicise and promote their UNESCO World Heritage Sites attract more tourists who are interested in cultural heritage in the first place, but all other tourists also experience a certain kind of socio-cultural pressure to pay a visit to some of these sites, due to their carefully created "must see" status (Poria, Reichel and Cohen 2011).

Tourism, by its very nature, relies on the consumption of the resources of the natural and the cultural environment (Mustonen 2006). Not surprisingly, in the postmodern era, tourism has become one of the fastest growing industries in the world, due to an increasing interest in postmaterial consumption (Inglehart 1997), i.e. the consumption of experiences and services that improve one's personal quality of life (Scarbrough 1995). The increasing centrality of culture is also reflected in the rapid growth of the number of cultural attractions (such as museums, visitor centres, protected monuments) and cultural events (e.g. festivals, exhibitions, concerts, theatre plays or re-enactment of historic events) which are increasingly being used as the core components of urban and rural destination development strategies as well as image creation and diversification programmes (Richards 2001). In the field of tourism, cultural consumption predominantly refers to visiting managed cultural attractions and attending cultural events, i.e. activities that generate revenue, although the broadest interpretation of culture also includes experiencing the daily life of the destination (Richards and Bonink 1995). The role of culture as a consumption component varies by destination and by visitor segment, leading to an interesting contradiction in certain cases: although culture as a destination asset and a key component of its milieu may have a decisive impact on the motivation of tourists to visit the place, their cultural consumption (i.e. spending on entrance fees to cultural attractions or tickets to cultural events) may only account for a small proportion of their total expenditure (including accommodation, food, local transportation and shopping) (Kundi 2013; Eusébio, Carneiro and Kastenholz 2013).

In contemporary consumer societies, a person's identity is expressed by their lifestyle (Miles 2000), and lifestyle is manifested through consumption (Räsänen 2003). Participation in cultural tourism offers two intertwined ways of distinguishing oneself through lifestyle choices: by becoming a tourist, which is associated with decisions to choose certain destinations, transport modes and services, and by consuming culture, e.g. attending certain cultural events or visiting particular cultural attractions. Of course, not every act of cultural consumption is necessarily part of tourism mobility: even in the postmodern world, there are people who are not interested or not able to travel, and choose to find the meanings that they are searching for in other forms of consumption (Mustonen 2006).

Cultural tourism is a significantly complex practice (Sharpley 2002), representing a wide range of motivations, most of which tend to focus on the basic human need for experiences (Michalkó and Rátz 2005) and novelty (Urry 2002). According to Richards (1996: 24), cultural tourism is *"all movements of persons to specific cultural attractions, such as museums, heritage sites, artistic performances and festivals outside their normal place of residence."* Although this definition is rather technical and emphasises a European, built heritage- and art-based approach to the cultural tourism product, it is suitable for the current research project, since it is in harmony with the current concept of cultural tourism in Hungary (MTH 2005). However, since modern tourism has become an established part of everyday life, consumption and culture, it is rather challenging to differentiate it from other leisure activities (McCabe 2002), and often the participants themselves do not consider their activities, such as going to the theatre in the nearest town or enjoying an open-air concert in the neighbouring village, as 'tourism'. Furthermore, this misconception is often shared by tourist destination planners and local decision-makers who tend to overlook the market opportunities in their environs.

In most developed destinations, visitors can benefit from the complexity of postmodern culture and have the opportunity to choose from simultaneously offered high and low, traditional and modern, mass and elite cultural activities (Smith 2003). Although visitors' choices are influenced by their socio-demographic characteristics, education and social background, among others, they are also affected by individual interests and one's sense of personal or group identity. The gap between the different forms of culture has become increasingly blurred: for most customer segments, the mutual exclusivity of elite and mass cultural activities has been replaced by the fusion of contemporary and traditional forms (Richards 2007).

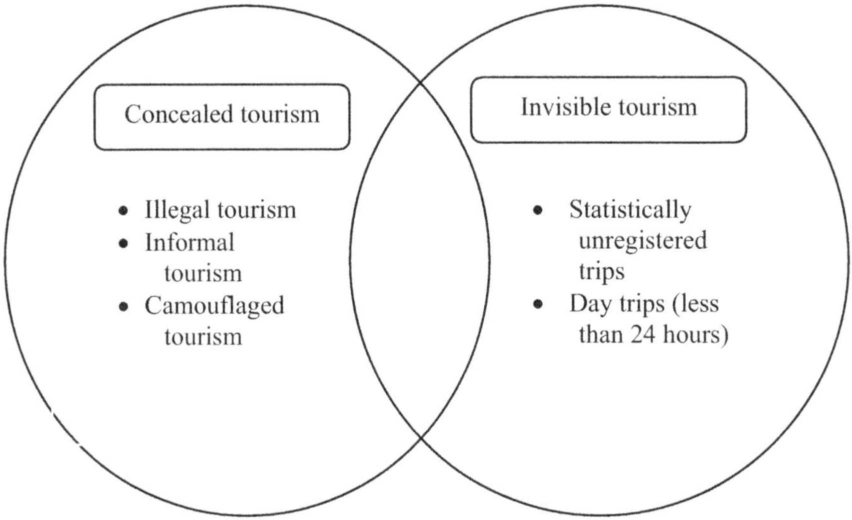

Figure 1: The concept of hidden tourism. (Michalkó and Rátz 2013)

Modern cultural tourists are generally seen as authenticity-seekers: as opposed to enjoying staged experiences in artificially created environments, they are motivated to gain experiences through building personal relationships and creating cultural encounters with locals (Kundi 2013). However, a parallel trend can also be observed, especially in urban cultural tourism and in visitor attraction development, where various material and immaterial resources of culture become tourist products in highly artificial cultural settings, providing cultural consumption experiences to well-informed visitors (Halewood and Hannam 2001; Buchmann et al. 2010).

In Hungary, a significant number of culturally motivated domestic trips take place within the framework of invisible tourism (Figure 1) which includes all forms of travel that belong to the liminal zone of conventional tourism activities (Irimiás and Michalkó 2013). This can mainly be attributed to the fact that although there is a limited amount of statistical information available on culture-motivated domestic tourist mobility (e.g. Rátz 2006), data collection is occasional and random, and the existing data are unsuitable both for comparative analysis of cultural events' and destinations' visitation patterns and for planning purposes at the local and the national levels. Decision-makers often ignore the demand characteristics of day-trippers and VFR tourists, since they do not use registered accommodation services or tour operators and, consequently, are missing from official tourist statistics.

In our understanding, the concept of *'hidden tourism mobility'* contains two forms: *'concealed tourism'* and *'invisible tourism'*, both of which might be subdivided into further categories. Within the first group, we may differentiate between *'illegal tourism'* that includes e.g. tour operation, tour guiding or accommodation services provided without the required permits and authorisations; *'informal tourism'* that includes legal tourism services offered in the grey zone (e.g. without registering every guest to partially avoid taxation or without issuing formal invoices following each commercial transaction); and *'camouflaged tourism'* such as travel with illegal or immoral motivations (e.g. sex, abortion, euthanasia or smuggling) disguised as a holiday or business trip.

In the second group, we find all kinds of tourism activities that take place outside the statistical registration system; although the composition of this form of tourism depends on each country's data collection methods, trips shorter than 24 hours and VFR tourism generally belong here. This sort of tourism mobility often eludes the attention of tourism marketers and planners, especially in the domestic market: partly as a consequence of the increasingly blurred boundaries between everyday leisure and tourism which makes the distinction of these concepts seem purely theoretical, and partly due to the lack of systematic market research.

Although there might be an overlap between the two forms, in the case of *'concealed tourism'* forms, it is in the interest of all participants to keep the real nature of their activities or transactions hidden, while in the case of *'invisible tourism'*, only the characteristics of the consumption process move these activities beyond the conventional system of the statistically measured tourism phenomenon. The overlapping area thus shows a great variety of trips, including such examples as day-trippers or VFR visitors using unlicensed guides or cross-border smuggling taking place at unpatrolled border crossings.

The spatial impacts of hidden tourism may be significant, due partly to travellers' spending on commercial articles and services and, in the framework of Visiting Friends and Relatives (VFR) tourism, partly to the additional spending of local hosts (on items such as festival tickets, restaurants, visitor attraction admission tickets, etc.).

Research methods

The study aimed to explore the consumption of cultural events realised within the framework of invisible tourism mobility in Hungary, based on the assumption that a significant proportion of the Hungarian population's tourism-related cultural consumption remains hidden as a consequence of inadequate data collection, despite the economic and social contribution of culturally motivated trips to the individuals' quality of life and the destinations' and attractions' demand and revenue characteristics (Michalkó and Rátz 2005). The research focused on respondents' attendance at cultural events, since previous studies suggested that domestic cultural tourism demand in Hungary was predominantly generated by events (e.g. festivals, concerts, theatre performances etc.) (Sulyok 2010; Sulyok and Polgár 2010). In order to investigate the hidden aspects of Hungarians' cultural event consumption associated with leisure travel activities, a questionnaire survey was carried out in Hungary between October and December 2012, with a sample size of 500 persons. The survey content and structure were developed by the authors based on the literature of cultural consumption and cultural tourism, and the questionnaire was tested in April 2012 among persons who had participated in cultural tourist activities during the previous year. The data were collected by BA in Tourism and Hospitality students of the Kodolányi János University of Applied Sciences, who had been trained previously and had received detailed survey manual. Multistage sampling was used to select the survey participants: at the first stage, in order to be included in the sample, respondents were required to be at least 18 years old and have a higher than average cultural consumption level (based on indicators defined in the 2003 survey of the Sociological Research Institute of the Hungarian Academy of Sciences (Dudás and Hunyadi 2005)). At the second stage, quotas for age and gender distribution were established for each surveyor, who could use convenience sampling methods to fill their personal quotas. The completed sample consisted of 50-50% male and female respondents, with 50% being 39 years old or younger. To enable the authors to verify the reliability of data collection process, the contact information (telephone number) of the respondents was registered separately (in order to ensure the anonymity of responses). A randomly selected 10% of the survey participants were contacted after the completion of the survey to confirm their personal contribution.

The analysis of the respondents' place of permanent residence indicated an over-representation of the Hungarian capital city, Budapest, in the sample: 34.8% lived there (in reality the city represents about 20% of the country's population). Concerning their family status, 47.2% of the respondents were married or living with a partner, and 52.8% were single, divorced or widowed.

48.8% had at least one child. With regard to their level of education, the survey participants proved to be more educated than the Hungarian population in general, explained by the sampling method that required a higher than average level of cultural consumption: 36.2% had BA or MA degree and 49.2% finished at least secondary school (in the total Hungarian population, only app. 20% completed higher education – Harsányi and Vincze 2012). The majority of the respondents considered their own financial status average (58.7%), slightly better than average (22.5%) or slightly little worse than average (15.6%), and less than 2-2% perceived it as much better or much worse than average. Among the other demographic variables, only education level had an influence on the survey participants' economic situation (those who completed higher education were more likely to perceive their own financial situation as better than average).

The collected data were analysed by SPSS 17.0 software, inconsistencies discovered during data cleaning led to the removal of 0.8% of all the questionnaires. The following chapter thus presents the findings based on the analysis of 496 responses.

Research results

Due to the sampling technique, the majority of the survey participants considered culture as a significant, primary travel motivation (i.e. the most important factor that influences the selection of a destination or the timing of a trip). Cultural event consumption also played a quite important role as a leisure activity (39.1% claimed that cultural events were among their most important leisure programmes, while only 1.7% declared a low level of importance of cultural activities in their leisure time). The significance of cultural consumption, especially as a tourist experience, is also demonstrated, to a certain extent, by the fact that 47.7% of the respondents did not perceive any change in the frequency of their attendance at cultural events since 2008 and 25.9% experienced an increase, despite the negative impacts of the global financial crisis. The correlation analysis suggests a weak link between the significance of culture as a leisure and tourist motivation and the actual change in cultural tourism consumption (Pearson's R=0.290, approx. sig.=0.000): although the consequences of the financial crisis were most probably experienced by all the survey participants (the majority of whom have average financial income), those with strong cultural motivation were more likely to make an effort to maintain their cultural consumption level at the price of making economic sacrifices in other areas of their life. An alternative way of coping with the crisis, as reflected by the data of the Hungarian Central Statistical Office as well (KSH 2013ab), was to replace longer holidays with shorter visits, often day trips, to cultural attractions or events, a change in consumer behaviour that could move the participants away from the official, registered tourism phenomenon towards the informal or the invisible spheres of tourism.

Since 2008, 90.1% of the respondents attended some kind of cultural event outside their place of residents. Those who are more active consumers of culture at home in their leisure time were also most willing to travel for cultural programmes, predominantly in the framework of domestic tourism (Kendall's tau-b=0.590, approx. sig.=0.000).

Type of event	Attended at least once a year since 2008 outside their permanent place of residence (%*)	Primary motivation for travel (%**)
Theatre play	54.2	73.6
Pop (rock, jazz, etc.) concert	50.7	73.2
Movie, cinema	45.3	66.1
Gastronomy festival	43.8	69.5
Cultural festival	42.6	69.9
Celebration of national holiday	30.8	56.8
Classical concert	15.5	57.1
Folk dance	12.6	54.9
Circus	9.6	63.2
Operetta	8.1	63.6
Opera	6.9	60.7

Figure 2: Types of cultural events as tourist attractions. (Own survey)
* - % of all respondents
** - of those respondents who attended that particular type of event

Figure 2 presents the most popular types of cultural events among the survey participants. As the data show, the survey participants were motivated to travel by a relatively wide range of cultural events, among which theatre plays and pop/rock/jazz concerts proved to be the most attractive, both in terms of their popularity and their role as primary attractions: in both cases, more than 50% of the respondents travelled at least once a year since 2008 to enjoy a theatre performance or a popular music concert, and for more than 70% of them, these cultural events were the key reasons to select a particular destination at a certain time. Movies as well as culinary and cultural festivals also played an important role in stimulating culturally motivated travel (although it shall be noted here that some of these 'festivals' do not correspond with the criteria defined by the Hungarian Festival Association summarised by Márta (2008), as a consequence of the relatively recent recognition of festivals' positive economic and social impacts by many small or medium-sized Hungarian settlements, and the subsequent explosion of the number of events called festivals).

Not surprisingly, certain forms of the performing arts such as operetta or opera seemed to attract much smaller segments of cultural tourists than broader forms such as theatre plays in general or popular music concerts. The popularity of both opera and operetta was slightly higher among female respondents (Pearson's Chi-Square=9.256 and 8.751, respectively, with sig.<0.05), but none of the other demographic variables seemed to have an impact.

With the exception of cultural and gastronomy festivals that are typically several days long, all the cultural events listed in Figure 2 almost exclusively motivate day trips in Hungary, due to the relatively small distances within the country, and the relatively high cost of accommodation compared with the ticket price of the events. This is particularly true in those cases when the participants decide to travel specifically for a given concert or play (i.e. when the event is their primary motivation), since during such trips the additional attraction of general sightseeing programmes, relaxation or other leisure activities is completely missing from the group of factors that define the length of stay and the overall trip characteristics.

Per capita spending proved to be rather low, even taking into consideration the limited spending power of Hungarians: 65.5% of the respondents spent less than 5,000 HUF (app. 16 EUR), and only 11.1% spent more than 10,000 HUF (app. 32 EUR). This is partly explained by the geographical closeness of the events and the survey participants' residence: 25% travelled less than 40 km for a cultural programme, although more than 50% travelled more than 100 km (with the largest distance being 421 km). Consequently, most trips (58.1%) did not generate overnight stays, and even those who spent at least one night at the visited destination were most likely to stay at friends or relatives as opposed to using commercial accommodation services (Figure 3), and 70% paid less than 5,000 HUF for accommodation. Concerning food and beverage services, food stalls available on the location of events proved the be the most popular choice among respondents (36.7%), followed by purchasing food in stores in the destination (30.5%) and consuming meals in restaurants (27.6%). It is particularly true for younger survey participants at longer music festivals that they tried to compensate for the relatively high admission prices by decreasing their other expenses.

These consumption characteristics are strongly related to the impacts of the global economic crisis in Hungary: in recent years, many active cultural consumers have been forced to renounce longer trips and more comfortable services in order to maintain the level of cultural activity that they were accustomed to. The findings also confirm that invisible – i.e. statistically unregistered – mobility constitutes a significant component of cultural tourism consumption.

Type of accommodation	**%**
Home of friends or relatives	39.3
Hotel	16.2
Campsite	13.7
Guesthouse	10.3
Own property (second home)	7.8
Hostel	5.3
Spent the night outdoors	3.3
Rural accommodation	2.8
Rented apartment	1.3

Figure 3: Accommodation used by respondents who spent at least one night at the visited cultural destination. (Own survey)

The majority of cultural events visited by the survey respondents generate very moderate revenues for the destinations since, in the absence of promoting these events as components of complex tourist packages, the visitors' spending is limited to buying the admission tickets and their demand remains in the sphere of invisible tourism mobility (Kundi 2013). The missed opportunity of creating longer stays and higher revenues may also be related to participants' lack of awareness of the visited area's sights and activities (McKercher et al 2006), highlighting the significance of destination level awareness building prior departure. In addition, VFR travellers' interest and behaviour may also be influenced in the destination through their hosts (Backer 2007), although this requires well-planned co-operation among the event organisers, the local DMOs and the tourist service providers.

Figure 4 presents those events that were listed by at least 1% of the survey participants as their most memorable cultural experience in recent years. As the figures indicate, even the most often mentioned single event – the popular multicultural VOLT Festival characterised by its wide variety of musical styles – was named by less than 5% of the respondents, and the total list included almost as many events as there were survey participants ('theatre', the first item represents several unidentified performances jointly). The majority of memorable events were of local significance, and the listing of gastronomic festivals (such as the Meat Jelly Festival or the Sausage Festival) alongside electronic music (Balaton Sound) and folklore festivals (Summerfestival) reflects a heterogeneous interpretation of the notion of 'culture'.

Most memorable event	**% (of the total sample)**
Theatre	6.0
VOLT Festival	4.7
Balaton Sound	3.4
Sziget Festival	3.2
Flower Carnival, Debrecen	1.5
Meat Jelly Festivál, Miskolc	1.5
Hegyalja Festivál	1.2
Summerfestival International Folklore Festival	1.2
Szeged Open Air Festival	1.2
Valley of Arts	1.2
Pannonia Festival	1.0
Békéscsaba Sausage Festival	1.0

Figure 4: The most memorable cultural experiences. (Own survey)

Content analysis was used to identify the key words used by respondents to explain their selection of memorable events. Using the increasingly popular illustration technique of a 'word cloud' where the size of a word indicates its prominence, Figure 1 summarises the key components of an event's memorableness. Some of the most often mentioned words merely expressed satisfaction (e.g. 'great') or repeated the question (*'I selected this event as my most memorable cultural experience, because it was a memorable experience for me'*). However, such key words as 'love', 'friends' and 'family' highlight the significance of interpersonal factors in shaping the experience, supported by the fact that 97.5% of the respondents attend cultural events in the company of others, mainly friends (43.6%), family members (31.1%) or both friends and family (25.3%). Festivals are traditionally considered as celebrations, i.e. inherently community events that are best enjoyed together, although 'programme', 'performance', 'festival' or 'music' also underline the importance of the actual cultural product offered to visitors. The data analysis suggested that the memorableness of an event also depended on its date: as memories tend to fade, it is not surprising that respondents were more likely to recall one of their latest culturally motivated trips as their most memorable cultural experiences or one of those events that they had attended repeatedly (confirmed also by the key words 'regular' and 'recent').

Figure 5: Components of a memorable cultural event. (Authors)

The geographical distribution of the most memorable cultural experiences' location, not surprisingly, indicates the dominance of the capital city, Budapest (Figure 6) (only those sites are included in Figure 6 that were mentioned by at least 1% of those respondents who could recall a 'most memorable' cultural event). The rest of the sites show a great variety of destinations, ranging from popular summer holiday resorts situated along Lake Balaton (Zamárdi, Balatonfüred) through major cities with rich cultural life (Debrecen and Miskolc are Hungary's second and third largest cities after Budapest, respectively) to classical cultural tourism destinations (Sopron and Eger are both among the most popular choices for culturally-motivated city trips). However, the relatively low % values in Tables 3 and 4 suggest that respondents' memorable experiences are distributed among a large number of events, the majority being of only local importance (a similar finding was reported by Sulyok in 2010 in a study assessing the festival-going characteristics of the Hungarian population).

Although only mentioned by 1-1% of the respondents, two locations on the list, Kapolcs and Etyek, shall be highlighted in this analysis, since both represent a new approach in cultural development: the creation of cultural attractions and a new local identity by urban actors in a rural environment (Csurgó 2004). Kapolcs, a village in Western Hungary with a population of 370 persons, is well-known in Hungary for the 'Valley of Arts' festival that grew from a single concert organised in 1998 by an artist second home-owner into an 'all-arts' festival spread out to the neighbouring villages, attended by app. 120,000 visitors in 2012 and 2013 (MTI 2013). In Etyek, a similarly small village near Budapest, a well-known media personality who had moved to the settlement initiated an event in 2003 with a wine-gastronomy-culture theme that, in ten years, grew into a popular festival attracting 30-35,000 visitors (until its transformation into four seasonal events in 2013) (Fütő 2012). Both festivals are based on factors such as authenticity, heritage, traditional gastronomy and traditional trades, and the local people take part in organising the programmes, creating a certain sense of community. The locations themselves possess a symbolic character, since both have preserved the rural lifestyle, and represent nostalgic values for the predominantly urban audience. However, the development of these festivals also illustrate the phenomenon of urban pressure (Overbeck and Terluin 2006) where urban consumption values are introduced to rural areas by urban actors, building experiences for urban cultural consumers and constructing new forms of local identity that are used to revalorise these places.

Location	**%**	**Location**	**%**
Budapest	27.3	Baja	1.2
Zamárdi	5.2	Békéscsaba	1.2
Sopron	3.0	Miskolc	1.0
Debrecen	1.7	Kapolcs	1.0
Eger	1.7	Etyek	1.0
Balatonfüred	1.2		

Figure 6: Location of the most memorable cultural event. (Own survey)

Since the Hungarian capital city proved to be the most important cultural tourism destination in this research (similarly to previous studies, e.g. Sulyok 2010), the consumption characteristics of Budapest respondents were further analysed. However, their choices showed a very similar pattern to that of the overall sample: in addition to theatre performances in major cities, the same popular music festivals, traditional cultural festivals and gastronomic events were mentioned. Consequently, the existence of an established set of 'must-visit' cultural events seems to be confirmed in Hungary, with gastronomy and popular music being the most attractive themes, although it also remains true that only few festivals are able to actually generate travel demand.

Discussion

The findings of the survey suggest that respondents perceive the concept of culture as a rather complex one, one that is able to incorporate an extensive range of activities from visits to the theatre through culinary festivals to circus shows. The currently available Hungarian cultural tourism product seems to confirm this mosaic-like composition of postmodern culture, simultaneously offering high and popular cultural pursuits for consumption, thus it is able to satisfy the needs of the 'omnivorous' cultural consumer (Peterson 1992) who is equally likely to search for classical concerts and for street art.

The preferences expressed by the respondents towards various cultural events suggest the parallel existence of two opposite trends in Hungarians' cultural tourism choices. Certain survey participants, particularly in the youngest respondent segment, seemed to be keen to follow the current cultural trends, in order to gain social prestige by demonstrating their up-to-date knowledge of the latest developments. Choices made by others however revealed an alternative consumption pattern focusing on the search for authentic and individual experiences (similarly to the findings of Michael (2013) in her research with young people deeply involved in urban cultural scenes). Nevertheless, cultural consumption in tourism in Hungary still seems to be structured by social differences, i.e. demand is highly influenced by the economic resources and the socio-demographic characteristics of the tourists.

The festivals attended by the respondents may be classified into three groups, based on the characteristics of their core cultural elements: (1) traditional, established festivals with a long history, embedded in the commonly recognised cultural tourist product of the country, (2) festivals highlighting their "Hungarianness", being organised around a theme that reflects a nationalistic approach to national identity, and (3) festivals with a trendy, international theme, aiming to bring up-to-date, global culture in reach for the Hungarian customers. (However, in the last group, these themes are generally reflections of the Western European or American manifestations of cultural globalisation; the phenomenon of multiple globalization, as highlighted by Goldstein-Gidoni (2005), has not really reached the mainstream Hungarian cultural festival market yet).

An interesting example of the transformation of the Hungarian cultural consumption scene is the shifting demand of domestic visitors from the internationally acclaimed, Best European Major Festival Award winner (2012) Sziget Festival to the younger, hipper Balaton Sound, adopting a practice of conspicuous consumption (attendance at the latter event has become a highly desirable way of creating and expressing social prestige and status, especially within peer groups, communicated via social media sites). Although Sziget is the best known festival among Hungarians (Sulyok 2010), as its audience grew from 43,000 in 1993 to a record 390,000 in 2009 (362,000 in 2013) (Sziget Kft. 2013), the event changed significantly: as it was gaining acclaim in the international market, it was also losing its original 'being among friends' atmosphere and became a professionally designed consumer product. By 2013, ticket prices reached the level of major European festivals, app. 60% of the visitors came from abroad and, as a consequence, many Hungarians did not consider themselves any more among its target customers.

As the findings indicated, culturally motivated trips are closely related to Visiting Friends and Relatives (VFR) travel in Hungary. This might be explained by economic reasons, since staying with friends or relatives as opposed to using commercial accommodation services is an economical solution; however, the constraints induced by the relatively low discretional income of Hungarians may have a limiting effect on cultural event consumption decisions, but may also have a beneficial impact on personal and family relations. In addition, those VFR tourists who are active cultural consumers (and who are most likely to classify themselves as leisure or cultural tourists – Backer 2007) may also encourage their hosts to participate in cultural events and engage in various tourist activities (e.g. eating out, visiting cultural attractions), thus creating a specific cultural multiplier effect.

Conclusions

The survey carried out in order to explore culturally motivated tourism mobility in Hungary confirmed the original premise of the research according to which a significant number of domestic cultural trips take place within the framework of invisible tourism. Although certain festivals and other cultural events may play a key role in attracting visitors to destinations, cultural tourism consumption is affected by several other factors as well, and is often connected to VFR tourism where friends and relatives serve both as a source of information on local cultural events and as a means to an economical way of travelling.

Another angle of the study is to assess the opportunities of small-scale destinations to benefit from the invisible tourism mobility of cultural consumers. Although major cultural festivals are featured among the key products identified by the Hungarian National Tourism Development Strategy (MTH 2005), the potential of minor cultural attractions and events often remains unnoticed, decreasing their ability to appeal to investors, larger numbers of visitors or even to local residents who may fail to acknowledge the cultural richness of their own surroundings. Further research will be necessary to understand how these events could be developed and promoted in a way that would increase their competitiveness in the Hungarian cultural economy.

Recognizing the dynamic and complex nature of the tourism system, the paper highlights the need to reconsider the demand patterns of tourism consumption and the way they are understood and interpreted. Since the concepts of leisure and tourism are more and more blurred as a consequence of growing mobility and the resulting gradual extension of daily life beyond traditional geographical boundaries, tourism consumption is increasingly taking place in a sphere where it remains invisible to destination decision-makers. From a practical point of view, this transformation process brings about significant changes in destination marketing and management, while theoretically it requires a re-interpretation of the notion of tourism and tourists.

References

Backer, E. (2007): VFR Travel: An Examination of the Expenditures of VFR Travelers and their Hosts. In: Current Issues in Tourism, 10(4), 366-377.

Bihagen, E. and Katz-Gerro, T. (2000): Culture Consumption in Sweden: The Stability of Gender Differences. In: Poetics, 27(5-6), 327-349.

Buchmann, A., Moore, K. and Fisher, D. (2010): Experiencing Film Tourism. Authenticity & Fellowship. In: Annals of Tourism Research, 38(1), 229-248.

Chan, T.W. and Goldthorpe, J.H. (2006): Social Stratification and Cultural Consumption: Music in England. In: European Sociological Review, 23(1), 1-19.

Csurgó, B. (2004): Urban Pressure – A Recent Phenomenon: The Valley of Arts. In: Eastern European Countryside, 10, 155-165.

Dudás, K. and Hunyadi, Zs. (2005): Találkozások a kultúrával 6. A hagyományos (színház, hangverseny, kiállítás) és a modern tömegkultúra (mozi, könnyűzenei koncert) helye és szerepe a kulturális fogyasztásban. Budapest: Magyar Művelődési Intézet.

Eusébio, C., Carneiro, M.J. and Kastenholz, E. (2013): The Economic Value of Cultural Tourism: Determinants of Cultural Tourists' Expenditures. In: Smith, M. and Richards, G. (eds.): The Routledge Handbook of Cultural Tourism. Oxon: Routledge, 116-126.

Fütő, B. (2012): Egy korszak lezárult, nem lesz több Kezes-Lábos és Pincefesztivál. http://www.boraszportal.hu/bortre/20120904/egy-korszak-lezarult-nem-lesz-tobb-kezes-labos-es-pincefesztival, 04.09.2012.

Goldstein-Gidoni, O. (2005): The Production and Consumption of 'Japanese Culture' in the Global Cultural Market. In: Journal of Consumer Culture, 5(2), 155-179.

Halewood, C. and Hannam, K. (2001): Viking Heritage Tourism. Authenticity and Commodification. In: Annals of Tourism Research, 28(3), 565-580.

Harrison, J. (2003): Being a Tourist: Finding Meaning in Pleasure Travel. Vancouver: UBC Press.

Harsányi, G. and Vincze, Sz. (2012): A magyar felsőoktatás néhány jellemzője nemzetközi tükörben. In: Pénzügyi Szemle, 57(2), 226-245.

Inglehart, R. (1997): Modernization and Postmodernization: Cultural, Economic and Political Change in 43 Societies. Princeton: Princeton University Press.

Irimiás, A. and Michalkó, G. (2013): Religious Tourism in Hungary – An Integrative Framework. In: Hungarian Geographical Bulletin, 61(2), 175-196.

KSH (2013a): Jelentés a turizmus 2012 évi teljesítményéről. Budapest: KSH.

KSH (2013b): Nemzetközi turisztikai kereslet, 2012. IV. negyedév. In: Statisztikai Tükör, 7(13), 1-2.

Kundi, V. (2013): Fesztiválok városokra gyakorolt gazdasági és társadalmi-kulturális hatásainak elemzése. A győri Magyar Táncfesztivál és a Miskolci Operafesztivál példáján keresztül. PhD értekezés. Győr: Széchenyi István Egyetem, Regionális- és Gazdaságtudományi Doktori Iskola.

Mackay, H. (1997) (ed.): Consumption and Everyday Life. Milton Keynes: The Open.

Márta, I. (2008): Regisztráció és minősítés? PPT prezentáció. http://mail.efmk.hu/vandorgyules/eloadasok/2nap_20081121_szekciok/5os_fesztivalok/2008okt_%20REGISZTRACIO_es_MINOSITES.ppt, 18.02.2014.

McCabe, S. (2002): The Tourist Experience and Everyday Life. In: Dann, G.M.S. (ed.): The Tourist as a Metaphor of the Social World. Wallingford: CABI, 61-76.

McCracken, G. (1990): Culture and Consumption: New Approaches to the Symbolic Character of Consumer Goods and Activities. Bloomington: Indiana University Press.

McKercher, B., Mei, W.S. and Tse, T.S.M. (2006): Are Short Duration Festivals Tourist Attractions? In: Journal of Sustainable Tourism, 14(1), 55-66.

Michael, J. (2013): It's Really Not Hip to Be a Hipster: Negotiating Trends and Authenticity in the Cultural Field. In: Journal of Consumer Culture, June 25, doi: 10.1177/1469540513493206.

Michalkó, G. and Rátz, T. (2013): Rejtett dimenziók a Kárpát-medence turizmusában. In: Frisnyák, S. and Gál, A. (eds.): Kárpát-medence: természet, társadalom, gazdaság. Szerencs – Nyíregyháza: Bocskai István Gimnázium – Nyíregyházi Főiskola Turizmus és Földrajztudományi Intézet, 463-476.

Michalkó, G. and Rátz, T. (2005): A kulturális turizmus élmény-gazdaságtani szempontjai. In: Enyedi, Gy. and Keresztély, K. (eds.): A magyar városok kulturális gazdasága. Budapest: MTA Társadalomkutató Központ, 123-141.

Miles, S. (2000): Youth Lifestyles in a Changing World. Buckingham: Open University.

MTH (2005): Nemzeti Turizmusfejlesztési Stratégia. Budapest: Magyar Turisztikai Hivatal.

MTI (2013): Hobo 180 dalt énekelt el tíz nap alatt. http://hvg.hu/kultura/20130804_Hobo_180_dalt_enekelt_el_tiz_nap_alatt, 11.02.2014.

Mustonen, P. (2006): Postmodern Tourism – Alternative Approaches. Turku: Turku School of Economics.

Overbeck, M.M.M. and Terluin, I.J. (2006) (eds.): Rural Areas under Urban Pressure. Case Studies of Rural-Urban Relationships across Europe. The Hague: Agricultural Economics Research Institute.

Peterson, R.A. (1992): Understanding Audience Segmentation: From Elite and Mass to Omnivore and Univore. In: Poetics, 21(4), 243-258.

Poria, Y., Reichel, A. and Cohen, R. (2011): World Heritage Site – Is It an Effective Brand Name? A Case Study of a Religious Heritage Site. In: Journal of Travel Research, 50(5), 482-495.

Räsänen, P. (2003): In the Twilight of Social Structures: A Mechanism-based Study of Contemporary Consumer Behaviour. Turku: University of Turku.

Rátz, T. (2006): A húsvét szerepe a magyar lakosság utazási magatartásának befolyásolásában. In: Turizmus Bulletin, 10(1), 30-38.

Richards, G. (2007): Introduction: Global Trends in Cultural Tourism. In: Richards, G. (ed.): Cultural Tourism – Global and Local Perspectives. New York: The Haworth Hospitality Press, 1-24.

Richards, G. (2001): The Development of Cultural Tourism in Europe. In: Richards, G. (ed.): Cultural Attractions and European Tourism. Oxon: CABI Publishing, 3-30.

Richards, G. (1996) (ed.): Cultural Tourism in Europe. Wallingford: CABI.

Richards, G. and Bonink, C. (1995): Marketing Cultural Tourism in Europe. In: Journal of Vacation Marketing, 1(2), 172-180.

Richards, G. and Queirós, C. (2005): ATLAS Cultural Tourism Research Project 2004 – Survey Report. Arnhem: ATLAS.

Scarbrough, E. (1995): Materialist-Postmaterialist Value Orientations. In: van Deth, J. W. and Scarbrough, E. (eds.): The Impact of Values. Oxford: Oxford University Press, 123-159.

Sharpley, R. (2002): The Consumption of Tourism. In: Sharpley, R. (ed.): Tourism and Development: Concept and Issues. Clevedon: Channel View Publications, 300-318.

Smith, M. (2003): Issues in Cultural Tourism Studies. London: Routledge.

Storey, J. (1999): Cultural Consumption and Everyday Life. New York: Oxford University Press Inc.

Sulyok, J. (2010): A magyar lakosság fesztiválIátogatási szokásai. In: Turizmus Bulletin, 14(3), 2-11.

Sulyok, J. and Polgár, J. (2010): A Kulturális Turizmus Éve 2009 témaév legfontosabb eredményei. In: Turizmus Bulletin, 14(3), 33-39.

Sziget Kft. (2013): 362 ezren voltak a Szigeten. http://index.hu/kultur/zene/fesztival/2013/08/12/hivatalosan_362_ezren_voltak_a_szigeten/, 15.02.2014.

Thrane, C. (2000): Everyday Life and Cultural Tourism in Scandinavia: Examining the Spillover Hypothesis. In: Loisir et Société, 23(1), 217-234.

UNWTO (2013): Tourism Highlights, 2013 Edition. http://dtxtq4w60xqpw.cloudfront.net/sites/all/files/pdf/unwto_highlights13_en_hr.pdf, 21.02.2014.

Urry, J. (2002): The Tourist Gaze, 2nd ed. London: Sage.

WTO (1989): The Hague Declaration on Tourism. Madrid: WTO.

Towards a New Role Model of the Contemporary Architectural Tourist

Jan Specht

"Tourists are not homogeneous." (Mo et al. 1993: 319)

Classification is a precondition for all kinds of statistical measurements, decision-making processes and a target-oriented marketing. It almost seems that, from an economic point of view, what cannot be classified cannot be measured and what cannot be measured does not exist. Tourism, as an important element of many national and regional economies, is no exception to this rule. Therefore, in both science and practice, tourists are, according to their primary purposes of travel, often put into fixed categories such as business, leisure, sun-and-beach, visiting friend and family etc. However, not least when it comes to urban tourism, one might ask if this concept is still (or ever was) reasonable. For instance, one might come to a city for business reasons or an event, while still spending a large part of his stay with the consumption of all kinds of appealing urban elements.

In tourism an objective classification is not easy (or even possible), as eventually it all depends on the tourist's gaze or perception. The gaze, in turn, depends on a wide range of factors, such as a tourist's culture, education, age or gender. According to Urry (2002: 94) "tourist sites can be classified in terms of three dichotomies: whether they are an object of the romantic or collective tourist gaze; whether they are historical or modern; and whether they are presented as authentic or inauthentic." But what would this mean for the tourists visiting such sites? Could they be classified in the same way? And how about architectural tourism? How could tourists consuming architecture as an attraction be classified? Conventional architectural classification approaches are of limited use in this regard, as a tourist's gaze or perception might not correspond with the technical classification criteria that are usually applied. An example is the classification of architecture by age or era. Reconstructed historical buildings (e.g. Church of our Lady in Dresden, Germany; see Figure 1), recently built architectures using historical styles or elements (e.g. Qianmen Street in Beijing, China; see Figure 2 and 3) or still unfinished buildings which are decades under construction (e.g. Sagrada Família in Barcelona, Spain; see Figure 4) might, based on their date of completion, all be classified as contemporary. However, most tourists would still perceive them as historical structures. While neither making a claim to be complete nor to be conclusive, the following paper aims to provide approaches for the classification of tourists related to (contemporary) architecture.

Figure 1: Rebuilt Church of Our Lady in Dresden, Germany: The remaining parts of the original are visible as dark spots within the new structure. (Author 2006)

Figure 2: Qianmen pedestrian street in Beijing, China: Popular shopping area for more than 500 years. (Author 2010)

Figure 3: Qianmen pedestrian street in Beijing, China: "Contemporary" tourism attraction, featuring "renewed" buildings, resembling the style of the late Qing Dynasty. (Author 2010)

Figure 4: Sagrada Família in Barcelona, Spain: Designed by Antoni Gaudí, the Roman Catholic church is under continuous construction since 1882. (Author 2004)

About types and roles of visitors

In tourism, in particular in an urban context, architecture might serve in various capacities, including this of an attraction (Specht 2009: 98). Goeldner and Ritchie (2009: 280) believed that "such cultural media as painting, sculpture, graphic arts, architecture, and landscape architecture constitute an important motivation for travel." However, referring to mass tourism, Schwarzer (2005: 18) claimed that "architecture might be the entrée for a trip, but in the end it is just one course of a long menu." In fact, instead of being attracted by one type, tourists are often rather motivated by a mixture of different types of attractions. This, however, makes it difficult to separate one from another, and to form distinct groups of tourists. Plaza (2006: 453) noted in this regard that "the fact that cities like London, Madrid or New York have several excellent museums and other forms of art and entertainment, makes it difficult to discern precisely what is the focus of tourist attention. Bilbao's offer of one specific museum [the Guggenheim] makes the city an almost perfect laboratory for testing the impact of this cultural investment."

In fact, even museums and other forms of art and entertainment are often just a small part of a city's mix of attractions. A tourist, interested in museums, may also be attracted by special events or the local cuisine, while, taken individually, none of these attractions might be sufficient as a sole motivator to visit the destination. Once again, the appeal of the mixture is decisive. A visitor interested in contemporary architecture might also be looking for historical monuments and further cultural elements and attractions. Therefore, Weiermeier (2002: 3) suggested that "cultural goods and services as parts of a tourism or larger cultural cluster must ... play a different role than culture or cultural goods as the sole motivator and/or prime decision parameter or prime satisfier in the destination choice and destination evaluation process." Likewise Law (2002: 26) argued that "the demand by leisure tourists to travel to cities also has various elements from culture to entertainment, although in some cases there may be joint demand." Shovala and Ravehb (2004: 742) believed that the urban tourism product was too large to be entirely consumed during an average visit to a city. Instead, tourists had to decide which of the attractions to visit or to skip.

The result was the creation of "typical consumption patterns of the tourism product based on the preferences and limitations of different tourist types." Hence, most notably when it comes to urban destinations, a rigid and sole allocation of a tourist to one specific type or purpose is not enough. Instead, it appears appropriate to use a more flexible approach, assigning a tourist with various alternating roles, according to the different purposes of his visit and his pattern of consumption. In this context, Mazanec (1997: 114) asked for a replacement of "the trivial single-item classification (sightseeing tourist, culture-seeker, museum visitor)" with "a multivariate activity pattern." Cohen (2004: 29) claimed, "there also exist many forms of partial tourism, in which travelling for novelty and change is combined in varying degrees and forms with other non-instrumental or even instrumental purposes." For instance, a visitor spending some days in Barcelona, Spain attending a fair, might at the same time also visit friends, enjoy a concert, check out the city's cultural offerings and spend some time at the beach. Hence, depending on the method of classification, the same visitor could, for example, be called an "urban tourist", a "business traveller", a "cultural or art's related tourist", a "tourist visiting friends or relatives (VFR)", a "recreational tourist" or a "sun lover" – all at the same time (see Goeldner and Ritchie 2009: 11; Hughes 2000: 56; Van Harssel 1995: 129; Yiannakis and Gibson 1992: 291). Therefore, some approaches ask for the primary interest of a tourist, or the main reason of his journey, in order to enable a clear attribution to one specific type or group. Yet, regarding urban tourism, such "clear attribution" might often not only be difficult, but also imprecise and misleading, e.g. for an appropriate tourism marketing.

In an article about historic theme parks, Moscardo and Pearce (1986: 470) pointed out that "there is no one motive for travel, and one cannot talk about 'the tourist' as if it were one role only." Referring to Cohen (1979; 1984), Pearce (1985) and Smith (1977) they further elaborated about "evidence supporting the idea that there are many travel-related roles, that is many different types of tourist." Cohen (2004: 35) stated that different roles may overlap "along a single dimension or along several dimension." Hence, the same tourist might correspond to different types or roles, and the architectural tourist might just be one of them.

Building an architecture-related role model of visitors

The Planning and Transportation Committee of the City of Toronto (2003: 6) called architectural tourism "an emerging international travel market"; however, assuming that, "the number of people who might potentially be motivated to visit Toronto solely because of its architectural product is probably small – perhaps less than 10,000 per year unless tied to a major event or conference." Yet, the Council understood architecture as an important piece of the puzzle of an integrated destination and suggested:

> "Greater access to our [Toronto's] architecture probably would enhance the visit and contribute to decisions to travel for tens of thousands potential visitors. It would also

> be a selling feature in attracting international conferences and business events for design professionals as well as for other professions employing highly educated people with interests in culture." (Planning and Transportation Committee of the City of Toronto 2003: 6).

However, who are these people attracted by architecture in general and contemporary architecture in particular? Hughes (2000) first distinguished between two general types of journeys:

- **Instrumental** (business or conference, education, religion or visiting friends)
- **Non-instrumental** (holiday)

Hence, while instrumental journeys are primarily dedicated to a specific purpose, according to Hughes (2000: 35) non-instrumental ones "are to do with 'change' – that is travel to and stay at a different place regardless of the things done or seen." However, as discussed before, both types might have strong overlaps. A tourist might spend, for instance, the evenings of a business trip in the form of a 'non-instrumental holiday'. For Hughes (2000: 35), "a desire to see and learn about other cultures or the opportunity to see famous buildings and sites … is still non-instrumental … it is a desire to get away rather than the attraction of particular places that distinguishes most holidays. The 'push' is more important than the 'pull'." Yet, this classification is only applicable to a certain degree of interest. Visitors to the Great Pyramid of Giza or the Guggenheim Bilbao, for example, might very well be driven by the desire to visit a specific place and object. Hence, such visitors are not primarily 'pushed' by a desire for change, novelty or escape, but rather 'pulled' by specific attraction(s).

Referring to arts tourism, Hughes (2000: 127) therefore proposed a more specific approach of classification. Based on the degree of cultural interest and cultural intent, he distinguished between five different categories of arts-related tourists (see Figure 4). With a few changes, Hughes' (2000) approach could also be adapted to a typology of architectural tourists, based on their interest and intent to visit architecture. Furthermore, the same logic could be used for further areas, such as culture, food or music. Hence, Hughes (2000) provided a scale to indicate the intensity of the relationship between a tourist and a specific area of interest (arts, in his particular case). However, the approach gave no indication regarding the interdependencies and hierarchies between different areas of interest and the related types of tourists. For instance, from the types of "arts tourists" presented in Figure 5, it is not possible to conclude which kinds of art are concerned, or if any of the given types are interested in or intend to attend other cultural or non-cultural attractions.

Type of arts-related tourist	Level of interest	Level of intent	Force of attraction
Arts-core	Pre-interest in attending	Main purpose	Attraction
Arts-peripheral (incidental)	Pre-interest in attending	Secondary purpose	Attraction or amenity
Arts-peripheral (accidental)	No pre-interest in attending	Not a purpose	Not an attraction, possibly an amenity
Unintentional	No pre-interest in attending	Not a purpose (no deliberate decision to attend)	Not an attraction or amenity
Non-arts related tourist	No pre-interest in attending	Not a purpose (does not attend)	Indirect attraction or amenity

Figure 5: Types of arts-related tourists based on Hughes (2000: 127).

In a text about "the heritage resource as seen by the tourist" Peterson (1995: 242) proposed a classification of four types of visitors to heritage sites:

- **Aficionados** – Preservationists, heritage professionals or well qualified amateurs who are interested in the historic resource in great depth
- **Event visitors** – Visiting a heritage site for an event, such as art festivals, concerts, historical festivals etc. (most often locals, not tourists)
- **Tourists** – Visitors, who are out of their normal routine, are away from home and visiting historic sites
- **Casual visitors** – Using historic site for leisure purposes (parks etc.), while the site is important for its grounds, not for its history

Although not explicitly specified, Peterson's approach does, similarly to Hughes' (2000), also include dimensions of interest and intent. In his dissertation about "architectural tourism and its influence on urban design", Shaw (2007: 79) adapted Peterson's approach for his research and claimed that "architecture also has these classifications in that some buildings are visited for their aesthetic value, completely aside from their function or historical significance."

McKercher and du Cros' (2002) typology of the cultural tourist has similarities to Peterson's (1995) approach and Hughes' (2000) typology of the arts-related tourist. Yet, McKercher and du Cros (2002: 144) used the dimensions of "importance of cultural tourism in the decision to visit a destination" and "experience sought", leading to five types of cultural tourists (see also Figure 6):

- **The purposeful cultural tourist** – Cultural tourism is the primary motive for visiting a destination and the tourist has a very deep cultural experience
- **The sightseeing cultural tourist** – Cultural tourism is a primary reason for visiting a destination, but the experience is less deep
- **The serendipitous cultural tourist** – A tourist who does not travel for cultural reasons, but who, after participating, ends up having a deep cultural experience
- **The casual cultural tourist** – Cultural tourism is a weak motive for travel and the resulting experience is shallow
- **The incidental cultural tourist** – This tourist does not travel for cultural reasons, but nonetheless participates in some activities and has shallow experiences

In some way, McKercher and du Cros' (2002) dimension of "importance of cultural tourism in the decision to visit a destination" combined Hughes' (2000) dimensions of "interest" and "intent". However, the dimension of "experience thought" was an addition to Hughes' (2000) approach, as it went beyond the desire and decisional process to visit a specific destination or attraction, looking at the experience and hence the satisfaction during and following the tourist's visit. Likewise to Hughes' (2000) approach, McKercher and du Cros' (2002) model could be adapted to different areas of interest or types of tourists, including the architectural tourist. Yet, it still did not provide indications regarding their interdependencies and hierarchies. For instance, depending on his specific interest and intent, a cultural tourist might accord top priority to historical monuments, while having a deep experience at the same time (purposeful cultural tourist). On the other hand, he might be less keen on contemporary architecture, but in passing by, still experience some interesting buildings (casual or serendipitous cultural tourist). Hence, in order to understand the different roles that one and the same tourist might take during a journey, interdependencies and also different levels of potential interests, intentions and, as far as possible, experiences might need to be taken into consideration.

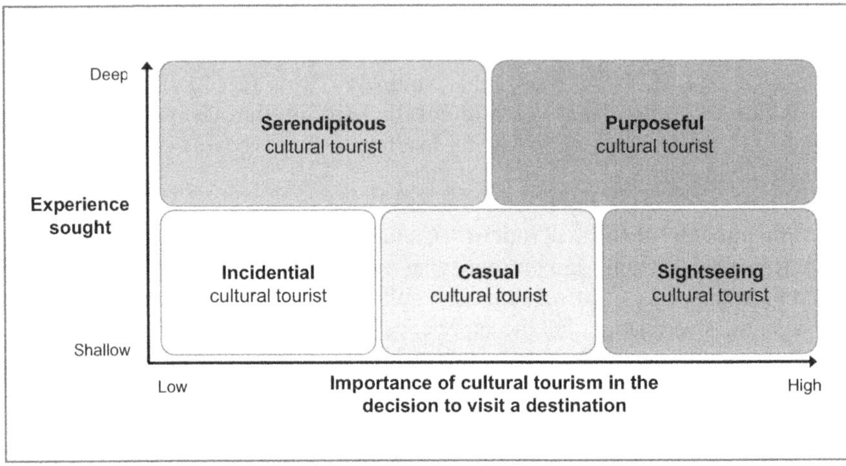

Figure 6: Types of cultural tourists based on McKercher and du Cros (2002: 140).

For Wood (2002), cultural tourism formed part of the tourism market on the same hierarchical level as rural tourism, nature tourism, sun-and-beach tourism, business travel and fitness/wellness and health (as cited in Ritchie and Crouch 2003: 50). Whereas Robinson and Novelli (2005) at first distinguished between two categories:

- **Mass tourism** – Conventional tourism involving large number of tourists in staged settings
- **Niche tourism** – Special interests, culture and/or activity based tourism involving small number of tourists in authentic settings (9)

For Robinson and Novelli (2005), cultural, environmental, rural, urban and other forms of tourism were particular "micro-niches" within the category of niche tourism. They further classified heritage tourism as part of cultural tourism, while art, for instance, belonged to urban tourism. Potential overlaps have not been taken into consideration (e.g. heritage tourism in an urban context). On the other hand, Smith (1998) clearly distinguished cultural tourism and historical tourism which, according to Ashworth (2000), was almost synonymous to heritage tourism. He argued that cultural tourism was experience and activity based, including "a vestige of a vanishing lifestyle that lies within human memory", while historical tourism was related to monuments, ruins and other architectural structures that stress "the glories of the past" (Ashworth 2000: 5).

As the literature review demonstrated, the classification of tourism types and tourist orientations depends to a large extent on the situational context of research as well as the perspective and understanding of the individual authors. In tourism, classification may be useful for many different reasons. However, given the complexity and multitude of requirements and situations, an all-embracing classification approach is just not possible. Hence, without claiming to be representative, Figure 7 proposes an excerpt of a model, which is putting architectural tourism (or the architectural tourist) in a more comprehensive hierarchical system. This classification approach shall demonstrate the possible interdependencies with related, super- and subordinate areas. Hence, an architectural tourist might be interested in contemporary and/or historical architecture and belong to the superordinate group of the cultural tourist. A cultural tourist, belonging to the superordinate group of the "general" tourists can, but does not need to be interested in other areas too. Depending on the purposes of a visit and pattern of consumption, during a journey he might take different roles, which belong to different groups or types of tourism.

Building on this classification (see Figure 7) as well as Hughes' (2000) typology of the arts-related tourist (see Figure 5), the following approach (see Figure 8) represents a proposal for a role model of tourists related to (contemporary) architecture.

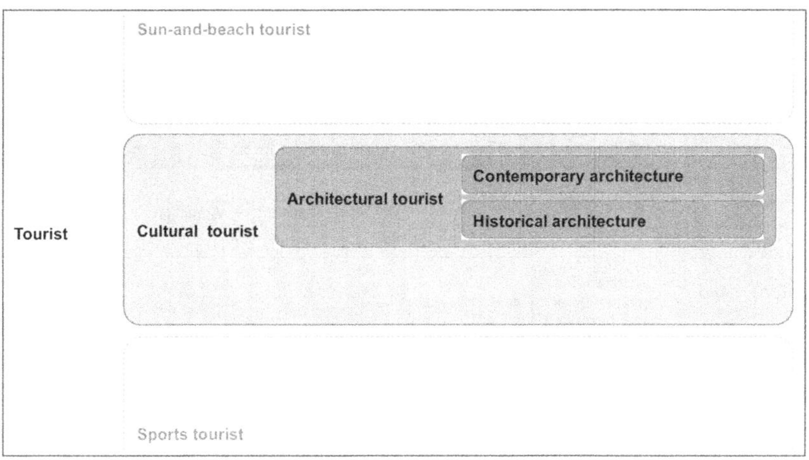

Figure 7: Simplified hierarchical classification of the architectural tourist. (Author 2012)

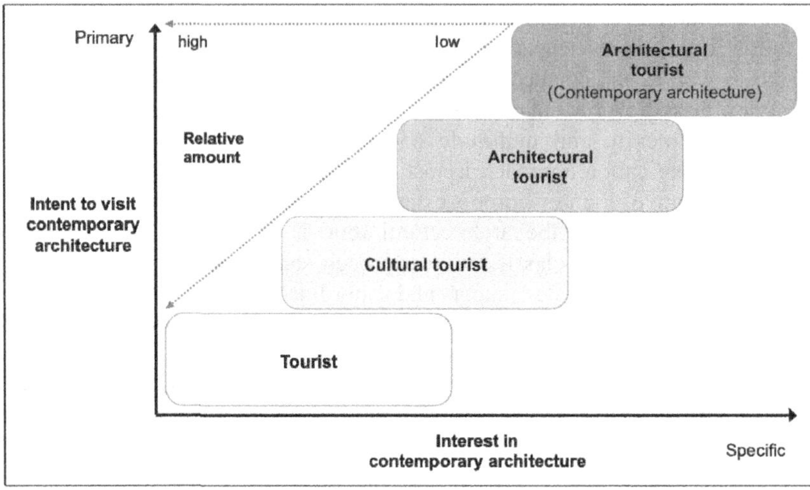

Figure 8: Roles of tourists related to contemporary architecture. (Author 2012)

Using the dimensions of "interest in contemporary architecture" and "intent to visit contemporary architecture" leads to four hierarchical types of tourists that are more or less related to contemporary architecture (see Figure 8 and 9).

Roles of tourists	Field(s) of interest	Level of interest in contemporary architecture	Level of intent to visit contemporary architecture	Force of attraction of contemporary architecture	Relative amount of tourists
Architectural tourist (contemporary architecture)	Contemporary architecture	Specific	Main purpose	Attraction	Low
Architectural tourist	Architecture (contemporary and historical)	Specific-general	One of the main purposes	Attraction or amenity	Low-middle
Cultural tourist	Culture (arts, architecture, music etc.)	General	Secondary purpose	Indirect attraction or amenity	Middle
Tourist	Various fields	Non	Not a purpose (no deliberate decision to attend)	No or indirect attraction or amenity	High

Figure 9: Roles of tourists related to contemporary architecture. (Author 2012)

The main purpose of the architectural tourists, who might range from expert to "well qualified amateur", is to visit historical and/or contemporary architectures (see Peterson 1995: 242). Hence, before or during the visit of a destination the architectural tourist will – due to his specific interest and intent – search on his own initiative for information about the architectures on site. Conversely, the "regular" tourist might rather accidentally or incidentally attend such structures or needs to be guided. Yet, this does not mean that contemporary architecture is per se not an attraction for roles other than the architectural tourist. Instead, the touristic significance of contemporary architecture depends on very different aspects (or variables) which might as well be relevant for cultural tourists or tourists in general. For instance, the Jewish Museum in Berlin (see Figure 9) is hosting, in two neighbouring buildings, permanent as well as changing exhibitions about the Jewish history. While one of these buildings is historical, the other – designed by "star-architect" Daniel Libeskind and finished in 1999 – is of contemporary nature (some call it "Deconstructivism").

Figure 10: Jewish Museum in Berlin, Germany (interior view): Contemporary architecture hosting exhibitions about Jewish history. (Author 2011)

Offering such a variety of features, it is only natural that the museum attracts very different roles of tourists. For instance, culturally interested tourists might come for the exhibitions, while for some of them the spectacular form of the building is just an interesting or even disturbing shell. In contrast, for architectural tourists, this very form or the special combination of features might be the main forces of attraction (see Specht 2014: 47). Some "regular" tourists might just feel attracted by the general fame of the museum, which then again is also born by its exceptional architecture. For some of these roles the museum is one of the main reasons for their visit to Berlin. For others it is just one of many activities during a holiday, business trip or visiting friends and family. Developers, marketers and managers need to be aware of these different roles, their interdependencies, requirements, sources of information and patterns of consumption. Otherwise, important measures regarding the development and marketing of attractions and destinations are left to chance, while important groups (or roles) of tourists will be ignored or not be reached properly. The more specific the level of interest is, the lower is the relative amount of tourists belonging to this role (see Hall and Mitchell 2005: 74). It is therefore all the more important to be aware of other roles with an explicit or implicit interest in specific experiences.

Conclusions

From the viewpoint of a destination as well as an attraction (or of these who are responsible for their development, management and marketing) it is important to know about specific consumers and target groups. Yet, while reasons to visit a sun-and-beach destination might still be comparatively clear or unidimensional, the reasons for urban tourism can be multifarious. Cities are attractive to visitors because of their overall atmosphere. Architecture, amongst others, forms an important part of this. However, few classification approaches have been made in order to specify, who exactly is consuming contemporary or historical architectures within a destination. Who understands architecture as the determining factor for the choice of a destination and who is a rather incidental consumer? Furthermore, traditional classification approaches often tend to only search for single or main reasons for travelling. However, in urban destinations, a rigid allocation of a tourist to only one specific type or purpose is often not possible. Based on a broad literature review, the present paper suggests a flexible approach, assigning tourists with different alternating roles, according to their intention(s) of visit, different interests and patterns of consumption. While a possible role model of the contemporary architectural tourist was discussed, the approach proposed in the present paper might also be adapted for further research areas, such as, for instance, tourism related to theatre, art or music.

References

Ashworth, G. J. (2000): Historical Tourism. In: Jafari, J. (ed.): Encyclopedia of Tourism. London, United Kingdom: Routledge, 277-278.

Cohen, E. (1979): Rethinking the Sociology of Tourism. In: Annals of Tourism Research, 6(1), 18-35.

Cohen, E. (1984): The Sociology of Tourism: Approaches, Issues, and Findings. In: Annals of Tourism Research, 10(1), 373-392.

Cohen, E. (2004): Who is a Tourist? A Conceptual Clarification. In: Cohen, E (ed.): Contemporary Tourism: Diversity and Change. Amsterdam, Netherlands: Elsevier, 17-36.

Goeldner, C.R. and Ritchie, J.R.B. (2009): Tourism: Principles, Practices, Philosophies. Hoboken, NJ: Wiley.

Hall, C.M. and Mitchell, R. (2005): Gastronomic Tourism: Comparing Food and Wine Tourism Experiences. In: Novelli, M. (ed.): Niche Tourism: Contemporary Issues, Trends and Cases. Oxford, United Kingdom: Elsevier Butterworth Heinemann, 73-88.

Hughes, H. (2000): Arts, Entertainment and Tourism. Oxford, United Kingdom: Elsevier.

Law, C.M. (2002): Urban Tourism. The Visitor Economy and the Growth of Large Cities (2nd ed.). London, United Kingdom: Continuum.

Mazanec, J.A. (1997): Segmenting City Tourists Into Vacation Styles. In: Mazanec, J.A. (ed.): International City Tourism: Analysis and Strategy. London, United Kingdom: Pinter, 114-128.

McKercher, B. and du Cros, H. (2002): Cultural Tourism: The Partnership Between Tourism and Cultural Heritage Management. New York, NY: Haworth Hospitality Press.

Mo, C.-M., Howard, D.R. and Havitz, M.E. (1993): Testing an International Tourist Role Typology. In: Annals of Tourism Research, 20(2), 319-335.

Moscardo, G.M. and Pearce, P.L. (1986): Historic Theme Parks: An Australian Experience in Authenticity. In: Annals of Tourism Research, 13(3), 467-479.

Pearce, P.L. (1985): A Systematic Comparison of Travel-Related Roles. In: Human Relations, 38(11), 1001-1011.

Peterson, K.I. (1995): The Heritage Resource as Seen by the Tourist. In: Van Harssel, J. (Ed.): Tourism: An Exploration. Englewood Cliffs, NJ: Prentice Hall. 242-249.

Planning and Transportation Committee of the City of Toronto (2003): Architecture Tourism Potential - All Wards. In: Report No. 1, Clause No. 5, 02/2003, http://www.toronto.ca/legdocs/2003/agendas/committees/plt/plt030324/it017.pdf, 03.11.2012.

Plaza, B. (2006): The Return on Investment of the Guggenheim Museum Bilbao. In: International Journal of Urban and Regional Research, 30(2), 452-467.

Robinson, M. and Novelli, M. (2005): Niche Tourism: An Introduction. In: Novelli, M. (ed.): Niche Tourism: Contemporary Issues, Trends and Cases. Oxford, United Kingdom: Elsevier Butterworth Heinemann, 1-11.

Schwarzer, M. (2005): Architecture and Mass Tourism. In: Ockman, J. and Frausto, S. (eds.): Architourism: Authentic, Escapist, Exotic, Spectacular. Munich, Germany: Prestel, 12-31.

Shaw, G.B.C. (2007): Tourism by Design: An Analysis of Architectural Tourism and its Influence on Urban Design from 1997 to 2007. (Doctoral Dissertation). University of California. Available from ProQuest Dissertations and Theses Database. (UMI Number: 3329667).

Shovala, N. and Ravehb, A. (2004): Categorization of Tourist Attractions and the Modeling of Tourist Cities: Based on the Co-Plot Method of Multivariate Analysis. In: Tourism Management, 25(6), 741-750.

Smith, V.L. (1989): Introduction. In: Smith, V.L. (ed.): Hosts and Guests: The Anthropology of Tourism (2nd ed.). Philadelphia, PA: University of Pennsylvania Press, 1-17.

Specht, J. (2009): The Role of Architecture in Tourism Destination Development and Branding. In: Krakover, S. and Uriely, N. (eds.): Tourism Destination Development and Branding: Eilat 2009 Conference Proceedings: Eilat, Israel: Ben-Gurion University of the Negev, 98-106.

Specht, J. (2014): Architectural Tourism: Building for Urban Travel Destinations. Wiesbaden, Germany: SpringerGabler.

Urry, J. (2002): The Tourist Gaze: Leisure and Travel in Contemporary Societies (2nd ed.). London, United Kingdom: Sage.

Van Harssel, J. (1995): Tourism: An Exploration. Englewood Cliffs, NJ: Prentice Hall.

Weiermair, K. (2002): The Integration of the Local Setting in Tourist Products: What Is the Importance of Architecture? Abstract of a presentation for the 4th Tourism Summit, Chomanix Mont-Blanc, France, 11.-13. December 2002.

Wood, M.E. (2002): Ecotourism: Principles, Practices and Policies for Sustainability. Paris, France: United Nations Environment Programme.

Yiannakis, A. and Gibson, H. (1992): Roles Tourists Play. In: Annals of Tourism Research, 19, 287-303.

Notes on Contributors

Melodena Stephens Balakrishnan is Professor of Marketing and Brands, Karlshochschule International University and Associate Professor at the University of Wollongong in Dubai. Her areas of research are Middle East North Africa, crisis management, branding, place marketing and social entrepreneurship for which she has won several competitive research grants and published on the same. She has an intercultural perspective having lived in India, USA, Taiwan and UAE. She has 20 years of experience in industry and academia. She is the Founder and President of the Academy of International Business (MENA), which she began in 2009. She is the Editor of a Case Book Series – Actions and Insights that looks at organizations operating in the MENA region. She enjoys working on bridging the industry-academic gap and mentoring start-ups.
mstephensb@karlshochschule.de

Felicjan Bylok is Professor of Sociology and a specialist of the field of the sociology of consumption. He serves as Director of the Institute of Sociology and Psychology of Management in the Technical University of Częstochowa. For many years he has been actively participating in scientific congresses, conferences and symposiums in the field of the sociology of consumption, economic sociology and the sociology of organization. The scientific and research works of Prof. Dr. hab. Felicjan Bylok consist of almost 160 papers published in both Polish and foreign journals, as well as collective works. Aside from this, he is the author of a multitude of papers in the sphere of consumer behaviour, prosumption, sustainable consumption, ethics of consumption, consumer culture and consumer society.
bylokfelicjan@gmail.com

Leszek Cichobłaziński is an Assistant Professor of Human Resources Management and Negotiation at the Management Faculty of the Częstochowa University of Technology, Poland. His main scholarly interest is in human resources management. His research focuses on the anthropology of organization, organizational semiotics and communication with his educational background in Sociology from Jagiellonian University/Kraków as well as a Doctorate in Liberal Arts. He has worked as an Adjunct Professor in the Speech

Department at Southern Illinois University, USA, and as a visiting lecturer at the Perugia University, Italy. In the recent past, he has shifted his research focus to tourism in a cooperation with the local government in Częstochowa in the frame of the EU projects COESIMA and INTERREG III C.
lech@zim.pcz.pl

Ulrich Gehmann studied Biology, Business Administration, and History. Manager in industry and international consulting Founder of the research group formatting of social spaces, and of the journal New Frontiers in Spatial Concepts, University of Karlsruhe (KIT), Germany. Publications on mythological issues and their impacts on recent sociocultural reality, spatial issues, and virtual worlds, Museum projects dealing with evolution, history, and their processes. Lecturer at Karlshochschule International University; partner in a German consulting firm active in the EU-Commission.
ugehm@t-online.de

Sourav Kargupta got his PhD degree from the Jadavpur University, Kolkata, India in 2014, working at the Centre for Studies in Social Sciences, Calcutta. His doctoral thesis concerns the possibility of a located feminist ethics and a critique of the intentional subject. He has previously worked in an academic project at the Martin Luther University, Germany. He has published on critical theory, literature and the philosophy of social sciences. His recent publications include, "Feminist Justice Beyond Law: Spivakian "Ab-Use" of Enlightenment Textuality in Imagining the Other," in an edited volume.
souravkargupta@googlemail.com

Ian King is Professor of Aesthetics and Management at the University of the Arts, London. He has a background in international music, theatre and academia. He has written and published widely in journals across a number of disciplines. His most recent book is entitled: Experiencing Organizations: New Aesthetic Perspectives, published by Libri in 2013. His research interests include: Aesthetics, Continental Philosophy and Organization Studies.
i.king@fashion.arts.ac.uk

Wendelin Küpers is Professor of Leadership and Organization Studies at Karlshochschule International University in Karlsruhe, Germany. Combining a phenomenological and cross-disciplinary orientation, his research focuses on embodied, emotional and creative, respectively aesthetic dimension in organizational life-worlds. In his current research and teaching he is focusing on

more responsible and wiser forms of organizational and leadership towards more integral and sustainable 'inter-practices'.
wkuepers@karlshochschule.de

Viktória Kundi is Associate Professor at Kodolányi János University of Applied Sciences, Székesfehérvár – Budapest, Hungary. She has a BA in Tourism from KJUAS and an MA in Marketing from Széchenyi István University, Hungary. She was awarded a PhD in Regional Sciences in 2013 at Széchenyi István University for a thesis on festivals' economic and socio-cultural impacts on cities. In addition to her academic work, she is also an active tour guide. She is member of the Hungarian Geographical Society and the Hungarian Tour Guides' Association. Her current research interests include cultural consumption, and cultural and economic impact analysis. Her key publications are in connection with her doctoral thesis.
kundiviki@gmail.com

Erica Liu is currently the programme leader of BA (Hons) Interior Architecture & Design in the University of Hertfordshire. Before joining the University, Erica was an interior and exhibition designer in the Far East for over 10 years. Erica continued her profession in the UK and obtained a PhD in Cultural Studies. She is keen to support young people and women in getting a career in the construction industry and acts as a consultant for the Pinkspiration Social Enterprise. Erica advocates multi-disciplinary collaboration and her projects have won 19 national awards. Her research interests include place branding and vernacular practice in architecture.
e.liu2@herts.ac.uk

Fernando Peña López is Associate Professor of Private Law at the University of A Coruña (Spain). His research has been mainly dedicated to the European Consumer Protection Law and to the Law of Torts. As a member of a Research Group on Consumer Protection at his university, he has been publishing papers concerning different topics within this area of Law for more than ten years. The most representative outcome of his research group activity in terms of knowledge transfer is the volume, «Consumer Claims» (3rd. Edition 2010), which is one of the most consulted legal books about consumer protection in Spain.
fernando.pena@udc.es

Gábor Michalkó is Scientific Advisor at the Geographical Institute of the Hungarian Academy of Sciences, and Professor of Tourism at Corvinus

University of Budapest and Kodolányi János University of Applied Sciences, Székesfehérvár – Budapest, Hungary. He was awarded a PhD in Geography from University of Debrecen in 1998, and a DSc from the Hungarian Academy of Sciences in 2009, for his contribution to tourism geography. His recent research interests include urban tourism, shopping tourism, health tourism, human ecology of tourism, and the relationship between tourism and quality of life. He has published 8 books and nearly 150 scientific articles, his research findings were presented at many international conferences.
michalko.gabor@csfk.mta.hu

Florin Mureşanu is an architect with a masters degree in Integrated Urban Planning at the "Ion Mincu" University of Architecture and Urbanism, Bucharest. He lectures in urban planning and land use management at the same university. With a PhD. in urban sciences, and a postdoctoral research in cultural anthropology at the Babeş-Bolyai University, in Cluj-Napoca, his investigative studies span away from architecture, towards the interdisciplinary field of urban development and cultural landscape.
gomarchgo@yahoo.com

Monica Mureşanu is an architect with a masters degree in Conservation and Rehabilitation of Built Heritage at UAUIM, Bucharest and a research masters degree in Cultural and Social History of Architecture and Urban Forms in the XIXth and XXth centuries at École Nationale Superieure d'Architecture de Versailles and Université de Versailles Saint-Quentin-En-Yvelines, France. With a PhD. in Architecture and Building Restoration she is currently lecturing at the "Ion Mincu" University of Architecture and Urbanism in Bucharest in the field of technical sciences.
monicamuresanu@yahoo.com

Roy A. Partain is an assistant professor of law at Soongsil University, in Seoul, South Korea. His research draws from legal philosophy, law & economics, and other substantive areas of law to examine the impact of technological innovations on society and its legal orderings. Energy law, environmental law, and related subjects have been a primary focus. His legal research has also engaged the political discourse and social narratives that provide the substrate upon which legal orderings and norms are built.
http://ssrn.com/author=1529022

Tamara Rátz is Professor of Tourism, and Director of the Institute of Tourism and Business Studies at Kodolányi János University of Applied Sciences,

Székesfehérvár – Budapest, Hungary. She was awarded a PhD in 2000 from Budapest University of Economic Sciences and Business Administration, Hungary, for a thesis on the socio-cultural impacts of tourism development at Lake Balaton. She is the author or co-author of more than 180 publications on tourism, including a number of books on the impacts of tourism, attraction and visitor management, and health tourism and quality of life. Her current research interests include cultural and heritage tourism development, and creativity and innovation in niche tourism development.
tratz@kodolanyi.hu

Stephan Sonnenburg is Professor for Creativity and Performative Management at the Karlshochschule International University in Karlsruhe, Germany. He is Dean of the Faculty 'Management and Performance'. Stephan Sonnenburg has broad research interests in the field of creativity, marketing, branding and management within which he examines its performative and transformative potential.
ssonnenburg@karlshochschule.de

In Germany, **Jan Specht** studied architecture and engineering followed by a Master of Business Administration with a focus on tourism management. He worked on major real estate projects around Europe and the Middle East as well as a researcher and lecturer at different European universities. Jan received a scholarship from the EU Science and Technology Fellowship Programme China and was doing research at Sun Yat-sen University in Guangzhou. During his doctoral studies at the International Graduate School of Girona (Spain) Jan investigated the role of contemporary architecture in urban travel destinations. After two years at IUBH in Munich he is now professor of tourism and hospitality management at DHBW in Ravensburg.
specht@dhbw-ravensburg.de

Desmond Wee is Professor for Tourism Sciences and Spatial Theories at the Karlshochschule International University in Karlsruhe, Germany. He is Head of the Bachelor Programme International Tourism Management. Desmond Wee uses reflexive, interpretive and visual methodologies to explore how tourism is performed in the everyday through emerging notions of identity, embodiment and intimacies.
dwee@karlshochschule.de

Made in the USA
Monee, IL
13 September 2026

62973763R00184